Traders and Gentlefolk

Traders and Gentlefolk

The Livingstons of New York,
1675–1790

Cynthia A. Kierner

Cornell University Press

Ithaca and London

For my parents
&
for Tom

Contents

Maps and Tables

Acknowledgments

Traders and Gentlefolk is both more and less than a collective biography of four generations of colonial Livingstons. This book does not tell the full story of each member of the Livingston family, nor does it discuss every aspect of the lives of the Livingstons who appear in its pages. It does examine the evolution of elite values and culture in colonial and Revolutionary America, showing how New York's most successful traders became gentlefolk without abandoning their entrepreneurial values, how these gentlefolk forged a distinct elite culture, and how the American Revolution occasioned a questioning and ultimate rejection of elite political authority.

Over the years, many people and institutions have helped to make this volume possible. At the University of Virginia, Stephen Innes was a model adviser, who, along with Michael F. Holt, David Levin, and D. Alan Williams, offered suggestions to guide me through my early revisions. Philip Morgan's thorough critique of the manuscript in its early stages set an agenda for subsequent revisions, while Kevin M. Sweeney's detailed comments on the revised version substantially improved the finished product. I am also grateful for the critical insights of Patricia Bonomi, Lisa Kannenberg, Christopher Lee, David Narrett, Eugene Sheridan, and John Smail, each of whom read all or part of the manuscript. At Cornell University Press, Peter Agree was a patient and encouraging editor who, happily, saw merit in an unpolished project.

Several scholars and friends have contributed less directly, but no less significantly, to this project's completion. I am especially grateful to Candice Bredbenner, Mary Hill Cole, Richard Hamm, Martin Havran, and Lex Renda for their friendship and moral support, which considerably eased the burden of writing and revising. Both Jean Butenhoff Lee and Elisabeth Cawthon offered timely advice, for which I am most appreciative. Finally, the best of my students at the University of North Carolina at Charlotte remind me constantly that history is fun—or at least that it should be.

My research has also benefited from the knowledge and skill of librarians and archivists at several facilities, all of which are acknowledged in my notes. But certain people and institutions deserve my special gratitude. At the New-York Historical Society, Thomas Dunning shared his vast knowledge of New York history and its sources; his expertise enabled me to exploit more effectively the Society's voluminous manuscript holdings. At the American Antiquarian Society, Georgia Barnhill helped me obtain the book's illustrations. At the libraries of the University of Virginia and the University of North Carolina at Charlotte, the Inter-Library Loan staffs processed my many requests in a cooperative and efficient manner.

Other institutions have provided financial support that enabled me to undertake and complete this project. The Corcoran Department of History at the University of Virginia supported me for five years during the earliest stages of my work, and two faculty research grants from the Foundation of the University of North Carolina at Charlotte funded subsequent research. In addition, the New Jersey Historical Commission, the Society of the Cincinnati in Virginia, and the Beveridge Research Grant Program of the American Historical Association have provided funding at various points along the way. I thank these organizations and institutions for their generous support.

Portions of this book appeared in slightly different form in the *Hudson Valley Regional Review*, 4 (1987): 38–55; *New York History*, 70 (1989): 133–52; and Jean Hunter and Paul Mason, eds., *The American Family: Historical Perspectives* (Pittsburgh: Duquesne University Press, 1991). I thank the editors of these publications for their permission to reprint this copyrighted material.

Finally, I acknowledge with gratitude and affection the less tangible contributions of the three people to whom I dedicate this volume. My parents, Robert and Beatrice Kierner, have always encouraged my academic interests. For their constant support I am truly grateful. My husband, Thomas Bright, has been a model of patience and understanding. Although he never read the manuscript, he never doubted the worth of this project or my ability to complete it. Without his confident encouragement, this book might not have been possible.

CYNTHIA A. KIERNER

Charlotte, North Carolina

Abbreviations

AAS   American Antiquarian Society. Worcester, Mass.

Albany Minutes   *Minutes of the Court of Albany, Rensselaerswyck and*
                         Schenectady. 3 vols. Ed. A.J.F. Van Laer. Albany,
                         1926–32.

Assem. J.   *Journal of the Votes and Proceedings of the General*
                         Assembly of the Colony of New-York. 2 vols. New York,
                         1764–66.

Assem. J., 1766–76   *Journal of the Votes and Proceedings of the General*
                         Assembly of the Colony of New-York, from 1766 to 1776,
                         Inclusive. Albany, 1820.

Cal. Coun. Min.   *Calendar of Council Minutes, 1668–1783.* Ed. Berthold
                         Fernow. Albany, 1902.

Cal. Hist. MSS.   *Calendar of Historical Manuscripts in the Office of the*
                         Secretary of State, Albany, N.Y. 2 vols. Albany, 1865–
                         66.

Cal. S.P.   *Calendar of State Papers, Colonial Series, America and*
                         West Indies. 42 vols. London, 1860–1953.

Coun. J.   *Journal of the Legislative Council of the Colony of New-*
                         York, 1691–1775. 2 vols. Albany, 1861.

DHNY   *The Documentary History of the State of New York.* 4 vols.
                         Ed. E. B. O'Callaghan. Albany, 1849–51.

DRNY   *Documents Relative to the Colonial History of the State of*
                         New York. 15 vols. Ed. E. B. O'Callaghan and
                         Berthold Fernow. Albany, 1853–87.

Early Records   *Early Records of the City and County of Albany and Colony*
                         of Rensselaerswyck. 4 vols. Ed. A.J.F. Van Laer.
                         Albany, 1916–19.

Abbreviations

Hist. Statistics of the U.S.	*Historical Statistics of the United States: Colonial Times to 1970.* 2 vols. Washington, D.C., 1975.
Livingston-Redmond MSS.	Livingston-Redmond Manuscripts. Franklin D. Roosevelt Library. Hyde Park, N.Y. microfilm.
Livingston-Welles Corres.	Johnson Family Papers, William Livingston–Noah Welles Correspondence. Yale University. New Haven, Conn.
Mass. Hist. Soc.	Massachusetts Historical Society. Boston, Mass.
MCNY	Museum of the City of New York.
NY Col. Laws	*The Colonial Laws of New York from the Year 1664 to the Revolution.* 5 vols. Albany, 1894.
NY Gen. & Bio. Rec.	*New York Genealogical and Biographical Record*
NY Hist.	*New York History*
NYHS	The New-York Historical Society. New York, N.Y.
NYPL	New York Public Library. New York, N.Y.
SPG Archives	Society for the Propagation of the Gospel in Foreign Parts Archives. London. microfilm.
WMQ	*William and Mary Quarterly*

Traders and Gentlefolk

Introduction

Historians have not been kind to New York's colonial leaders. In 1909, Carl Becker described them as political intriguers who sought only patronage and power. More recently, Patricia Bonomi has shown them to be the factious leaders of a factious people, notable mainly for their unenlightened self-interest and lack of idealism.[1] New York's colonial elites have never been conceded the wisdom, public spirit, and gentility usually associated with the South's colonial gentry, nor have they won points for humanitarianism and benevolence, like the Quaker grandees of eighteenth-century Philadelphia. Unlike the New England Puritans and their descendants, New York's first citizens are known more for materialism than for morality. Although they did succeed in business as merchants and as landed entrepreneurs, wealth seems to have been their only distinguishing quality.[2] Alone among America's colonial elites, New York's apparently lacked the more admirable cultural attributes of an Anglo-American aristocracy.

Endemically factious, the elite of New York reflected the cultural, economic, and regional divisions in its community. Because the colo-

---

[1] Carl Becker, *History of Political Parties in the Province of New York* (Madison, Wis., 1909), esp. chap. 1; Patricia U. Bonomi, *A Factious People: Politics and Society in Colonial New York* (New York, 1971).

[2] On the business activities of New York's colonial leaders, see Virginia D. Harrington, *The New York Merchant on the Eve of the Revolution* (New York, 1935); and Sung Bok Kim, *Landlord and Tenant in Colonial New York: Manorial Society, 1664–1775* (Chapel Hill, N.C., 1978).

[1]

ny was unusually heterogeneous, its elite was unusually contentious. The colonial leaders divided into political factions to pursue their conflicting interests, and they have, therefore, seemed unprincipled and self-serving to both scholars and contemporaries. Social pluralism and political factiousness thus shaped the public demeanor of New York's colonial elite and gave its members their unsavory reputation.

In reality, elites elsewhere were no more altruistic. Homogeneity provided the social basis for political consensus in the notably harmonious Virginia colony. Social homogeneity allowed the eighteenth-century Virginia gentry to present themselves as enlightened leaders who governed in the community's best interests. Indeed, Virginia's gentlemen could profess disinterested public-spiritedness only because nearly all white Virginians shared their economic, racial, and political interests.[3] New York's colonial leaders were no more self-interested; they were just less homogeneous.

At the same time, New York's strategic importance within the British Empire created unique opportunities for ambitious men and thus raised the stakes of political controversy. English authorities realized that New York's proximity to French Canada made frontier defense a top priority. They also knew that maintaining the friendship of the Five Nations of the Iroquois Confederacy was crucial if Britain hoped to contain or defeat the French in America. Because the Iroquois occupied the area between New York and New France, imperial authorities made New York's governors responsible for frontier diplomacy. Not surprisingly, the governors generously rewarded men who promoted good relations with the Indians and used their influence to facilitate the implementation of imperial military and defense policies.[4]

---

[3] Edmund S. Morgan, *American Slavery, American Freedom: The Ordeal of Colonial Virginia* (New York, 1975), book 4. For a useful discussion of a similar situation in contemporary South Carolina, see Robert M. Weir, "'The Harmony We Were Famous For': An Interpretation of Pre-Revolutionary South Carolina Politics," *WMQ*, 3d ser., 26 (1969): 473–501.

[4] For discussions of the politics and problems of frontier diplomacy, see Daniel K. Richter, "Cultural Brokers and Intercolonial Politics: New York-Iroquois Relations, 1664–1701," *Journal of American History*, 75 (1988): 40–68; Allen W. Trelease, *Indian Affairs in Colonial New York: The Seventeenth Century* (Ithaca, N.Y., 1960), chaps. 9–11; Stephen Saunders Webb, *1676: The End of American Independence* (New York, 1984), pp. 251–404.

Patronage, perquisites, and frontier policy were among the many issues that divided New York's political leaders throughout the colonial era. But while New York's governing class was less cohesive than most, its provincial elite was less peculiar overall than traditional accounts have led us to believe. Like their New England neighbors, New York's colonial leaders valued both religion and morality and consistently sought to pass on more than a little of each to their sons and daughters. Like the southern gentry, they too came to prize gentility and forged a distinctly genteel elite culture in the closing decades of the colonial era. Moreover, New York's colonial leaders were not bereft of the public spirit that animated Quaker humanitarianism. Although they may have been less genteel than southerners, less moralistic than New Englanders, and less philanthropic than the Philadelphia Quakers, New York's leaders exhibited all these characteristics during the colonial era.

Over the course of the eighteenth century, a discernible elite ethos developed throughout British colonial America. Morality, gentility, and philanthropy were all components of that ethos, as were the more widely shared bourgeois values usually associated with the Protestant ethic. The strength of these individual components, or characteristics, may have been subject to regional, religious, or ethnic variations. Nevertheless, the diaries of Virginia's Landon Carter show that New Englanders had no monopoly on self-conscious morality and introspection. On the other hand, Governor Thomas Hutchinson of Massachusetts was a shining example of northern gentility and public spirit.[5]

This book examines the values and culture of New York's colonial elite and argues that, their factiousness notwithstanding, they had much in common with their social peers elsewhere in British America. Indeed, New York's leaders exemplified most of the salient features of America's emerging elite ethos. Like most of their counterparts throughout provincial America, they sought to combine the values of the Protestant ethic with those of the aristocratic ideal,

[5] Bernard Bailyn, *The Ordeal of Thomas Hutchinson* (Cambridge, Mass., 1974), esp. pp. 9–31; Jack P. Greene, ed., *The Diary of Landon Carter of Sabine Hall, 1752–1778*, 2 vols. (Charlottesville, Va., 1965). Greene's *Landon Carter: An Inquiry into the Personal Values and Social Imperatives of the Eighteenth-Century Virginia Gentry* (Charlottesville, Va., 1967) provides a useful overview of the diaries.

steering the middle course between the Calvinist's austerity and the gentleman's luxury.

Using the Livingstons of New York as exemplars, this book shows both continuity and change in the values and culture of America's provincial leaders. Individually and collectively the Livingstons were representative, if not typical, of the ideals to which their class aspired. Taken together, the interests and activities of four generations of colonial Livingstons provide the basis for establishing some general conclusions about elite life in provincial New York—and in colonial America. A prolific family involved in virtually every aspect of provincial life, the Livingstons were merchants, landowners, and lawyers; they were among the most successful of America's early entrepreneurial families. Politically, they were one of New York's most active and influential families during the colonial and Revolutionary eras.

Like Robert Livingston—who emigrated from Scotland to America in 1674—the founders of many great colonial families began their lives in the New World as ambitious and hardworking merchants or planters.[6] Of middling social origins, they came to America to make their fortunes, their ambitions nurtured by a social ethic that found virtue in industry, and evil in idleness and frivolity. While a combination of industry, talent, and good fortune made many prosperous, patronage and personal connections were the surest keys to success in colonial America. Politics, trade, and land-ownership were the routes to wealth and prominence, but more often than not success in all three of these enterprises depended on personal contacts with highly placed individuals. For instance, kinship or friendship with a prominent merchant could yield credit, capital, and useful trading connections. Political patrons could be even more useful. Winning the favor of the colony's governor could result in appointment to political office. The governor's extensive land-granting powers compounded his importance as a potential source of wealth and influence.[7]

---

[6] On the middling origins of New York's leading colonial families, see Bonomi, *Factious People*, p. 8.

[7] Stanley N. Katz, *Newcastle's New York: Anglo-American Politics, 1732–1753* (Cambridge, Mass., 1968), pp. 40–42; Kim, *Landlord and Tenant*, chaps. 1–2. On the use of personal connections in the world of trade, see, for instance, Bernard Bailyn, *The New England Merchants in the Seventeenth Century* (Cambridge, Mass., 1955), pp. 35–36, 79–

Introduction

Arriving in New York without family, friends, or patrons, Robert Livingston immediately began to forge the personal and political connections he needed to become a successful merchant, landowner, and politician. Within four years he had married into Albany's leading family and acquired several local political appointments. Livingston's wife, Alida Schuyler, provided him with the connections he needed to be a person of consequence in the colony. Her brothers became his fur-trading partners and political allies; Alida herself became his most trusted business manager and adviser. By 1686, Livingston had used his growing political influence to persuade Governor Thomas Dongan to grant him 160,000 acres in the Hudson River valley. This land, which came to be known as the Manor of Livingston, eventually became the cornerstone of the Livingstons' commercial enterprises.

Over four generations, personal connections continued to shape the Livingstons' business and political endeavors, though Robert and Alida's successes made the prosperity of their descendants less dependent on the goodwill of governors and other strangers. Kinship networks readily translated into political and commercial networks. Later generations of Livingstons often found political allies among their kin, and as their family tree grew, so too did the volume and scope of the family's business.

The first three chapters of this book show how three generations of American Livingstons made their fortunes in politics, commerce, and land, respectively. Because all three generations were committed to the pursuit of material wealth, the overwhelming majority of Livingston men chose careers in trade. Nevertheless, over the course of the eighteenth century, the decline of the fur trade and a corresponding rise in the demand for foodstuffs made trade and landownership increasingly interdependent as business enterprises. Livingston Manor thus became an invaluable source of grain products, lumber, and iron—the staples of the Livingstons' export and local trades. At the same time, the Manor's growing tenant population provided an expanding market for the merchandise the

---

80, 87–91; Harrington, *New York Merchant*, esp. pp. 51–53, 57–60, 194–95, 238; Jacob M. Price, *Capital and Credit in the British Overseas Trade: The View from the Chesapeake, 1700–1776* (Cambridge, Mass., 1980), p. 50; John J. Waters, Jr., *The Otis Family in Provincial and Revolutionary Massachusetts* (Chapel Hill, N.C., 1968), pp. 65–66, 115–16, 125–31.

Livingstons imported from Great Britain, the West Indies, and else-where.

Sustained success in business brought social and financial security, both of which were reflected in changes in elite material culture during the late colonial era. By mid-century, the Livingstons—like many established merchants and planters throughout provincial America—had begun building fine Georgian homes, which they filled with family portraits and expensive English furnishings. They gathered with their social peers for high tea or for the annual social season. They sought to give their children genteel educations, send-ing sons to college and having daughters tutored in music, French, and dancing. They also cultivated civic-mindedness and phi-lanthropy as marks of leadership and beneficence that distinguished a governing class from the rest of their society.[8]

These newly genteel merchants and planters had not rejected their ancestors' legacy. Instead, they became gentlefolk without abandoning their prior commitment to the work ethic and its eco-nomic imperatives. Robert and Alida Livingston had given their sons only practical vocational training; their son Philip sent his sons to college to turn them into gentlemen, but he also sent them off to merchants' stores or lawyers' offices to learn practical and profitable occupations. By the 1740s, the Livingstons had begun to enjoy the diversions of New York City's social season, but at the same time Philip was building an ironworks on his estate, a facility that his son, Robert Livingston, Jr., would enlarge and expand over the next four decades.

While the elite's inherited economic values thus survived this cul-tural challenge, their political values changed perceptibly during the eighteenth century. Because the elite's new social ethic stressed both gentility and public service, colonial politicians began to see them-selves as gentlemen-leaders wisely and selflessly in pursuit of the common good. The first Robert Livingston had practiced politics for profit, frankly expecting to get offices, land grants, and government contracts in return for his political loyalty. By contrast, his grandsons saw political leadership as the social responsibility of the rich, the

[8] Richard L. Bushman, "American High-Style and Vernacular Cultures," in Jack P. Greene and J. R. Pole, eds., *Colonial British America: Essays in the New History of the Early Modern Era* (Baltimore, 1984), pp. 349–67; Carl Bridenbaugh, *Cities in Revolt: Urban Life in America, 1743–1776* (New York, 1955), chap. 8.

wise, and the well-born. They equated politics with public service and claimed to be a disinterested governing class exercising political authority to promote the general welfare.

Elite values and culture thus changed markedly during the decades preceding the War of Independence. The fourth, fifth, and sixth chapters of this book examine the changing world of New York's elite during the late colonial and Revolutionary eras. Chapter 4 explains the development of their culture of gentility and public-spiritedness, while Chapter 5 argues that the ideal of the gentleman-leader was particularly influential within the ranks of the colony's political opposition, a faction led by key members of the Livingston family during the late colonial era. Most members of this Livingston-led opposition supported American independence in 1776, unlike the overwhelming majority of their political opponents. A combination of whiggish principles and political ambition led the Livingstons to ally themselves with urban artisans and middling farmers in defense of American liberties. Nevertheless, as Chapter 6 shows, the Livingstons were reluctant revolutionaries. As conservative Whigs, they opposed the democratic reforms the Revolution spawned and soon grew disillusioned with the world the revolutionaries made.

Because it coincided with the rise of aristocratic values in America, the experience of the Revolution was doubly traumatic for provincial leaders, such as the Livingstons, who cast their lot with the patriot cause. Inherently antiauthoritarian, the spirit of the Revolution urged Americans to question custom and tradition and to insist that their governors be accountable and responsive to the governed.[9] By the 1770s, however, America's gentlemen-leaders believed that they alone possessed the wisdom, experience, and public spirit necessary to ensure good government. Responding to the whims and interests of the lesser sort ran counter to their political values. In the end, the Revolution marked America's rejection of these aristocratic political values, as well as the old elite's withdrawal from the circles of political power.

Over four generations, the Livingstons collectively and individually epitomized the continuities and changes in elite values and culture during the colonial and Revolutionary eras. Robert and Al-

---

[9] Edmund S. Morgan, *Inventing the People: The Rise of Popular Sovereignty in England and America* (New York, 1988), part 3.

ida Livingston had been the quintessential founders of a great colonial family. Congenital merchant-entrepreneurs, they combined their talents to amass a fortune in commercial and landed wealth as well as political influence. Their son Philip was the ideal developmental landlord. Philip Livingston improved his estate, used its produce to enhance his trade, and began building the ironworks that would secure his descendants' financial futures.

Philip's son and namesake, in turn, was a public-spirited entrepreneur whose superior education and wide-ranging interests were the hallmarks of America's late colonial gentry. A Yale graduate, successful merchant, elder of the Dutch Reformed church, New York City alderman, member and later speaker of the provincial assembly, the younger Philip Livingston attained intercolonial recognition as a Whig pamphleteer and signer of the Declaration of Independence. He combined the elite's new commitment to public service and cultural refinement with its older entrepreneurial priorities.[10]

The Revolution's achievement of popular government deterred future generations from continuing their family's tradition of political leadership. Chancellor Robert R. Livingston was the best his family's fourth generation could offer Revolutionary America, but he found himself unable to adapt to an increasingly undeferential political world. Indeed, as chancellor and diplomat, he had the political career of a man whose ego and education urged him to public service but whose anachronistically aristocratic temperament prevented him from finding his niche in post-Revolutionary America. Like most of his peers, Robert R. Livingston was unwilling to submit either himself or his principles for popular approval. He remained chancellor until 1809 and as minister to France was the main negotiator of the Louisiana Purchase. But these were appointive positions that enabled him to serve his country from outside the mainstream of popular politics.[11]

The experience of four generations of the Livingston family illustrates the process of elite formation, gentrification, and withdrawal that occurred throughout America during the colonial and Revolu-

[10] *Dictionary of American Biography*, s.v., "Livingston, Philip"; William H. W. Sabine, ed., *Historical Memoirs . . . of William Smith*, 2 vols. (New York, 1958), 2:159–60.

[11] See George Dangerfield, *Chancellor Robert R. Livingston of New York, 1746–1813* (New York, 1960).

tionary eras.[12] Despite its peculiarities, New York's elite followed an evolutionary pattern that was replicated throughout provincial America; they also embraced an elite ethos shared by governing classes in other Anglo-American colonies. For these reasons, the Livingstons' story suggests parallels and comparisons between New York and other colonies while charting the rise and eventual decline of aristocracy in America.

---

[12] This process is best described in John M. Murrin, "Political Development," in Greene and Pole, eds., *Colonial British America,* pp. 408–56.

[1]

Politics for Profit

R obert Livingston carried with him to America talent, ambition, and a decidedly middling personal background. His family traced its ancestry to a Saxon thane who had settled in Scotland late in the eleventh century; by the sixteenth century, as lords of Linlithgow and Callendar, the family's senior branch was among the first rank of Scottish nobility. Robert, however, descended from the family's cadet branch, many of whose members became clergymen and prospered through the patronage of their highly placed cousins.[1]

Robert's father, John Livingstone, was a third-generation minister, a leading Presbyterian who could not accept the reimposition of the episcopacy that accompanied the Stuart Restoration of 1660. The Reverend John Livingstone never had fared well with the bishops, who refused his ordination in 1625 and thereafter suspended him repeatedly for nonconformity. In the 1630s, he had corresponded with John Winthrop, Jr., and contemplated emigrating to New England, but instead he remained in Scotland and served, with his father, in the antiepiscopal General Assembly of 1638. Livingstone was a member of all but one of the subsequent Presbyterian assemblies, and during the English Civil War he emerged as a leading Scottish advocate of radical ecclesiastical change. When both king and bishops were restored to Scotland, Livingstone refused to sub-

---

[1] Edwin Brockholst Livingston, *The Livingstons of Livingston Manor* (New York, 1910), pp. xxvi–xxix, 2–20.

scribe to the oath of allegiance and was banished for his recalcitrance.[2]

Livingstone's subsequent exile profoundly influenced the future
of his youngest son, Robert, who was nine years old when the family
fled to the Netherlands in 1663. Robert spent the remainder of his
youth in the prosperous port city of Rotterdam, one of the
Netherlands' leading commercial centers. Seventeenth-century Rotterdam was an ideal place for a young man to learn the business of
trade, and Robert took advantage of the commercial opportunities
the city offered. By 1670, at the age of sixteen, he had begun his
trading career and posted a respectable net profit of 8,000
guilders—roughly £723 sterling—for his first year's work. He presumably continued his business until shortly after his father's death
in 1672, when he left the Netherlands.[3]

Robert returned to Scotland briefly but apparently found little
opportunity there for an aspiring merchant. An overwhelmingly
agricultural country with only a limited overseas trade, Scotland
must have seemed dreadfully dull and constraining to a youth accustomed to living in a dynamic commercial community. The former
exile wasted little time before deciding to try his luck in America. On
28 April 1673, the nineteen-year-old Livingston sailed from Green-
ock on the ship *Catharine*, bound for Charlestown, Massachusetts.[4]

Robert Livingston came to America to make his fortune. He chose
to come to Massachusetts, in particular, because he hoped his own
career there might benefit from his father's good reputation.
Livingston knew the importance of patronage and influence, and he
spent the rest of his life cultivating and exploiting advantageous
personal relationships. His New England connections, limited
though they were, gave him his start in America. The connections he

---

[2] Ibid., pp. 21–49; *Dictionary of National Biography*, s.v. "Livingstone, John." Robert
Livingston dropped the final vowel from his surname once he arrived in America.

[3] Robert Livingston, untitled account book, 1670, Livingston-Redmond MSS., reel
1. Currency conversion based on tables in John J. McCusker, *Money and Exchange in
Europe and America, 1600–1775: A Handbook* (Chapel Hill, N.C., 1978), pp. 44–60.
Lawrence H. Leder and Vincent P. Carosso estimated that Livingston's profit was
equivalent to $3,300 in American currency in 1956. See "Robert Livingston (1654–
1728): Businessman of Colonial New York," *Business History Review*, 30 (1956): 21.

[4] Livingston's own account of his passage to America is his "Journaol of our good
intended Voyage," 1673, Livingston-Redmond MSS., reel 1.

later made for himself in the colony of New York helped him to fulfill his most ambitious aspirations.

Robert Livingston made his fortune in politics, and he advanced his political fortunes by cultivating the goodwill of New York's colonial governors. In early colonial New York, politics was a business, and self-interest was a legitimate justification for political activity. Like many other colonial courtiers, Livingston earned the governors' favor by making himself an invaluable subordinate and adviser. Over the course of his career in New York, he represented the governors' interests in the assembly and on the frontier; he lent the government money and advanced supplies to the provincial military forces. For all of these services, the governors rewarded him handsomely. Robert Livingston performed public service primarily to benefit his own private interests; his political career exemplified the conflation of the public and private spheres in the early modern era.

Yet, Livingston's political career, which spanned five decades, also exemplified the changes that occurred in colonial politics during his own lifetime, especially the rise of the lower house and the evolution of a stable, if factious, provincial political order. Livingston began his career as a gubernatorial client, or courtier, at a time when the governor's authority in New York was absolute and when the absence of a representative assembly severely restricted access to political influence and power. Gubernatorial rule aggravated the social divisions that plagued colonial New York; in 1689, widespread discontent culminated in New York's version of the Glorious Revolution, known as Leisler's Rebellion. By 1691, imperial authorities had deposed Leisler's rebels, but the home government also authorized New Yorkers to elect representatives to a new provincial legislature. The creation of the assembly institutionalized the competing interests of a heterogeneous population and in so doing gave rise to the factiousness that would be characteristic of New York politics for the remainder of the colonial era.

In the 1720s, Robert Livingston ended his days in politics as speaker of the provincial assembly at a time when that body, in New York and elsewhere, was effectively challenging the governor's exclusive power to determine government policy. With the rise of the assembly came a certain amount of political stability. New York's politics remained factious, but factional rivalries in the legislature gradually replaced the more violent factional confrontations that had occurred during the days of Leisler. In the eighteenth century, the rise of the assembly enabled more men to enter the political elite, but by then the profits of politics had declined substantially since Livingston's early days as a gubernatorial client.[5]

Robert Livingston had entered the governor's circle only gradually, as a result of his ability to establish and to exploit a series of business and family connections at various levels of provincial society. In Massachusetts, Livingston presumably had hoped to capitalize on his father's godly reputation. As it turned out, he stayed in the Bay Colony just long enough to secure a loan from John Hull, a Boston merchant, in October 1674. By January 1675, Livingston had settled in the town of Albany, New York, a predominantly Dutch fur-trading community.[6]

In 1675, Albany was a frontier town of several hundred people, a septangular wedge protected by a wooden stockade, carved from the vast wilderness of the upper Hudson Valley. This community evolved from a trading post erected in 1624 by the Dutch West India Company on the west bank of the Hudson River, approximately 160 miles north of Manhattan Island. A half-century after its founding, Albany remained true to its commercial origins. Two trading posts standing at the town's northern and southern ends suggested the Indians' enormous importance to the local economy. When Robert Livingston arrived in Albany in 1675, the town remained the premier fur-trading center in British colonial America.[7]

[5] Generally, see John M. Murrin, "Political Development," in Jack P. Greene and J. R. Pole, eds., *Colonial British America: Essays in the New History of the Early Modern Era* (Baltimore, 1984), pp. 416–41. On New York, in particular, see Robert C. Ritchie, *The Duke's Province: A Study of New York Politics and Society, 1664–1691* (Chapel Hill, N.C., 1977); and Patricia U. Bonomi, *A Factious People: Politics and Society in Colonial New York* (New York, 1971).

[6] John Hull to Livingston, 30 Jan. 1679, Livingston-Redmond MSS., reel 1: A. J. F. Van Laer, ed. and trans., *Early Records*, 3:329.

[7] The best contemporary description of late seventeenth-century Albany is John Miller, *A Description of the Province and City of New York . . .*, in *Historic Chronicles of New Amsterdam, Colonial New York and Early Long Island*, vol. 1 (Port Washington, N.Y., 1968), pp. 29–31 and fig. 3. See also Jasper Danckaerts, *Journal of Jasper Danckaerts, 1678–1680*, ed. Burleigh J. Bartlett and J. Franklin Jameson (New York, 1913), pp. 216–17; Donna Merwick, "Dutch Townsmen and Land Use: A Spatial Perspective on Seventeenth-Century Albany," *WMQ*, 3d ser., 37 (1980): 53–78; Stefan Bielinski, "The People of Colonial Albany, 1650–1800," in William Pencak and Conrad Edick Wright, eds., *Authority and Resistance in Early New York* (New York, 1988), pp. 1–10.

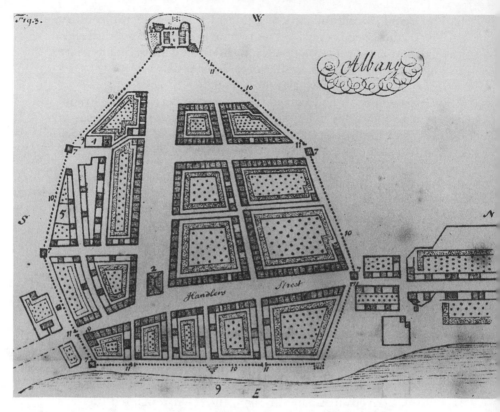

Map 1. Albany in 1695. Reprinted from John Miller, *A Description of the Province and City of New York* (London, 1843), fig. 3. Courtesy of the American Antiquarian Society.

In Albany, Livingston could use his unusual personal background to its greatest advantage. Once he arrived in New York, he found his bilingualism especially valuable. On the one hand, Livingston's fluency in Dutch enabled him to fit easily into Albany's Dutch community, where he could engage in the fur trade and associate with some of the colony's oldest and wealthiest families. On the other hand, Livingston's Scottish origins, his obvious ambition, and his willingness to live among the Dutch, together with his linguistic skills, made him a potentially valuable liaison for the English colonial governors downriver in New York City.

English colonial authorities distrusted the Albany Dutch but knew that they needed their cooperation to defend the frontiers of English America. The English initially had conquered New Netherland in 1664, but in 1673 Dutch rule briefly had been reinstated. By 1674, New York was again back in English hands, but the colony's English proprietor, James, Duke of York, worried that the disaffection of the Albany Dutch might leave its borders vulnerable to French and Indian invasions. Because James wanted to ensure the loyalty of the Albany Dutch, he specifically ordered his governor, Major Edmund Andros, to provide for the defense of the frontier without unduly harassing the colony's Dutch inhabitants.[8] To handle this ticklish situation, Andros clearly needed a reliable mediator in Albany who would not arouse the suspicion of the insular Dutch burghers.

Livingston thus had timed his arrival in Albany perfectly. When Andros arrived in New York in October 1674, Livingston was still in Massachusetts; by the following August, however, the governor had appointed him clerk of the court of Albany and ex officio secretary to the Albany commissioners for Indian affairs, who handled New York's frontier diplomacy.[9] Andros may have encountered Livingston through a mutual acquaintance, Domine Nicholas Van Rensselaer who, like the governor, had arrived in New York in October 1674. Andros helped Van Rensselaer get appointed pastor of Albany's Dutch Reformed congregation. Subsequently, the domine hired Livingston to be his private secretary. Van Rensselaer had come to New York primarily to succeed his deceased brother, Jeremias, as overseer of Rensselaerswyck, a one-million-acre family estate in the upper Hudson Valley. Livingston became Van Rensselaer's manorial secretary in August 1675, at approximately the same time he received his Albany appointments. Together, these three positions brought Livingston a combined annual salary of 800 guilders, or nearly £73 sterling.[10] More important than the salary,

---

[8] Duke of York's instructions to Andros, 1 July 1674, *DRNY*, 3:216–19. On the perceived importance of frontier policy in the 1670s, see Stephen Saunders Webb, *1676: The End of American Independence* (New York, 1984), esp. pp. 355–59.

[9] Proclamation of Governor Andros, 31 Oct. 1674, *DRNY*, 3:227; Minutes of the court of Albany, 8 Aug. 1675, Livingston-Redmond MSS., reel 1.

[10] Lawrence H. Leder, "The Unorthodox Domine: Nicholas Van Rensselaer," *NY Hist.*, 35 (1954): 166–68; and Lawrence H. Leder, *Robert Livingston, 1654–1728, and*

however, was the opportunity that officeholding provided for making important contacts at both the local and provincial levels.

Using his Albany offices, Robert Livingston was able to meet and serve influential people both inside and outside of Albany. He worked diligently at his clerical tasks, rarely missing a court session and systematically recording the proceedings of conferences with the Indians. Because he was intimately acquainted with the court of Albany, Livingston also earned both fees and friends in exchange for legal advice and services. In his first three years in Albany, he acted as attorney for the plaintiffs in five cases heard before the Albany magistrates. In four of those cases, he acted on behalf of men who wielded considerable influence in the colony: Frederick Philipse, a member of the governor's council and arguably the wealthiest man in New York; Captain Anthony Brockholls, the governor's friend and commander of the fort of Albany; and Captain Matthias Nicolls, the provincial secretary. All of Livingston's clients won their suits and undoubtedly appreciated his assistance.[11]

Livingston also used his local offices to maintain and improve his contacts with New York's colonial governors. Because Albany was a frontier community, fortifications and Indian relations were among local government's foremost priorities. Although frontier defense and diplomacy were also of vital interest to the colony as a whole, a combination of distance, poor communications, and the insularity of the Albany Dutch often made it difficult for the governors to keep abreast of frontier matters. As a local official, Livingston was privy to all sorts of information that would be useful to his superiors in the provincial capital. Seizing his opportunity, he decided to become the government's Albany correspondent. As town clerk and secretary

the Politics of Colonial New York (Chapel Hill, N.C., 1961), pp. 15–16. Currency conversion based on tables in McCusker, *Money and Exchange,* pp. 44–60. Leder argues that Livingston obtained the Rensselaerswyck appointment on 24 August 1675 and that this job was the first he received. Nevertheless, because Livingston recorded the minutes of the court of Albany on 8 August 1675, it appears that he secured his Albany appointments before being hired by Van Rensselaer (Livingston-Redmond MSS., reel 1).

11 Lawrence H. Leder, ed., *The Livingston Indian Records, 1666–1723* (Gettysburg, Pa., 1956); *Albany Minutes,* 2:67–68, 77, 84, 334, 340–41. On Philipse, see Thomas J. Archdeacon, *New York City, 1664–1710: Conquest and Change* (Ithaca, N.Y., 1975), p. 40.

for Indian affairs, Livingston became familiar with all aspects of local defense and Indian relations. He dutifully sent the governors English translations of his Dutch minutes of important conferences with the Indians, and he kept them up-to-date with all the news from Albany.[12]

Gradually, Livingston became a valued adviser to New York's governors, who rewarded him amply for his services. His growing influence in Albany and in the provincial capital were mutually reinforcing. In time, he became a mediator for both the town and the central government. For instance, as early as 1678, the court of Albany chose Livingston, along with Dirck Wessels and Marte Gerritse, to travel to New York to meet with Governor Andros, who had returned recently from England. In the capital, the trio greeted Andros and gave him the latest news from the frontier.[13] Although Livingston was a relative newcomer to Albany, the town officials evidently recognized the value of choosing him, the governor's client, as one of their emissaries. Mediators like Livingston played vital roles in the governance of colonial America, particularly in frontier areas beyond the reach of imperial authorities. In New York, the services of such mediators were especially critical because the security of English America depended on continuing good relations with the neighboring Five Nations of the Iroquois Confederacy. During his early years in Albany, Livingston thus performed services of imperial significance. He acted as a link between Albany and the capital, supplying the governors with defense and diplomatic news and making sure that the town's garrison and trading post were supplied adequately.[14]

[12] Leder, ed., *Livingston Indian Records*, pp. 9–10; Allen W. Trelease, *Indian Affairs in Colonial New York: The Seventeenth Century* (Ithaca, N.Y., 1960), p. 212; Robert Livingston to Captain Anthony Brockholls, 13 May 1678, July 1681, in *Cal. Hist. MSS.*, 2:68, 96.

[13] *Albany Minutes*, 2:348.

[14] Daniel K. Richter, "Cultural Brokers and Intercolonial Politics: New York-Iroquois Relations, 1664–1701," *Journal of American History*, 75 (1988): 48–60. For the importance of frontier mediators in other colonies, see, Stephen Innes, *Labor in a New Land: Economy and Society in Seventeenth-Century Springfield* (Princeton, 1983), pp. xix–xx, 19–21; Gregory Nobles, *Divisions Throughout the Whole: Politics and Society in Hampshire County, Massachusetts, 1740–1775* (New York, 1983), chap. 1; Kevin Sweeney, *River Gods and Lesser Dieties: The Williams Family of Western Massachusetts* (Chapel Hill, N.C., forthcoming).

At the same time, Livingston also was using his contacts in New York and in New England to begin his career in the fur trade. Because he initially lacked ties to anyone of importance in New York, Livingston's New England contacts shaped the first phase of his commercial career in Albany. While he was in Massachusetts, he may have met John Pynchon of Springfield, an important New England fur trader. Shortly after he arrived in Albany, Livingston certainly did become acquainted with Timothy Cooper, Pynchon's fur agent in the Hudson Valley. The Albany Dutch distrusted Cooper, a New Englander, and the townsmen's suspicions hampered his business. Cooper realized that the Albany traders would accept a Dutch-speaking agent far more readily. He also knew that Livingston could use his position as secretary for Indian affairs to gain access to the Iroquois trade. Therefore, Cooper proposed an arrangement whereby Livingston would procure the furs while he and Pynchon supplied the capital. Livingston, who had little money himself, seized this opportunity to begin his career as a fur trader. Although he did have some minor dealings with New York merchants, during his first few years in Albany Livingston acted primarily as a middleman in Pynchon's commercial network.[15]

This first phase of Livingston's trading career was not successful. Like many colonial traders, he became tangled in the ubiquitous web of credit. He quickly ran up large debts with his New England patrons and then repeatedly made excuses to postpone paying what he owed. One explanation for Livingston's failure to meet his New England obligations was the fact that he had extended credit to people in New York, who now were either unwilling or unable to repay him. Consequently, during the late 1670s, Livingston's business affairs in both New York and New England were dangerously unsettled. Between 1675 and 1679, Livingston appeared frequently before the Albany magistrates as both creditor and debtor. His litigiousness betokened desperation. By 1678, Pynchon had sent his brother-in-law, Elizur Holyoke, to Albany to collect what Livingston owed. Fortuitously, Livingston was not in town when Holyoke ar-

---

[15] By the mid-seventeenth century, furs were scarce in Massachusetts, and the Bay Colony's fur traders had moved west into the Hudson Valley in hopes of continuing their trade. See Innes, *Labor in a New Land*, pp. 29–33; Leder and Carosso, "Robert Livingston," pp. 22–24.

rived, but his absence did not prevent the New Englander from threatening to make Livingston's financial problems public unless Pynchon's demands were satisfied. Although Livingston was unable to pay Pynchon, Holyoke seems to have held his tongue. Still, by the late 1670s it was widely rumored in Albany that Livingston had exhausted his credit and was on the verge of financial ruin.[16]

Livingston's social life and official responsibilities must have aggravated his financial problems by distracting him from the business of trade. In 1676, he was summoned to appear before the Albany magistrates for breaking a borrowed violin during the course of an evening's revelry. Between 1677 and 1678, he also considered courting and marrying at least two different women.[17] Livingston's social activities were probably costly, and they certainly distracted him from his more substantive concerns. Meanwhile, his official responsibilities required constant attendance at court sessions and Indian conferences, and his political ambitions led him to travel occasionally to the provincial capital—diversions that his financial situation ill afforded.

By 1679, Livingston had been in New York for four years and had met and served some of the colony's most influential citizens. The contacts he made in New York had, thus far, brought him several minor offices, a reasonably good salary, and a commercial career that was far from successful. Livingston was impatient for success. As early as 1677, he had considered marrying a wealthy widow in order to extricate himself from his financial difficulties. Although at least one of Livingston's friends applauded this "great plan," the marriage never took place.[18] Two years later, Livingston married for both love and money.

As it turned out, Livingston's association with Domine Nicholas Van Rensselaer brought him his most valuable and long-lived New York connection. In 1675, Van Rensselaer, Livingston's patron, had

---

[16] Leder and Carosso, "Robert Livingston," pp. 22–24; *Albany Minutes,* 2:129, 175–76, 189–90, 218–19, 230–31, 240, 266–67, 335, 343–44. See also Timothy Cooper to Livingston, 3 Oct. 1678, Livingston-Redmond MSS., reel 1; and Elizur Holyoke to Livingston, 3 Oct. 1678, 20 Oct. 1679, ibid.

[17] *Albany Minutes,* 2:176; Richard Bingley to Livingston, 30 Oct. 1677, Livingston-Redmond MSS., reel 1; William Shaw to Livingston, 8 Oct. 1678, ibid.

[18] Richard Bingley to Livingston, 30 Oct. 1677, Livingston-Redmond MSS., reel 1.

married Alida Schuyler, the daughter of Philip Pieterse Schuyler, one of Albany's leading citizens. When Van Rensselaer died in November 1678, Livingston had known Alida nearly four years and apparently held her in high regard. Robert and Alida married within eight months of the domine's death. Unquestionably, Livingston recognized the benefits of marrying into one of Albany's leading families. Nevertheless, even the earliest letters exchanged by him and Alida indicate that theirs was a truly affectionate union.[19]

The marriage was the turning point of Livingston's early career. Marriage brought him important family and political connections, new trading partners, an enlarged estate, and —most important— a wife who proved to be an agreeable companion and a capable business partner. Although Livingston, as a virtual orphan in America, was subject to no parental constraints in choosing a wife, his choice would have elated even the most demanding of parents. Alida Schuyler Van Rensselaer was the third of ten children of Philip Schuyler and Margaretta Van Schlectenhorst. Schuyler had risen from humble origins to become a prosperous merchant and land-owner and the founder of Albany's most prominent family; his wife was the daughter of a director of Rensselaerswyck and in her own right a successful Albany fur trader. Alida's elder sister, Gertrude, had married Stephanus Van Cortlandt, a future member of the governor's council and first proprietor of Cortlandt Manor. Her brother Peter was already an established fur trader with substantial influence in Albany politics. He too would become a councillor and marry a Van Rensselaer. Alida's parents probably had arranged her own marriage to Nicholas, who was more than twice her age and had arrived in New York just months before their nuptials. When Alida was free to marry again in 1678, her family apparently did not contest her choice of a Scottish immigrant with uncertain prospects.[20]

---

[19] See, for instance, Robert Livingston to Alida Livingston, 6 Nov. 1680, ibid., reel 6; Alida Livingston to Robert Livingston, 16 Nov. 1680, translated in Linda Biemer, ed., "Business Letters of Alida Schuyler Livingston, 1680–1726," *NY Hist.*, 63 (1982): 188.

[20] Biemer, ed., "Business Letters," pp. 184–85. For a more detailed treatment of Alida's life, see Biemer, *Women and Property in Colonial New York: The Transition from Dutch to English Law, 1643–1727*, Studies in American History and Culture 38 (Ann Arbor, Mich., 1983), pp. 59–74.

Even before his marriage took place, Livingston's business situation improved markedly. Personal connections shaped the flow of trade and credit in colonial America, and kinship ties were especially important for forming commercial networks. Because he had had no kin in America, Livingston initially had relied on his New England contacts for business and credit. Now he was able to sever his ties with the New Englanders and start over with the help of his newly acquired family. Thus Robert Livingston began the second phase of his trading career, as a general merchant in Albany, with the help of his future in-laws. In 1678, he began trading with Alida's brother-in-law, Stephanus Van Cortlandt of New York City. For the next few years, Van Cortlandt, an import merchant, supplied Livingston with merchandise for his store in Albany. During this time, Alida's brother Brant Schuyler, appears to have acted as Livingston's fur agent, and another Schuyler brother, David, was his partner in at least one commercial venture. But Livingston's impending marriage also brought him new business contacts outside the Schuyler family circle. For instance, in April 1679, James Graham, a fellow Scot and perennial officeholder, solicited Livingston's services as a factor. Graham also asked Livingston to take on his younger brother as an apprentice, a sure sign of Livingston's sudden rise to respectability.[21]

By 1680, Livingston was able to settle his debts with Pynchon and Cooper, freeing himself to concentrate on his expanding New York enterprises. His Albany business grew quickly, and by July 1681 his many clients collectively owed him more than 15,000 guilders—the equivalent of £1,337 sterling. Livingston continued to be a frequent litigant in the Albany courts, but after 1678—with one minor exception—he always appeared as a plaintiff seeking to enforce the payment of debts owed him.[22]

[21] Leder, *Robert Livingston*, pp. 37–39; Livingston's account with Stephanus Van Cortlandt, 1679–1680, Livingston-Redmond MSS., reel 1; Albany excise book, June 1680, ibid.; James Graham to Livingston, 7 Apr. 1679, ibid. On the importance of kinship in colonial business, see, for instance, Bernard Bailyn, *The New England Merchants in the Seventeenth Century* (Cambridge, Mass., 1955), pp. 35–36, 79–80, 87–91; Virginia D. Harrington, *The New York Merchant on the Eve of the Revolution* (New York, 1935), pp. 51–52, 194–95, 238.

[22] Leder, *Robert Livingston*, pp. 38–39; *Lyste van Shuldenaers Getrocken uyt myn Grootboeck*, 1 June 1681, Livingston-Redmond MSS., reel 1. Currency conversion based on tables in McCusker, *Money and Exchange*, pp. 44–60. On 7 June 1681, Pieter Ryver-

Livingston's new connections and improved reputation also enabled him to secure credit in London and thus begin his career in the transatlantic trade. By 1683, London merchant Jacob Harwood had sent Livingston his first cargo on consignment. For roughly a decade, Livingston acted as Harwood's factor, selling his cargoes, which usually consisted of English textiles and other goods suitable for the Indian trade. Livingston sold the goods, deducted his costs plus a 5 percent commission, and credited the remaining proceeds—usually in furs and bills of exchange procured in the West Indian trade—to the account of his London supplier. Under such an arrangement, the consignor assumed the risks of purchasing and shipping the cargo, but he also took the lion's share of the profits. By 1692, however, Livingston was importing goods on his own account, a practice that was far more profitable, but also far more risky, than acting as another merchant's factor. Livingston was willing to take risks; he soon abandoned the consignment trade entirely.[23]

Livingston's ability to import goods on his own account suggests that he had begun to develop a reputation in England that would merit him the credit of his commercial correspondents. At the same time, his success in New York was bringing him a wider circle of London contacts. For instance, in 1686, Livingston began a new business relationship with John Blackall, who like Harwood was a London merchant with a deep interest in the New York fur trade. By then Livingston was in a position to promote the business of his friends in London. He persuaded his mother-in-law, Margaretta Van Schlectenhorst, to consign a case of beaver to Blackall and promised to recommend the Londoner to other Albany friends and associates. Livingston had, in effect, secured Blackall's credit in exchange for promoting his business in New York. Blackall was duly appreciative; he promised Livingston to "make it my bussiness to retalliate the Same kindness to you as it lies in my way."[24] Once dependent on

---

dingh unsuccessfully sued Livingston for 38 guilders that Nicholas Van Rensselaer owed to an Amsterdam merchant (*Albany Minutes*, 3:127). At the time, Livingston was administering Van Rensselaer's estate.

[23] Harwood's invoices, 10 May 1683, 19 Mar., 25 June 1687, 12 Apr. 1692, Livingston-Redmond MSS., reel 1; Memorandum of Livingston's case with Harwood, [1695], ibid.

[24] John Blackall to Robert Livingston, 1 Jan. 1686, Livingston-Redmond MSS., reel

family connections for business contacts, by 1686 Livingston had himself become a useful contact for London traders.

At the same time, Livingston's new Schuyler connections and commercial success also were paying political dividends by increasing his potential value as an ally and adviser to New York's colonial governors. Shortly after his marriage, Livingston began to exploit his newfound influence in order to reap the material benefits of gubernatorial favor. Livingston had entered the governor's service expecting to be rewarded, and in colonial America land was the customary reward for political loyalty. In 1680, he began to extract compensation for his services, requesting and receiving Governor Andros's permission to buy 2,000 acres of Indian land on the east side of the Hudson River.[25]

Gubernatorial patronage was a prerequisite for amassing acreage in New York during the colonial era. Because the governor alone had the power to grant unclaimed lands, his patentees were invariably his loyal friends and political supporters. The land-granting process had several distinct stages, and at every stage the success of the venture depended on the continued support of the governor. First, an aspiring landowner petitioned the governor and council for a license to purchase a specific tract of land from the Indians. If the governor agreed, the petitioner then negotiated with the Indians, procured their deed, and applied to the governor and council for a survey of the land he had purchased. After the survey had been made, the buyer again petitioned the governor, this time requesting that his title to the land be confirmed by royal letters patent. If the governor refused any of these requests, the petitioner's quest for land would be fruitless. On the other hand, the monetary costs of acquiring land were relatively inconsequential. The petitioner had to pay the Indians for the land, and he also had to pay government clerks for recording, copying, and filing documents at each stage of the application process. In both cases, however, the sums involved were minimal, compared to the land's eventual value.[26]

---

1. Following Dutch custom, Alida's mother and her contemporaries in New Netherland/New York did not adopt their husbands' surnames.

[25] Andros's answer to Livingston's petition, 12 Nov. 1680, *DRNY*, 13:546.

[26] Payments to the Indians varied widely, and many patentees defrauded them by

New York's early governors freely traded grants of land for political loyalty. During the first decade of English rule, King Charles II had instructed the colony's governors to reward their supporters with "all advice and encouragement to promote our service," and they duly responded by creating several relatively small manors and independent patents. Under Dutch rule, however, the governors of New Netherland had established a precedent for giving much larger tracts of land—known as patroonships—to deserving petitioners.[27] Of the Dutch patroonships, only Rensselaerswyck survived intact after 1664, but that million-acre family estate became an ideal for New York's most ambitious land speculators. Livingston was especially ambitious, and Alida's previous connection to the patroonship gave him a golden opportunity to attain his objectives. In the end, therefore, Robert Livingston's marriage to Alida Schuyler Van Rensselaer indirectly led to the creation of Livingston Manor.

Although Nicholas Van Rensselaer died intestate, the court of Albany awarded Alida the exclusive right to administer his estate. When Livingston married Alida in 1679, he immediately took possession of that estate, including two valuable farms, and proceeded to manage Van Rensselaer's legacy on his wife's behalf. Livingston later claimed to have paid Van Rensselaer's debts in New York, totaling 5,831 guilders, and demanded part of the domine's share in Rensselaerswyck as his own compensation. Van Rensselaer, however, also had amassed enormous debts in the Netherlands, and these Livingston did not attempt to pay. Instead, he insisted that Van Rensselaer's American and European estates were distinct entities and that Alida held no claim to the latter. Under the Dutch custom of community property in marriage, this distinction was dubious at

---

taking more land than they actually purchased. A 1710 law, however, standardized clerical fees at roughly £70 for processing any grant not exceeding 2,000 acres. Although recipients of larger grants paid higher rates after 1710, a grant's size had no bearing on the fees charged in 1686, when Livingston received his patent (Fees for Grants of Land by Act of Oct. 1710, ibid., 7:923).

[27] Charles II's private instructions to Nicolls et al., 23 Apr. 1664, *DHNY*, 3:60. On the Dutch patroonships and early English land grants, see Sung Bok Kim, *Landlord and Tenant in Colonial New York: Manorial Society, 1664–1775* (Chapel Hill, N.C., 1978), pp. 3–20.

best; the Van Rensselaers knew that they were being hoodwinked.[28]

Despite the weakness of his case, Livingston's association with the Schuyler family gave him enough political leverage to force Governor Thomas Dongan (1682–88) to take him seriously. But Dongan, who wanted to alienate neither the Schuylers nor the Van Rensselaers, postponed deciding Livingston's case for as long as possible. Meanwhile, Livingston himself began to cultivate Dongan's goodwill and to make contingency plans to acquire other land in the event that his attack on Rensselaerswyck proved futile.

In July 1683, Livingston acquired his first landholdings in the Hudson Valley, when he concluded the 2,000-acre purchase Andros had authorized nearly three years earlier. Shortly thereafter, he also purchased two adjoining houses in Albany and a pasture outside the town's northern gate.[29] On 4 November 1684, Governor Dongan secured Livingston's investments by issuing royal patents confirming his title to all four of his recent acquisitions. On the same day, Dongan also issued another patent to seven Albanians for more than 180,000 acres of unsettled land located north of Albany at Saratoga. Livingston was among the patentees, as were two of the Schuyler brothers.[30]

By issuing these patents, Dongan undoubtedly was trying to appease Livingston and his in-laws in order to facilitate the settlement of the Rensselaerswyck affair. But Livingston was not yet satisfied. In

[28] *Albany Minutes*, 2:347–56, 379–80. The best account of this dispute and its resolution is Leder, *Robert Livingston*, chap. 2. See also A. J. F. Van Laer, ed. and trans., *Correspondence of Maria Van Rensselaer, 1669–1689* (Albany, N.Y., 1935), for the Van Rensselaer family's perspective.

[29] Andros's answer to Livingston's petition, 12 Nov. 1680, *DRNY*, 13:546; Deed of the Mohegan Indians to Livingston, 12 July 1683, *DHNY*, 3:612–13; *Early Records*, 2:15–16, 16–17n., 200–201, 250–51; *Memoriael Van d Incidente onkostin Int Repareeren van myn huys*, 8 Dec. 1683–Oct. 1684, Livingston-Redmond MSS., reel 1. On land as a reward for political service, see Innes, *Labor in a New Land*, pp. 29, 32, 34; Richard S. Dunn, *Puritans and Yankees: The Winthrop Dynasty of New England, 1630–1717* (Princeton, 1962), pp. 72–75, 78, 86, 108–12, 191, 248–49; John J. Waters, Jr., *The Otis Family in Provincial and Revolutionary Massachusetts* (Chapel Hill, N.C., 1968), pp. 50–51, 55–56, 61–62, and especially Theodore B. Lewis, "Land Speculation and the Dudley Council of 1686," *WMQ*, 3d ser., 31 (1974): 255–71.

[30] Dongan's patents to Livingston, 4 Nov. 1684, Livingston-Redmond MSS., reel 1; *Early Records*, 2:343–49. On the Saratoga patent, see also George W. Schuyler, *Colonial New York: Philip Schuyler and His Family*, 2 vols. (New York, 1885), 2:96.

June 1685, he asked Dongan for permission to buy an additional 200 or 300 acres at Taghkanic near the Massachusetts border, claiming that the 2,000 acres he had purchased previously was "much Contrare to Expectation, very Little being fitt to be Improoved." Dongan immediately granted Livingston's petition, allowing him to buy 200 acres of Indian land "provided the said land be not disposed of to any others." By 10 August, Livingston had concluded his deal with the Mohegans. Ten days later, Dongan gave him a patent that confirmed his title to 600 acres at Taghkanic instead of the originally agreed upon 200.[31]

Tripling Livingston's Taghkanic landholdings was Dongan's way of rewarding him for finally coming to terms with the Van Rensselaer family. On 19 July 1685, in the governor's presence, the disputants had ended their six-year-old controversy. The Van Rensselaers forgave the rents due them for Livingston's use of their farms, and they released Robert and Alida from liability for Nicholas's unpaid debts. In addition, Livingston received a settlement of 800 schepels of wheat, worth approximately £120. Robert and Alida, in return, renounced their claims both to Nicholas's own land and to Rensselaerswyck.[32]

Perseverance and political leverage had enabled Livingston to parlay an extremely dubious legal case into £120 and several hundred acres, but his ultimate compensation came when Dongan issued him yet another patent on 22 July 1686. This patent united Livingston's previous purchases on the Hudson and at Taghkanic to form "the Lordshipp and Manor of Livingston," the first of several manors that would come to dominate the Hudson River valley. Although twenty miles of Indian land separated Livingston's two tracts, Dongan's patent treated them contiguously. By sleight of hand, the governor had transformed 2,600 acres into 160,000.[33]

[31] Livingston's petition and Dongan's response, 3 June 1685, *DHNY*, 3:617; Deed of Mohegan Indians to Robert Livingston, 10 Aug. 1685, ibid., 3:617–19; Dongan's patent to Livingston, 20 Aug. 1685, ibid., 3:620–22.

[32] S. G. Nissenson, *The Patroon's Domain* (New York, 1937), p. 302; Leder, *Robert Livingston*, p. 32. One Dutch schepel is equivalent to three-fourths of an English bushel (*Albany Minutes*, 3:105n.); conversion of grain to cash value is based on the price table in Kim, *Landlord and Tenant*, p. 195.

[33] Dongan's patent to Livingston, 22 July 1686, *DHNY*, 3:622–27; Leder, *Robert Livingston*, p. 35. Leder persuasively argues that this transaction was an addendum to the formal resolution of the Van Rensselaer affair.

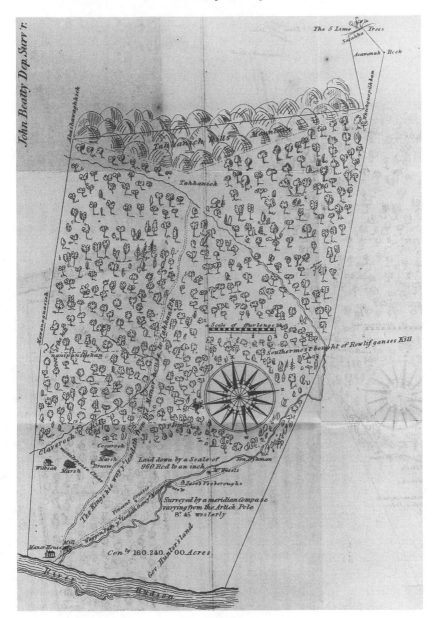

Map 2. John Beatty's survey of Livingston Manor, 1714. Reprinted from E. B. O'Callaghan, ed., *The Documentary History of the State of New York*, vol. 3 (Albany, 1850), facing p. 690. Courtesy of the American Antiquarian Society.

Although it is unclear whether the governor or his patentee instigated this fraudulent inflation of the original purchases, obviously
both men were shrewd enough to understand what was happening.
The Dongan patent of 1686 was the greatest gift that Livingston
received from any governor during his half-century of political service. Dongan probably had two reasons for presenting so handsome
a gift to Livingston: first, to compensate him more fully for relin-
quishing his troublesome claims to Rensselaerswyck; and second, to
ensure Livingston's future political allegiance. Livingston did remain loyal to Dongan, just as he attempted to cultivate good relations with all his successors. He understood that the governor could
be a mighty patron or a deadly enemy, and he played the political
game accordingly.

Livingston's relations with New York's early governors were orderly and harmonious. Governors Andros and Dongan had given
him both land and offices, and Livingston, in return, lent them his
political support and his services as frontier mediator. By the late
1680s, Livingston also had begun to lend money to the provincial
government. His services as frontier mediator and government
creditor were especially critical from the 1680s until 1713, when
England and France were nearly constantly at war and when New
York was consistently threatened by French and Indian invaders.

Nevertheless, the events of 1689–91 taught Livingston that politics was not all patronage and profits. In 1688, New York had become part of the Dominion of New England, King James II's plan to
centralize imperial administration by uniting the northern colonies
under one royal governor—Sir Edmund Andros, Livingston's former benefactor. The English deposed the Catholic James later that
year, replacing him with the Protestant William and Mary. When
news of the Glorious Revolution reached Boston, the New Englanders responded by deposing Andros and overthrowing the Dominion government. For the time being, New Yorkers remained
quiescent, but on 31 May 1689 the city militia and a mob of supporters seized the fort of New York. Andros's lieutenant governor, Francis Nicholson, fled to England, and within a few days Jacob Leisler
emerged as the rebels' leader. The insurgents created a council of
safety and elected Leisler commander-in-chief of the militia and
captain of the fort. Leisler then took steps to undermine the influ-

ence of the governor's favorites, who of course opposed the rebellion.[34]

When instructions arrived from England addressed to "Francis Nicholson . . . and in his absence to such as for the time being take care for Preserving the Peace and administring the Lawes," Leisler assumed that he was their proper recipient and that the home government had in effect recognized the legitimacy of his administration. The protests of the governor's council notwithstanding, Leisler proceeded to form a new council and to issue writs for the election of an assembly to raise funds to defend the colony against an expected French invasion. In fact, Leisler's legislature was not legitimate, since at this point New York's government did not include an elective assembly.[35]

As a leading anti-Leislerian, Livingston partook of both the spoils and the perils of sustained factional warfare. From 1675 through 1688, he had enjoyed the patronage of friendly governors, but when Jacob Leisler and his followers overthrew the Dominion of New England in 1689, Livingston lost his patrons and suffered the wrath of their foes. In New York City, Leisler's Rebellion was primarily an ethnic revolt, the protest of a Dutch community whose social status and economic opportunities had declined precipitously since the English conquest. In Albany, however, ethnicity was not the central issue, mainly because both the town of Albany and its surrounding county were overwhelmingly Dutch and the area's non-Dutch settlers were neither influential nor wealthy enough to challenge the authority of the leading Dutch families.

In Albany County, those who supported Leisler's Rebellion did so for either personal or economic reasons. For instance, people living in the town of Schenectady resented Albany's monopoly over the Indian fur trade, a privilege bestowed on the Albanians by the English colonial administration. Many of Schenectady's inhabitants decided to support Leisler's revolt when his chief lieutenant, Jacob Milbourne, promised to rescind the Albany monopoly. The citizens

---

[34] Useful accounts of Leisler's Rebellion in New York City include Archdeacon, *New York City*, pp. 38–57; Ritchie, *Duke's Province*, chap. 9; and John M. Murrin, "English Rights as Ethnic Aggression: The English Conquest, the Charter of Liberties of 1683, and Leisler's Rebellion in New York," in Pencak and Wright, eds., *Authority and Resistance in Early New York*, pp. 56–94.

[35] William III's instructions to Nicholson, 30 July 1689, *DRNY*, 3:606.

of Albany, who of course wanted to keep their monopoly, they correctly viewed Leisler as a threat to their commercial privileges.[36] Consequently, the little support Leisler and Milbourne could command within the town of Albany came from men who had suffered personal setbacks as a result of the patronage policies of the English administration. The Leislerian Johannes Provoost had been the clerk of the court of Albany until Andros gave that job to Robert Livingston in 1675; Provoost held an official position in Albany during Leisler's brief administration. Richard Pretty, likewise, had been subcollector of the excise at Albany until 1680, when Andros removed him from office and appointed Livingston as his successor. In return for his support, Leisler appointed Pretty sheriff of Albany County.[37]

While the opponents of the English regime prospered during Leisler's ascendancy, their adversaries suffered. In Albany, the Leislerians made Livingston the target of their most venomous abuse, either because they resented his speedy rise to prominence or because they realized that his position in Albany was less secure than that of the long-established Dutch patrician families.[38] The Leislerians accused Livingston of treasonously opposing the accession of William and Mary because he—like many prominent colonials—prudently waited for confirmation from England before openly shifting his political loyalties. On 1 March 1690, Leisler ordered his men to arrest Livingston for Jacobitism. Fortuitously, the anti-Leislerian Albany Convention had already decided to send him to New England to solicit help defending the northern frontier against an expected French invasion. Livingston thus was able to leave New York before Leisler's subordinates had a chance to enforce the arresting order. Although the evidence against him was ambiguous at best, with a charge of treason lodged against him and with his enemies in power, Livingston was forced to remain in exile in New England for more than a year. In his absence, the Leislerian authorities harassed his wife, searched his house, and eventually confiscated his estate.[39]

---

[36] Livingston to Andros, 14 Apr. 1690, ibid., 3:708. On 24 April 1690, the Leislerian assembly did pass a law that abolished all monopolies (*NY Col. Laws*, 1:218).

[37] Leder, *Robert Livingston*, pp. 40, 69; Ritchie, *Duke's Province*, p. 218.

[38] See Alice P. Kenney, "Dutch Patricians in Colonial Albany," *NY Hist.*, 49 (1968): 249–83, on deference and elite authority among the Albany Dutch.

[39] Leder, *Robert Livingston*, pp. 65–76.

During Leisler's Rebellion, Livingston sorely regretted the loss of his patrons. He wrote to Andros in London, hoping that the displaced governor could persuade the home government to step in and suppress the rebellion. Livingston explained that all Andros's loyal supporters were now suffering under Leisler: [Stephanus Van] Cortland[t] is fled; poor Colonel [Nicholas] Bayard, . . . W[illia]m Nicolls, and severall more, he keeps close and in dark prisones, and causes Bayard to be carried . . . [through] the Fort by porters, with irons on, in triumph." The exiled New Yorker entreated Andros to tell the king that if a new royal governor did not arrive soon "this countrey will be Lost."[40]

While he anxiously awaited news from England, Livingston arranged for his family to join him in Connecticut in December 1690. They spent the following winter in Fairfield and returned to New York only in April 1691, when Leisler and Milbourne had been replaced with a new royal governor from England and were themselves in prison awaiting trial for treason. Livingston witnessed the execution of Leisler and Milbourne in New York on 16 May and was the only anti-Leislerian publicly rebuked from the scaffold. Milbourne noticed Livingston in the crowd of onlookers and declared ominously, "You have caused the King [that] I must now die. But before gods tribunal I will implead you for the same."[41] Although Livingston did not record his reaction to Milbourne's threat, the trial and execution of Leisler and Milbourne polarized a political community already deeply divided by the experience of the recent rebellion. The legacy of Leisler's Rebellion shaped the course of New York politics for the next two decades. In the ongoing battle between the friends and foes of Leisler, Livingston would always be among the most prominent members of the anti-Leislerian party.

Although Livingston continued to regard the governor's favor as a "weapon to wage war," the painful experience of 1689–91 had taught him that even that very powerful "weapon" was not invincible. Governors could be ousted, or recalled to England. Later, in the vindictive and unstable political environment of post-Leislerian New York, Livingston also learned that the governor's influence could be used to his detriment as well as to his advantage.[42] For the rest of his

[40] Livingston to Andros, 14 Apr. 1690, *DRNY*, 3:708–10.

[41] Leder, *Robert Livingston*, pp. 75–76; Dying speeches of Leisler and Milbourne, 16 May 1691, *DHNY*, 2:380.

[42] The quotation appears in Philip Livingston to Robert Livingston, 8 Feb. 1721, in

life, Livingston tried to remain on friendly terms with New York's governors. Failing that, he continued to employ the two defensive strategies he had used, with limited success, during Leisler's ascendancy. First, he withdrew temporarily from the political arena—if not from the province itself—hoping that his absence would make him a less convenient target for the revenge of his enemies. Second, he complained to imperial authorities and waited anxiously for a change in the colonial administration.

In the two decades following Leisler's Rebellion, Livingston remained politically active, sitting briefly on the governor's council (1698 and 1701) and in the lower house (1709–11) and serving as government creditor and military contractor. For Livingston, business and politics were inseparable; success in business had given him the financial resources to become a government creditor, and the provincial government relied heavily on the resources of private citizens, particularly in times of war.

Although Robert Livingston was an expansionist who championed British imperial interests as a matter of principle, like many other ambitious colonials, he spent the better part of his career lending money and merchandise to the government, expecting to profit, however belatedly, from his investments.[43] In 1687 and 1688 alone, Livingston had advanced Governor Dongan more than £2,000 in goods to maintain the Albany garrison. Later, as victualer of the forces at Albany during King William's War (1689–97), he continued to provision the troops without payment, extending considerable credit to the provincial government.[44] Livingston waited years for the government to fulfill its financial obligations, but eventually he profited from his government contracts. In addition, his status as a government creditor often gave him significant leverage when he requested political favors.

---

which Philip indicates that it was one of his father's favorite axioms (Livingston-Redmond MSS., reel 4).

[43] On the expansionist verus nonexpansionist cleavage in New York's colonial politics, see Marc Egnal, *A Mighty Empire: The Origins of the American Revolution* (Ithaca, N.Y., 1988), chap. 3. The Pynchon and Williams families of western Massachusetts performed similar financial services for their provincial government. See Innes, *Labor in a New Land*, esp. pp. 27–29; Nobles, *Divisions throughout the Whole*, pp. 32–34.

[44] New York council minutes, 30 April 1688, *Cal. S. P.*, 1685–88, no. 1727; Statement of Livingston's case and proofs, 19 Sept. 1695, *DRNY*, 4:132–37; Livingston to Earl of Bellomont, 5 Aug. 1698, Livingston-Redmond MSS., reel 1.

Under ideal circumstances, provisioning imperial troops was profitable both for the governor and for his merchant clients. The governor sold the contract to local merchants, who then advanced their own funds to feed, clothe, and pay the soldiers. In 1691, Livingston and Stephanus Van Cortlandt paid Governor Henry Sloughter ten shillings a year per man, at a time when the home government allowed the provisioners to spend five pence a day per man to fulfill their contractual obligations. The provisioners kept as profit whatever they were able to save from the government's allowance, and they were also entitled to claim 8 percent interest on credit they advanced to maintain the soldiers. Because English authorities often put off paying their colonial debts, profits from interest could be substantial. For instance, by 1695, after four years of provisioning, Livingston claimed £1,500 in interest alone on his unpaid accounts.[45]

But circumstances for government creditors were rarely ideal, perhaps least of all so in Livingston's New York. With Britain and France at war nearly constantly between 1689 and 1713, the governments both in London and in New York amassed enormous debts at an alarming rate. Neither the imperial fiscal system nor its colonial counterpart was equipped to sustain almost a quarter-century of expensive warfare; corruption in high places made New York's financial problems even more serious, particularly during the administrations of governors Fletcher (1692–98) and Cornbury (1702–8).[46] When the government was unwilling or unable to fulfill its financial obligations, the provisioners' personal finances obviously suffered. By 1701, the government owed Livingston £3,400, and he claimed that public service was ruining his private business. Livingston complained to the Board of Trade, "I have so far exhausted my estate in the King's service, that I am not only become disabled to carry on my trade of Merchandize, but must be totally ruin'd without your Lordships' redress."[47]

[45] Leder, *Robert Livingston*, pp. 78–79; Statement of Livingston's case and proofs, 19 Sept. 1695, *DRNY*, 4:132–37.

[46] On Fletcher and Cornbury, respectively, see James S. Leamon, "Governor Fletcher's Recall," *WMQ*, 3d ser., 20 (1963): 535–42; and Charles Worthen Spencer, "The Cornbury Legend," NYHS *Proceedings*, 13 (1914): 309–20. For a near-contemporary appraisal of each, see William Smith, Jr., *The History of the Province of New-York*, ed. Michael G. Kammen, 2 vols., (1757; Cambridge, Mass., 1972), 1:95–99, 103, 117.

[47] Livingston to Board of Trade, 21 June 1701, *DRNY*, 4:884.

If Livingston was typical, public creditors in colonial America often had to go to extraordinary lengths to collect what the government owed them. By 1693, Livingston found himself in a very difficult position. Over the last two years, he had advanced more than £2,000 to the provincial government, none of which had been repaid; moreover, he was still owed more than £3,000 for expenditures he had made on behalf of Governor Dongan in the 1680s. Livingston petitioned Governor Benjamin Fletcher for compensation, but the best Fletcher could do was to issue him warrants promising him a portion of that year's custom duties. Unfortunately, the customs service was mismanaged and corrupt, and Livingston found it impossible to redeem his warrants. With his own creditors growing impatient, he finally asked and received permission to travel around the colony personally collecting delinquent taxes. Livingston went tax-collecting twice and collected nearly £1,000 of the money owed him. Meanwhile, the governor and council continued to issue him warrants that were virtually worthless.[48]

Despite his difficulties, in May 1694, Livingston allowed Fletcher to renew his victualing contract.[49] Undoubtedly, he realized that retaining the governor's favor by continuing to supply these essential services was his only hope of receiving just compensation. To have quit provisioning the troops, particularly in wartime, would have been tantamount to writing off the substantial sums the government still owed him. In May 1694, Livingston apparently still hoped that Fletcher would pay his accounts; by autumn, however, he had become impatient and he believed that his chances of getting satisfaction in New York were hopeless.

On 10 December, Livingston sailed for England to present his case to the Lords of Trade and Plantations. He spent more than a year in England, making contacts and lobbying for a satisfactory settlement. Livingston's demands were quite straightforward: reimbursement for the nearly £3,000 he had lent to the New York government,

[48] For a more detailed account, see Leder, *Robert Livingston*, chap. 5. On New York's early colonial tax system, see Bonomi, *Factious People*, pp. 79–81. On the imperial customs service before the creation of the Board of Trade in 1696, see Charles M. Andrews, *The Colonial Period of American History*, 4 vols. (New Haven, 1937), vol. 4, chap. 7. As Andrews repeatedly noted, the colonial customs service was created primarily to regulate trade, not to raise revenue.

[49] New York council minutes, 14 May 1694, *Cal. S. P.*, 1693–96, no. 1043.

replacement of ten barrels of powder seized during Leisler's administration, royal confirmation of his Albany offices, and appropriation of an official salary—retroactive to 1676—for his services as Indian secretary.[50]

After spending what must have been a frustrating and expensive year in England, the Lords of Trade vindicated Livingston on every issue, but the tangible results of this moral victory fell far short of his expectations. Most disappointing was that the home government approved Livingston's accounts but then ordered that they be paid by the New York government. In England, Livingston received only £668 sterling in interest from the royal paymaster; the Lords of Trade directed the New York government to pay the remaining £501 sterling in interest owed on Livingston's accounts. Similarly, although Livingston received royal warrants confirming both his Albany offices and a £100 salary for the Indian affairs post, the Crown ordered New York authorities to pay his entire annual salary.[51]

When Livingston returned to New York in August 1696, he was therefore once again at the mercy of Governor Fletcher, who by now was his personal and political enemy. Fletcher resented Livingston's having gone over his head by appealing to his London-based superiors, and he knew Livingston had disparaged his administration in order to get the backing of his political opponents in England. The governor was determined to prevent Livingston from getting what he wanted. He denied Livingston's petitions for redress, asserting that he had exaggerated his monetary claims and invented the secretaryship for Indian affairs simply to increase his own personal income. On Fletcher's recommendation, the council ignored Livingston's vouchers and warrants and referred the matter to the Crown for reconsideration. Because cases of this type could be lost for years in the quagmire of imperial administration, Fletcher had in

[50] Case of Robert Livingston, 22 Aug. 1695, Livingston-Redmond MSS., reel 1. Leder argues that the secretaryship of Indian affairs did not exist independently of the Albany clerkship until 1696, when Livingston "decided to take advantage of the naiveté of the Lords of Trade and the Privy Council concerning intra-colonial administration to gain for himself an extra title and another salary." See his introduction to *Livingston Indian Records*, p. 8.

[51] Leder, *Robert Livingston*, chap. 6, provides a more detailed account of Livingston's stay in England. The decisions of the Lords of Trade and of the King-in-Council appear in *Cal. S. P.*, 1693–96, nos. 2085, 2147–49, 2225, 2241–42.

effect nullified what little Livingston had gained by his trip to England. Frustrated and embittered, Livingston temporarily withdrew from politics, hoped for a new governor, and wrote to English authorities denouncing Fletcher and demanding satisfaction.[52]

Although Fletcher's successor, the Earl of Bellomont, initially sympathized with Livingston, he was unable to raise enough money in either New York or England to satisfy his claims. Between 1698 and 1701, Livingston continued to provision the troops at Albany, and his claims against the government mounted.[53] Worse still, Bellomont sympathized with the Leislerians, Livingston's archenemies, and gave them the majority of seats on the provincial council. Livingston and his brother-in-law Peter Schuyler also sat on Governor Bellomont's council, and while he lived the governor was able to enforce a truce between the continually feuding factions. But on 5 March 1701 Bellomont died, leaving New York in chaos and Livingston at the mercy of his political opponents. His prominence as a government creditor made him an especially inviting target.

Out of power since 1691, the Leislerians were eager for revenge. As a particularly active and influential member of the anti-Leislerian faction, Livingston had good reason to fear his enemies' vengeance. Indeed, as early as November 1700, the Leislerian councillors had prevailed on Bellomont to remove Livingston from his Albany excise post, accusing him without justification of embezzlement and corruption. Next, the Leislerian assembly had persuaded the governor to refuse payment of £800 interest on funds that Livingston had lent the government. The following January, the councillors voted to suspend Livingston's salaries for his Albany offices and to put off paying the back salary he claimed "till his Majesty's pleasure be known." Then, in March, the Leislerian councillors resolved to convene the assembly, as scheduled, in April, despite the anti-Leislerians' protests that Bellomont's death had dissolved the legislature, which had been summoned by the governor's writ.[54]

---

[52] Leder, *Robert Livingston*, chap. 6–7. Fletcher's Tory patrons in England had fallen from power by mid-1695. Livingston therefore courted the newly ascendant Whigs—Fletcher's enemies—among them Fletcher's eventual successor, the Earl of Bellomont.

[53] Bellomont to Board of Trade, 28 June, 21 Oct. 1698, 17 Oct. 1700, *DRNY*, 4:331–32, 399, 723; Generall Account of Victualling his majesties forces, 1 May 1698–1 Nov. 1700, Livingston-Redmond MSS., reel 1.

[54] Bellomont to Board of Trade, 23 Nov. 1700, *DRNY*, 4:776–77; New York Coun-

Bellomont's death left the Leislerian councillors and assemblymen completely free to attack their political opponents. The Leislerians continued to withhold Livingston's salary and arrears; they also demanded that Livingston and Schuyler present their victualing accounts to the assembly on the grounds that they allegedly had overcharged the government in order to pad their own profits. Livingston refused to relinquish his account books to an openly hostile legislature, and in August 1701 the assembly retaliated by passing a law to confiscate his estate. Meanwhile, the Leislerians consolidated their power by expelling their opponents from the legislature. Outside the assembly they also intensified their attacks on their most outspoken anti-Leislerian critics. For instance, in January 1702, a Leislerian court convicted Nicholas Bayard of treason and sentenced him to death, although Bayard's only crime was disparaging the Leislerian leaders in his letters to the home government. Livingston's situation was less critical than Bayard's, but he also suffered the wrath of the Leislerians. In April the council resolved to enforce the confiscation act against his estate and to suspend him from the provincial council.[55]

To Livingston, the political situation in 1701 was ominously reminiscent of Leisler's Rebellion. "Our governm[en]t here," he lamented, is "much out of frame, our parties being more divided I think than eleven years ago. . . . The Councell, Assembly, & indeed the whole Province, [are] divided & in a foment."[56] Even the arrival of Lieutenant Governor John Nanfan in May 1701 did little to arrest the political vendetta that had erupted in New York. Nanfan tried to

---

cil minutes, 30 Jan. 1701, *Cal. S. P.*, 1701, no. 350; Remonstrance of Peter Schuyler and Robert Livingston, 31 Mar. 1701, Livingston-Redmond MSS., reel 2; Schuyler and Livingston's approval of Col. Smith's paper, 14 Apr. 1701, ibid.; Smith, Schuyler, and Livingston to Board of Trade, 30 Apr. 1701, *DRNY*, 4:857–61.

55 *Assem. J.*, 1:115–21; *Coun. J.*, 1:159; *NY Col. Laws*, 1:462–65; Petition of the Protestants of New York to King William, 30 Dec. 1701, *DRNY*, 4:933–42; Nanfan and council to Board of Trade, 21 Jan. 1702, ibid., 4:942–43; *Cal. Coun. Min.*, pp. 167, 170; Nanfan's reasons for suspending Robert Livingston, 27 Apr. 1702, *DHNY*, 3:629–30. On the Bayard trial, see Adrian Howe, "The Bayard Treason Trial: Dramatizing Anglo-Dutch Politics in Early Eighteenth-Century New York City," *WMQ*, 3d ser., 47 (1990): 57–89. Bellomont's successor, Lord Cornbury, later exonerated Bayard.

56 Livingston to Fitz-John Winthrop, 14 Apr. 1701, Mass. Hist. Soc. *Collections*, 6th ser., 3 (1889): 67.

restrain the Leislerians, but they were determined to have revenge and he was too weak to stop them.

In 1701–2, Livingston was in danger of losing everything he had gained in New York over the past quarter-century. His enemies on the council and in the assembly sought to destroy his reputation and deprive him of his estate. His political influence had evaporated with the Leislerian ascendancy and the loss of his patrons. Yet Livingston did not flee New York in 1701, as he had in 1690, because this second Leislerian challenge was far more formidable than the first. In 1689–91, the anti-Leislerians knew that Leisler's regime had not been sanctioned by the Crown and that the legislature convened by Leisler was illegal because at that time New York had no elective assembly. By contrast, in 1701, the Leislerian councillors and assemblymen had attained their offices legitimately, and any laws they chose to pass would stand unless specifically disallowed by the King-in-Council. Consequently, Livingston withdrew from politics, but he remained in New York, where he could keep an eye on his opponents while he and the other anti-Leislerians wrote repeatedly to England asking that a new governor be sent to restore order. By the autumn of 1701, they had learned that King William had chosen Edward Hyde, Viscount Cornbury, to succeed Bellomont. Cornbury arrived in New York in May 1702, and the brief Leislerian revival was over.[57]

Cornbury's arrival brought Livingston safety but not satisfaction. Although the governor's council verified his financial claims and dismissed all the charges against him, Cornbury himself delayed settling Livingston's case, unwilling or unable to repay the government's outstanding debts. Finally, in 1703 Livingston decided it was time to return to London to seek restitution. After an encounter with French privateers on the high seas, he arrived in England that July, bearing thirty-five documents attesting to the legality of his claims. Livingston did not return to New York until 1706. For three years, he presented his petitions and vouchers to the Board of Trade and the Lords of the Treasury and cultivated potential patrons who could support his cause. Politicking was tedious business, but

---

[57] Livingston to Board of Trade, 21 June 1701, *Cal. S. P.*, no. 567; John Riggs to Livingston, 22 Nov. 1701, Livingston-Redmond MSS., reel 2; Nicholas Bayard to Livingston, David Jamison to Livingston, and William Sharpas to Livingston, all 24 Nov. 1701, ibid.

Livingston ultimately was rewarded for his perseverance. He received payment, in England, for the £2,300 sterling he demanded. In addition, Queen Anne issued new commissions to confirm him in his Albany offices, and she also confirmed his salary as secretary for Indian affairs. The home government approved all of Livingston's claims, save a belated request for £394, New York currency, that was referred to the provincial council.[58] Thus, after years of travail and uncertainty, he successfully concluded this most frustrating phase of his career as a government creditor.

Livingston's interest in imperial affairs never waned, but when he returned to New York in 1706 he apparently decided to give up politics in order to concentrate on his personal business. Until 1709, he avoided politics, appearing before the governor and council only to request unsuccessfully recognition of his new royal commissions and payment of his salary as Indian affairs secretary. In 1709, Livingston did nominally reenter the political arena as an assemblyman representing Albany County, but only to secure statutory repeal of the 1701 act that threatened his estate with confiscation. Early in the first session, Livingston introduced his bill, which passed in both houses. He represented Albany in the next assembly, which convened in September 1710, in order to ensure that the newly arrived Governor Robert Hunter would recommend his bill to the Board of Trade for royal approval. After securing Hunter's recommendation in November, Livingston left the assembly, possibly expecting never to return.[59]

After 1706, Livingston intended to expand and diversify his various business interests. As early as 1690, he had begun investing in ships, purchasing a half-interest in the *Margriet,* a vessel that journeyed to Madagascar, Barbados, and Virginia to trade in slaves, sugar, and tobacco.[60] Within a few years, Livingston acquired shares

---

[58] Livingston's affairs in London were extraordinarily complicated. For a lucid account of his maneuvers and the proceedings of the government, see Leder, *Robert Livingston,* pp. 187–97. At this time, the New York pound was worth approximately one-third less than the English pound sterling (McCusker, *Money and Exchange,* pp. 162–65). Hereafter, all references will be to New York pounds unless otherwise noted.

[59] *Assem. J.,* 1:242–43, 264–65, 271–88; Hunter to Board of Trade, 10 Nov. 1710, *Cal. S. P.,* 1710–11, no. 487.

[60] *Rek vant Ship de Margriet,* 1690, Livingston-Redmond MSS., reel 1. On New

in four more ships, three of which he owned in partnership with his brother-in-law Peter Schuyler. Two of these ships were sloops, small ships that Livingston and Schuyler used to transport goods between Albany and New York, particularly during their stint as military contractors.[61] In 1710 Livingston purchased a 34-foot sloop of his own, which he named *Caledonia* in remembrance of his native Scotland. Ownership of his own sloop placed him among the elite of the merchants of Albany County and even distinguished him as the head of one of New York's leading commercial families. Toward the end of the seventeenth century, only six or seven sloops sailed the Hudson River, and most of them were owned by merchants based in New York City. Even as late as 1765, Albany County had only thirty-five sloops consistently employed in the Hudson River trade, and most of those seem to have been owned in shares rather than by individual traders.[62]

Commissioning the *Caledonia* was part of Livingston's most ambitious entrepreneurial scheme, a plan to eliminate the middlemen at both ends of his trade in furs, by dealing directly with the Indians on the frontier and by shipping his cargoes out of his own trading house downriver in New York City. To this end, in 1707, Livingston purchased the "Great Island" in the Mohawk River, where he planned to establish a private trading post where he could deal directly with the local Indians. Then, in 1709, he became a freeman of the city of New York in order to be permitted to conduct overseas trade in his own name in that city. Livingston had owned land in Manhattan since 1693 and had built a new house there in 1697, but

---

York's early trade with Madagascar, see Jacob Judd, "Frederick Philipse and the Madagascar Trade," *New-York Historical Society Quarterly,* 55 (1971): 354–75; James G. Lydon, "New York and the Slave Trade, 1700 to 1774," *WMQ,* 3d ser., 35 (1978): 376–77.

[61] Accounts of the *Orange,* 1694, Livingston-Redmond MSS., reel 1; Account of money Disbursed by Robt. Livingston for the Materialls and workmanship of three new vessels, 2 Oct. 1694, ibid.

[62] David Arthur Armour, "The Merchants of Albany, New York: 1686–1760" (Ph.D. diss., Northwestern University, 1965), pp. 50–52; Indenture between Evert Pells and Robert Livingston, 8 June 1710, Livingston-Redmond MSS., reel 3; Inventory of Furniture, Tackle & Apparrell belonging to . . . the *Caledonia,* 10 July 1710, ibid.; I. N. Phelps Stokes, *The Iconography of Manhattan Island, 1498–1909,* 6 vols. (New York, 1915–28), 4:396; Dongan's report on New York, 22 Feb. 1687, *DHNY,* 1:160; James and John Montressor, *The Montressor Journals,* ed. G. D. Scull (New York, 1882), p. 33.

only when he was freed of his government contracts did he decide to become a permanent member of the city's mercantile community.[63] Unlike most Albany traders, who employed New York merchants to receive and ship their goods in return for a small commission, Livingston decided to control both ends of his Hudson River trade.

At the same time, Livingston gradually attempted to exploit the potential of his Hudson Valley manor. Like New York's other great landowners, he responded to the growing demand for foodstuffs by building mills to attract settlers and thereby increase his trade. In 1699, Livingston erected both a gristmill and a sawmill on Roeloff Jansen's Kill near the Hudson River. Livingston's gristmill was the first built on the east side of the Hudson. He spent approximately £800 building both mills, but they more than repaid his investment. Serving tenants and nontenants alike, the mill brought new business to the Manor and was directly responsible for the establishment of a new general store there. Mill owners often became the leading storekeepers in rural areas because farmers needed mills to grind their grain and—in a cash-poor economy—they also traded their grain for tools, dry goods, and other items their families needed. The mills thus helped the Livingstons to become Albany County's leading rural merchants. Supervising the mills and stocking the store became full-time occupations for Alida Livingston, who spent increasingly more time at the Manor attending to its expanding enterprises.[64]

Within a few years, however, Livingston's growing interest in his landed estate led him back into the business of government. In 1710, Governor Robert Hunter offered him what appeared to be a golden opportunity to profit from his relatively unimproved and under-populated Hudson Valley manor. The home government had instructed Hunter to set up a naval stores industry in the Hudson Valley, and he had brought with him 2,000 Palatine refugees who

[63] Leases and releases of Jan and Bata Clute to Robert Livingston, 25 June, 26 June, 12 Aug., 25 Sept. 1707, Livingston-Redmond MSS., reel 2; Account of Expences for building my house at N[ew] Yorke, 20 Apr.–3 July 1697, ibid.; Certificate of the Mayor and Aldermen of the City of New York, 13 Dec. 1709, ibid., reel 3; Leder, *Robert Livingston*, pp. 202, 211.

[64] Duncan Campbell's account of Iron Work for the Mills, 15 Mar. 1699, Livingston-Redmond MSS., reel 2; Biemer, ed., "Business Letters," pp. 183–207; John J. McCusker and Russell R. Menard, *The Economy of British America* (Chapel Hill, N.C., 1985), p. 322.

were expected to work producing naval stores in exchange for their paid passage to America. Hunter needed suitable forested land; Livingston had thousands of uncleared acres. In September 1710, the two men concluded a mutually beneficial transaction whereby Livingston sold the queen's government 6,000 acres for £400, a sum not much less than what he had paid for his original 160,000 acres. In November, Hunter also awarded Livingston an exclusive contract to provide the Palatines with everything they needed for their work and their subsistence. Livingston built a brewery and a baking-house, which—along with the Manor mills and store—supplied the Palatines' necessities. At the Manor, Alida supervised the baking, brewing, and provisioning while Robert attended to their business in New York and Albany.[65]

Despite Livingston's earlier difficulties as a government creditor, Hunter's proposal for settling and maintaining the Palatines on Manor land was too tempting to refuse. For Livingston, the long-term benefits of the Palatine project were substantial. When the naval stores project collapsed for lack of funds in 1712, at least forty-eight Palatine families came to settle at Livingston Manor; the descendants of these early tenant farmers comprised a majority of the Manor's colonial population.[66] The one hundred Palatine families who remained in their four original settlements, formerly part of the Manor, also helped Livingston's business. Like his own tenants, these farmers often sold Livingston their wheat and regularly purchased merchandise at his general store.[67]

[65] Deed of Robert and Alida Livingston to Hunter, 29 Sept. 1710, *DHNY*, 3:644–51; Contract between Hunter and Livingston, 13 Nov. 1710, ibid., 3:653–55. Tar had been produced in Albany County at least as early as 1682, and for several years the home government had considered New York a potential source of naval stores (*Albany Minutes*, 3:236; Cornbury to Board of Trade, 29 Sept. 1702, *DRNY*, 4:976). On the Palatine experiment, see Walter Allen Knittle, *Early Eighteenth Century Palatine Emigration: A British Government Redemptioner Project to Manufacture Naval Stores* (Philadelphia, 1937).

[66] Palatine Debtors who Live in the mannor, 23 Feb. 1726, Livingston-Redmond MSS., reel 4. Most of these tenants or their descendants also appear in the Livingston Manor rent ledger, 1767–84, Livingston Family Papers, NYHS, reel 15.

[67] Posts . . . for goods Sold out of the Shop upon Trust, Mar. 1712–Mar. 1714, Livingston-Redmond MSS., reel 3; Debts due by the Palatines Living in the 4 Villages, 26 Dec. 1718, 1 Jan. 1721, 1 Feb. 1722, 23 Feb. 1726, ibid., reels 3 and 4; Palatine Debtors who Live in the mannor, 23 Feb. 1726, ibid., reel 4; Wheat from the Palatines [for] our Sloop, Mar. 1719, ibid. For the population distribution of the Palatines after

The arrival and settlement of the Palatines marked the turning point in the development of Livingston's Manor trade. According to Robert Livingston's ledgers, in 1696, only 11 of 238, or less than 5 percent, of his Hudson Valley clients resided at the Manor; by 1710, the 18 Manor debtors he listed still accounted for only 8 percent of the total. Between 1710 and 1714, however, the number of debtors at the Manor nearly doubled, from 18 to 32, with the latter accounting for almost 18 percent of Livingston's clients in the valley.[68]

As the Manor's population continued to grow, Livingston increasingly concentrated his valley business among its tenant farmers. By 1726, he had 114 clients living at the Manor, and he seems to have curtailed his trade with more distant communities in the Hudson Valley. In 1726, Livingston's Manor clients comprised two-thirds of the valley debtors listed in the ledgers; on the other hand, Livingston listed no accounts with people living in Schenectady, Rensselaerswyck, and Ulster and Dutchess counties, all areas with which he had previously conducted an extensive trade. Livingston's tenants also accounted for an increasing proportion of the monetary value of his outstanding accounts. In 1710, Manor residents accounted for roughly 17 percent of the money that valley residents owed Livingston. By 1714, that proportion had increased to approximately 50 percent of the total. By 1726, some 114 Manor residents were indebted to Robert Livingston for a total of £796, a sum that represented nearly 60 percent of the combined value of all outstanding valley debts that Livingston recorded in his ledger.[69]

Thus, while the naval stores project itself failed dismally, its long-term results for Livingston were beneficial. In the short term, however, both Livingston and Hunter suffered the ill effects of having underwritten a project that lacked adequate financial backing from the home government. Expecting reimbursement from England, Hunter had advanced £32,071 to set up the naval stores experiment, and Livingston had lent him at least £10,000 in supplies and provi-

---

1712, see the Rev. J. F. Haeger's *Noticias Parochiales*, 19 May 1715, 20 July 1717, SPG Archives, Letter Book A, vols. 10 and 12; Account of the German families, 1718, *DHNY*, 1:692.

[68] Lists of debtors drawn out of Ledger F, 20 Jan. 1710, 15 Dec. 1714, Livingston-Redmond MSS., reel 3.

[69] Ibid., 20 Jan. 1710, 15 Dec. 1714, 30 Mar. 1726, ibid., reels 3–4.

sions.[70] But funding from England never arrived, and New York's provincial treasury was virtually bankrupt. Hunter spent the first five years of his administration trying to keep himself and his government solvent; he spent the next two years compensating Livingston for his frustrations and trying to help him recover his investments. For instance, while Livingston awaited payment of the money the government owed him, Hunter gave him a patent that verified the disputed northern boundary of Livingston Manor and provided for its separate representation in the provincial legislature. Predictably, Livingston was elected to fill the Manor's new legislative seat. In 1717, he took his place among the members of New York's seventeenth assembly.[71]

Livingston wanted an assembly seat for the Manor in order to guarantee that he would be on hand when the legislators discussed payment of outstanding government debts. He entered the assembly in 1717—as he had in 1709 and 1710—primarily to protect his personal interests. With Hunter's assistance, he was able to prevail on the assembly to allocate money to pay most of his accounts. He also used this opportunity to persuade both Hunter and the assemblymen to redefine the boundary between Albany and Dutchess counties so that the Manor would lay entirely within the former and its proprietor would be spared the expense of paying taxes in two counties. In the next legislative session, Livingston's election to the speakership was a tribute to his political service and skill, as well as recognition of his status as elder statesman and the governor's trusted ally.[72]

Until he retired from politics in 1726, Livingston enjoyed cordial relations with New York's governors. Livingston's estate was secure, his accounts were paid, and his position was firmly established; he

[70] Account of the moneys paid by Hunter, Dec. 1717, *Cal. S. P.*, 1717–18, no. 235; Livingston's account for subsistence of the Palatines, 26 Mar. –24 June 1711, *DHNY*, 3:668. The latter documents Livingston's claim of £4,000 for three months' provisions; he held the provisioning contract for more than one year.

[71] Hunter's patent to Livingston, 1 Oct. 1715, *DHNY*, 3:690–702. His son Philip supervised the voting at the Manor in the 1717 election. See Philip's letters to his father, 22 Apr. and 25 Apr. 1717, Livingston-Redmond MSS., reel 3. On Hunter's difficulties with the assembly, see Bonomi, *Factious People*, pp. 81–85; Leder, *Robert Livingston*, chap. 14.

[72] *Coun. J.*, 1:597; *Assem. J.*, 1:395, 405, 407, 412–13; *NY Col. Laws*, 1:957–85; Philip Livingston to Robert Livingston, 20 May 1717, Livingston-Redmond MSS., reel 3.

no longer needed a patron. Having learned his lesson, Livingston refrained from further involvement with government contracts. In 1713, the signing of the Treaty of Utrecht ended Queen Anne's War and thus made his services less critical. Moreover, he now had no need to serve the governors financially because—as speaker until 1725—his political services were substantial.

Indeed, Livingston's political influence reached its zenith under Hunter's successor, Governor William Burnet, who arrived in New York in 1720. Burnet shared Livingston's commitment to British imperial interests, as well as several mutual friends and acquaintances. The new governor was Hunter's friend and political ally; he also married a New Yorker, Mary Van Horne, who was the first cousin of Livingston's son-in-law Cornelius Van Horne of New York City.[73] Although there is no evidence that Livingston promoted the match, the inclusion of the governor in his own extended family must have reinforced his growing political influence. The relationship between Livingston and Burnet was a partnership of near-equals who shared common views and interests.

As speaker of the assembly, Livingston used his position in the lower house to promote the governor's legislative programs. Of these the most controversial was Burnet's plan to eliminate New York's trade with French Canada—a plan first proposed by Livingston himself and approved in principle by Governor Hunter in 1720. Livingston, Hunter, and Burnet all believed that trade fostered friendship between Europeans and Indians; they also knew that the Indians bought large quantities of English manufactures. Because ending the Canada trade would have deprived the French of the English goods that the Indians wanted, Livingston and the governors argued that such an arrangement would force the western tribes to trade only with the English, thus leaving French Canada isolated and without allies.[74]

This plan was opposed both by the Albany merchants, who traded with Canada, and by their suppliers, the import merchants in New York City. But the merchants were outnumbered in the assembly, where Livingston and Lewis Morris were able to secure a majority in

[73] C. S. Williams, *Jan Cornelis Van Horne and His Descendants* (New York, 1912), pp. 6, 34, 54.
[74] Livingston to Peter Schuyler, 23 Aug. 1720, *DRNY*, 5:559–61; Hunter to Board of Trade, 20 July 1720, ibid., 5:552.

favor of Burnet's legislation.[75] The law passed in 1720 prohibited certain enumerated "Indian goods" from being transported north of Albany, in the hope that this trade would be redirected from Canada to the west, where it would become the basis for an English alliance with the western Indians. But Burnet's law proved unenforceable; for every illegal trader the government caught, many others got through to their Canadian destination. Therefore, in 1726, Burnet requested and got a seemingly more practical law that sought to tax the Canada trade out of existence by imposing double duties on all goods going north of Albany. By then, however, merchants in both New York and London were lobbying against the governor's policies. The Crown finally disallowed all the trade laws in 1729.[76] By then, Livingston was dead and Burnet had been recalled to England.

Despite his principled support of British imperial interests, Robert Livingston valued public life primarily as a source of private profits. Livingston's generation looked upon politics as a business. He and his contemporaries would not have understood the notions of public service and noblesse oblige that informed the public careers of many of their descendants.

Livingston found politics fascinating for the material rewards it brought and for the personal challenge it offered, but he did not view political activity as a means to establish an honorable public identity. Indeed, Livingston's activities as a government creditor earned him a reputation for excessive greed and unscrupulous jobbery—certainly not honorable personal qualities. In 1696, Governor Benjamin Fletcher claimed that Livingston was "known by all men to have neither religion nor morality . . . [and] would rather be called knave Livingston than poor Livingston." Lord Cornbury accused him of being "guilty of the most notorious frauds by which he improv'd his estate." Both Fletcher and Cornbury, themselves corrupt and unscrupulous, were hardly reliable witnesses. But Governor

[75] On the rivalry between the landed and commercial interests in New York politics, particularly in the 1720s, see Bonomi, *Factious People*, pp. 87–97. Among Albany merchants, even Philip Livingston detested the new trade laws, though he never said so publicly. See his letters to his father, 8 Feb., 20 Feb. 1721, 15 May 1724, Livingston-Redmond MSS., reel 4.

[76] *Assem. J.*, 1:445, 447–48; *NY Col. Laws*, 2:8–10, 2:351; Report of the King's Council, 19 Nov. 1729, *DRNY*, 5:897–99. See also Thomas Eliot Norton, *The Fur Trade in Colonial New York* (Madison, Wis., 1974), pp. 137–51.

Robert Hunter, Livingston's friend and an honest man for the times, also described him as "the most selfish man alive" because of his tenacity in recovering debts owed him.[77]

In all his years in provincial politics, Livingston never seemed to mind such insults. Instead, he returned them in kind and played the political game to the best of his ability. Political name-calling was commonplace in Livingston's New York, and people participating in factional politics could expect their reputations to suffer. Livingston was the product of an age and a place noted for its unsavory business and political practices. He was no more avaricious than most of his contemporaries, though ultimately more successful.

In every sense, Robert Livingston was a self-made man. He made his own fortune, as well as his own contacts and connections, upon which the success of his early career, in particular, depended. Livingston had no kin in America, but marriage to Alida Schuyler brought him a circle of prominent relations. At the same time, he used his personal connections and talents to forge a network of patron-client relations among the colony's political leaders. Livingston relied heavily on the goodwill of his patrons, whose support enabled him to garner prestige, wealth, and influence. Together with Alida, he founded a family business that would grow to magnificent proportions in later generations.

Robert and Alida bequeathed to their six children wealth, landholdings, social status, and an impressive network of public and personal connections. Over the years, politics and patronage had brought them land and tenants, offices and influence, public fame and private profits. Indeed, Robert Livingston's success in politics enabled him to bequeath to his children the luxury of abstention. His sons would have less need for public attachments because he himself would be their greatest patron.

[77] Fletcher to the N.Y. agents, 20 Dec. 1696, *Cal. S. P.*, 1696–97, no. 522; Edward Hyde, Earl of Clarendon (formerly Lord Cornbury) to Lord Dartmouth, 8 Mar. 1711, *DHNY*, 3:656–57; Hunter to Francis Nicholson, 22 Oct. 1711, ibid.

[2]

The Family Business

O ver four generations, the story of the Livingstons' family business demonstrates the persistence of entrepreneurial values
throughout the colonial era. The entrepreneurial ideal of the
founding generation of colonial Livingstons lauded industry, so-
briety, and above all success. Such values impelled successive generations to expand and diversify the enterprises established by Robert
and Alida.

The growth of the Livingstons' family business was symptomatic
of more general changes in New York's colonial economy. New
York's economy was dynamic and expansive; a growing population
meant increased productivity, which in turn led to a remarkable
growth in colonial commerce. As trade grew, it became more diversified, as colonial merchants experimented with new products and
new markets. At the same time, they also developed industrial enterprises to complement their commercial interests. The growth of the
Livingstons' commercial fortune thus encouraged them to build the
mills and the ironworks that put them on the cutting edge of industrial development in eighteenth-century America. On the other
hand, the growth of the family itself helped them expand their
trading networks by delegating various commercial tasks to willing
sons and brothers.

Robert Livingston's success in politics and trade enabled him to
give his children the advantages he himself had lacked when he

arrived in New York in 1675. Between 1680 and 1698, Alida Livingston gave birth to nine children, six of whom survived to adulthood. Those four sons and two daughters received educational training that would enable them to prosper as members of an Anglo-Dutch colonial community. Later, they benefited from their parents' many business and political contacts. Finally, Robert and Alida used their wealth to help their adult children establish their own households, and when they died they left to their offspring their landed and commercial fortunes. Education, connections, and material wealth were Robert and Alida's legacy to the second generation.

But Robert and Alida also passed on to their children the bourgeois values usually associated with the Protestant ethic. While they used the fruits of their own success to promote their children's future prospects, they also expected their children to work diligently, to become self-sufficient as adults, and to maintain their own households. Robert Livingston wrote three wills between 1690 and his death in 1728; how he disposed of his real and personal property tells us something about his values.[1] Livingston's revisions consistently rewarded industry and self-reliance, while punishing indolence, extravagance, and dependence. Although Robert and Alida left no written record of the lessons they taught their children, Robert's wills suggest that they expected the younger Livingstons to find virtue in work and evil in idleness.

When the Livingston children were coming of age, their family's fortunes were by no means secure. Consequently, Robert and Alida sought to give their children practical educations that would enable them to live independently, without parental assistance. The Livingstons' four sons and two daughters learned their earliest lessons at home. In 1690, Robert's will appointed Alida "tutrix" of their minor children, and because he was often away from home she was probably responsible for most of their early education. Alida taught her children to read and write both English and Dutch, though their letters suggest that sons were better trained in the use of both languages. Children also received religious and moral instruction, and sons and daughters alike learned basic arithmetic, an

[1] Wills of Robert Livingston, 3 Mar. 1690, 24 Jan. 1710, 10 Feb. 1721, Livingston-Redmond MSS., reels 1, 3, and 4, respectively. See also the codicil to Livingston's will, 22 Sept. 1722, ibid., reel 4.

accomplishment necessary both for trade and for efficient household management.[2]

While the Livingstons' four sons left home at an early age to receive their formal schooling, their sisters Margaret and Joanna remained at home until they married. At home, the Livingston daughters learned how to cook, sew, and manage a household. Although Alida's participation in the family business was permanent and ongoing, she and Robert expected their daughters to be involved in trade only as "deputy husbands," filling in for absent men when doing so could advance their family's material interests.[3] Alida therefore taught her daughters only the fundamental business skills they needed to discharge their duties competently when they acted as deputy husbands. This relative decline of female entrepreneurship in the Livingston family was symptomatic of a gradual drift toward more rigidly defined sex roles throughout colonial America. Unlike their mother, Margaret and Joanna would not be full-fledged businesswomen, but neither would they be the idealized ornamental wives of the late colonial era.[4]

Surviving letters indicate that both Margaret and Joanna were thoroughly acquainted with their husbands' business interests. In 1700, Margaret Livingston (1681–1758) married Colonel Samuel Vetch, a Scottish soldier who had arrived in New York just one year earlier. Joanna Livingston (1694–1733) married New York City merchant Cornelius Van Horne in 1720, three years after Robert and Alida had put an end to Henry Beekman's courtship of their younger daughter. Margaret Livingston Vetch actually began trading on

[2] Will of Robert Livingston, 3 Mar. 1690, ibid., reel 1. The Dutch believed that both boys and girls should learn the fundamentals of reading, writing, and arithmetic—unlike the English, who were far less interested in educating girls and young women. See William Heard Kilpatrick, *The Dutch Schools of New Netherland and Colonial New York* (Washington, D.C., 1912), pp. 216–27.

[3] The concept of the "deputy husband" is taken from Laurel Thatcher Ulrich, *Good Wives: Image and Reality in the Lives of Women in Northern New England, 1650–1750* (New York, 1980), chap. 2.

[4] For parallels elsewhere, see Lois Green Carr and Lorena S. Walsh, "The Planter's Wife: The Experience of White Women in Seventeenth-Century Maryland," *WMQ*, 3d ser., 34 (1977): 542–71; Joan R. Gunderson and Gwen Victor Gampel, "Married Women's Legal Status in Eighteenth-Century New York and Virginia," ibid., 39 (1982): 133–34. On the changing gender conventions of the late colonial era, see Ruth H. Bloch, "American Feminine Ideals in Transition: The Rise of the Moral Mother, 1785–1815," *Feminist Studies*, 4 (1987): 103, 108–16.

her own during her husband's frequent absences, and she continued trading intermittently after his death in 1732. Customs records reveal that she imported dry goods in 1707, sent beaver skins to Boston in 1708, and imported rum in 1721 and wine in 1748. Family correspondence shows that Margaret also traded within New York, exploiting her family connections to obtain credit and contacts. Margaret's family and business associates neither condemned nor applauded her commercial activities; as a widow with young children, she was merely filling in for a permanently absent husband and father.[5]

Margaret's trading ventures were occasional and unforeseen by her parents, but Robert and Alida expected their sons to become self-supporting by working permanently in useful occupations. Consequently, Margaret and Joanna's brothers left home between the ages of nine and twelve in order to receive their formal educations. Once his sons returned home, Robert Livingston used his wealth and influence to help establish them in their respective occupations.[6] All four sons ultimately chose careers in trade, and Livingston helped them get the experience and connections that they needed to succeed by allowing each son at some time to act as his business agent. Livingston also sought to advance his sons politically, using his influence to win them offices. They did not, however, inherit their father's fascination with government and politics; unlike him, they played only limited roles in New York's colonial politics.

Robert Livingston had expected his eldest son, John (1680–1720), to succeed him as the family's nominal leader. Indeed, as early as 1690, Livingston had entailed the Manor to his eldest son so that both the identity of the family estate and the prestige of its proprietors would be preserved.[7] But Livingston also expected John to work for a living and probably envisioned for him a career in the Anglo-American trade. Between 1691 and 1693, John lodged in the

---

[5] Henry Douglas to Philip Livingston, 27 May, 27 Dec. 1709, Livingston-Redmond MSS., reel 6; Joanna Livingston Van Horne to Robert Livingston, 8 July 1725, ibid., reel 4; Henry Livingston to Robert Livingston, Jr., 11 Oct. 1742, ibid., reel 7; Jean P. Jordan, "Women Merchants in Colonial New York," *NY Hist.*, 58 (1977): 420.

[6] For a good summary of their early lives, see Lawrence H. Leder, "Robert Livingston's Sons: Preparation for Futurity," *NY Hist.*, 50 (1969): 238–39, 242–47.

[7] Will of Robert Livingston, 3 Mar. 1690, Livingston-Redmond MSS., reel 1.

New London, Connecticut, home of Fitz-John Winthrop, while he studied with a local tutor. After returning from Connecticut, John spent a year in New York City studying with another tutor, Joseph Davis. In 1695, he journeyed with his father to London, where he served a mercantile apprenticeship in the office of William Bridgman. The following year, John returned to New York with his father and assumed his duties as an agent in his parents' commercial network.[8]

By 1701, however, John had left the family business, married Mary Winthrop, and moved to Connecticut. Marrying the only child of Connecticut's governor brought John some impressive political contacts, but he was much more interested in trade than in politics. Despite his father-in-law's influence, John's political career in Connecticut consisted of only two years in the provincial legislature. Instead, John Livingston planned to make his fortune quickly by investing his marriage settlement in an illegal trading venture to Canada. His partner in this venture was Colonel Samuel Vetch, who had become part of the Livingston family by marrying John's sister Margaret just one year earlier. This scheme proved disastrous, despite the partners' initial optimism. The authorities seized their ship, the *Mary,* and confiscated its cargo.[9]

The seizure of the *Mary* in 1701 nearly ruined John Livingston, though he continued to regard himself as a merchant, to dabble in trade, and to speak optimistically of his chances for future profits. Later, following Vetch's example, he tried his luck as a soldier and considered embarking on a new career in the military. John served under his brother-in-law in Queen Anne's War and in 1712 asked his father to "use all [his] Interist" with Governor Hunter to get him a "Seuperiour Command" in the British army. John never got his commission, and when the war ended in 1713, he left the army to manage his father-in-law's estates. John remarried after Mary Winthrop

[8] Leder, "Robert Livingston's Sons," pp. 238–39; Fitz-John Winthrop to Robert Livingston, [Dec. 1691], in *The Winthrop Papers,* Mass. Hist. Soc. *Collections,* 6th ser. (Boston, 1892), 3:511–12; A List of John Livingstones Cloathes . . . to be boarded at Mr. Davies house . . . , 5 Apr. 1693, Livingston-Redmond MSS., reel 1; Journall of our voyage to England . . . , 1694–95, trans. A. J. F. Van Laer, ibid.; John Livingston to Robert Livingston, 12 May 1698, ibid., reel 2.

[9] *The Public Records of the Colony of Connecticut,* 15 vols. (Hartford, 1850–90), 5:1, 17, 29, 37; G. M. Waller, *Samuel Vetch: Colonial Enterpriser* (Chapel Hill, N.C., 1960), pp. 58–63.

Livingston died in 1713; his new wife was Elizabeth Knight of Boston. In 1720, John Livingston died at the age of forty.[10]

Philip Livingston (1686–1749), Robert and Alida's second son and eventual heir, was far more successful than his older brother. Alone among the Livingston sons, Philip was educated in New York entirely. Robert probably expected his second son to earn his living as an Albany trader. After studying briefly with a Dutch tutor, Philip spent a year in the Huguenot community of the New Rochelle, where he learned French to facilitate his entry into the growing trade with French Canada. He probably then served a mercantile apprenticeship in Albany, before beginning his career as a general merchant and fur trader. From 1707 on, Philip also acted as his father's unofficial deputy for his local offices. Robert undoubtedly remembered the valuable contacts he himself had made through his early involvement in Albany's local government. Now a prominent Albanian in his own right, Robert could use his position to help his son forge contacts among the town's leading citizens.[11]

When John Livingston died in 1720, Philip became the heir both to the Manor and to his father's political legacy. Consequently, shortly after John's death, Robert Livingston prevailed on Governor William Burnet to appoint Philip to succeed him as clerk of the court of Albany and secretary for Indian affairs; the following year, Robert also advised his son to cultivate the governor's goodwill in order to win a seat on the provincial council. The influence of the father and the courtiership of the son, together, proved successful; in May 1725, Philip began his twenty-four-year career as a member of the governor's council.[12]

---

[10] Waller, *Samuel Vetch*, pp. 190, 201–2, 237–38; John Livingston to Robert Livingston, 27 May 1712, Livingston-Redmond MSS., reel 3. For examples of John's unwarranted optimism with regard to his financial future, see his letters to his father, 7 Oct. 1701, 16 July, 9 Sept., 9 Oct. 1717, ibid., reels 2–3.

[11] William A. Brat to Robert Livingston, 15 Nov. 1697, Livingston-Redmond MSS., reel 2; Philip Livingston to Robert and Alida Livingston, 12 June 1700, ibid.; [Mr. Tuck?] to Robert Livingston, 15 Sept. 1701, ibid.; Joel Munsell, ed., *The Annals of Albany*, 10 vols. (Albany, 1850–59), 5:152.

[12] Philip Livingston to Robert Livingston, 8 Feb. 1721, Livingston-Redmond MSS., reel 4; King's commission to Philip Livingston, 30 July 1721, ibid., reel 6; George Bampfield to Livingston, 11 Sept. 1721, ibid., reel 4; Robert Livingston's petition to Burnet, 17 Nov. 1720, *Cal. S. P.*, 1720–21, no. 303; Burnet to Board of Trade, 26 Nov. 1720, ibid.; Samuel Vetch's petition to the Board of Trade, 16 Feb. 1721, ibid.,

Unlike his father, however, Philip always preferred business over politics; throughout his life he considered himself first and foremost a merchant. In 1724, for instance, Philip had refused to stand for a vacant Albany assembly seat because, though he believed he could win the election, he thought that attending the legislature would hurt his business. He explained to his father, "While the Assembly Sitts its comonly the best trade here, which must be attended as well as a farmer his plow." Later in life, Philip was obsessed with improving his estate in order to enhance his children's patrimony. Politics, by comparison, seemed neither necessary nor productive. After his father's death in 1728, Philip's letters rarely mentioned political matters, and while he undoubtedly believed that his family's importance merited a seat on the provincial council, he attended only a third of the council's meetings during his twenty-four-year tenure.[13]

When Philip did participate in politics, he did so as his father had, primarily to make a profit. In particular, he was able to use his influence as secretary for Indian affairs to acquire thousands of acres of unimproved land in the Mohawk River valley.[14] Philip believed that his own use of politics for profit was not exceptional; indeed, he believed that self-interest determined the public conduct of most of the leading men in the colony. In New York's factional politics, he contended, "we Change Sides as Serves our Interest best, not the Countries." Even in wartime, he believed, New York's political leaders had "more Regard how to fill their Purces than how to Secure our Country."[15]

Perhaps because he regarded self-interest as the main end of political activity, or because he remembered the difficulties his father had

---

no. 385; Burnet to Board of Trade, 7 Nov. 1724, ibid., 1724–25, no. 392; Royal warrant, 31 May 1725, ibid., no. 639; *Cal. Coun. Min.,* p. 299.

[13] Philip Livingston to Robert Livingston, 25 Mar. 1724, Livingston-Redmond MSS., reel 4; *Coun. J.,* 1:521–2:1043 passim. See Philip's letter to his son Robert Livingston, Jr., 20 July 1741, for his sense of his own responsibility as patriarch and provider (Livingston-Redmond MSS., reel 7).

[14] Ingagement of the Sachims of the Upper Castle of the Maquase, 25 Jan. 1729, Rutherfurd Collection, NYHS, vol. 2; Release of five Indians to Philip Livingston et al., 2 May 1729, ibid., vol. 1; Patents to Philip Livingston et al., *Cal. Coun. Min.,* pp. 326, 331, 333, 344. See also Ruth L. Higgins, *Expansion in New York with Especial Reference to the Eighteenth Century* (Columbus, Ohio, 1931), pp. 67–88.

[15] Philip Livingston to Jacob Wendell, 17 Oct. 1737, 26 Feb. 1747, Livingston Papers, MCNY, box 2.

faced as a factional leader, Philip Livingston avoided taking a clear public position on the pivotal issues of his time. For instance, during Burnet's administration he privately criticized the same trade laws his father so wholeheartedly supported. Philip was an Albany merchant and, as he repeatedly complained to his father, Burnet's trade regulations severely curtailed his business. Yet, although he freely expressed his dissatisfaction in private, in public Philip pretended to be the governor's friend and supporter. Clearly, he wished to avoid antagonizing Burnet, who at the time was considering elevating him to the provincial council. Moreover, Philip probably did not want to embarrass his father publicly by opposing the policies he had done so much to establish.[16]

The ambiguous stance that Philip assumed in the 1720s fore-shadowed his conduct during the Morris-Cosby dispute of the 1730s, when he remained publicly uncritical of Governor William Cosby, though he genuinely sympathized with the Morrisite opposition. That dispute began over a seemingly minor issue, Governor William Cosby's attempt to deprive Council President Rip Van Dam of his salary. Cosby took his case against Van Dam to the provincial Supreme Court, where he wanted the case decided in equity. When the court ruled that they could not exercise equity jurisdiction, the governor replaced Chief Justice Lewis Morris with one of his own supporters, James DeLancey. DeLancey then decided the case in Cosby's favor, and Van Dam lost his salary without benefit of trial by jury. Meanwhile, Cosby proceeded to remove Morris's supporters from other provincial offices. Morris and his allies responded, in 1734, by helping John Peter Zenger establish the *New-York Weekly Journal*, the province's first opposition newspaper. The Morrisites founded the *Journal* expressly to criticize Cosby's government. Within a year the governor had the printer Zenger arrested for seditious libel.[17]

---

[16] Philip Livingston to Robert Livingston, 8 Feb., 20 Feb. 1721, 4 Jan., 15 May, 25 May, 16 June 1724, Livingston-Redmond MSS., reel 4. As late as 1726, Burnet recommended Philip to the governor of Canada as "my particular friend" (Burnet to Longueil, 5 July 1726, *DRNY*, 5:802).

[17] Two different but complementary accounts of the Morris-Cosby dispute are Patricia U. Bonomi, *A Factious People: Politics and Society in Colonial New York* (New York, 1971), chap. 4, and Eugene R. Sheridan, *Lewis Morris, 1671–1746: A Study in Early American Politics* (Syracuse, N.Y., 1981), chap. 8.

Lewis Morris and his adherents contended that Cosby's attempt to deprive Van Dam of his salary endangered the citizen's right to property, while the governor's decision to silence his opponents ultimately jeopardized both the freedom of the press and the independence of the judiciary. Privately, Philip Livingston agreed that "if Mr. Van Dam had Sufferd himself tamely to be devourd [by Cosby], certainly another Morcell, . . . would have followd, [and] no person could expect to have escapd . . . the arbitrary proceedings [that] had been establishd to the ruin of the whole Province." In March 1734, Philip privately decried the "arbitrary steps" Cosby had taken, yet that November he was in attendance when the council unanimously ordered Morrisite printer John Peter Zenger's arrest for seditious libel. Philip probably saw the futility of opposing the resolution in the council, where Cosby commanded a majority. He did stop attending the council's meetings after Zenger's arrest, but because he feared that the governor's vengeance would threaten both his land titles and his council seat, Philip did not openly criticize Cosby. Confidentially, however, he continued to support the Morrisites, and encouraged their efforts "to Settle our Liberty on a Solid foundation."[18]

Philip's younger brother Robert (1688–1775) shared his ambivalence toward politics as well as his propensity for waffling on key political issues. Although this Livingston son had spent ten years in Edinburgh and London training for a career in law, he, like Philip, made his fortune in trade and land speculation and viewed politics as at best an unproductive sideline. As a young man in his twenties recently returned from the Inns of Court, this Robert Livingston had learned the limits of political influence—even when that influence was as great as his father's seemed to be during the administration of Governor Robert Hunter. When the younger Robert repeatedly complained that he could not attract enough business to support himself by the law alone, his father counseled him to cultivate Hunter's favor in order to get a patronage appointment. But the governor was uncooperative, and in 1713, Robert reported, "I very seldom wait on [him] for I dont see any advantage to be reap'd by being over courteous." Unable to support himself by his legal

[18] Philip Livingston to Samuel Storke, 13 Mar. 1734, Livingston Family Letters, AAS; *Coun. J.*, 1:642; Livingston to James Alexander, 7 Jan. 1735, Rutherfurd Collection, NYHS, vol. 2.

practice, by 1717 Robert had begun trading in order to supplement his income. Gradually, he abandoned the law entirely.[19]

As a result of his father's early decision to entail the Manor to his eldest son, young Robert could not expect to retire when his parents died and live off his inheritance. The elder Livingston's first will, in 1690, gave his third son a farm at the Manor that he and his heirs held from its proprietor in fee tail—or, in other words, in exchange for a nominal quitrent. In 1710, Livingston's second will gave Robert two Manor farms in fee tail, as well as a waterfront lot in New York City. Eleven years later, Livingston revised his will again. By then, John's death had made Philip his principal heir; Philip would receive the Manor, as well as the house in Albany where he currently resided. But in this third and final will, Livingston's unexpected decision to divide the Manor resulted in the sole partition of the family estate during its first century. In 1721, the elder Robert Livingston conveyed to his third son, Robert, 13,000 acres in the southwestern corner of Livingston Manor—a tract that came to be known as Clermont, or the Lower Manor.[20]

According to family tradition, Clermont was Robert's reward for thwarting an Indian plot to massacre the inhabitants of Albany County, but it was more likely a sign of parental recognition that this son had made good. Robert and Alida consistently had encouraged their sons to be industrious and self-reliant, and when Robert had complained of his inability to support himself by the law alone they urged him to supplement his income by becoming involved in trade. As a result of his willingness to work diligently to improve his situation, Robert rose in his parents' estimation. By the 1720s, he was a successful and self-sufficient New York City merchant.[21] Although Robert and Alida had spared no expense to prepare him for a career

[19] Robert Livingston (1688–1775) to his father, 28 Mar. 1713, 25 July 1717, Livingston-Redmond MSS., reel 3; Alida Livingston to Robert Livingston, 10 July, 12 Oct. 1717, in Linda Biemer, ed., "The Business Letters of Alida Schuyler Livingston, 1680–1726," *NY Hist.*, 63 (1982): 195, 203–4; Leder, "Robert Livingston's Sons," pp. 246–47.

[20] Wills of Robert Livingston, 3 Mar. 1690, 24 Jan. 1710, 10 Feb. 1721, Livingston-Redmond MSS., reels 1, 3, and 4, respectively.

[21] Robert Livingston (1688–1775) to Robert Livingston, 28 Mar. 1713, 25 July 1717, ibid., reel 3; Alida Livingston to Robert Livingston, 10 July, 12 Oct. 1717, in Biemer, ed., "Business Letters," pp. 95, 203–4; Edwin Brockholst Livingston, *The Livingstons of Livingston Manor* (New York, 1910), p. 144.

in law, success in his chosen profession ultimately outweighed his disregard for parental planning.

Despite the uncertainty of his early prospects, Robert Livingston of Clermont—as he came to be known—had never considered getting deeply involved in provincial politics. In 1717, the elder Robert Livingston persuaded Governor Burnett to appoint his third son clerk of the court of chancery. In 1726 and 1727, young Robert succeeded his aged and ailing father as the Manor's representative in the provincial legislature, but he probably did not play an important role in the assembly's proceedings. In the 1730s, Robert, like his elder brother Philip, privately supported the Morrisites without publicly opposing Governor Cosby. When Lewis Morris went to London in 1734 to present his case to the home government, Robert Livingston of Clermont was among the 297 New Yorkers who donated money to help pay his expenses. Nevertheless, he was not among the public leaders of the Morrisite party.[22]

When his interests were threatened directly, however, Robert Livingston of Clermont did consider defending them politically, as was the case when, in the 1750s, the majority party threatened to tax unimproved land. As one of the colony's leading speculators, Robert certainly opposed this project, and he considered returning to the assembly to fight its implementation. Nevertheless, when Philip's eldest son refused to vacate the Manor's assembly seat, Robert Livingston of Clermont did not stand for election elsewhere. He continued to involve himself in politics intermittently behind the scenes, but like Philip he never became an important political leader.[23]

Gilbert (1690–1746), the youngest Livingston son, also chose a career in trade, though his parents had sent him to Northampton, Massachusetts, to study with the Reverend Solomon Stoddard, possibly to prepare him to enter the ministry. Robert and Alida appar-

[22] *Cal. Coun. Min.*, p. 280; *Assem. J.*, 1:545–72 passim; Names of those agreeing to sustain Col. Morris, [1734], Rutherfurd Collection, NYHS, vol. 1.

[23] James Alexander to Cadwallader Colden, 5 Dec. 1751, 21 Jan. 1752, in *The Letters and Papers of Cadwallader Colden*, 9 vols. (New York, 1918–37), 4:303–4, 307–8; Beverly McAnear, ed., "Mr. Robert R. Livingston's Reasons against a Land Tax," *Journal of Political Economy*, 48 (1940): 63–90. On speculative holdings belonging to Robert Livingston of Clermont, see Indenture between shareholders in the Hardenbergh Patent, 15 Nov. 1749, Livingston Family Papers, NYHS, reel 26.

ently accepted Gilbert's decision to choose his own vocation. When Gilbert decided to become first a surveyor and then a merchant, his father helped him begin both careers by employing him, successively, as his surveyor and commercial agent.[24]

Robert Livingston also used his political influence to help his youngest son obtain several potentially lucrative public offices. In 1717, Robert helped Gilbert and his partner, Francis Harison, to purchase the farm of the New York City liquor excise. Three years later, he prevailed on Governor Burnet to appoint Gilbert register of the court of chancery. Despite his father's patronage, however, Gilbert Livingston did not prosper. By 1721, he and Harison were unable to pay what they owed the government from their customs farming operation. Robert Livingston secured Burnet's support for a bill designed to extricate Gilbert from his financial difficulties.[25] Nevertheless, Gilbert's irresponsibility, extravagance, and poor business judgment had by then driven him to bankruptcy and lost him the respect of his parents.

Although Robert paid Gilbert's debts after his disastrous stint as a customs farmer, a 1722 codicil to his will curtailed his youngest son's inheritance and placed the remainder under Philip's trusteeship. Robert had sold half of his Saratoga holdings—intended as Gilbert's portion of his estate—to satisfy his son's creditors. Now, the remainder of the Saratoga land would be shared by all five surviving Livingston siblings. Similarly, all five children would share the proceeds from the sale of the Albany house that Robert originally had devised to Gilbert. According to the terms of the 1722 codicil, Gilbert in his own right would receive only a farm at Canastoga. Robert maintained that Gilbert had only himself to blame for "his miserable Circumstance wherein by his folly he has involved him

24 Munsell, ed., *Annals of Albany,* 5:186; Survey of Livingston Manor, 27 Mar. 1710, Livingston Family Papers, NYHS, reel 28; John Cast to Robert Hunter, 17 Mar. 1711, *DRNY,* 5:212–13; Gilbert Livingston to Robert Livingston, 11 Jan., 13 June, 16 July, 23 Aug. 1712, 4 Jan., 26 June 1717, Livingston-Redmond MSS., reel 3.

25 *Cal. Coun. Min.,* p. 280; Philip Livingston to Robert Livingston, 8 Feb. 1721, Livingston-Redmond MSS., reel 4; *Assem. J.,* 1:455, 457–59, 463, 469, 480, 486–89; Burnet to Board of Trade, 21 Nov. 1722, *Cal. S. P.,* 1722–23, no. 349; Lawrence H. Leder, *Robert Livingston, 1654–1728, and the Politics of Colonial New York* (Chapel Hill, N.C., 1961), pp. 244–49. The bill limited Gilbert's liability to £300, though his share of the farm originally had cost £750. The disruption of trade during the Spanish war was partly responsible for the farmers' problems.

Self." Gilbert, his father believed, was both ungrateful for the advantages he had enjoyed and unwilling to work to resolve his financial difficulties. By contrast, John, the eldest Livingston son, was also chronically indebted, but he, unlike Gilbert, had taken responsibility for his financial problems and regularly informed his father of his progress toward solvency. Consequently, John was still his father's principal heir when he died, still heavily indebted, in 1720.[26]

John was unsteady and unfortunate, but Gilbert was arrogant and irresponsible. When he requested his father's financial assistance in 1721, Gilbert had the temerity to demand that he be given a farm, two slaves, Philip's Albany residence, and the secretaryship for Indian affairs to enable him to live in a "Reputable mannor." Robert's angry response to these requests juxtaposed Philip's exemplary conduct with that of his foolish and pathetic brother. "As for the house at Albany," Robert retorted, "I think it would be unreasonable to Turn out the Bro[the]r who has lived frugal & been Very Diligent and Carefull in his Bussiness, and . . . turn in [he] who has been quite the Reverse. Neither do I think it either Reasonable or Prudence to take the office of Secretary of the Indian affairs out of y[ou]r Bro[the]r Philip's hands who understands it & . . . let you have it who understands nothing of such matters."[27]

Gilbert's virtual disinheritance limited his family's future prospects by forcing them into exile in Ulster County, where they lived off the patrimony of his wife, Cornelia Beekman Livingston. Gilbert was by no means poor, but unlike his brothers he lacked the financial resources necessary to establish each of his nine sons in fruitful careers or to promise them a substantial patrimony.

Consequently, most of Gilbert's sons left home to fend for themselves as they grew into adulthood. The eldest, Robert Gilbert, did become a successful merchant; the second son, Henry, became the business assistant and political protégé of his sonless uncle Henry

[26] Robert Livingston's Resolution on Son Gilberts Proposes, 15 Sept. 1721, Livingston-Redmond MSS., reel 4; Codicil to Livingston's will, 22 Sept. 1722, ibid. On John's financial status in 1720, see the letter of his second wife Elizabeth Knight Livingston to Robert Livingston, 6 July 1721, ibid., as well as the abstract of his will in William S. Pelletreau, comp., *Abstracts of Wills on File in the Surrogate's Office, City of New York,* 17 vols. (New York, 1893–1909), 2:154–55.

[27] Gilbert Livingston to Robert Livingston, 14 Sept. 1721, Livingston-Redmond MSS., reel 4; Robert Livingston's Resolution on Son Gilberts Proposes, 15 Sept. 1721, ibid.

Beekman and, through his uncle's patronage, became an important man in Dutchess County. But the other seven brothers lived modestly in relative obscurity. Only James, who farmed 115 acres in Dutchess County, resided permanently in New York. Philip Gilbert emigrated to Curaçao, where he died in 1751 at the age of twenty-five. Gilbert, Jr., was first a soldier, then a ship master; he fled New York in 1743 to escape debtors' prison. Samuel and Cornelius also became ships' masters, and worked occasionally for their prosperous ship-owning cousins. Johannes was a soldier; William's activities are unknown. Clearly, the size of Gilbert's family—thirteen children in all—compounded the effects of his diminished patrimony.[28]

Gilbert himself retired to the assembly temporarily when bankruptcy forced him to abandon trade. When his brother Philip inherited the Manor in 1728, he gave Gilbert the family's assembly seat, perhaps in the hope that attending legislative sessions would keep him occupied and out of trouble. Gilbert retained the Manor seat until 1737, when Philip apparently decided that his own eldest son should serve a political apprenticeship in the provincial assembly. Although Gilbert had initially taken an interest in the affairs of the legislature, during his last six years there he rarely attended the assembly's sessions, and when he did attend he was not actively involved in the proceedings.[29] Clearly Gilbert had no genuine interest in politics. Nevertheless, having access to a family-controlled seat in the assembly had given him an opportunity to retire from his failed business with a degree of grace and dignity.

The elder Robert Livingston had used politics and political connections to win status, wealth, and land grants; because his sons inherited the fruits of his labor, they could afford to forgo the trials and uncertainties of politics. Despite Robert's attempts to promote the public careers of his progeny, none of his sons followed him into

[28] See George B. Kinkead, "Gilbert Livingston and Some of His Descendants," *NY Gen. & Bio. Rec.*, 84 (1953): 6–12. The experience of Gilbert's sons paralleled that of New England's middling families. See, for instance, Philip J. Greven, *Four Generations: Population, Land, and Family in Colonial Andover, Massachusetts* (Ithaca, N.Y., 1970), pp. 123–24, 156–57, 211–14, and Robert A. Gross, *The Minutemen and Their World* (New York, 1976), pp. 74–89.

[29] Gilbert Livingston to Robert Livingston, 14 Sept. 1721, Livingston-Redmond MSS., reel 4; Robert Livingston's Resolution on Son Gilberts Proposes, 15 Sept. 1721, ibid.; Codicil to Robert Livingston's will, 22 Sept. 1722, ibid., reel 4; *Assem. J.*, 1:574–701 passim.

the business of politics. Robert Livingston had been first a politician and then a merchant, though he had consistently tried to use his influence in public life to benefit his private business. His sons, on the other hand, all chose to be merchants but remained relatively free from political entanglements.

Significantly, the sons of the Schuyler brothers and Stephanus Van Cortlandt—Robert Livingston's closest business and political associates—also were far less involved than their fathers had been in the political affairs of the colony. Perhaps their fathers' many difficulties convinced them that politics was often more troublesome than useful, that public life often was detrimental to private business and material interests. Moreover, Burnet's departure in 1728 left his supporters patronless and out of power for more than a decade, and the deaths of Peter Schuyler and Robert Livingston—in 1724 and 1728, respectively—seriously weakened their factional leadership. Lewis Morris emerged as the new leader of what was left of the Hunter-Burnet faction, although his departure for New Jersey in 1736 left its members again without a dominant leader. Perhaps the faction's declining political fortunes discouraged the younger Livingstons, Schuylers, and Van Cortlandts from assuming the mantle of leadership once Morris left the colony. Although they generally supported this faction—whose members identified with the landed interest and advocated an aggressive defense policy—the next generation of Livingstons, Schuylers, and Van Cortlandts were never among its outstanding leaders.[30]

In wealth and status, however, these families remained in the first rank of provincial society. When Robert Livingston died in 1728, he left his offspring a handsome patrimony. Daughters Margaret and Joanna each received one fifth of their father's Saratoga holdings, as well as a lot and house in New York City. Livingston had conveyed the houses to his daughters shortly after they married. His will gave Margaret £100 for repairs and alterations; Joanna received £200,

---

[30] Philip Livingston and Philip Van Cortlandt were members of the provincial council for twenty-four and sixteen years, respectively. Of thirteen male Schuylers in the next generation, only Philip, son of Johannes, sat in the assembly (1728–45), while none was a member of the council. Unlike their fathers, even these most active members of the second generation were not among the colony's most visible and influential political leaders. On the declining fortunes of the Livingston-Schuyler-Morris party after Burnet's departure, see Bonomi, *Factious People*, esp. pp. 97–103.

perhaps because her house was smaller than her sister's. Livingston also bequeathed a slave to each daughter. Margaret inherited a "slave girl" named Isabel, while Joanna was given a "slave man" named Dego.[31]

Each of Livingston's heirs also received one-fifth of his land at Saratoga, though Philip controlled Gilbert's share in trusteeship for his hapless brother. All five children shared the revenues generated by an Albany house originally intended for Gilbert. In addition, Gilbert got the Canastoga farm and a "slave boy" named Jupiter. Robert inherited three slaves, as well as the 13,000 acres that became known as Clermont; his father devised the land to him and his heirs in entail, on the condition that it never be alienated. Philip received the remainder of the Manor—also in entail—as well as six slaves and the lot and house in Albany where he currently resided.[32]

Although Robert Livingston's daughters inherited land, his will showed the extent to which he followed English inheritance practices rather than the more egalitarian Dutch customs. According to Dutch custom, testators divided their estates equally among all their surviving children regardless of sex or birth order; sons and daughters alike usually received equal portions of both real and personal property. Following English custom, however, Robert Livingston practiced a modified version of primogeniture, discriminating in favor of the eldest son and against both daughters. Margaret and Joanna received shares of the Saratoga land only because their brother Gilbert had angered their father; Robert gave the land to his daughters in order to punish the irresponsible Gilbert. Moreover, because English law, unlike Dutch law, did not allow married women to own property, the land that Livingston devised to Margaret and Joanna belonged not to them but to their husbands.[33]

31 Will of Robert Livingston, 10 Feb. 1721, Livingston-Redmond MSS., reel 4; Deed of the house and 2 Lotts in Dok Street . . . to Joanna Van Horn[e], 9 Aug. 1722, ibid.; Samuel Vetch's account with Robert Livingston, 1702–20, ibid., reel 2.

32 Will of Robert Livingston, 10 Feb. 1721, ibid. On the slaveholdings of the colonial Livingstons, see Roberta Singer, "The Livingstons as Slaveholders: The 'Peculiar Institution' on Livingston Manor and Clermont," in Richard T. Wiles, ed., *The Livingston Legacy: Three Centuries of American History*, (Annandale, N.Y., 1987), pp. 67–97.

33 See David E. Narrett, "Dutch Customs of Inheritance: Women and the Law in Colonial New York City," in William Pencak and Conrad Edick Wright, eds., *Authority and Resistance in Early New York* (New York, 1988), pp. 27–55, and "Preparation for

Perhaps that is why Robert Livingston never considered giving his daughters a piece of Livingston Manor; after all, his bequest to his third son, Robert, showed that he did not oppose dividing the family seat as a matter of principle.

The final will and testament of the first Robert Livingston would act as a model for future generations. Land-rich colonial Livingstons customarily would convey land to daughters as well as to sons, but the daughters' portions were sometimes smaller and more remote and never included shares of the estate that bore the family name. Similarly, Robert and Alida's descendants continued to favor eldest sons over their younger brothers, keeping their family seats in entail for the remainder of the colonial era. Only when the prospect of an irresponsible heir threatened the future of the family seat did Robert and Alida's grandson abolish the entail on Livingston Manor.[34]

Inheritance, along with family size, shaped the varied experiences of the second generation of colonial Livingstons and gave rise to three distinct branches within the Livingston family. Gilbert and most of his descendants could not be counted among New York's colonial elite. Robert of Clermont and his son Robert R. Livingston clearly were members of that elite, who profited by their inheritance as they expanded their land and commercial interests. But Philip was by far the most successful of the second-generation Livingstons. Using his six sons as business agents, Philip took advantage of his vast resources and developed colonial New York's most ambitious family business. Through his own efforts and with the help of his

Death and Provision for the Living: New York Wills, 1665–1700," *NY Hist.*, 57 (1976): 423–24, 434–35. For a comparison of married women's rights under Dutch and English law, see also Linda Briggs Biemer, *Women and Property in Colonial New York: The Transition from Dutch to English Law, 1643–1727*, Studies in American History and Culture 38 (Ann Arbor, Mich., 1983), chap. 1. Some manorial families—most notably the Van Cortlandts—perpetuated Dutch inheritance customs well into the English era. See Sung Bok Kim, *Landlord and Tenant in Colonial New York: Manorial Society, 1664–1775* (Chapel Hill, N.C., 1978), pp. 88–89.

[34] See, for instance, Will of Philip Livingston, 15 July 1748, Livingston-Redmond MSS., reel 6; Will of Robert Livingston, Jr., 31 May 1784, Livingston Family Papers, NYHS, reel 3. Philip conveyed the Manor to his eldest son but divided the rest of his estate equally among his remaining sons and daughters. His eldest son and heir, Robert Livingston, Jr., divided the Manor among his five sons but gave each of his daughters land at Saratoga.

kin, Philip Livingston became colonial New York's quintessential merchant-entrepreneur.

The career of Philip Livingston, as both son and father, is a case study of the operation of a successful colonial family business. Under his aggressive leadership, the second and third generations of Livingstons improved and expanded the family business launched by Robert and Alida. Although Philip became the second lord of Livingston Manor when his father died in 1728, he continued to regard himself as a merchant and a citizen of the town of Albany. Philip designated himself "Lord and Proprietor of the Manor of Livingston" only in his tenants' leases. He preferred the simpler— and, he believed, more appropriate—title "merchant of Albany." Philip enjoyed trade, and he was a shrewd and successful businessman. He also believed that he was obliged to continue working in his vocation until the end of his life in order to ensure his nine children's future prosperity.[35] Consequently, he did not move from Albany to the Manor until 1743, when he was in his fifty-eighth year. By then he had grown sons to whom he could entrust his Albany interests, and he could turn his own attention to developing an iron industry at Livingston Manor.

Like his parents, Philip had begun his career in the Albany fur trade, but he also recognized the growing importance of agriculture in the economy of the Hudson Valley. As early as 1679, the people of Albany had deemed the grain trade vital to their local economy because "the [fur] trade with the Indians daily weakens and diminishes . . . and cannot possibly support this place." In 1687, Governor Dongan ranked the grain-importing English West Indies, with fur-importing England and the Netherlands, as the colony's most important trading partners. In 1705, New York's merchants claimed that wheat was the "principall staple" of their trade, "excepting the small trade of peltry which is now so diminished as scarce worth regarding." By 1715, some 48 percent of New York's exports went to the food-importing sugar islands of the West Indies.[36]

---

[35] Philip Livingston to Robert Livingston, Jr., Dec. 1740, 20 July 1741, Livingston-Redmond MSS., reel 7.

[36] *Albany Minutes*, 2:407; Dongan's report on New York, 22 Feb. 1687, *DHNY*, 1:160; Petition of the merchants of the City of New York, Feb. 1705, *DRNY*, 4:1133;

New York merchants depended on the West Indian trade to pay for their English imports. Provincials sent their flour, bread, and meat to the island colonies and returned home with the sugar, molasses, dye woods, and cocoa that—along with local furs and timber—formed the nucleus of their export trade to England. Although New Yorkers found new markets for their foodstuffs as the century progressed, the islands continued to be their single most important export market throughout the remainder of the colonial era. Nearly half of the vessels that entered or cleared the port of New York between 1715 and 1765 were employed mainly in the West Indian trade.[37]

The development of the Livingstons' family business mirrored the evolution of New York's colonial economy. The Livingstons responded to changing commercial circumstances, shifting their interests from furs to grain and developing that vast commercial hinterland of Livingston Manor. Robert Livingston had built a gristmill and a sawmill on Roeloff Jansen's Kill in the 1690s; he later added a second gristmill on the same site to absorb the business generated by the Palatine farmers. Earlier he had built both a brewery and a baking-house at the Manor so that he could provision the Palatines with beer and bread manufactured at his own facilities. Although the family later abandoned the brewery, both Philip Livingston and his son and heir Robert Livingston, Jr., later exported bread made at the Manor baking-house from grain ground at the family mills.[38]

Hist. Statistics of the U.S., 2:1180. On the movement of the fur trade from the Hudson to the Mohawk Valley and the gradual decline of its overall importance to New York's economy, see Thomas Eliot Norton, *The Fur Trade in Colonial New York* (Madison, Wis., 1974), chaps. 5–6.

[37] William I. Davisson and Lawrence J. Bradley, "New York Maritime Trade: Ship Voyage Patterns, 1715–1765," *New-York Historical Society Quarterly*, 55 (1971): 317; Cornbury to Board of Trade, 1 July 1708, *DRNY*, 5:57–58. The best summary of the commerce of the grain-exporting middle colonies is John J. McCusker and Russell R. Menard, *The Economy of British America* (Chapel Hill, N.C., 1985), pp. 189–200. See also Paul G. E. Clemens, *The Atlantic Economy and Maryland's Eastern Shore: From Tobacco to Grain* (Ithaca, N.Y., 1980), esp. chap. 6.

[38] On early brewing and baking at the Manor, see Alida Livingston to Robert Livingston, 10 July 1710, 17 July, 29 Oct. 1711, 24 Apr. 1712, in Biemer, ed., "Business Letters," pp. 195, 197, 199. On the Livingstons' subsequent exportation of bread, see, for example, Philip Livingston to Robert Livingston, Jr., 24 Mar. 1739, Livingston-Redmond MSS., reel 7; Freight Lists of the Cargo on Board the *Jameaca Packet*, 8 Sept. 1745, ibid., reel 6; Account of Goods sent to Newyork [on] the Sloops *Polly* and *Catte & Dolle*, Mar. 1766–Nov. 1768, Livingston Family Papers, NYHS, reel 28.

Both Philip and his son continued to develop the family land, building more mills and recruiting tenants from Scotland and the German states in order to increase its productivity.[39]

As a young man, Philip had benefited from his father's business experience and connections. As we have seen, Robert had sent Philip to New Rochelle, where he learned French to prepare for a career in the Canada trade. Later, Robert probably was instrumental in securing for his son a mercantile apprenticeship, most likely in the store of one of his Schuyler uncles. By 1709, at the age of twenty-three, Philip had begun his own trading business in Albany. Robert used his influence to enable his son to begin a commercial correspondence with James Douglas, a London merchant who had been the elder Livingston's friend and business partner during his second visit to England. Philip sent grain to Douglas's brother and agent, Henry, in New York City, in exchange for textiles and other English manufactures. Thus, Philip began his trade in Albany as his father had, with the help of his family and working through an agent in New York City.[40]

As a novice merchant, Philip's business contacts varied. Early in his career, he sold his furs to the province's leading fur merchant, Stephen DeLancey of New York City. By 1714, however, he was dealing primarily with Henry Cuyler, a former resident of Albany who had moved downriver to New York. In the 1720s, Philip also employed his younger brother Robert as his agent in Manhattan, although by then grain was displacing furs as his most important export commodity. Philip's New York City correspondents paid his accounts in imported goods which he, in turn, sold in Albany County.[41]

[39] Philip Livingston to Jacob Wendell, 21 Apr. 1739, Livingston Papers, MCNY, box 2; Philip Livingston to John DeWitt, 5 Mar. 1741, Livingston-Redmond MSS., reel 9; Robert Livingston, Jr., to Gulian Verplanck, 20 Dec. 1749, Robert R. Livingston Papers, NYHS, reel 1. Philip built a second gristmill—and probably a sawmill—at Ancram in the 1740s. See John Waddell to Robert Livingston, Jr., 24 Mar. 1752, Livingston-Redmond MSS., reel 7.

[40] William A. Brat to Robert Livingston, 15 Nov. 1697, Livingston-Redmond MSS., reel 2; Philip Livingston to Robert and Alida Livingston, 12 June 1700, ibid.; [Mr. Tuck?] to Robert Livingston, 15 Sept. 1701, ibid.; Henry Douglas to Philip Livingston, 12 Apr. 1709, ibid., reel 6. The elder Livingston had formed a partnership with James Douglas for the disposal of £940 in dry goods in New York (Invoice of . . . Merchandize . . . bound for New York, 10 Apr. 1706, ibid., reel 2).

[41] Stephen DeLancey to Philip Livingston, 22 Dec. 1710, ibid., reel 6; Henry Cuyler to Philip Livingston, 20 May 1714, 12 Apr. 1715, ibid.; Philip Livingston to Robert Livingston, 21 Aug. 1725, ibid., reel 4.

During this same period, however, Philip's business ties with his father were both varied and extensive. In Albany County, he performed many business services for Robert, particularly during the latter's frequent sojourns in the provincial capital. Philip often collected his father's local debts and Manor rents; occasionally, he saw to the prosecution of delinquent tenants and debtors. He also acted as his father's wheat agent in the Hudson Valley, buying grain to be ground at the Manor mills and then exported or used to fulfill provisioning contracts.[42] Finally, Philip also served as his father's general agent in Albany—just as his brother Robert and brother-in-law Cornelius Van Horne acted as the elder Livingston's agents in New York City. Philip shipped furs, produce, and lumber to Manhattan, and beginning in 1717 he marketed his father's cattle each year in Albany County and its vicinity.[43]

Although Robert Livingston's personal influence had helped his son to establish a substantial trade, family ties did not guarantee the continued success of Philip's business. Direct trade between father and son increased as Philip himself became a prominent member of the colony's merchant community. But in trade between kin, the values of the marketplace generally outweighed the emotional bonds of family loyalty. Thus Robert and Philip traded as equals and—in the interest of profits and efficiency—afforded each other no special favors. In 1717, for instance, when his father sent him some "Indifferent" pelts, Philip demanded that he pay a reduced rate for such inferior goods. Philip also earned his father's patronage by matching or besting the terms of his competitors. He knew that in order to purchase his father's wheat he must "follow the prices of others." Similarly, in disposing of his imported goods, Philip repeatedly assured his father that his own prices were "as cheap as

[42] See, for example, Philip Livingston to Robert Livingston, 13 June 1712, 1 Apr., 12 May, 25 May, 17 June 1713, 18 Feb., 3 Mar., 30 Mar., 7 Apr. 1714, 8 Feb. 1717, ibid., reel 3; same to same, 14 Jan. 1720, 15 Feb. 1722, ibid., reel 4; Robert Livingston to Philip Livingston, 28 Dec. 1714, ibid., reel 6.

[43] Philip Livingston to Robert Livingston, 1 Apr. 1713, 8 July, 6 Nov. 1717, ibid., reel 3; same to same, 15 Feb. 1722, 16 June 1724, 19 Nov. 1725, ibid., reel 4; Account of Fatt Catle Sent to Albany, Nov. 1719, ibid.; Robert Livingston's accounts with Philip Livingston, Jan.–Feb. 1724, Feb.–Nov. 1726, ibid.; Robert Livingston's accounts with Cornelius Van Horne, Oct. 1721–June 1722, ibid.; Robert Livingston to Van Horne, 18 July 1723, 1 May 1724, 8 July 1725, ibid.; Robert Livingston (1688–1775) to Robert Livingston, 28 Mar. 1713, ibid., reel 3.

can be had from Mr. [Stephen] D[e]Lancey," one of his leading competitors. "I begg you to buy from me before others," he wrote to his father in 1724. Clearly, the elder Livingston's trade with his sons was competitive and discriminating.[44]

As a father, Philip later used his own business connections to improve the prospects of his sons, who in turn took up their responsibilities in his growing commercial network. Philip used his considerable personal influence to give each son promising beginnings in business by securing for them apprenticeships in prestigious trading establishments. He personally trained his eldest and fourth sons, Robert and Philip, respectively, for the Albany trade, using his influence to get Robert passes to trade in Canada and Philip clerical posts in Albany's local government.[45] Two other sons, John and Peter Van Brugh Livingston, went to Europe and apprenticed in the London office of Samuel Storke, Philip's longtime trading partner. Peter later moved on to Jamaica to learn the sugar business and became, for a time, his father's West Indies commercial agent.[46] Of Philip's six sons, only William did not become a merchant. He too, however, prospered through his father's influence, which won him an apprenticeship in the office of James Alexander, New York's most prominent lawyer.

Henry, the fifth son, received the most thorough commercial training. Like his father and his eldest brother, he began his education by studying French in New Rochelle to prepare for a career in the Canada trade. After three years in New Rochelle, Henry began his practical education by working, as his older brothers had, in his

44 Philip Livingston to Robert Livingston, 25 Aug. 1717, ibid., reel 3; same to same, 25 Mar., 21 Apr., 15 May 1724, 21 Aug. 1725, ibid., reel 4; Robert Livingston (1688–1775) to Robert Livingston, 11 Feb. 1713, ibid., reel 3.

45 Philip Livingston to Robert Livingston, Jr., 20 May 1724, ibid., reel 7; Passes issued to Robert Livingston, 8 Mar. 1727, 6 Aug. 1730, *Cal. Hist. MSS.*, 2:498, 512; *Early Records*, 4:176; Joel Munsell, ed., *The Annals of Albany*, 10 vols. (Albany, 1850–59), 10:120, 132.

46 Philip Livingston to Samuel Storke, 20 Nov. 1734, 2 June 1735, Livingston Family Letters, AAS; Philip Livingston to Jacob Wendell, 23 May, 9 Nov. 1738, 21 Apr. 1739, Livingston Papers, MCNY, box 2; Peter Van Brugh Livingston to Robert Livingston, Jr., 26 Feb. 1735, Livingston-Redmond MSS., reel 7; Jacob Lansing, Jr., to Robert Livingston, Jr., 9 June 1739, ibid.; Joseph Mico to Robert and Peter Van Brugh Livingston, 3 May 1740, ibid. See also William I. Roberts III, "Samuel Storke: An Eighteenth-Century London Merchant Trading to the American Colonies," *Business History Review*, 39 (1965): 147–70.

father's Albany store. In 1738, he then began a three-year apprenticeship in the Boston store of his father's friend, Jacob Wendell.
When Henry finished his stint with Wendell, Philip Livingston
proudly declared that his son, at the age of twenty-two, was now "a
Compleat merchant." Nevertheless, he then sent Henry to Europe to
make the Grand Tour and, more important, to forge his own transatlantic business connections. Henry ultimately settled in the West
Indies, where his New York contacts helped him to establish himself
in the sugar trade.[47]

Although all of his sons except Henry eventually settled in New
York City, Philip probably had envisioned the creation of a far-flung
commercial network with his sons acting as his agents and trading
partners throughout Europe and America. Philip had educated his
sons to play specialized roles in his growing business, in order to
make his trade more self-sufficient and systematic. Albany, New
York, the West Indies, London, and Boston were his main commercial outlets, and Philip had trained at least one son to specialize in
each of those branches of trade.

Philip also tailored his sons' commercial training to suit New
York's changing economy. Although he himself was one of the colony's leading fur traders, he recognized that by the time his own sons
were coming of age the fur trade was declining. By the 1730s, the
French had built two trading posts at Detroit and Niagara that provided stiff competition for the New York fur traders. Moreover, the
English had erected a trading post of their own at Oswego to compete with the French, but competition from Oswego also hurt Albany's trade, particularly by the mid-1730s when the Oswego men
decided to avoid the Albany middlemen and deal directly with London.[48] These changing economic circumstances shaped Philip's

[47] Henry Livingston to Henry Van Renssealer, 21 June 1736, Misc. MSS., Henry
Livingston, NYHS; Philip Livingston to Storke and Gainsborough, 12 June 1738,
Livingston Family Letters, AAS; Philip Livingston to Jacob Wendell, 7 Mar. 1738, 13
Mar. 1739, 29 May 1742, Livingston Papers, MCNY, box 2; Henry Livingston's in-
voice for sugar and molasses, 18 Aug. 1752, ibid., box 1; Henry Livingston to Robert
Livingston, Jr., 5 Mar. 1774, Livingston-Redmond MSS., reel 7; Philip Livingston to
Jacob Wendell, 5 Jan. 1745, Misc. MSS., Philip Livingston, NYHS; William Walton
and Co. to James Beekman, 30 Nov. 1751, in Philip L. White, ed., *The Beekman
Mercantile Papers*, 3 vols. (New York, 1956), 2:552; Virginia D. Harrington, *The New
York Merchant on the Eve of the Revolution* (New York, 1935), pp. 194–95.
[48] Norton, *Fur Trade*, pp. 149–50; Roberts, "Samuel Storke," pp. 166–68.

plans for his sons' futures. Only his oldest son and eventual heir, Robert Livingston, Jr., received extensive training in the fur-trading business; he had completed his education by 1727, before the outlook for the Albany fur traders had become so dismal.

Philip had long been involved in the grain trade, but by the late 1730s several factors compelled him to make it the main focus of his business. First, the decline of the fur trade encouraged him to look elsewhere for big profits. Second, since New York's growing population was producing more grain than ever before, exporting foodstuffs became an attractive alternative for the fur merchants of the Hudson Valley—particularly for those who, like Philip Livingston, owned tenanted estates in prime grain-producing regions. Beginning in 1739, the Spanish war made the trade in foodstuffs even more inviting, as the arrival of military and naval personnel in the West Indies generated a great demand for provisions. Finally, grain, unlike furs, was not among the articles enumerated by the Navigation Acts for export exclusively to England. Consequently, the potential growth of the colonial grain market seemed virtually limitless.

Concentrating on the grain trade therefore enabled Philip to experiment with new trade routes, to capitalize more fully on his landed estate, and to survive handsomely the problems that beset his trade in furs. Like the Maryland farmers who turned to grain in the 1750s to offset their dependence on an unstable and debt-ridden tobacco trade, New Yorkers increasingly looked to grain as a means to diversify their interests and earn credits on their habitually overdrawn accounts in England.[49]

While the first Robert Livingston had traded mainly with London and the West Indies, Philip and his sons experimented with other markets that introduced new commodities to their trade. For instance, Philip's extensive trade with the West Indies led to his involvement in the African slave trade. In the 1730s and 1740s, he was one of New York's leading importers of slave labor from the sugar islands, and also one of few New Yorkers who imported slaves directly from Africa before the abolition of the Spanish Asiento in 1748. In 1738, Philip bought a one-third share in a voyage to Guinea, where two hundred slaves were purchased and consigned to

[49] See Clemens, *Atlantic Economy.*

his son Peter Van Brugh Livingston and his partner in Jamaica. New York's direct trade with Africa grew significantly after 1748, and the Livingstons continued to be among the colony's leading Africa traders.[50]

Philip and his sons also expanded their trade into new markets in Europe and America. By the 1740s, southern Europe and the Wine Islands were increasingly important markets for colonial grain exports. The Livingstons used the English contacts they had formed during their fur-trading days to exploit Europe's demand for American foodstuffs. Samuel Storke of London informed them when the Iberian grain crops failed, so that they could tap that market ahead of their competitors. On such occasions, the Livingstons either shipped their grain directly to Spain or Portugal or sent it to Storke, who forwarded it to his agents in Gibraltar, Barcelona, and Cadiz.[51]

Like many other colonial merchants, the Livingstons also expanded their coastal trade and used their growing trade with the mainland colonies to complement their European commercial interests. For instance, in 1741 Philip sent bread and flour to Newfoundland, where his cargo was exchanged for fish that was later traded for wine in Madeira. Although by the 1740s many New York City merchants were trading with Madeira, Philip was one of very few Albanians to import wine directly from that island. Philip sold his wines locally or reexported them elsewhere. In 1740, for example, he sent grain and wine to South Carolina, where he traded for rice, which he in turn exported to Amsterdam.[52]

Yet the differences between Philip's business and his father's were more quantitative than qualitative. Like his father, Philip supple-

[50] Philip Livingston to Storke and Gainsborough, 25 Apr. 1738, Livingston Family Letters, AAS; A Book of Trade for the Sloope *Rhode Island*, Dec. 1748–July 1749, Misc. MSS., B. V. *Rhode Island*, NYHS; James G. Lydon, "New York and the Slave Trade, 1700 to 1774," *WMQ*, 3d ser., 35 (1978): 375–94.

[51] Philip Livingston to Storke and Gainsborough, 7 June, 20 Nov., 28 Nov. 1734, Livingston Family Letters, AAS; Philip Livingston to Robert Livingston, Jr., 12 Sept., 3 Dec. 1740, Livingston-Redmond MSS., reel 7; Roberts, "Samuel Storke," pp. 160–61.

[52] David Arthur Armour, "The Merchants of Albany, New York: 1686–1760" (Ph.D. diss., Northwestern University, 1965), p. 215; Harrington, *New York Merchant*, pp. 200–201. On the growing importance of the coastal and southern European trades, in general, see McCusker and Menard, *Economy of British America*, pp. 79–80, 89–98; Clemens, *Atlantic Economy*, pp. 176–83.

mented his export trade with extensive shipping interests. He owned or co-owned at least eight vessels, which made frequent voyages to Europe, the West Indies, and the mainland colonies. Most of these he owned in partnership with his sons.[53] Like his father, Philip also relied heavily on the members of his family as business partners and commercial agents. The Livingston sons benefited from their father's wealth and connections, just as Philip and his own brothers had done a generation earlier.

Each of Philip's sons acted at some time as his agent, supplier, or business representative, but the two eldest—Robert Livingston, Jr., and Peter Van Brugh Livingston—were involved most extensively in their father's business. After trading at Albany for several years, by 1734 twenty-six-year-old Robert Livingston, Jr., had moved his business to New York City, where he soon formed a partnership with his brother Peter. Philip helped his sons begin their business by persuading his London correspondents, Storke and Gainsborough, to send them their first cargo on credit.[54]

In addition to pursuing their own independent trade, Robert and Peter disposed of their father's grain, lumber, and furs and in return sent him West Indian sugar products and English manufactures. Typically, they traded foodstuffs for sugar and coin or bills of exchange, which they then used toward purchasing English goods to be marketed in New York or Albany County. Peter left for Jamaica in 1736 and for several years acted as agent at Kingston.[55] Robert, who was the agent in New York City, corresponded regularly both with his father and with Storke and Gainsborough in London. Philip supplied the produce for their trade and sold imported goods at his

[53] Philip Livingston to Robert Livingston, 20 Aug. 1717, Livingston-Redmond MSS., reel 3; Philip Livingston to Robert Livingston, Jr., 3 Dec. 1740, 19 Mar. 1743, ibid., reel 7; Philip Livingston to Storke and Gainsborough, 20 Nov. 1734, 28 July 1735, Livingston Family Letters, AAS; Book of Trade for the Sloope *Rhode Island*, Dec. 1748–July 1749, Misc. MSS., B. V. *Rhode Island*, NYHS; Patricia Joan Gordon, "The Livingstons of New York, 1675–1860: Kinship and Class" (Ph.D. diss., Columbia University, 1959), p. 99.

[54] Philip Livingston to Samuel Storke, 7 June 1734, 2 June, 13 Nov. 1735, Livingston Family Letters, AAS; Shipping insurance for a cargo from Storke and Gainsborough to Robert & Peter Livingston & Company, 16 Aug. 1735, Livingston-Redmond MSS., reel 7.

[55] Peter Van Brugh Livingston to Storke and Gainsborough, 28 Sept. 1736, Livingston-Redmond MSS., reel 7. Peter had returned to New York by November 1739, when he married Mary Alexander.

stores at Albany, Schenectady, and the Manor.[56] After the dissolution of their partnership in the late 1730s, Robert and Peter continued to act separately as their father's New York agents, shipping his grain and flour to the West Indies and Europe. Robert also became the main distributor of Philip's iron after the opening of the Manor forge in 1743.

When Philip died in 1749, his eldest son, Robert Livingston, Jr., inherited both the Manor and his father's position as de facto head of the family business. Like his father and grandfather before him, Robert Livingston, Jr., relied heavily on his kin—first his brothers and later his sons—to run the New York end of his trade. As Robert admitted to his brother Peter in 1751, "I am out of the way of trade [and] herefore am the more obliged to you."[57] Peter marketed his brother's grain and iron products, much as he and Robert had done earlier for their father.

Robert's relations in the provincial capital also used their influence in official circles to enable him to participate in the wartime profiteering that flourished in New York and elsewhere during the French and Indian War. In 1755, General William Shirley, governor of Massachusetts and commander-in-chief of the British forces in America, selected the firm of Peter Van Brugh Livingston and his brother-in-law William Alexander, along with Lewis Morris III of New York and John Erving of Boston, to provision military expeditions to Crown Point and Niagara. In New York, the provisioning contract became a Livingston family affair. Peter was charged with procuring most of the goods, while his brother Robert became his most productive supplier. Robert supplied the partners with cattle, grain, and iron from the Manor and the surrounding region.[58]

---

56 Accounts of Robert Livingston, Jr., with Manor store, 20 May 1735, 16 Apr. 1737, 13 Feb. 1741, ibid.; Philip Livingston to Robert Livingston, Jr., 24 Mar. 1739, ibid.; John DeWitt to Robert Livingston, Jr., 17 Aug. 1739, ibid.; Henry Van Rensselaer, Jr.'s account with Robert & Peter Livingston & Co., 28 May 1735–8 Sept. 1737, Misc. MSS., Robert & Peter Livingston & Co., NYHS.

57 Robert Livingston, Jr., to Peter Van Brugh Livingston, 26 June 1751, Welch-Livingston Collection, NYHS.

58 Livingston and Alexander to Robert Livingston, Jr., 22 July 1755, Livingston-Redmond MSS., reel 7; Peter Van Brugh Livingston to Robert Livingston, Jr., 15 Aug. 1755, 3 Mar., 6 Mar. 1756, ibid.; William Alexander to James Stevenson, 3 Jan. 1756, Rutherfurd Collection, NYHS, vol. 3; Robert Livingston, Jr., to William Alexander, 10 Feb. 1756, William Alexander Papers, NYHS, vol. 2. On provisioning and war

Because both the troops and the fighting were concentrated in New York, provisioning was a big business. The partners' transactions for eighteen months of service totaled more than £115,000 sterling.[59] Shirley's decision to award such a valuable contract without consulting officials in New York became a political issue that contributed to his own recall and the subsequent displacement of the four partners in August 1756. While it lasted, however, the arrangement had been lucrative, though the partners—like the first Robert Livingston—were forced to plead their case in London in order to obtain full compensation for their services.[60]

Robert Livingston, Jr., continued to rely on his brothers as business agents until his sons came of age and replaced their uncles in the family commercial network. Although we know little about the type of apprenticeships Robert's sons served, it is clear that he expected them to become either merchants or lawyers after they completed their formal education. Robert's eldest son, Philip, died within a year of his graduation from Harvard College in 1755 and thus never participated in the Livingston family business. Peter R. Livingston, the second son, attended both Harvard and the College of New Jersey. Walter Livingston and Robert Cambridge Livingston—Robert's third and fourth sons, respectively—studied at

---

profiteering, in general, see Gary B. Nash, *The Urban Crucible: Social Change, Political Consciousness, and the Origins of the American Revolution* (Cambridge, Mass., 1979), pp. 235–46; Kevin Michael Sweeney, "River Gods and Related Minor Deities: The Williams Family and the Connecticut River Valley, 1637–1790" (Ph.D. diss., Yale University, 1986), esp. chap. 6.

[59] Shirley's warrants to William Alexander, 5 Dec. 1755, 22 June 1756, Rutherfurd Collection, NYHS, vol. 3; Extract of all warrants made payable to Erving, Alexander, Morris, and Livingston, or either of them, in Mr Johnston's List, [1756], William Alexander Papers, NYHS, vol. 2; Extract of all warrants made payable to Erving, Alexander, Morris, and P V B Livingston, or either of them, in Mr Mortier's List, [1756], ibid.; Petition of William Alexander et al., to the Lords of the Treasury, July 1757, ibid.

[60] Bonomi, *Factious People*, pp. 175–76; Charles Howard McIlwain, Intro. to *An Abridgement of the Indian Affairs . . .* , by Peter Wraxall (Cambridge, Mass., 1915), pp. cvii–cxi; Lord Loudoun to Peter Van Brugh Livingston, 23 Aug. 1756, Rutherfurd Collection, NYHS, vol. 3; Petition of William Alexander et al., to the Lords of the Treasury, July 1757, William Alexander Papers, NYHS, vol. 2; Powers of attorney granted to the "Earl of Sterling" by his associates in America, 3 Sept., 11 Sept. 1759, ibid. While in England, Alexander unsuccessfully sought official recognition of his claim to the earldom of Stirling. See Alan Valentine, *Lord Stirling* (New York, 1969), chap. 4.

the College of New Jersey, Cambridge, and the Inns of Court, successively. Their younger brothers, John and Henry, followed them to New Jersey and studied for several years at Princeton but left the college without graduating. After leaving college at least four of the five surviving Livingston brothers acted at some time as their father's commercial agent.[61]

Robert Livingston, Jr., sent all his sons to college, but he expected them to work for their livings once their university days were over. For instance, by 1763, Walter Livingston had spent four years in Europe, and his father was impatient for him to return to New York to begin working in some useful occupation. Robert wrote to his son, requesting that he return home "as its high time for him to be put in away of business." Walter returned to New York shortly thereafter, taking up his new responsibilities as a merchant and agent in the Livingston family business.[62]

Robert Livingston, Jr., may have summoned Walter home to New York to fill the void left in the family business by the downfall of his eldest surviving son, Peter R. Livingston. In 1758, the twenty-one-year-old Peter had left college to begin his mercantile career and for a while acted as his father's New York agent.[63] As the heir and protégé of the third lord of Livingston Manor, Peter's future seemed bright, but his career turned out to be disastrous. His story suggests that a young man needed more than connections and a prestigious name to succeed in the business of trade.

Although Peter R. Livingston could have supported himself and his family by acting as his father's agent, he preferred to get involved in riskier projects that seemed to offer greater immediate profits.

[61] John Livingston (1750–1822) appears to have been the exception, though he later did help oversee his father's enterprises at the Manor. On the education of the sons of Robert Livingston, Jr., see John Langdon Sibley and Clifford K. Shipton, *Sibley's Harvard Graduates: Biographical Sketches of those who attended Harvard College* (Boston, 1873–), 13:619, 14:183–84, 190; James McLachlan, *Princetonians, 1748–1768: A Biographical Dictionary* (Princeton, 1976), pp. 274–79; Robert Livingston, Jr., to James Duane, 26 July, 30 Nov. 1762, Duane Papers, NYHS, box 1. Christened simply as "Robert Livingston," the fourth son of the third lord of the Manor adopted "Cambridge" as his middle name both to honor his alma mater and to distinguish himself from the other Roberts in his numerous extended family.

[62] Robert Livingston, Jr., to James Duane, 26 July, 30 Nov. 1762, 22 Nov. 1763, 9 Nov. 1764, Duane Papers, NYHS, box 1.

[63] Peter R. Livingston to Oliver Wendell, 3 Nov. 1758, Livingston Papers, MCNY, box 1.

Peter's schemes to get rich quickly never paid off; in fact, his involvement in illegal trade during the French and Indian War caused him irreversible financial problems. In 1761, Peter sent his ship, the *Dove*, to the French sugar islands to dispose of a cargo of lumber and provisions. The ship arrived safely in the islands, landed its cargo, and took on a load of sugar, coffee, and rum for the return voyage to New York. But the *Dove* never arrived in New York because British authorities seized it in the Caribbean and confiscated both the ship and its contents. The loss of the *Dove* was a tremendous blow to Peter's finances and to his reputation. To make matters worse, he also was unable to collect the debts owed him by merchants in the French and Spanish colonies. Because his trade with them had been illegal, he could take no legal action against them. Meanwhile, his debts to legitimate trading partners mounted. By 1771, Peter's debts to his father alone amounted to roughly £13,000.[64] Like his great-uncle Gilbert, he received financial help from his family but was thereafter excluded from his father's patronage. Like Gilbert, Peter had proved himself reckless and incompetent and therefore unfit to participate in the family business.

Peter's abysmal wartime career underlined the importance of talent and restraint—as well as connections, capital, and credit—in entrepreneurial life. New York's successful risk-takers—the privateers, illegal traders, and aggressively developmental landlords and industrialists—were usually men who had made their fortunes in a dependable trade and then chose to reinvest some of their profits in riskier sorts of business ventures. Robert Livingston, Jr., recognized the importance of getting one's foothold in a dependable trade before gambling on less predictable enterprises, and after the seizure of the *Dove* he advised his son Peter "to follow [instead] the European business which is attended with the least trouble, no difficulties and a Certain Small proffitt to answer the maintaining [of] a family."[65] Robert expected his sons to work at a dependable, respect-

[64] Colden to Jeffrey Amherst, 16 Apr. 1762, in *The Letters and Papers of Cadwallader Colden,* 9 vols. (New York, 1918–37), 6:149–51; Deposition of George Moore, 22 Apr. 1762, ibid.; Robert Livingston, Jr., to James Duane, 3 May 1762, Duane Papers, NYHS, box 1; Peter R. Livingston to Oliver Wendell, 22 Nov. 1762, Livingston Papers, MCNY, box 1; Peter R. Livingston to Robert Livingston, Jr., 14 Apr., 8 Nov. 1769, Livingston-Redmond MSS., reel 8; Bond of Peter R. Livingston, 7 July 1771, ibid.

[65] Robert Livingston, Jr., to James Duane, 3 May 1762, Duane Papers, NYHS, box 1.

able trade before they experimented with the more exciting but less predictable branches of business that clearer heads regarded as a way to supplement their income instead of the main source of their subsistence. Peter, however, preferred gambling and experimentation to steady, dependable work. When his experiments failed, even his impressive social and political connections were not enough to enable him to revive his sagging fortunes.

Luckily, Robert Livingston, Jr., had more capable sons to whom he could delegate his commercial responsibilities. Between 1765 and 1769, Walter Livingston and Robert Cambridge Livingston did most of their father's business in New York City. As partners, the Livingston brothers imported European manufactures and luxury items from the London firm of Neate, Pigou & Booth. They then either shipped their imported merchandise to their father at the Manor or marketed these items elsewhere on their own account. As their father's agents in New York, Walter and Robert Cambridge were also responsible for disposing of the produce that came their way from Livingston Manor.

Although Walter and Robert Cambridge traded with many partners both inside and outside of their family circle, their business with their father was by far the most extensive. In 1767, for example, Robert Livingston, Jr., sent his sons 1,472 casks of flour and grain, 342 tons of pig iron, and lesser quantities of bread, butter, and furs. That year Robert's sloop, the *Polly,* made thirteen trips to his sons' wharf in New York, returning laden with goods to be used at the Manor or sold in the Albany County stores. The arrangement was profitable and convenient for all parties. Robert disposed of his produce and had a constant supply of imported items; his sons, after four years in business together, posted a net profit of £4,100 when they formally dissolved their partnership in 1769.[66] Thereafter, Robert Cambridge Livingston continued to conduct his father's business until 1775. Then, Henry, the youngest Livingston brother, succeeded him as his father's agent in New York until 1776, when British troops occupied the city.[67]

---

[66] Walter and Robert [Cambridge] Livingston, Waste Book, 1765–69, Livingston Family Papers, NYHS, reel 16; Walter and Robert [Cambridge] Livingston, Ledger, 1765–74, ibid.; Account of Goods Sent to New York . . . for Acct of Robt. Livingston Junr Esqr & Consign'd to Walter and Robt. [Cambridge] Livingston, Mar. 1766–Nov. 1768, ibid., reel 28.

[67] Account of Robert Livingston, Jr., with [Robert Cambridge Livingston], Apr.–

Robert Livingston, Jr., and his sons thus embraced the entrepreneurial vision of Philip, the second lord of Livingston Manor, whose ambition and foresight had transformed his Hudson Valley estate into the cornerstone of the Livingston family business. During Philip's lifetime, growing numbers of tenants and neighboring farmers brought grain to be ground at the Manor gristmill, while Manor sawmills produced boards for local sale or export. Later, the addition of an iron forge and Philip's purchase of a share of the nearby Salisbury "ore hill" made the Manor the potential source of yet another valuable commodity. Robert Livingston, Jr., exploited that potential, gradually expanding the ironworks begun by his father.

By the middle decades of the eighteenth century, many colonial merchant-entrepreneurs were investing in industrial projects, though few were as ambitious as the ironworks at Livingston Manor. Colonial merchants long had engaged in milling and shipbuilding as logical extensions of their trade. Involvement in the West Indian trade likewise encouraged merchants to invest in sugar refineries and rum distilleries—both of which became increasingly numerous in New York during the eighteenth century.[68] But by mid-century, the growth of colonial wealth and population also persuaded some local entrepreneurs to invest in other industries to produce consumer goods for a rapidly expanding domestic market. Some of these new industries, like iron-making, involved the exploitation of natural resources—a capital-intensive process that had not been viable in the early colonial period, when capital was scarce and the home market for domestic manufactures was extremely limited.[69]

Philip Livingston built New York's first permanent ironworks at Ancram, on Roeloff Jansen's Kill fourteen miles east of the Hudson River. He erected one blast furnace at Ancram in 1743 and added a forge two years later; after 1749, his son and heir, Robert

---

Dec. 1769, Livingston-Redmond MSS., reel 8; Accounts of Sales, 1773, 1774, ibid.; Henry Livingston to Robert Livingston, Jr., 20 Nov. 1775, 26 Mar. 1776, ibid.

[68] Harrington, *New York Merchant*, pp. 146–48. By the 1760s there were eight sugar refineries in New York, one of which belonged to Peter Van Brugh Livingston. By 1767 the province's lower counties contained seventeen distilleries including one owned by John Livingston, brother of Robert Livingston, Jr.

[69] See McCusker and Menard, *Economy of British America*, pp. 277–81, 309–26; E. N. Hartley, *Ironworks on the Saugus: The Lynn and Braintree Ventures of the Company of Undertakers of the Ironworks in New England* (Norman, Okla., 1957), chap. 2, pp. 262–70. On New York's earliest ironworks, see Irene D. Neu, "The Iron Plantations of Colonial New York," *NY Hist.*, 33 (1952): 3–24.

Livingston, Jr., added at least two more forges, both located at Livingston Manor.[70] During the quarter-century preceding the Revolution, Robert expanded the ironworks and diversified its products. In addition to pig and bar iron, Robert's ironworks manufactured nails, kettles, pots, musket shot, carriage wheels, chimney backs, stoves, and other assorted items. The Livingstons were New York's premier iron producers through the Revolutionary era. Indeed, during most of the colonial period they enjoyed a virtual monopoly of the province's iron industry.[71]

Despite the rich deposits of iron ore in New York's highlands and their accessibility to relatively inexpensive river transportation, New Yorkers lagged far behind most other colonists in exploiting their natural resources. Unlike many other provincial legislatures, the New York assembly made no effort to encourage iron production, though they did grant monopolies, offer bounties, and levy duties to promote other manufacturing enterprises.[72] More important, many of New York's most conveniently located ore-producing areas were

[70] Robert may have built his forges in defiance of the Iron Act of 1750, which prohibited construction of new plating forges and steel furnaces in the colonies though it did not proscribe the expansion of existing iron-making facilities. See Roberta S. Singer, "'Iron Will Not Decay': The Ancram Ironworks, 1749–1790," in Wiles, ed., *The Livingston Legacy*, pp. 302–3. Most scholars agree that the Iron Act was unenforceable and widely disregarded; by 1775, there were at least 82 furnaces and 175 forges in British colonial America, many of which probably were constructed after 1750. See Oliver M. Dickerson, *The Navigation Acts and the American Revolution* (Philadelphia, 1951), pp. 47–48; Arthur C. Bining, *British Regulation of the Colonial Iron Industry* (Philadelphia, 1933), esp. chaps. 4–5; McCusker and Menard, *Economy of British America*, p. 326.

[71] Robert Livingston, Jr., to James DeLancey, 15 June 1755, *DHNY*, 3:811; Robert Livingston, Jr.'s accounts with Walter and Robert [Cambridge] Livingston, Mar.–Apr. 1767, and with Robert [Cambridge] Livingston, Apr.–Dec. 1769, Livingston-Redmond MSS., reel 8; John Stevenson to Robert Livingston, Jr., 12 Sept. 1773, ibid.; Sale of sundry items by Robert Livingston, Jr., 30 June 1768, Livingston Family Papers, NYHS, reel 1. On the Livingstons' dominance of New York's colonial iron business, see Neu, "Iron Plantations of Colonial New York."

[72] The provincial government granted monopolies for linseed oil (1694, 1712), porpoise-hunting (1714, 1726), sugar refining (1720), and lampblack (1724). In 1764–65, bounties were offered to encourage the production of hemp. Between 1728 and 1734, the government imposed a duty on empty casks and barrels brought to New York from other colonies in order to protect local coopers; beginning in 1734, shipping and shipbuilding were promoted by levying tonnage duties on incoming ships built neither in Britain nor in New York (*N.Y. Col. Laws*, 1:339, 752–53, 839–40, 2:7–8, 242, 311–12, 423–24, 843–47, 852–54, 3:440–42, 737–39, 796).

included in the large land grants made by the colony's early governors. The proprietors of these grants were usually wealthy men already engaged in various entrepreneurial activities, and most had little inclination or incentive to invest their time and money in an enterprise that was both risky and experimental.

As early as 1739, however, Philip Livingston had planned to develop an ironworks at Livingston Manor. Clearly, Philip was exceptional in his willingness to invest in such an uncertain new industry. In 1741, he estimated the cost of building and stocking his Ancram ironworks at more than £4,500, New York currency. In addition, the project absorbed a great deal of Philip's time, both in planning and implementation. In particular, he had great difficulty procuring experienced skilled laborers to operate his furnace and forge. Philip and his sons scoured the colonies from New England to Maryland and even considered sending to Germany for a founder. Nevertheless, Philip believed that "the Iron Manufactory is the most advantagious business if well manag[e]d" and that success in that industry would enable him to spend most of his remaining years at the Manor, where he would "Enjoy [his] Brook . . . and lay up an Everlasting treasure" to ensure his family's financial future. Unlike most of his social peers, Philip Livingston correctly believed that the profits from his ironworks would ultimately far outweigh his expenditures in time and money, that his potential gains would easily repay his initial effort.[73]

Besides a large initial capital investment, iron production required large quantities of land and natural resources that, in landlord-ridden New York, only the great magnates could command. Each blast furnace needed nearly 3,000 acres of forest land to ensure the continuous supply of charcoal necessary for iron-making. Ore fields had to be located within a reasonable distance from the ironworks to avoid excessive transportation costs. Limestone, used as a flux to rid

[73] Philip Livingston to Jacob Wendell, 16 Aug. 1739, 16 Aug. 1740, 16 Mar. 1741, Livingston Papers, MCNY, box 2; Philip Livingston to Robert Livingston, Jr., 20 July 1741, 18 Oct., 11 Nov. 1742, 30 Jan. 1745, Livingston-Redmond MSS., reel 7. The scarcity of skilled labor also had hindered the development of earlier colonial ironworks (Hartley, *Ironworks on the Saugus*, pp. 57, 269–70). Livingston's belief that manufacturing could bring him steady, dependable profits to support a genteel style of living presaged similar attitudes among nineteenth-century industrialists. See Robert F. Dalzell, Jr., *Enterprising Elite: The Boston Associates and the World They Made* (Cambridge, Mass., 1987), chaps. 1–2.

the iron of impurities, also had to be readily accessible, as did running water to drive the blast and hammer. The ironworks at Ancram admirably met all these requirements. As Philip Livingston boasted in 1740, the site he chose had "the most naturall conveniencys as to the Stream & wood that is in America, and also a very good bed of ore." Philip was also part owner of the Salisbury, Connecticut, "ore hill," located only twelve miles from Ancram.[74] Thus he built the Livingston ironworks on a creek in the midst of family-owned forests, where its proximity to the Hudson River decreased the cost of transporting the finished product.

Like most successful colonial ironworks, the Ancram establishment was an "iron plantation" similar to the company towns of the nineteenth and twentieth centuries. Although no contemporary description of the Ancram ironworks survives, the German immigrant Peter Hasenclever wrote a detailed description of his three iron plantations in eighteenth-century New Jersey, which must have been similar to the Livingstons' facilities. At each of his ironworks, Hasenclever employed a founder, a forgeman, and various semiskilled and unskilled workers. These ironworkers lived in dwellings provided by their employer. According to Hasenclever, the quality and location of the employees' residences, as well as their wages, varied according to the level of skill their jobs demanded. His Charlottenburg ironworks, for instance, was equipped with "six large frame dwelling-houses fill'd with brick and clay, 37 good and comfortable log-houses, besides a number of smaller houses in the woods for the wood-cutters and colliers." Other buildings within the iron-making community filled the needs of the ironworks and the people who ran it. Sawmills, charcoal sheds, and casting houses, in addition to the furnace and forge, formed the nucleus of the industrial operation. Some iron plantations also had churches, schools, and taverns; for the workers' convenience and the employer's profit, most included a general store and perhaps a gristmill.[75]

Like the inhabitants of iron plantations elsewhere, the workers at

[74] Philip Livingston to Robert Livingston, Jr., 10 June 1740, Livingston-Redmond MSS., reel 7; Philip Livingston to Jacob Wendell, 16 Aug. 1740, Livingston Papers, MCNY, box 2; Neu, "Iron Plantations," pp. 5–8; James A. Mulholland, *A History of Metals in Early America* (University, Ala., 1981), pp. 70–73.

[75] Peter Hasenclever, *The Remarkable Case of Peter Hasenclever . . .* (London, 1773), esp. p. 67; Neu, "Iron Plantations," p. 3; Mulholland, *History of Metals*, pp. 71–72.

Ancram were entirely dependent on the goods and services provided by their employer. Although Hasenclever did not indicate whether his employees had either farms or gardens, Livingston's ironworkers doubled as tenant farmers; they tilled his land, ground their grain at his Ancram gristmill, and spent their wages at his nearby store. Perhaps because the Ancram workers divided their time between farming and iron-making, the Livingstons were able to pay them far less than Hasenclever paid his employees in New Jersey. Many of the workers at Ancram were New Englanders adversely affected by the growing land scarcity in western Massachusetts. The Livingstons may have been able to pay these workers less by giving them access to the land they presumably wanted.[76]

Low labor costs and efficient marketing made the Ancram ironworks successful. Robert Livingston, Jr., sold most of his iron goods locally; after manufacturing the iron at the Manor, he shipped it on his own sloop to his sons downriver in New York City. Because his transportation costs were minimal and his workers' wages generally low, it is reasonable to assume that Livingston's total costs to produce and transport a ton of pig iron did not exceed £5 2s.5d. In 1767, Livingston sold his pig iron in New York at an average price of £9.8s. per ton, making his profit for each ton sold £4 5s.7d., or nearly 84 percent. Thus, his return on his investment was substantial, even after deducting his sons' 10 percent commission. In 1767, Livingston sent his sons 342 tons of pig iron, but in a good year his furnace could be much more productive. For instance, during the prosperous 1750s, annual production at the Ancram ironworks averaged

[76] Wheat book of Robert Livingston, Jr., 1765–66, indicates that the gristmill at Ancram was used by men described elsewhere as ironworkers (Livingston-Redmond MSS., reel 7). The Livingstons paid their colliers between 11s.3p. and 12s.6p. per 100 bushels of coal, while colliers at Hasenclever's ironworks received 20s. for only 96 bushels; Hasenclever paid his ore-diggers 15s. per ton, while the Livingstons' ore-diggers generally received far less. See Hasenclever, *Remarkable Case of Peter Hasenclever*, pp. 79, 81–82; Philip Livingston's agreement with Ebeneezer Loomis, 14 Apr. 1748, Livingston-Redmond MSS., reel 6; Agreement between Robert Livingston, Jr., and Jedidiah Moore, 20 Oct. 1757, ibid., reel 7; Agreement between Robert Livingston, Jr., and William Smith et al., 21 Nov. 1775, ibid., reel 8; Agreement between Robert Livingston, Jr., and John Loomis, Misc. MSS., Robert Livingston, Jr., NYHS; Diary and Account Book of Charles DeWitt, 1749–80, Misc. MSS., B. V. DeWitt, NYHS. On land scarcity in eighteenth-century western Massachusetts, see Gregory Nobles, *Divisions throughout the Whole: Politics and Society in Hampshire County Massachusetts, 1740–1775* (New York, 1983).

474 tons of pig iron, 186 tons of bar iron, and 9 tons of iron converted to other castings.[77]

Like his father Philip, Robert Livingston, Jr., relied heavily on his
brothers, and later his sons, for various commercial services. With
their help as agents and marketers, the family business prospered.
In 1765, in the midst of an economic depression, Robert
Livingston, Jr., estimated the weekly profits of his iron-making and
milling operations at £100, which he believed was "more then
any [other] Gentlemen in America can this day say."[78] Robert
Livingston, Jr., may have exaggerated his income, but his Manor
had indeed become an immensely profitable agricultural-industrial
complex. By facilitating the distribution and marketing of Manor
produce, kin played a vital role in encouraging the development of
the family land.

Landed magnates like Philip Livingston and Robert Livingston,
Jr., both dominated and developed New York's economy during the
colonial era. New York's landed gentry were also aggressive entrepreneurs. Upon receiving his inheritance in 1749, Robert
Livingston, Jr., thus retired to his estate not to live a life of idleness
and frivolity but to direct the family business from its nerve center at
Livingston Manor.

The Livingstons were clearly innovators who constantly searched
for new markets, new commodities, and new projects to broaden
and diversify their trade. At the same time, they consistently chan-
neled their resources into areas that complemented their established
enterprises. As the premier mill-owners of the upper Hudson Valley,

[77] Neu, "Iron Plantations of Colonial New York," pp. 5–8; James DeLancey to
Board of Trade, 1 Dec. 1757, *DRNY*, 7:335; Account of Iron Made at Ancram,
Livingston Manor, 1750–56, ibid., 7:336; Account of Goods Sent to Newyork, . . . for
Acct of Robt. Livingston Junr Esqr & Consign'd to Walter and Robt. [Cambridge]
Livingston, Mar. 1766–Nov. 1768, Livingston Family Papers, NYHS, reel 28; Walter
and Robert [Cambridge] Livingston's account of Sales of 342 Tons pigg Iron, 1767–
68, Robert R. Livingston Papers, NYHS, reel 1; John Stevenson's account with Robert
Livingston, 1769–75, Livingston-Redmond MSS., reel 8. All figures are converted to
New York currency.

[78] Robert Livingston, Jr., to James Duane, 30 Nov. 1765, Duane Papers, NYHS, box
1.

the proprietors of New York's first successful ironworks, and the creators of an increasingly far-flung and diversified commercial network, the Livingstons were one of colonial America's leading entrepreneurial families. They were also New York's archetypical developmental landlords during the colonial era.

[3]

The Family Land

When the first Robert Livingston received the patent for his manor in 1686, the area it embraced was undeveloped and inhabited only by a few Indians. Livingston was a land speculator, and the Manor was his prize acquisition. He thought of his land as an investment for the future, an estate that would in time become an asset to his family's business. Yet Livingston also knew that land-ownership conferred social status. As early as 1690, social and dynastic considerations prompted him to entail the 160,000-acre estate to his eldest son, a strategy designed to preserve the identity of the Manor and prestige of the proprietary family.

Over the course of the eighteenth century, Livingston Manor lived up to the first Robert's expectations. The Manor became a successful business enterprise, a rural community, and a symbolic representation of the ideals and identity of the proprietary family. The Manor represented the family's economic future and the fulfillment of their entrepreneurial ideals. It also came to symbolize their social ambitions and their desire to become part of a distinctive and respected elite akin to the contemporary English gentry.

By mid-century, New York's landed magnates were merchant-entrepreneur-aristocrats whose residence on their estates both enhanced their personal wealth and fostered their family's identification with the manors that bore their names. Significantly, it was the iron industry that was largely responsible for transforming the proprietor of Livingston Manor into a country squire and his estate into a residential family seat. During the first Robert's lifetime, the Manor had been simply one of many branches of the family's business interests. After Philip Livingston inherited the Manor in 1728, he looked upon the family land as a hinterland for his Albany trade— until he built his blast furnace there in 1743. Philip decided to move to the Manor to oversee the construction and operation of his iron-works; likewise, his son Robert Livingston, Jr., later devoted himself to improving the Manor's industrial facilities, "building all new, as fast as I could, when this estate fell in my hands."[1]

The Livingstons and their peers in New York were not quasi-feudal grandees who wasted their income in idleness and ostentation; they were landed capitalists who reinvested their profits in order to continue developing their estates. New York's landed magnates supplied the capital, credit, and initiative necessary to trans-form acres of untapped wilderness into rural communities and prof-itable business ventures. In the process, they drew many lesser folk into their economic orbits as tenant farmers and hired laborers, habitually indebted clients and dependents. After 1750, however, some of these lesser folk grew resentful of their landlord's economic privileges. The resulting unrest on the Livingstons' land jeopardized both the interests and the identity of the proprietary family.

Land speculation was a way of life for elites in New York and elsewhere during the colonial era. Speculators regarded frontier land as a sound investment; costing little, it was nonetheless an ap-preciating asset that could be passed on to future generations. Be-cause New York's provincial government did not tax unimproved land, incentives to settle and cultivate remote speculative holdings were minimal.[2] Consequently, in 1774, Governor William Tryon re-

---

[1] Robert Livingston, Jr., to James Duane, 30 Nov. 1765, Duane Papers, NYHS, box 1.

[2] Robert R. Livingston argued the opposite. See Beverly McAnear, ed., "Mr. Robert R. Livingston's Reasons against a Land Tax," *Journal of Political Economy*, 48 (1940): 90. Although Livingston's motives were obviously suspect, some historians have taken him at his word. See, for instance, Sung Bok Kim, "A New Look at the Great Land-lords of Eighteenth-Century New York," *WMQ*, 3d ser., 27 (1970): 599–604. Kim contends that the great landowners did settle and improve their land, but his argu-ment is based overwhelmingly on the status of the great manors by the mid-eigh-teenth century, or more than fifty years after their patents had been issued. More recently, Bernard Bailyn has argued that land speculators played a crucial role in the settling and developing of British America. Nevertheless, while these speculators did

ported that the Mohawk, Schoharie, and Susquehanna valleys had been neither settled nor improved, though speculators, abetted by royal governors, had received patents for these lands decades earlier.[3]

The Livingstons were avid participants in the great land grabs that swelled New York's frontiers during the eighteenth century. Robert and Alida's elder sons, Philip and Robert of Clermont, were among the province's leading land speculators. Robert Livingston of Clermont owned more than 460,000 acres in the Hardenbergh Patent on the west side of the Hudson River, in addition to smaller holdings elsewhere. Philip Livingston used his influence as secretary for Indian affairs to acquire expansive holdings in the Mohawk Valley; when he died in 1749, he bequeathed to each of his eight younger children nearly 20,000 acres there and elsewhere in New York and western New England. To varying degrees, Philip's sons continued their family's speculative tradition. His son and namesake, New York City merchant Philip Livingston, owned more than 120,000 acres of unimproved land in New York when he died in 1778, in addition to his lesser holdings in New Jersey, Connecticut, Albany, and Manhattan. By contrast, William Livingston was probably the most cautious and the least affluent of the third-generation Livingston brothers. Yet even he owned 10,000 acres in speculative holdings, in addition to the 20,000 acres conveyed to him by his father.[4]

---

recruit settlers for their land, in New York they seem to have been most successful only after land became scarce in accessible freehold tenure areas. See Bailyn, *The Peopling of British North America: An Introduction* (New York, 1986), pp. 65–70.

[3] Tryon to Lord Dartmouth, 11 June 1774, *DRNY*, 8:441. On the geographic progression of land speculation, see Ruth L. Higgins, *Expansion in New York with Especial Reference to the Eighteenth Century* (Columbus, Ohio, 1931), esp. pp. 70–80.

[4] The most significant of the voluminous documents pertaining to the Livingstons' speculative holdings during the colonial period are: The Ingagement of the Sachims of the Upper Castle of the Maquase, 25 Jan. 1729, Rutherfurd Collection, NYHS, vol. 2; Release of five Indians to Philip Livingston et al., 2 May 1729, ibid., vol. 1; Philip Livingston to Abraham Van Horne and William Provoost, 28 June 1731, ibid.; Peter Wraxall, *An Abridgement of the Indian Affairs . . .*, ed. Charles Howard McIlwain (Cambridge, Mass., 1915), pp. 185–86; Patents to Philip Livingston et al., 1736–43, *Cal. Coun. Min.*, pp. 326, 331, 333, 344; Indenture between shareholders in the Hardenbergh Patent, 15 Nov. 1749, Livingston Family Papers, NYHS, reel 28; Robert R. Livingston, Jr., to John R. Livingston, 18 May 1779, Misc. MSS., John R. Livingston, NYHS; Lands . . . belong[ing] to the estate of Governor Livingston, [1790], William Livingston Papers, Mass. Hist. Soc., reel 3; Schedule of Lands belonging to the Estate of William Livingston, 1794, ibid., reel 6A; Account of the Division of the Lands of

Large-scale land speculation antedated settlement in nearly every part of New York north of Manhattan Island. Unlike the more remote frontier regions, the manors and patents of the Hudson Valley were ideally situated for settlement and development even during the seventeenth century. Even before the English conquest, New York and Albany had been the colony's most important centers of population. As the population of New Netherland / New York grew, settlers flowed from both north and south into the Hudson River valley.[5] Easily accessible to both Albany and Manhattan by cheap, efficient water transportation, the fertile Hudson Valley fast became New York's commercial farming region. The gradual improvement and settlement of Livingston Manor was symptomatic of this much more general regional development.

By 1700, the four manorial families of Van Rensselaer, Livingston, Van Cortlandt, and Philipse controlled most of the best land in the Hudson Valley. These great landowners generally avoided selling their land, preferring to rent it instead to tenant farmers. Because the great landlords owned so much land and were unwilling to sell it, newcomers found it difficult to purchase land in colonial New York. Some contemporaries believed that the colony's monopolistic land system discouraged people from settling in New York, which in turn impeded economic development. As early as 1698, the Earl of Bellomont had complained to the Board of Trade that because New York was "given away to about thirty persons" it could not compete effectively with neighboring colonies for settlers. Because land was cheap in both New Jersey and Pennsylvania, he observed, "what man will be such a fool as to become a base tenant to [New York's] mighty Landgraves?"[6]

In 1726, Cadwallader Colden—the colony's surveyor-general—

Philip Livingston, the Signer, 1794, Philip Livingston Papers, NYPL, box 4. The best summary of Livingston landholdings appears in Patricia Joan Gordon, "The Livingstons of New York, 1675–1860: Kinship and Class," (Ph.D. diss., Columbia University, 1959), pp. 65–66, 82, 142–88. See also Higgins, *Expansion in New York*, esp. pp. 67–88; and Milton M. Klein, "The American Whig: William Livingston of New York" (Ph.D. diss., Columbia University, 1954), pp. 721–41.

[5] See Patricia U. Bonomi, *A Factious People: Politics and Society in Colonial New York* (New York, 1971), pp. 20–24.

[6] Bellomont to Board of Trade, 21 Oct. 1698, *DRNY*, 4:397–98. See also Bellomont to Board of Trade, 28 Nov. 1700, *Cal. S.P.*, 1700, no. 953. Cornbury expressed similar complaints; see his letter to the Board of Trade, 30 June 1704, *DRNY*, 4:1112.

asserted that the inequities of the provincial land system forced even native New Yorkers to look elsewhere for their subsistence. Colden lamented that the huge patents were generally uncultivated, "while the people in other parts of the Province have for some time wanted land for their Children & have been Oblidged to send them into the Neighbouring Colonys." Colden reiterated this concern in 1732, noting that people were leaving New York "to avoid the dependence on landlords, and to enjoy lands in fee [simple] to descend to their posterity that their children may reap the benefit of their labour and Industry." Recent studies of the towns of Flatbush and Newtown support Colden's observation, with adjacent New Jersey as the emigrants' most popular destination. Tenancy, as Colden noted, was the last resort for the "better sort" of farmers, who could afford to purchase land elsewhere.[7]

Although the population of New York's manors and land grants did increase during the eighteenth century, it did so less dramatically than that of other areas having comparable agricultural and commercial potentials. Like Livingston Manor, southeastern Pennsylvania was largely unsettled until the 1680s, but the population density of that region rose to more than twenty people per square mile by 1760. By comparison, an average of 6.5 people inhabited each square mile of Manor land in 1767. Similarly, between 1690 and 1770 the white population of Pennsylvania as a whole increased at nearly twice the rate of that of New York.[8]

Overall, then, New York's manorial system probably did impede

[7] Colden to Secretary Popple, 4 Dec. 1726, *DRNY*, 5:806; Colden to William Cosby, 1732, *DHNY*, 1:384; William John McLaughlin, "Dutch Rural New York: Community, Economy, and Family in Colonial Flatbush" (Ph.D. diss., Columbia University, 1981), pp. 86–92, 99–101; Jessica Kross Erlich, "A Town Study in Colonial New York: Newtown, Queens County, 1642–1790" (Ph.D. diss., University of Michigan, 1974), pp. 182–90.

[8] *Hist. Statistics of the U.S.*, 2:1168. My calculation of the Manor's population density is based on the Livingston Manor rent ledger, 1767–84, Livingston Family Papers, NYHS, reel 15, which lists 285 tenant households occupying 141,000 acres, or 220.3 square miles. Of the original 160,000-acre grant, 6,000 acres had been conveyed to Governor Hunter in 1710 and 13,000 had been partitioned by the first lord of the Manor as a bequest to his son Robert. The rent ledger lists only heads of households, and I have assumed that an average household consisted of five people. For demographic data on southeastern Pennsylvania, see James T. Lemon, *The Best Poor Man's Country: A Geographical Study of Early Southeastern Pennsylvania* (Baltimore, 1972), pp. 46, 58–62.

Table 1
Tenant families at Livingston Manor,
1696–1784

Year	Number
1696	11*
1715	53*
c. 1750	220*
1767	285
1775	339
1784	355

*Conservative estimates. The figure for 1696 includes only Livingston's debtors at Livingston Manor. The 1715 and c. 1750 estimates are based on militia lists and do not include people with duplicate surnames.

Sources: *Lyste van Debiteurs geextraheert uyt myn Grootbook*, 31 Dec. 1696, Livingston-Redmond MSS., reel 2; Muster Roll, Livingston Manor Company, 30 Nov. 1715, *DHNY*, 3:704; A List of the Independent Company of Foot of the Manour Livingston, c. 1750, Livingston-Redmond MSS., reel 7; Livingston Manor rent ledger, 1767–84, Livingston Family Papers, NYHS, reel 15.

settlement somewhat, despite the best efforts of the landlords to encourage economic development. At Livingston Manor, settlement was dispersed, with the areas adjacent to the waterways, mills, and ironworks being the most densely populated. As Table 1 indicates, by 1775, some 339 tenant families inhabited the Manor's 220 square miles of forested land, an area ten times the size of Manhattan Island.

From the beginning, the Hudson Valley landlords had land and capital, but they needed labor in order to develop their land and make it commercially successful. Thus, in 1710, the first Robert Livingston had accepted Governor Robert Hunter's proposal to settle the Palatines on his land, a plan that increased both his milling and retail trades and eventually fostered the growth of a stable tenant community at Livingston Manor. Subsequent proprietors of both Livingston Manor and Clermont occasionally solicited tenants from Europe. Like New York's other great landlords, they may have sent their agents to Manhattan to meet incoming ships and arrange leases with newly arrived immigrants.[9] To make their proposition

[9] Apparently, this practice was commonplace. See "Information for Europeans intending to remove from Europe to America," c. 1765, William Smith Papers, NYPL, box 2.

more attractive, the Livingstons offered all new leaseholders an initial rent-free period—usually two years—in exchange for the clearing and cultivation of unimproved land.

The proprietors' recruitment efforts, coupled with the scarcity of land in nearby southern New England, caused the Manor's population to increase markedly over the course of the eighteenth century. Table 1 shows that Robert Livingston had approximately 11 tenants in 1696; by 1715, he had more than 50, many of whom were refugees from the Palatine settlements. By 1767, the Manor's population had risen to 285 tenant families. Collectively, these tenants leased more than 30,000 acres from Robert Livingston, Jr., and paid him more than £1,500 worth of wheat in annual rent. In the 1670s, the entire province of New York had exported only 60,000 bushels of wheat annually; by the 1760s, each year the tenants of Livingston Manor alone produced approximately 50,000 bushels, one-tenth of which Robert Livingston, Jr., claimed as rental income.[10]

For some New Yorkers, tenancy must have been an attractive option. The Livingstons offered land and credit to aspiring farmers— and therefore provided real opportunities to the young and destitute. At least before 1763, the presence of the French and their Indian allies limited settlement in New York north and west of Albany. Livingston Manor, like the colony's other tenanted estates, was safe from the violence of the frontier and easily accessible to mills and inexpensive water transportation.

The Livingstons offered prospective tenants fertile acreage in the colony's most productive grain-producing region, as well as the facilities necessary to process their wheat and send it off to market. In exchange for these conveniences, however, the tenant probably compromised his ability to secure the greatest possible return on his produce. The Livingstons' leases reserved for the landlord the preemptive right to purchase all his tenant's grain and required the leaseholder to do all his grinding at the Manor mills, where he paid one-tenth of his produce for the miller's services. At this rate, a good

---

[10] Livingston Manor rent ledger, 1767–84, Livingston Family Papers, NYHS, reel 15. Combined annual rent for 285 tenants in 1767 was 5,000 bushels of wheat. Cash values and acreage calculated according to wheat prices and farm sizes in Sung Bok Kim, *Landlord and Tenant in Colonial New York: Manorial Society, 1664–1775* (Chapel Hill, N.C., 1978), pp. 189, 195. On the volume of New York's early grain exports, see Edmund Andros to Lords of Trade, 1678, *DHNY*, 1:90.

harvest could mean as much as £700 in grain as clear profit for the proprietor and his miller, not including rents, which unlike milling tolls did not fluctuate according to crop yields.[11]

Overall, the Livingstons' economic power was ubiquitous in their bailiwick. Tenants depended on them for their land, for processing and marketing their crops, for supplying them with items from the general store that they needed for their subsistence. Tenants became indebted to their landlords for rent and for milling, but especially for the merchandise purchased at the general store. Most colonial families were not self-sufficient; particularly in commercial farming areas like the Hudson Valley, they depended heavily on merchants and shopkeepers for necessities they did not produce themselves.[12] As soon as the Palatine refugees settled on his land, Robert Livingston had stocked his store with textiles, stockings, hats, tools, and cooking utensils, all of which he imported from England. Because Livingston's store was the only one accessible to Manor tenants, he and his descendants had a reliable and growing rural clientele who purchased their imported goods, usually on credit. The store's trade in dry goods, tools, and cooking and dining utensils was particularly heavy. In the 1750s, the Manor store sold earthenware dishes at a 70 percent profit.[13]

In view of their dependence on the Livingstons and their resources, a surprising proportion of Manor tenants managed to avoid

[11] Mill gains, 1742–50, in Diary and Account Book of Charles DeWitt, 1749–80, Misc. MSS., B. V. DeWitt, NYHS. Most of the surviving leases are in the Livingston-Redmond MSS., reels 6–8, and Misc. MSS., Livingston Manor, NYHS.

[12] On consumption among rural people in colonial America, see Carole Shammas, "How Self-Sufficient Was Early America?" *Journal of Interdisciplinary History*, 13 (1982): 242–72. Evidence from Livingston Manor suggests that the Hudson Valley's farmers had outgrown the subsistence *mentalité* that James A. Henretta claims was pervasive in provincial America. See Henretta, "Families and Farms: *Mentalité* in Pre-Industrial America," *WMQ*, 3d ser., 35 (1978): 3–32; and James T. Lemon, "Comment on James A. Henretta's 'Families and Farms'" (with Henretta's reply), ibid., 37 (1980): 688–700. For a more recent—and more persuasive—interpretation, see Daniel Vickers, "Competency and Competition: Economic Culture in Early America," ibid., 57 (1990): 6–12.

[13] *Alt goet in'd Winkel & int Stowhuys* . . . , 4 Mar. 1713, Livingston-Redmond MSS., reel 3; Posts in the Genl. Journall for goods Sold out of the Shop upon Trust . . . , Mar. 1712–Mar. 1714, ibid.; Posts . . . in the Ledger on the Credit Side of [the] Shop . . . , Apr. 1717–June 1721, ibid.; Price of Earthen Ware Sold [at] Manor Livingston, Aug.–Sept. 1751, in Diary and Account Book of Charles DeWitt, 1749–80, Misc. MSS., B. V. DeWitt, NYHS.

becoming indebted. In 1716, of the sixty-seven adult men who resided at the Manor, only thirty-three had outstanding debts at
Livingston's general store. Tenants during the Revolutionary era
demonstrated a similar capacity to remain solvent. Between 1767
and 1784, 43 of the Manor's 357 tenants—or 12 percent—kept their
rent accounts entirely up-to-date; between 1782 and 1787, some 123
tenants—or 35 percent—had managed to avoid falling into debt in
their nonrental accounts.[14]

Most tenants were indebted to the Livingstons to some degree
because, in a cash-poor economy, most business was conducted on
credit. But a careful examination of the Livingston ledgers and account books reveals that tenancy was an extraordinarily variable
condition and that the significance of debt itself often is somewhat
ambiguous. On the one hand, small individual debts, by far the most
common, suggested a healthy business relationship, not debilitating
dependence. On the other hand, a very large book debt could be
misleading. Often a large debt reflected the debtor's higher status or
greater ability to satisfy his obligation. For instance, between 1714
and 1726, William White and Jacob Vosburgh were more indebted
to the first Robert Livingston than any other Manor tenants. Both
White and Vosburgh were among the more prosperous residents of
Livingston Manor. White was a storekeeper and Vosburgh was a
justice of the peace and an officer in the local militia. Both men used
Livingston as a source of credit; their indebtedness to him did not
signify unremitting poverty, but rather relative prosperity and their
creditor's confidence in their eventual ability to repay him.[15]

Of course, some tenants did suffer chronic, large-scale indebtedness that rendered them and their families utterly dependent on the
forbearance of their landlord-creditor. Gerrit Decker, a Manor tenant for more than forty years, was always heavily indebted to the

[14] Muster roll, Livingston Manor Company, 30 Nov. 1715, *DHNY*, 3:704; List of
debtors taken out of Ledger F, 26 Jan. 1716, Livingston-Redmond MSS., reel 3;
Livingston Manor rent ledger, 1767–84, Livingston Family Papers, NYHS, reel 15;
Account ledger of Robert Livingston, Jr., 1782–87, Livingston-Redmond MSS., reel
13.

[15] Lists of debtors taken out of Ledger F, 1710–26, Livingston-Redmond *MSS.*,
reels 3–4; Notice of execution of the bond of Johannes Bernhart, 4 Jan. 1721, ibid.,
reel 4; Muster roll, Livingston Manor Company, 30 Nov. 1715, *DHNY*, 3:704. On the
sociology of debt, see Alice Hanson Jones, *The Wealth of a Nation to Be: The American
Colonies on the Eve of the Revolution* (New York, 1980), pp. 141–53.

lord of the Manor. In 1740, Philip Livingston hired Decker's son as a plowman in order to help satisfy some of his outstanding debts, but Decker still had difficulty paying his rent. By 1767, he owed Robert Livingston, Jr., 298 bushels of wheat on a farm that he leased at a cost of 40 bushels annually. Decker's debts escalated during the Revolutionary era. Between 1767 and 1783, he paid his rent only once, and by 1784 he owed 938 bushels of wheat on his rent account. But Decker's case was not typical. In 1779, the tax assessors valued his estate at only £20, while the average for Manor tenants was £350.[16] Although Gerrit Decker never paid his debts, Livingston took no legal action against him.

New York's landlords were entrepreneurs who depended on the labor of their tenants to make their land both productive and profitable. Robert Livingston, Jr., did not press Gerrit Decker to pay his debts because Decker was more valuable to him as an indebted but productive tenant farmer than as an unproductive inmate of the local debtor's prison. Decker's case was not exceptional. Landlords routinely accepted their tenants' bonds for overdue debts rather than take forcible measures against them. Evictions were rare because they were fruitless. Evicting a tenant essentially nullified his debt by removing him from his creditor's sphere of influence. Eviction also deprived the landlord of his tenant's labor and the resulting produce.[17]

Landlord and tenant depended on one another for their livelihoods, but their mutual dependence did not make them equal partners. From the landlord's perspective, the ideal tenant—like the ideal factory worker—was tractable and industrious. Philip Livingston preferred Dutch tenants to English tenants because he believed the former were both less contentious and more productive. As he explained to a friend, the Dutch "generally prove more industrious and Raise wheat & the [English] run chiefly on stock which is not so profitable for us nor them."[18]

[16] Personal and land tax lists of the district of the Manor of Livingston, 2 Mar. 1779, New York State Library; Philip Livingston to John DeWitt, 28 June 1740, Livingston-Redmond MSS., reel 9; Livingston Manor rent ledger, 1767–84, Livingston Family Papers, NYHS, reel 15.

[17] For a more benign interpretation of landlords' leniency toward indebted tenants, see Kim, *Landlord and Tenant*, pp. 216–18.

[18] Philip Livingston to Jacob Wendell, 16 Mar. 1741, Livingston Papers, MCNY, box 2.

Because grain was the staple of New York's export trade, wheat production was crucial to the Livingstons' commercial interests. New York's leaseholding system was designed to benefit the landlord's trade by giving him unlimited access to his tenants' produce—hence his insistence on the preemptive right and the milling monopoly. Some tenants resented their landlord's monopoly privileges and occasionally resisted their implementation. In the winter of 1741, for example, Philip Livingston instructed his overseer, John DeWitt, to buy all the wheat he could because he expected an order to provision the fleet at Jamaica. Realizing that the price of wheat would rise in later months, Philip anticipated difficulties with his tenants, who quite sensibly would prefer to wait to sell their crops. Philip wanted DeWitt to purchase the wheat for 3s. per bushel, though the current market price was 3s.3d. Most tenants complied with these terms, but some refused to sell their produce, opting to wait until the prices rose. Philip threatened to evict the "Brutes" for their defiance and angrily instructed DeWitt "to insist on our Right to have the Refuzall of the wheat of our Tenants" at the price he had specified. The 1741 controversy over preemptive rights was unusual. Tenants usually accepted the landlord's preemptive privileges, and the Livingstons rarely acted on their threats to punish recalcitrant tenants.[19]

The landlord's monopoly privileges did lessen his tenants' bargaining power and autonomy, but the Livingstons knew that they needed their tenants' labor in order to make their estate profitable. Their dependence on tenant labor often made them somewhat more flexible in enforcing the terms of Manor leases. Moreover, because landlord and tenant were mutually dependent, their economic interests were sometimes compatible. For instance, both landlord and tenant benefited from the mills at Livingston Manor. The Livingstons used their mills to process grain for trade; the farmers who grew the grain also needed mills, and the Livingstons' easily accessible facilities undoubtedly reduced the costs and inconvenience of transporting their produce.[20] Overlapping economic in-

[19] Philip Livingston to John DeWitt, 2 Jan., 17 Jan., 10 Feb., 5 Mar. 1741, Livingston-Redmond MSS., reel 9; Petrus DeWitt to Philip Livingston, 23 Jan. 1749, ibid., reel 6.

[20] Kim has argued that the mills were "a great boon to . . . tenants and the people in adjacent areas" (*Landlord and Tenant*, p. 167). For a comparable situation, in which a single individual dominated an entire county both economically and politically, see Stephen Innes, *Labor in a New Land: Economy and Society in Seventeenth-Century Spring-*

terests thus often eased potential tensions between the Livingstons and their tenants.

Shrewd and aggressive as rural land developers, the Livingstons, as landlords, were not paternalistic. The lords of Livingston Manor were noted neither for compassion nor for benevolence. Indeed, the leading authority on landlord-tenant relations in the colonial Hudson Valley has concluded that the Livingstons were the "most authoritarian and tightfisted" of New York's great manorial families.[21]

Livingston tenants had the smallest farms but paid the highest annual rents—usually twenty to thirty bushels of wheat, or about one-tenth of their produce. In addition, each year most Manor tenants paid their landlord two "days riding"—usually to build or maintain roads or, later, to cut wood for the ironworks—as well as the anachronistic gift of four hens, which denoted their fealty and subservience to the lord of the Manor. The average Manor farm was eighty-four acres, a size comparable to the typical seventeenth-century New England farm but significantly smaller than other New York leaseholds. Undoubtedly, the Livingstons believed that tenants would cultivate smaller farms more intensively and thus provide them with a greater yield per acre.[22]

Of all New York's landed magnates, the Livingstons also collected their rents most assiduously. Between 1767 and 1774, Manor tenants averaged a delinquency rate of 25 percent, substantially lower than their counterparts on other New York estates. The Livingstons' leases generally remained valid for two concurrent lives—normally those of a husband and his wife—and when a lease was renegotiated

---

field (Princeton, 1983), esp. chap. 2. Innes argues persuasively that the presence of the singularly wealthy and powerful John Pynchon had both advantages and drawbacks for the community.

21 Kim, *Landlord and Tenant*, p. 233.

22 Ibid., pp. 188–96; Livingston Manor rent ledger, 1767–84, Livingston Family Papers, NYHS, reel 15; Robert R. Livingston to Robert R. Livingston, Jr., 12 Mar. 1762, Robert R. Livingston Papers, NYHS, reel 1; William Smith, Jr., *The History of the Province of New-York*, ed. Michael G. Kammen, 2 vols. (Cambridge, Mass., 1972), 1:215. For farm sizes in colonial New England, see Philip J. Greven, *Four Generations: Population, Land, and Family in Colonial Andover, Massachusetts* (Ithaca, N.Y., 1970), pp. 58–60; David Grayson Allen, *In English Ways: The Movement of Societies and the Transferal of English Local Law and Custom to Massachusetts Bay in the Seventeenth Century* (Chapel Hill, N.C., 1981), pp. 128–29.

after the death of both spouses, the new leaseholder paid an entry fine, often in the form of back rent. Between 1767 and 1784, the Livingstons rarely increased their rents when leases were renegotiated, but the soaring price of wheat in the 1760s assured the proprietors of larger real profits. Finally, while tenants were able to sell the improvements they made on their land, they were also required to pay all taxes on the land they improved.[23]

Manor tenants left few records of their daily lives, but the available evidence suggests that leaseholders were neither uniformly impoverished nor monolithically prosperous. Some leaseholders were artisans; others, like Archibald Thompson, identified themselves as merchants and owned land outside of Livingston Manor.[24] The overwhelming majority, however, were householders—farmers who grew wheat, planted vegetable gardens and orchards, and either owned livestock or rented it from their landlord. Their livelihood depended on the farms they rented.

Fragmentary evidence suggests that some tenants prospered while others languished. Simon Coen, a Manor tenant, was prosperous enough to lend £200 in cash to Philip Clum, the miller at neighboring Clermont. When he made his will in 1779, Johannes Finger, another tenant, bequeathed to his children a total of £151 in "hard money," plus unspecified personal possessions and a slave girl named Suze. Another Manor farmer, Bastian Lesher, owned four slaves. At the other end of the scale was Johannes Myer, a Manor resident who was arrested for vagrancy in Albany in 1773. Local authorities described Myer as a "helpless man" unable to maintain himself; they sent him back to the Manor, where he continued to reside and to amass debts through the Revolutionary era.[25]

Because few inventories of tenant estates have survived, New

---

[23] Livingston Manor rent ledger, 1767–84, Livingston Family Papers, NYHS, reel 15; Kim, *Landlord and Tenant*, pp. 213–14.

[24] William McDermott, ed., *Eighteenth-Century Documents of the Nine Partners Patent, Dutchess County, New York* (Baltimore, 1979), p. 338.

[25] Philip Clum's bond to Simon Coen, 1 Jan. 1777, Livingston Family Papers, NYHS, reel 28; William S. Pelletreau, comp., *Abstracts of Wills on File in the Surrogate's Office, City of New York*, 17 vols. (New York, 1893–1909), 8:340, 9:248–49; Abraham C. Cuyler to Robert Livingston, Jr., 21 Aug. 1773, Livingston-Redmond MSS., reel 8. Johannes Myer appeared in neither the 1779 nor the 1799 tax list nor was his name listed in the Manor rent ledger. Myer was, however listed as a debtor in the account book of Robert Livingston, Jr., where he was identified as a resident of the Manor.

York's 1779 tax list is our best source of information on the contours of tenant wealth. Using data from the tax list, Sung Bok Kim has shown that the estate of an average tenant farmer compared favorably with that of an average Hudson Valley freeholder.[26] Equally significant, however, is the fact that the tax list reveals wide variations in the property holdings of the Hudson Valley's colonial tenant farmers.

The 1779 tax list probably underestimates the average wealth of Livingston leaseholders. For one thing, as Table 2 shows, the Manor list includes 55 men who owned personal, but not real property; the vast majority of these men were not actual leaseholders and presumably not heads of households. For instance, Isaac Decker's personal property was assessed for £120, New England currency, in 1779, when he owned no real property. Two years later, he took out a lease at Livingston Manor. Similarly, Andries Frans Brusie had £239 in personal property in 1779, though he still lived with his parents. Five years later he started his own household, when he took over his father's Manor leasehold.[27]

By including some dependent young men like Brusie and Decker, the tax list diminishes the average property holdings of leaseholding heads of households. This problem is compounded by the fact that all tax records tend to give conservative estimates of estate values— unlike probate records, which yield far more accurate data.[28] Comparing tax and probate records is problematic. Nevertheless, a cautious comparison of New York tax lists and Connecticut probate data suggests that colonial tenants and freeholders lived in the same economic universe and that leaseholders were not a uniquely im-

---

[26] Kim, *Landlord and Tenant*, pp. 272–74. Among New York probate records, I found only thirteen estate inventories for Hudson Valley tenants for the entire period through 1790. None are for tenants from Livingston Manor. Estate inventories for Caleb Archer (1790), Barent Dutcher (1772), Roswell Lee (1779), Michael Shaw (1679), and Gerrit Van Den Bergh (1733) are in the New York State Library, Albany. Those for James Barnet (1768), Stephen Conckling (1784), Daniel Downing (1769), William Fowler (1731), Henry Hill (1775), Israel Kniffen (1750), Charles Mead (1772), and Nehemiah Purdy (1769) are in the collections of the New-York Historical Society. The 1779 tax list is located in the New York State Library.

[27] New York tax list, 1779, New York State Library; Livingston Manor rent ledger, 1767–84, Livingston Family Papers, NYHS, reel 15.

[28] The New York tax list for 1779 seems especially prone to underreporting personal wealth; 145 men were assessed for real property only, though common sense tells us they also must have owned some personal property.

Table 2
Real property holdings in Livingston Manor and Connecticut,
1770–1775 (£N.Eng.)

	Livingston Manor, 1775		Connecticut, 1770–74
	N	%	%
None	67*	12.6	21.5
£1–39	93	17.5	14.5
40–79	154	28.9	8.5
80–119	124	23.3	8.5
120–199	88	16.5	11.0
200–299	4	0.8	11.0
300–499	1	0.2	10.5
500–999	1	0.2	8.5
1,000+	0	0.0	6.0

Sources: New York tax list, 1779, New York State Library; Sung Bok Kim, *Landlord and Tenant in Colonial New York: Manorial Society, 1664–1775* (Chapel Hill, N.C.: University of North Carolina Press, 1978), pp. 270–71. Connecticut data reprinted, with permission, from Jackson Turner Main, *Society and Economy in Colonial Connecticut* (Princeton: Princeton University Press, 1985), p. 124. Livingston Manor data include tenants residing at Clermont, also known as the Lower Manor. Assessments for 1779 have been adjusted for wartime inflation to 1775 values. Currency conversions based on John J. McCusker, *Money and Exchange in Europe and America, 1600–1775: A Handbook* (Chapel Hill, N.C.: University of North Carolina Press, 1978), pp. 142, 165.

*Includes 55 men from personal property list who were not assessed for real property.

poverished class that had little in common with their freeholding neighbors.

Tables 2 and 3 describe tenant property holding at Livingston Manor alongside data from Jackson Turner Main's exhaustive analysis of probate records for contemporary Connecticut.[29] Compared

[29] Main adjusted his data to correct the age bias in favor of older—and thus more prosperous—inhabitants. As a result, his data, like the New York tax list, includes all adult men, and not only heads of households. Main estimated that young men in their twenties would account for roughly 35 percent of the adult male population, though the Manor's 55 nonleaseholding owners of personal property compose a much smaller fraction of the overall population. Thus, it seems likely that the 1779 tax lists excluded some poor young men who had little property and did not head their own households. In this sense, the New York data may be inflating the property holdings of Manor inhabitants, and this inflation, in turn, may have counteracted some of the conservative tendencies mentioned earlier.

Table 3
Personal property holdings in Livingston Manor and Connecticut,
1770–1775 (£N.Eng.)

	Livingston Manor, 1775		Connecticut, 1770–74
	N	%	%
£1–29	5	1.4	17.4
30–59	11	3.1	20.4
60–119	21	5.8	30.4
120–199	103	28.6	16.4
200–299	116	32.2	5.9
300–399	56	15.6	3.7
400–499	28	7.8	2.0
500+	20	5.6	3.9

Sources: New York tax list, 1779, New York State Library; Sung Bok Kim, *Landlord and Tenant in Colonial New York: Manorial Society, 1664–1775* (Chapel Hill, N.C.: University of North Carolina Press, 1978), pp. 270–71. Connecticut data reprinted, with permission, from Jackson Turner Main, *Society and Economy in Colonial Connecticut* (Princeton: Princeton University Press, 1985), p. 153. Livingston Manor data include tenants residing at Clermont, also known as the Lower Manor. Assessments for 1779 have been adjusted for wartime inflation to 1775 values. Currency conversion based on John J. McCusker, *Money and Exchange in Europe and America, 1600–1775: A Handbook* (Chapel Hill, N.C.: University of North Carolina Press, 1978), pp. 142, 165.

to their New England neighbors, Livingston Manor residents were less likely to be destitute, but they were also less likely to be affluent. More than two-thirds of all Manor residents owned real property— mainly improvements on their farms—worth between £40 and £199, New England currency. Of 532 people assessed at Livingston Manor and Clermont, roughly one-eighth had no real estate whatsoever, though only 6 held real property worth more than £199. By contrast, more than one-fifth of Main's Connecticut farmers held no real property at all, and more than one-third had real estates worth less than £40. At the same time, however, roughly one-third of the Connecticut residents would have owned real property worth more than £199; exactly one-fourth would have held real property in excess of £300.

Table 3 suggests that tenant farmers were far more likely to concentrate their assets in their personal estates and that the personal estate of the average Livingston tenant compared favorably with that of the average Connecticut farmer in the 1770s. Two-thirds of Main's Connecticut property holders had personal estates worth less than £120, New England currency. On the other hand, nearly 90 percent of all Manor residents had personal estates worth £120 or more—even after adjusting their personal property assessments to offset wartime inflation. The few tenant estate inventories that have survived suggest that livestock was by far the most valuable of tenants' personal possessions, accounting for an average of 40 percent of the estate's value at the time of the death of the leaseholder. Surviving tenant wills also indicate that livestock were the farmers' most important assets. Farmers invested in horses, cattle, and hogs especially, for their labor or their produce. They also looked on their livestock—along with the improvements on their farms—as their children's most substantial patrimony.[30]

The one surviving inventory of the personal property of a Livingston tenant suggests that even New York's less prosperous tenant farmers lived in middling material circumstances. Comfort Shaw leased a farm belonging to the Clermont branch of the Livingston family during the 1770s. Shaw apparently never paid his rent. By 1780, his account was ten years in arrears and his landlord, Margaret Beekman Livingston—widow of Robert R. Livingston—seized his personal estate as compensation. Seizure of a tenant's estate was very unusual, especially during the Revolution, when

[30] See estate inventories in note 26, above, as well as the wills of the following people, located in the New York State Library: Jonathan Austen (1766), Evert Bancker (1734), Jacob Blatner (1785), Dirck Brat (1763), Benjamin Brundage (1761), Hendrick Clapper (1772), Samuel Coeymans (1754), Philip DeForest (1774), Hendrick Douw (1749), Elsie Egbertse (1739), Cornelis Esselsteen (n.d.), Johannis Finger (1779), Abraham Fonda (1762), Francis Hardick, Jr. (n.d.), Jeremiah Hogeboom (1782), Hitchen Holland (1761), Philip Holsappel (1782), Philip Koons (1769), Omy LaGrange, Jr. (1724), Gerrit I. Lansing (1746), Bastian Lesher (1775), Martinus Loop (1786), Jacob Mesick (1774), Thomas Mesick (1782), Johan Michel Muche (1772), Cornelis Mulder (1744), Cornelis Muller (1746), Jeremiah Muller (1763), Killian Muller (1782), Henry Oothout (1738), Joseph Pixley (1760), Johan Emmerick Plese (1745), Conrad Reitser (1778), William Roe (1760), Jacob Schermerhorn (1760), Godfrey Schoonmaker (1781), Johannes Shirts (1773), Martinus Shoeck (1778), Abraham Slingerland (1784), Jurry Adam Smith (1747), Thomas Storm (1763), Anthony Ten Eyck (1775), John Upham (1773), John Upham, Jr. (1777), Jacobus Van Alen (1769), Tobias Van Deusen (1772), Catharina Van Hoesen (1780), Ariantie Van Voerdt (n.d.), Johannes Velder (1746), Abraham Witbeck (1784), Johannes Witbeck (1748), Johannes Witbeck (1750), and John Yates (1775).

widespread hardship made most creditors more lenient toward their delinquent clients. But Margaret Livingston decided to enforce Shaw's obligation; her decision to do so resulted in a detailed inventory of his personal possessions.

The inventory revealed that Comfort Shaw lived in a three-room house crowded with largely functional furnishings. The "large room," which served as kitchen, bedroom, and living area, contained a desk and two beds. The "little room" also had two beds. The "stair room" was furnished with three beds, a table, and a chest. The family's seven beds—three feather beds and four filled with straw— five feather pillows, five "fine blankets," and sundry related articles were valued at £31 2s., or approximately 18 percent of the value of Comfort Shaw's entire personal estate. Besides the beds, the house was sparsely furnished. Like common people throughout British America, the Shaws made comfortable beds and bedding one of their top priorities. Shaw also owned livestock worth £79; his seven horses, one cow, two hogs, ten sheep, and eleven geese accounted for nearly half the value of his total personal estate. The family also owned cooking and dining utensils—iron pots, pewter dishes and mugs, and a brass kettle—worth £4 10s. They kept their farming implements and produce in the barn and stored barrels of beef and pork in the cellar.[31]

Although his rent was ten years in arrears, Comfort Shaw was not a poor man by contemporary standards. His personal estate was worth 473.5 bushels of wheat, or £166 in 1775 New York currency. According to Kim's estimates, Shaw would have been among the least prosperous quintile of Livingston tenants. Nevertheless, although he owned less livestock than the average eighteenth-century Connecticut farmer, the total value of his personal estate—£127 in New England currency—was comparable to those of the Connecticut residents who Main studied. Therefore, in terms of the material circumstances in which he lived, Shaw was probably no worse off

---

[31] Inventory of the Goods and Chattles found . . . on the farm of Comfort Shaw . . ., 10 Feb. 1780, Livingston Family Papers, NYHS, reel 29. The Shaws' material circumstances were comparable to those of common people living in the Chesapeake. See Gloria L. Main, *Tobacco Colony: Life in Early Maryland, 1650–1720* (Princeton, 1982), pp. 167–76; Rhys Isaac, *The Transformation of Virginia, 1740–1790* (Chapel Hill, N.C., 1982), pp. 32–34, 74.

than most of his contemporaries on the other side of New York's eastern border.[32]

In eighteenth-century New York, land tenancy did not preclude economic mobility. Some tenants came to the manors virtually destitute but were able to subsist, or even to prosper, by exchanging their labor for the landlord's land and credit.[33] Others accumulated wealth in much the same way as contemporary freeholders. If tenancy had stifled opportunity, leaseholders would have stagnated economically, unable to amass wealth. The value of an individual tenant's estate would have remained relatively constant over time because he would have been unable to profit by the fruits of his labor.

In fact, Table 4 suggests that the wealth-holding patterns of Hudson Valley tenants conformed to patterns characteristic elsewhere in British colonial America. Tenant farmers, like freeholders, started out with relatively little as young men and then gradually accumulated both real and personal wealth. Their wealth levels peaked during middle age and then declined as they began to give property and marriage portions to their children, who had reached adulthood and were now leaving home to start their own families.[34]

Since other tenants were geographically mobile, this data probably underestimates the potential for upward mobility. Colonial tenant farmers were not tied to their land, and many Hudson Valley tenants availed themselves of the opportunity to start anew elsewhere. An average turnover rate of approximately ten years per Manor lease indicates that some Livingston tenants considered leaseholding

[32] Inventory of the Goods and Chattles found . . . on the farm of Comfort Shaw . . . , 10 Feb. 1780, Livingston Family Papers, NYHS, reel 29; Kim, *Landlord and Tenant*, p. 272; Jackson Turner Main, *Society and Economy in Colonial Connecticut* (Princeton, 1985), pp. 121, 235–38; John J. McCusker, *Money and Exchange in Europe and America, 1600–1775: A Handbook* (Chapel Hill, N.C., 1978), pp. 149–50, 164–65; Arthur Harrison Cole, *Wholesale Commodity Prices in the United States, 1700–1861: Statistical Supplement, Actual Wholesale Prices of Various Commodities* (Cambridge, Mass., 1938), p. 69.

[33] Bonomi, *Factious People*, pp. 196–200; Kim, *Landlord and Tenant*, pp. 134–39, 242–46. See also Innes, *Labor in a New Land*, pp. 39–43, 51–52.

[34] For the relationship between wealth and age elsewhere, see, Main, *Society and Economy in Colonial Connecticut*, pp. 70, 88–89, 109–10, 137–40, 311–12; Jones, *Wealth of a Nation to Be*, pp. 381–88. Although Table 4 suggests that tenants began to accumulate property again after they reached the age of sixty, the number of men in the over-sixty category is too small to be meaningful.

Table 4
Average property holdings by age: Livingston Manor,
1775 (£NY)

Age	Avg. Real Estate	Avg. Personal Estate	N
60+	248	311	6
50–59	108	258	28
40–49	133	344	37
30–39	77	200	61
20–29	76	174	37

Sources: N.Y. tax list, 1779, N.Y. State Library; ages based on baptismal records for Claverack (Dutch Reformed), Loonenburg (Lutheran), Rhinebeck/Red Hook (German Reformed), and Rhinebeck Flats (Dutch Reformed), published in *NY Gen. & Bio. Rec.,* 73–100 (1942–69).

a temporary expedient.[35] Because few tenants were forced to leave the Manor, and probably fewer uprooted their families simply to become tenants elsewhere, some departures were indicative of upward mobility and eventual landownership. Thus tenancy could be a temporary condition for the upwardly mobile, although it was more often the permanent status of the modestly successful.

Most tenant families who settled at Livingston Manor stayed there for generations, intermarrying with other longtime tenant families and forming the nucleus of a stable farming community. For instance, the Brusie family initially appears in the Manor records in 1710, when the first Robert Livingston listed Gabriel and Vincent Brusie as debtors residing at Livingston Manor. Although some of Gabriel's and Vincent's descendants presumably settled elsewhere, seven members of the Brusie family held leases at Livingston Manor by 1767.[36] Similarly, Johannes Rosman had settled at the Manor by 1715, when his name was included on the muster roll for the local militia. Rosman's descendants also proliferated on Livingston land. His son Conrad settled at the Manor, as did Conrad's three sons, Johannes, Jacob, and Jurry.[37]

[35] Livingston Manor rent ledger, 1767–84, Livingston Family Papers, NYHS, reel 15.
[36] Ibid.; List of debtors drawn out of Ledger F, 20 Jan. 1710, Livingston-Redmond MSS., reel 3.
[37] Muster roll, Livingston Manor Company, 30 Nov. 1715, *DHNY,* 3:704; "Bap-

Like many other longtime tenant families, the Rosmans often married within the Manor's leaseholding community. Jacob Rosman married Catharine Petrie, whose ancestor had also appeared on the muster roll for 1715. Both Johannes and Jurry Rosman also found wives among the Manor's residents, marrying Hannah Lesher and Helena Lesher, respectively, who were probably first cousins. The Leshers were a prolific Manor family whose founding member had come to the Hudson Valley during the Palatine migration. By 1767, the Livingstons' tenants included seven members of the Lesher family, including Helena's father and three brothers.[38]

While bonds of kinship thus united many Manor leaseholders, the Manor itself had no formal institutions to foster a sense of community among the tenant farmers. Despite the Manor's vast size, no courts convened within its borders; Manor residents had no access to political forums or local government. Although the tenants did have access to religious institutions, heterogeneity and dispersed settlement impeded the churches' ability to promote communal unity.

Most Manor residents attended Dutch Reformed services, although by the middle of the eighteenth century they divided among as many as five congregations. In 1716, the area's first Dutch Reformed congregation had been formed at Claverack, adjacent to the Manor's northern border, but churchgoers had to wait eleven years before they had a regular minister. In 1722, the first Robert Livingston built a church at Linlithgo, near his mansion at Livingston Manor, and six years later another church was built at Germantown, near Clermont. In 1731, the Dutch Reformed church at Rhinebeck opened to serve the growing population of Dutchess County. Finally, in 1746, another congregation was founded at Ancram, the site of the Livingstons' ironworks. Although the Ancram church never had a permanent minister, most congregations were

---

tismal Records of Zion Lutheran Church, Loonenburg, . . . New York," *NY Gen. & Bio. Rec.*, 82:166, 83:33, 39.

[38] "Baptismal Records of the Dutch Reformed Church of Claverack, Columbia County, New York," *NY Gen. & Bio. Rec.*, 83:12; "Baptisms of the German Reformed Church of Rhinebeck, . . . NY," ibid., 97:140; Walter Allen Knittle, *Early Eighteenth Century Palatine Emigration: A British Government Redemptioner Project to Manufacture Naval Stores* (Philadelphia, 1937), p. 287; Will of Bastian Lesher, 11 June 1775, New York State Library; Muster roll, Livingston Manor Company, 30 Nov. 1715, *DHNY*, 3:704; Livingston Manor rent ledger, 1767–84, Livingston Family Papers, NYHS, reel 15.

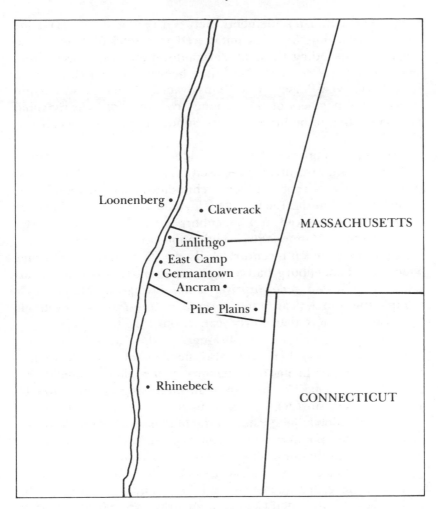

Loonenberg •
• Claverack
MASSACHUSETTS
• Linlithgo
• East Camp
• Germantown
Ancram •
• Pine Plains •
• Rhinebeck
CONNECTICUT

Map 3. Colonial churches: Livingston Manor and vicinity. Based on material
in Frederick Lewis Weis, *The Colonial Clergy of the Middle Colonies: New York,
New Jersey, and Pennsylvania* (Worcester, Mass., 1957); and Randall Balmer, *A
Perfect Babel of Confusion: Dutch Religion and English Culture in the Middle
Colonies* (New York, 1989), pp. 157–64.

able to fill their pulpits, though a single minister often served several
churches simultaneously. For instance, Domine Petrus Van Driessen
was pastor at Albany (1712–38), Kinderhook (1712–27), Linlithgo
(1722–37), and Fishkill (1727–31), while also serving as a missionary

to the nearby Indian settlements. Between 1730 and 1762, Domine George Wilhelmus Mancius ministered to a total of sixteen congregations, including those at Germantown and Rhinebeck; from 1737 until 1741, he divided his time between several churches in New York, New Jersey, and Pennsylvania. Under these circumstances, the members of the domine's congregations clearly could not expect him to be present every Sunday to conduct weekly services.[39]

A substantial minority of Manor residents were Lutherans, and by mid-century they too divided themselves among five local congregations. As early as 1708, Lutheran churches had been founded at Rhinebeck and in the Palatine settlement at East Camp. Additional congregations followed at Loonenburg (1712), Claverack (1716), and Livingston Manor (1764). Lutheran ministers were relatively scarce in the eighteenth-century Hudson Valley. Between 1751 and 1760, only Loonenburg had a regular pastor. This parish was located roughly ten miles upriver from Livingston Manor. East Camp—the church nearest to the Manor before 1764—was without a minister for more than thirty years, from 1729 to 1760.[40]

While most Manor residents belonged to the Dutch Reformed or Lutheran churches, there were also members of other denominations among the Livingstons' tenants. Some Manor families belonged to Rhinebeck's German Reformed congregation, and by 1772 they were sufficiently numerous to warrant the creation of a new congregation at Pine Plains in the Manor's southeastern corner. Members of less popular denominations presumably attended either Reformed or Lutheran services or did not go to church at all. In the 1750s, New Englanders who had settled in the Manor's eastern section complained that no nearby churches conducted services in English. These transplanted Congregationalists had no church of their

[39] Frederick Lewis Weis, *The Colonial Clergy of the Middle Colonies: New York, New Jersey, and Pennsylvania* (Worcester, Mass., 1957), pp. 268, 333; Randall Balmer, *A Perfect Babel of Confusion: Dutch Religion and English Culture in the Middle Colonies* (New York, 1989), pp. 157–64. In his will the first Robert Livingston also set aside a total of 100 acres for a house and farm "for the use of a Presbyterian minister of the established Church of Scotland, or for one of the churches of Holland which conform to the doctrine and discipline of the Synod of Dort . . ." (10 Feb. 1721, Livingston-Redmond MSS., reel 4).

[40] Weis, *Colonial Clergy*, pp. 178, 217–18, 234, 253, 298, 317.

own, but linguistic differences precluded their assimilation into local Dutch and German congregations.[41]

Just as Manor residents had no common place of worship, they had no secular gathering place comparable to a court house or town center. Because the Manor fell entirely under the jurisdiction of Albany County, Manor residents had only limited access to local government. Manor leases reserved the proprietor's right to convene courts leet and baron, but the Livingstons, like New York's other manorial families, never established these local institutions. The county court at Albany sat more than thirty miles from the Manor house and much farther from the homes of most of the tenants. Livingston Manor had no equivalent to New England's town meetings or Virginia's court days. Although Manor residents did elect constables, tax assessors, and collectors, local elections were infrequent and sparsely attended.[42]

By bringing people together and resolving local conflicts, churches, town meetings, and courts became crucial agents of socialization in colonial America. Churches, courts, and local government served as forums for airing grievances and for promoting a sense of communal unity and loyalty. Such institutions also acted as showcases for the power, influence, and beneficence of local elites and thus legitimized the authority of provincial community leaders.

The absence of local institutions at the Manor undermined the Livingstons' ability to portray themselves as legitimate local leaders. Like elites elsewhere in colonial America, the Livingstons represented local interests at the provincial level and made capital improvements, such as mills and storehouses, that were essential to the welfare of their community. Although the Livingstons performed these services mainly to advance their own interests, most other eighteenth-century American elites were no more altruistic. Local institutions gave most colonial leaders a forum they could use to publicize their usefulness and generosity and thereby cultivate the esteem of their social inferiors. Lacking access to such institutions,

---

[41] Ibid., p. 198; "Baptisms of the German Reformed Church of Rhinebeck"; Philip J. Schwarz, *The Jarring Interests: New York's Boundary-Makers, 1664–1776* (Albany, N.Y., 1979), p. 100.

[42] *NY Col. Laws*, 4:1056.

the Livingstons fulfilled the functions of local leaders without reaping the social rewards for their actions.

The presence of unifying community institutions also would have strengthened the personal bond between the Livingstons and their tenants. As it was, the landlord's contacts with his tenants were limited. Livingston Manor was vast; the proprietors' interests were varied. Consequently, the lords of the Manor employed resident managers whose manifold duties made them the most visible figures of local authority even after the Livingstons themselves settled permanently on their land. Charles DeWitt, estate manager for Robert Livingston, Jr., in the 1750s, supervised the collection of rents and taxes and mediated rent and toll disputes between millers and tenants, though Livingston himself seems to have presided over the negotiation of Manor leases. Likewise, Livingston apparently negotiated wage agreements with his workers at Ancram, but DeWitt routinely gave the workers their wages and purchased the farmers' produce, which he then delivered to the Manor house or shipped to New York City. On election day, it was DeWitt, not Livingston, who treated and canvased the voters.[43]

Robert Livingston, Jr., was an active landlord, who was deeply interested in the daily operation of his estate, but his decision to reside at the Manor did not transform him into an acknowledged community leader. Even after abandoning absenteeism, the Livingstons remained relatively isolated, both physically and culturally, from most of their tenants and dependents. Ironically, the most extensive interaction between Livingston and his tenants seems to have occurred after 1751, when farmers residing on his estate began to challenge his land titles and thus jeopardized the survival of Livingston Manor.

Beginning in the 1750s, a series of riots and disturbances occurred on the tenanted estates of the Hudson River valley. Squatters from New England and their New York tenant allies demanded better lease terms or—more serious still—challenged the validity of the great manorial patents. For Robert Livingston, Jr., decades of intermittent popular unrest raised the specters of financial loss, family

[43] Diary and Account Book of Charles DeWitt, 1749–80, Misc. MSS., B. V. DeWitt, NYHS.

dishonor, and mob rule. From 1751 until his death in 1790, the lord of Livingston Manor lived in near-constant fear of losing the family land.

Livingston's troubles began in the fall of 1751, when David Ingersoll of Massachusetts led a band of New England squatters into the Taghkanic region, the easternmost section of Livingston Manor. Ingersoll's expedition had the blessing of the General Court of Massachusetts, whose members sought to establish the Bay Colony's jurisdiction over this disputed border region. The squatters also won the support of some Livingston tenants who resided at Taghkanic. These tenants refused to pay their rents and joined with the New Englanders in laying out farms, claiming roughly 26,000 acres of Livingston Manor and neighboring Claverack for the colony of Massachusetts.[44]

The insurgents' actions alarmed Robert Livingston, Jr., who unsuccessfully appealed for assistance from the New York government. Finally, in the spring of 1752, Livingston took matters into his own hands by having squatter George Robinson arrested as a trespasser. Livingston also enlisted some loyal tenants to pull down Robinson's dwelling, but in January 1753 the insurgents retaliated by marching to Ancram, where they disrupted Livingston's iron business by arresting several workers. In May, six squatters and four Taghkanic tenants began to survey the Manor's eastern section—despite Livingston's threats and warnings—and in July a company led by tenant Joseph Pain destroyed more than 2,000 trees in the forests surrounding the Ancram ironworks.[45] In response, Livingston sent forty armed men to the farm of rebel leader Josiah Loomis with orders to destroy his crops and fences. The insurgents avenged Loomis's losses by arresting Robert Van Deusen and his son Johannes, two of Livingston's loyal tenants. Finally, on 28 July 1753,

[44] The most complete accounts of the agrarian conflicts of the late colonial era are Kim, *Landlord and Tenant*, chaps. 7–8; and Irving Mark, *Agrarian Conflicts in Colonial New York, 1711–1775* (New York, 1940), chaps. 4–5. My own brief account draws heavily on these studies, as well as on Bonomi, *Factious People*, chap. 6, and on Schwarz, *Jarring Interests*, chaps. 6–7.

[45] Livingston valued the timber destroyed by Pain at roughly £544. See his Acct. of Damage done by Joseph Pain and his Company, July 1753, Livingston-Redmond MSS., reel 7. Financially, Livingston stood to lose the most when the insurgents disrupted his ironworks. Consequently, the rioters made Ancram their frequent target.

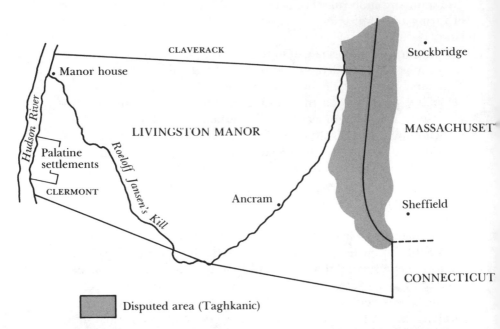

Map 4. New York's disputed eastern border: Livingston Manor. Adapted from *Landlord and Tenant in Colonial New York: Manorial Society, 1664–1775,* by Sung Bok Kim. Published for the Institute of Early American History and Culture. Copyright 1978, The University of North Carolina Press. Used by permission.

New York Governor George Clinton issued a proclamation that resulted in the arrest of several rebel leaders.

Clinton's proclamation restored order until early 1755, when rioting resumed in the eastern portion of Claverack, adjacent to Livingston Manor. When Albany County Sheriff Abraham Yates attempted to disperse the rioters, he was taken prisoner and dispatched to jail in nearby Sheffield, Massachusetts. Robert Livingston, Jr., and Claverack proprietor Henry Van Rensselaer then mobilized their loyal tenants to attack the insurgents. By April, the landlords' forces had captured and jailed several rebel leaders, killing one rebellious tenant as he fled from his attackers. In retaliation, the insurgents marched to Ancram, where they arrested eight ironworkers. In June, however, the governments of New York and Massachusetts agreed to an exchange of prisoners.

Meanwhile, the New Englanders and their tenant allies had been exploiting the shakiness of the proprietors' grants, purchasing rival deeds from the Stockbridge Indians, who claimed to be the land's rightful owners. In the summer of 1756, the insurgents returned to Livingston Manor and claimed ownership of the Livingstons' land by virtue of their Indian titles. Robert Livingston, Jr., responded to this latest challenge by initiating legal proceedings to evict his rebellious tenants. Undeterred, the insurgents persisted in their claims and began to survey the Taghkanic region in the spring of 1757. Vowing to oppose his enemies "with all my might," Livingston again sent a company of loyal tenants to fight them, and this time the landlord's forces routed their opponents. This decisive victory, plus a timely proclamation from Lieutenant Governor James DeLancey, put an end to the violence at Livingston Manor. In 1762, the insurgents did revive their claims to Livingston's land, but a proclamation by Lieutenant Governor Cadwallader Colden, calling for their arrest, prompted their withdrawal from Livingston Manor.[46]

New York's eighteenth-century agrarian conflicts derived from three disparate sources: the province's disputed eastern boundary, the ambiguities and possible illegalities contained in various New York land patents, and the potential antagonism inherent in the relationship between landlord and tenant. But the revolts of the 1750s arose more over disputed property rights than over tenant grievances, pitting landlords against the New Englanders and a few discontented leaseholders. Attempts to downplay the importance of the border and title disputes and to attribute the revolts primarily to tenant discontent founder on several key issues.[47] First, why did the tenants wait until the 1750s to rebel, when their supposed grievances were presumably as old as tenancy itself? Surely, even if tenants were dissatisfied with their condition and resentful of their landlords' prerogatives, they needed encouragement from the New England intruders before they were moved to rebellion.

[46] Robert Livingston, Jr., to Peter Van Brugh Livingston, 27 Apr. 1757, Rutherfurd Collection, NYHS, vol. 3; Robert Livingston, Jr., to James Duane, 15 Feb., 3 May 1762, Duane Papers, NYHS, box 1; Robert Livingston, Jr., to Peter R. Livingston and James Duane, 22 Mar. 1762, *DHNY*, 3:825–26; Colden's proclamation, 31 Mar. 1762, ibid., 3:827–29.

[47] The most notable of such attempts are Staughton Lynd, *Anti-Federalism in Dutchess County, New York: A Study of Democracy and Class Conflict in the Revolutionary Era* (Chicago, 1962), esp. chap. 3, and Edward Countryman, *A People in Revolution: The American Revolution in New York, 1760–1790* (Baltimore, 1981), pp. 48–55, 68.

Second, why were so few tenants actively involved in the riots? The embattled lord of Livingston Manor had every reason to exaggerate the unruliness of his tenants when he frantically tried to persuade the provincial government to intervene and restore order. Yet, in both his private and official correspondence Livingston consistently claimed that the New England squatters had caused all his troubles. For instance, in 1753 he complained to his brother-in-law William Alexander that the New Englanders "are . . . daily troubleing me & my Tennents," while admitting that "Some of the Latter are Indeed near as bad as the N. England people." Despite the rebelliousness of some of his own leaseholders, Livingston clearly believed that the New Englanders had instigated the rebellion. In 1755, he informed a Boston friend, "I Shall look upon all the Blood that may be Spilt in this Affair to lay at the doors of your People."[48]

Livingston's tenants also believed that the New Englanders were responsible for fomenting and encouraging the commotion at the Manor. For instance, in January 1755, one tenant farmer told Livingston that he had been approached by three men who had been sent by "the Boston people" to incite rebellion at the Manor. Robert Van Deusen, the loyal tenant evicted from his home by insurgents in October 1755, blamed the whole affair on "Eleaven or twelve strang[e] Men from New England." Although two Livingston tenants, Michael Halenbeck and Josiah Loomis, did become rebel leaders, even Loomis later admitted that the New England squatters were primarily responsible for orchestrating the violence at the Manor.[49]

In all, no more than fifteen Manor residents were known participants in the rebellions of the 1750s, and only eight of those can be identified as holders of leases at Livingston Manor. The remaining seven, whose surnames do appear in the Manor records, were probably either sons of Livingston tenants or kin who rented farms at

[48] Robert Livingston, Jr., to William Alexander, 26 Mar. 1753, William Alexander Papers, NYHS, vol. 1; Livingston to Jacob Wendell, 4 Mar. 1755, Livingston Papers, MCNY, box 3. For Livingston's repeated indictments of the New Englanders, see also his letters to Wendell, 12 Apr. 1753, 8 Feb., 29 July 1754, 27 Jan. 1755, ibid.; to James DeLancey, 7 Feb., 23 June 1755, *DHNY*, 3:774–75, 808–12; and to Sir Charles Hardy, 9 Nov. 1755, ibid., 3:814–15.

[49] Robert Livingston, Jr., to James DeLancey, 7 Feb. 1755, *DHNY*, 3:774–75; Robert Van Deusen to Robert Livingston, Jr., 29 Oct. 1755, ibid., 3:812; Josiah Loomis to Robert Livingston, Jr., 15 Apr. 1755, Livingston Papers, MCNY, box 3.

Claverack, the Manor's northern neighbor. Typically, New Englanders dominated the parties of rioters who caused trouble at the Manor in the 1750s. For instance, in February 1755, when twenty-one insurgents seized Sheriff Abraham Yates, only six members of this group seem to have been tenants at either Claverack or Livingston Manor, while the remaining fifteen were New England squatters. Similarly, of the thirty-one men accused of rioting at Taghkanic in May 1757, only two can be identified as Livingston's tenants, although another two were possibly sons of Manor lease-holders.[50]

In the 1750s, the Hudson Valley revolts were concerned primarily with disputed property rights, not tenant grievances, because it was on the issue of land titles that the landlords were the most vulnerable. The land titles of New York in general and of the Hudson Valley magnates in particular could be challenged effectively on various grounds, and Livingston Manor was particularly vulnerable to rival public and private claimants. Although they dared not admit it, the Livingstons must have known that most of their land had not been purchased from the Indians, but rather was bestowed gratuitously on their ancestor in 1686 by Governor Thomas Dongan. Moreover, New York's long-contested border with Massachusetts, coupled with the acute scarcity of vacant land in southern New England, made the Boston government sympathetic to the insurgents' cause.[51]

In the late 1730s, Philip Livingston implicitly had acknowledged the problems that both public and private title disputes could pose for his family when he began buying land adjacent to the Manor in western Massachusetts. By buying the land on the Manor's eastern border, Philip had hoped to protect his Taghkanic holdings from a

[50] Christopher Andries Brusie, Hendrick Brusie, Jonathan Darby, Michael Halenbeck, Josiah Loomis, Joseph Pain, Andries Janse Reese, and William J. Reese were Manor leaseholders. William J. Halenbeck, William S. Halenbeck, Andries Johannes Reese, Johannes Reese, Adam Shafer, Dirck Spoor, and Jacobus Van Deusen had either fathers or other kin who held leases at Livingston Manor. See Robert Livingston, Jr., to James DeLancey, 12 Feb. 1754, 5 Feb., 8 Mar. 1755, *DHNY*, 3:767–68, 782–84; Affadavit of Sheriff Yates, 13 Feb. 1755, ibid., 3:778; Affadavit of Peter R. Livingston et al., 21 Nov. 1755, ibid., 3:817–19; New York council minutes, May 1757, ibid., 3:821–23; Robert Livingston, Jr., to Jacob Wendell, 4 Mar. 1755, Livingston papers, MCNY, box 3.

[51] This argument has been expressed most forcefully in Schwarz, *Jarring Interests*, chaps. 6–7.

possible influx of New England squatters. After failing to find tenants to settle his new land, however, he sold his share to his partners in Massachusetts, who in turn gradually sold the land to Yankee farmers. Thus, despite Philip's efforts to protect his land, the unsettled boundary remained an inviting target for those who sought to challenge both his own title and the jurisdiction of the New York government.[52]

The insurgents' strategies revealed their awareness of the vulnerability of the Livingstons' title, as well as the primacy of title disputes in the origins of the revolts of the 1750s. These early rioters wanted to own the Livingstons' land, and not simply to rent it on agreeable terms; they never mentioned their supposed grievances with regard to the Livingstons' leasing policies. Enjoying the support of both the Indian claimants and the Massachusetts provincial government, the insurgents wisely chose legalism over class warfare as the most promising strategy for challenging New York's manorial patents. Their ultimate failure to have those patients invalidated should not obscure the fact that, for a time, the rebels came remarkably close to attaining their objective.

By contrast, in 1766, rural rioters challenged their landlords' leasing practices rather than their land titles. In 1766, agrarian unrest resurfaced mainly in the Philipse and Van Cortlandt holdings in Dutchess and Westchester counties but eventually extended northward to Claverack and Livingston Manor. In November 1765, tenants and squatters at Philipse's Highland Patent united, demanding better lease terms from their landlords. Tenant discontent soon spread to Cortlandt Manor, culminating in the uprising known as the Great Rebellion. In the spring of 1766, inspired by the Sons of Liberty and their fight against imperial oppression, tenants in the lower Hudson Valley rebelled, only to be repressed in June by British regulars dispatched by the provincial government.[53]

In 1766, Livingston Manor remained quiet until May, when Robert Livingston, Jr., learned that some of his tenants were plan-

---

[52] Philip Livingston to Jacob Wendell, 3 June 1737, 7 Mar., 5 Apr. 1738, 27 Jan., 13 Mar., 21 Apr., 10 May 1739, 27 Feb, 21 July 1740, 16 Mar. 1741, 15 Jan., 11 Mar., 29 May 1742, Livingston Papers, MCNY, box 2; George Clarke to Board of Trade, 24 May 1739, *DRNY*, 6:143–44; Schwarz, *Jarring Interests*, pp. 77–81, 264.

[53] Two detailed accounts of the Great Rebellion of 1766 are Kim, *Landlord and Tenant*, chap. 8, and Mark, *Agrarian Conflicts*, chap. 5.

ning to visit him to protest the terms of their leases. The tenants, however, delayed their visit until mid-June, when, according to one contemporary, approximately two hundred men "marched to murther the Lord of the Manor and level his house, unless he would sign leases for 'em agreeable to their form, as theirs were now expired and that they would neither pay Rent, taxes, &c, nor suffer other Tenants" to accept their landlord's terms. Walter Livingston dispersed the mob with the help of forty armed men, though the unrest did not subside until after Governor Sir Henry Moore's proclamation of 3 July, which authorized the use of troops to defeat and capture the conspirators at Claverack and Livingston Manor.[54]

Fragmentary evidence suggests that leaseholders participated more extensively in the 1766 riots than in those of the preceding decade. For instance, Captain John Montressor, a British soldier stationed in New York, reported that hundreds of Manor "tenants" stormed Livingston's mansion demanding better leasing conditions; unlike the insurgents of the 1750s, they were not challenging Livingston's land title, but protesting the conditions of tenancy. Governor Sir Henry Moore also regarded the 1766 episode as fundamentally different from New York's earlier agrarian uprisings. Moore's proclamation recognized the role that New England squatters played in the Great Rebellion, but the governor also reported to the Earl of Shelburne that the renewed unrest was not related to the ongoing border dispute between New York and Massachusetts. In 1766, even the squatters admitted that they were on New York soil, but they joined with a substantial number of tenants to protest the terms of the leases that the great landlords offered.[55]

Nevertheless, in 1766 as in the 1750s, the influence of the New England squatters must have been critical because in both cases the uprisings occurred exclusively on estates adjacent to the eastern colonies. While Robert Livingston, Jr., fretted over the latest developments on his property, his cousins at Clermont to the southwest experienced no such unpleasantness. While violence first erupted in the Philipse's Highland Patent in 1766, tenants at that family's Phil-

---

54 Robert R. Livingston to Robert Livingston, Jr., 14 May 1766, Livingston-Redmond MSS., reel 8; James and John Montressor, *The Montressor Journals*, ed. G. D. Scull (New York, 1882), pp. 375–76.

55 *Montressor Journals*, pp. 375–76; Sir Henry Moore's proclamation, 3 July 1766, *DHNY*, 3:830–32; Moore to Shelburne, 24 Feb. 1767, *DRNY*, 7:910–12.

ipsburgh Manor in western Westchester County also remained quiescent.

Even within Livingston Manor itself, between 1751 and 1766, the overwhelming majority of raids and riots occurred in the Taghkanic area, the easternmost portion of the Manor, adjacent to Massachusetts. Aside from the insurgents' march to the manor house in 1766, only three times during this entire period did they progress as far west as Ancram, about six miles from Taghkanic and the disputed New York–Massachusetts border. Moreover, most tenants at Ancram—both farmers and ironworkers—did not support the insurgents. When the latter invaded Ancram in January 1753, the tenants there "happened to be Advertised of it in the evening and armed themselves to stand in their Defence." Livingston feared an eventual bloodbath because, as he explained to his friend James Alexander, "My people are determined to defend themselves." In May 1755, when the rebels returned to Ancram to seize Livingston's ironworkers, the remaining inhabitants fled for safety rather than join the rioters. Similarly, when the insurgents returned to Ancram in October and arrested the Van Deusens, no Ancram residents actively supported their offensive.[56]

Most tenants simply wanted to be left undisturbed at their farms, fearing both the reprisals of their landlord and the violence of the insurgents. With the possible exception of the June 1766 uprising, the New Englanders, not the tenants, were the catalysts and the main participants in the revolts. But the squatters' presence on the Manor and their continued chiding of the "fools" who paid their rents provided an opportunity for unhappy tenants to revolt.[57] Inspired and encouraged by the Sons of Liberty in New York and by the rural rioters in the counties of Dutchess and Westchester, many Livingston tenants briefly availed themselves of this opportunity in June 1766, when they marched en masse to challenge their landlord's prerogatives.

The proprietary families emerged unscathed from the mid-eigh-

[56] Robert Livingston, Jr., to James Alexander, 22 Jan. 1753, Rutherfurd Collection, NYHS, vol. 3; Dirck Swart to Robert Livingston, Jr., 6 May 1755, *DHNY*, 3:791–92; Affadavit of Robert Livingston, Jr., 29 Oct. 1755, ibid., 3:792–93; Robert Van Deusen to Robert Livingston, Jr., 29 Oct. 1755, ibid., 3:812.

[57] Robert Livingston, Jr., to Jacob Wendell, 12 Apr. 1753, Livingston Papers, MCNY, box 3.

teenth-century revolts, and in 1773 an intercolonial commission left their landholdings intact when they fixed New York's eastern boundary twenty miles east of the Hudson River. Nevertheless, the defects in their original patents continued to haunt the valley's great landlords. After 1766, imperial authorities considered invalidating the patents in order to mollify Indian claimants and reward veterans of the recent French and Indian War.[58] During the Revolution, New England squatters and Manor tenants once again challenged the Livingstons' title, and in the post-Revolutionary era the tenants renewed their offensive against the claims of the proprietors. In 1795, some 210 Manor leaseholders unsuccessfully petitioned the state legislature for a revocation of the fraudulent Dongan patent of 1686. Employing the Revolutionary republican idiom, the petitioners claimed that they, as tenants, were subjected to "Terms and Conditions oppressive and burthensome to the last degree, unfriendly to all great exertions of Industry and tending to degrade [us] from the Rank the God of Nature destined all Mankind to move in, to be SLAVES and VASSALS."[59] Tenant dissatisfaction, which culminated in the Anti-Rent movement of the 1840s, had its roots in the New England invasions of the 1750s, but colonial tenants lacked both the unity and the political purpose of their successors.

During the colonial period, it had been the landlords who had used republican language to express their anxiety and hostility toward the forces that jeopardized their most sacred right, the right to property. Oddly enough, most scholars who have studied New York's agrarian revolts have neglected to analyze the motives and beliefs of the landlords who opposed them. Economic self-interest clearly played a major role in determining the landlords' response to the rebellions, but the proprietors believed they had more at stake than mere financial considerations. The rebels challenged not only their property rights but also their entire world view, which was premised on the notion of an organic, hierarchical society. As a result, the landlords' desire to protect both their fortunes and their

[58] Kim, *Landlord and Tenant*, pp. 408–12.

[59] Petition of Petrus Pulver et al., 7 Jan. 1795, *DHNY*, 3:839–41. Another unsuccessful petition was submitted by 153 Manor tenants in 1811 (Petition of a few Dam'd Rascals at the Manor of Livingston to the Legislature of New York, 1811, Livingston Family Papers, Columbia University, ser. II).

way of life acquired, as one scholar has noted, "a quasi-religious dimension."[60]

If Robert Livingston, Jr., was at all typical, New York's beleaguered landlords came to interpret their travails within the conspiratorial framework that intellectual historians associate with the Anglo-American republican tradition.[61] Livingston gradually came to see purposeful antipathy in everyone from the New England "levellers" to the seemingly unresponsive government of New York. Livingston's letters chronicle his growing sense of helplessness and isolation in dealing with what seemed to be a steadily deteriorating situation. Livingston had been accustomed to being lord and master on his own estate, and, in 1751, at the outset of the unrest, he was serenely confident in the social and political influence of his large family. He also believed that the government of Massachusetts could never countenance the insurgents' attack on the sacred right of property, which lay at the root of the eighteenth-century understanding of the concept of the civil liberty. As late as May 1753, when he met with the boundary commissioners from Massachusetts, Livingston continued to hope for the best from their government while decrying the reprehensible actions of its rebellious citizens. Soon thereafter, however, he was forced to admit that the Bay Colony's government sympathized with the insurgents' demands. Consequently, although he continued to urge his friends in New England to aid him in his struggle, Livingston increasingly pinned his hopes on getting support from the government of New York.[62]

New York's provincial government spent a good deal of time reviewing and evaluating Livingston's petitions, which elicited sympathy and verbal support but little decisive action.[63] The reluctance of

[60] Schwarz, *Jarring Interests*, p. 106.

[61] See, for instance, Bernard Bailyn, *The Ideological Origins of the American Revolution* (Cambridge, Mass., 1973), esp. pp. 144–59.

[62] Robert Livingston, Jr., to Jacob Wendell, 14 Sept. 1751, 16 Apr. 1752, 26 May 1753, Livingston Papers, MCNY, box 3. The report of the Massachusetts General Court of 11 September 1753 was extremely critical of Livingston and his claims and was probably instrumental in causing him to lose all hope of support from the Boston government (*DHNY*, 3:754–56).

[63] A representative sample of Livingston's petitions and letters to the New York authorities appear in *DHNY*, 3:727–823. New York's chief executives during this period were George Clinton (1743–53), Sir Danvers Osborne (1753), James DeLancey (1753–55), Sir Charles Hardy (1755–57), and James DeLancey (1757–60).

the government to take a firm stand, coupled with his brother William's discouraging reports from New York, undermined Robert's faith in the ability of the political process to safeguard his rights. New York's lethargy and Massachusetts's recalcitrance weakened his morale and eroded his sense of patriotism and public spirit. While New Yorkers prepared to fight the French in March 1755, Livingston complained that he "cannot think my Self in duty bound to assist either in Councill or purse to Carry on an offensive war against the [French] while I am threatened with an invasion from my Supposed friends at home."[64] His faith in the efficacy of political authority was restored somewhat by Lieutenant Governor James DeLancey's 1757 proclamation for the arrest of the Taghkanic rioters. Because DeLancey's directive quieted the insurgents, Livingston subsequently looked on proclamations as panaceas. When the squatters and their tenant allies began to grow restless again in 1762, he successfully pressed for another gubernatorial proclamation in hopes of preserving order.[65]

Besides the material issues at stake, the rioters threatened the three things Livingston and his peers held dearest: the right to property, the honor of their families, and the natural, stable social order in which they were preeminent. Property, of course, was central to liberty in an Anglo-American libertarian tradition that, at least prior to the Revolution, laid no claim to egalitarianism.[66] In 1735, Philip Livingston had condemned Governor William Cosby's "arbitrary proceedings" against Rip Van Dam and the Morrisites because, both by gratuitously deposing appointed officials and by challenging the land patents of his political enemies, Cosby's tyrannous behavior undermined the rights and liberties of all New Yorkers. Only strenuous opposition to such injustice, he believed, would "Settle our

---

[64] Robert Livingston, Jr., to Jacob Wendell, 12 Mar. 1755, Livingston Papers, MCNY, box 3. See also William Livingston's letters to his brother Robert, 4 Feb. 1754, 24 Dec. 1755, 13 June 1757, Livingston-Redmond MSS., reel 7.

[65] DeLancey's proclamation, 8 June 1757, *DHNY*, 3:821–23; Robert Livingston, Jr., to Peter R. Livingston and James Duane, 22 Mar. 1762, ibid., 3:825–26; Colden's proclamation, 31 Mar. 1762, ibid., 3:827–29; Robert Livingston, Jr., to James Duane, 3 May 1762, Duane Papers, NYHS, box 1. DeLancey had issued a proclamation in 1755, but it applied only to Robert Noble and his associates, who had seized Sheriff Abraham Yates at Claverack (*DHNY*, 3:785–87).

[66] Gordon S. Wood, *The Creation of the American Republic, 1776–1787* (Chapel Hill, N.C., 1969), pp. 70–75.

Liberty on a Solid foundation." Decades later, in the midst of the agrarian uprisings, Robert echoed his father's sentiments, though he looked to the rectitude of the New York government for protection from the licentious "N[ew] England people" and their tenant allies.[67]

Robert believed that the violence and anarchy that convulsed his estate would spread elsewhere to the utter ruin of all property rights. As he lamented to his brother-in-law William Alexander, "If I am not Speadily assisted by the Government I fear the Infection will very Soon be general and then no man that has an Estate in this Province or p[er]haps in north America, will be Safe or able to Call it his owne." In a similar vein, Robert Cambridge Livingston saw no irony in his own simultaneous condemnation of the Stamp Act and the rebellious farmers, both of which he believed posed serious threats to the liberty and property of his family.[68]

The attack on Livingston Manor was also an affront to the honor of the proprietary family. Consequently, the defense of the Livingston estate was conducted by an array of family members who had no material interest whatsoever in the survival of the family seat. When Robert Livingston, Jr., learned that the squatters had submitted their first petition to the Massachusetts General Court in October 1751, he quickly wrote to his four brothers in New York City to apprise them of his situation and ask their advice. Throughout the ensuing crisis, Robert relied heavily on his brothers for the latest news from the provincial capital as well as for their personal efforts to spur the government to action. William, the family lawyer, was particularly active in his brother's behalf, but on at least one occasion all four brothers met with the governor together to plead the case of their family.[69] Brother-in-law William Alexander also acted as Livingston's intermediary with the provincial government, and in

---

[67] Philip Livingston to James Alexander, 7 Jan. 1735, Rutherfurd Collection, NYHS, vol. 2.

[68] Robert Livingston, Jr., to William Alexander, 26 Mar. 1753, William Alexander Papers, NYHS, vol. 1; Robert Cambridge Livingston to Robert Livingston, Jr., 29 May 1766, Livingston-Redmond MSS., reel 8.

[69] William Livingston to Robert Livingston, Jr., 25 Nov. 1751, 4 Feb. 1754, 24 Dec. 1755, 13 June 1757, ibid., reel 7; John Livingston (1714–86) to Robert Livingston, Jr., 25 Nov. 1751, ibid.; Peter Van Brugh Livingston to Robert Livingston, Jr., 26 Nov. 1751, ibid.; Philip Livingston (1716–78) to Robert Livingston, Jr., 29 Nov. 1751, ibid.

the 1760s son-in-law James Duane added his legal expertise to the proprietor's cause. Robert R. Livingston—son of Robert of Clermont—met with the Massachusetts boundary commission at his cousin's behest in 1755, and eleven years later he assured his embattled relative that he would do all he could to help thwart the renewed challenge to his estate.[70]

The Livingstons' sense of family honor, which impelled Robert's relatives to come to his aid, also intensified as a result of the attacks on the family land. The actual process of defending the Manor entailed delving into the family's past and reexamining ancestral legacies. For example, the organization of Livingston's case against rebel leader Josiah Loomis was itself an exercise in family history. Of the twelve affadavits Livingston procured to support his case, eleven dwelt on the longevity of the Livingston title and the deponents' memories of Robert's father and grandfather in their capacity as lords of the Manor. Similarly, when James Duane prepared his father-in-law's case against the insurgents in 1767, he also stressed the historical claims of the Livingston family, which had devolved upon Robert Livingston, Jr., by virtue of entail and primogeniture.[71]

The defense of the Manor at times created an emotionally charged atmosphere within the Livingston family. Emotions ran highest when Catrina Van Brugh Livingston—Philip's widow and Robert's mother—died in 1756. On that occasion, New York merchant Philip Livingston stressed the need to maintain family unity and identity despite the death of "the best of Mothers." Although "this great bond of Union is Brouk," Philip wrote to his brother Robert, "the Same Brotherly Affection & Friendship that has so remarkably subsisted between us All, may continue as Long as Life." Brother-in-law William Alexander made the case for family solidarity even more forcefully. Perhaps reflecting on the family's current misfortunes, Alexander recommended that its members "see each other often and . . . cultivate friendship and harmony, for . . .

---

[70] Robert Livingston, Jr., to William Alexander, 26 Mar. 1753, William Alexander Papers, NYHS, vol. 1; Robert Livingston, Jr., to James DeLancey, 29 May 1755, *DHNY*, 3:803–4; Robert R. Livingston to Robert Livingston, Jr., 14 May 1766, Livingston-Redmond MSS., reel 8; James Duane to Robert Livingston, Jr., 24 Jan. 1767, ibid. Duane had married Livingston's eldest daughter in 1759.

[71] Affadavits of Ebeneezer Loomis et al., 23 Aug. 1753, Livingston-Redmond MSS., reel 7; James Duane to Robert Livingston, Jr., 24 Jan. 1767, ibid., reel 8.

the Credit, the Power, and the Interest of families chiefly depend on this."[72]

The uprisings of the mid-eighteenth century left Robert Livingston, Jr., obsessed with his personal responsibility to preserve the legacy of honor and influence attained by his forbears. His family and friends noticed that he had become extremely sensitive to anything that might threaten the interests of his family; they also reported that he suffered acute bouts of anxiety that rendered him temperamental and overbearing. As Robert Cambridge Livingston explained his father's condition in 1771, "The cause of [his violent temper] may be attributed to his Ideas being totally engrossed by, and incessantly fixed on, some plan to extricate himself from the imaginary difficulties he supposes surround him—which may be more particularly distinguished by the Bugbear-appellation of family-honor."[73]

The Hudson Valley revolts so terrified Robert Livingston, Jr., and his peers because such upheavals were utterly alien to the world in which they lived. Since Leisler's Rebellion, New York had been remarkably calm, especially in the countryside, and that tranquillity was reflected in the world view of New York's provincial elite. Before the 1750s, government officials and colonial gentlefolk rarely mentioned the common people in their official and private correspondence. Members of New York's colonial elite certainly knew that there were those less fortunate than themselves, but they did not really notice the middling and lesser sorts, as a group, until they began to cause trouble.

The Livingstons were entirely incapable of understanding the grievances against them. Robert Livingston, Jr., believed he held an inviolable title to his land and that, as a landlord, he rightfully enjoyed authority over his tenants. He also considered himself a good man who deserved the respect of those who, according to the natural order of society, were his underlings and dependents. In 1752, Livingston ejected his rebellious tenant, Josiah Loomis, not so much for his participation in the riots but because Loomis showed no signs

[72] Philip Livingston (1716–78) to Robert Livingston, Jr., 28 Feb. 1756, ibid., reel 7; William Alexander to [Robert Livingston, Jr.], 1 Mar. 1756, Rutherfurd Collection, NYHS, vol. 3.

[73] Robert Cambridge Livingston to James Duane, 29 June 1771, Duane Papers, NYHS, box 2.

of "Reformation." Livingston informed Loomis, "You deserve no Clemency at my hands, the whole being your own Wicked doings and nothing but your poverty has hitherto protected you." But Livingston had paid the bail and court fees of his loyal tenants who had been carried off by rioters to a Massachusetts jail. He had also petitioned for government intervention out of "Compassion to the Distressed state of the Poor people, who live on the Eastern parts of this Province."[74]

Surely, Livingston saw himself as the model of rectitude in dealing with his tenants, and nothing in his experience or education would have led him to believe that New York's leaseholding system was inherently wrong or inequitable. His cousin and close friend, Robert R. Livingston of Clermont, went so far as to argue that the tenancy system promoted industry and commerce by giving tenants larger farms than partible inheritance would allow ordinarily. He also believed that charging farmers rent encouraged them to produce more than they would otherwise, which enriched the tenants themselves, as well as the province. At the same time, he maintained, New York's "civil Constitution" protected the leaseholders from "Oppression."[75] Far from comprehending the grievances of their opponents, such men could only consider themselves victims of a vicious plot to destroy their way of life.

When Robert Livingston, Jr., had decided to live at his estate, the Manor became the social and emotional center of the proprietary family. Robert himself so identified his family's reputation and welfare with its landed estate that when his son Peter's insolvency prompted him to break the Manor's entail in 1771 he deemed it "the most difficult and interesting affair which has hitherto happend to my family." During Robert's lifetime, the Manor came to symbolize the prestige and solidarity of the Livingston family. Robert even forgave his daughters Alida and Catharine for marrying without his consent by allowing them to visit the Manor, thus signifying that

[74] Robert Livingston, Jr.'s notice of ejection to Josiah Loomis, 17 Jan. 1752, Livingston-Redmond MSS., reel 7; Robert Livingston, Jr., to James Alexander, 22 Mar. 1753, Rutherfurd Collection, NYHS, vol. 3; Robert Livingston, Jr., to James DeLancey, 29 May 1755, *DHNY*, 3:801–3; Robert Livingston, Jr., to Sir Charles Hardy, 23 Nov. 1755, ibid., 3:814–17.

[75] McAnear, ed., "Mr. Robert R. Livingston's Reasons against a Land Tax," p. 89.

their places in the family were not forfeit. Later, during the Revolution, the Manor provided a haven for any family member, regardless of political sympathies. Patriot, loyalist, and neutral Livingstons and their kin flocked to the Manor, where family ties overshadowed political preferences. Four of Robert's five surviving sons built homes of their own at the Manor; like their father, they settled permanently on their ancestral landholdings.[76]

Clermont, too, gradually became the acknowledged seat of the junior propertied branch of the Livingston family. In the 1730s, Robert Livingston of Clermont had built a large brick house on the banks of the Hudson River. Although he spent little time there before the 1750s, the estate was an important source of personal and family identity. Consequently, Robert Livingston of Clermont viewed a protracted land dispute with a neighbor, Martin Hoffman, as a call to defend both the fortune and the honor of his family. As the proprietor of Clermont explained to his brother Gilbert, "If I loose the Cause its true I shall loose the land & a thousand Pound in mony defending the Same. Tho' that be considerable yet I think the Family will loose more by the loss of our [priceless] reputation . . . and [it] will be a Slurr on the Family while wee and our Children live." Hoffman's challenge ultimately failed, and after Robert retired to Clermont the estate became a perennial family gathering place. His grandchildren—the ten children of Robert R. Livingston and Margaret Beekman—were frequent summertime visitors who as adults built their own homes on the banks of the Hudson within twenty miles of their grandfather's mansion.[77]

---

[76] Robert Livingston, Jr., to James Duane, 25 Feb. 1771, Duane Papers, NYHS, box 2; Peter R. Livingston to Robert Livingston, Jr., 25 Dec. 1769, Livingston-Redmond MSS., reel 8; James Duane to Robert Livingston, Jr., 26 Nov. 1770, ibid.; John Henry Livingston, "The Livingston Manor," Order of Colonial Lords of Manors in America, *Publications* 1 (1910): 24; Harold Donald Eberlein, *The Manors and Historic Homes of the Hudson Valley* (Philadelphia, 1924), pp. 78–79; Walter Livingston's account of money disbursed for building a house at Teviot Dale, July 1773–Apr. 1777, Livingston Family Papers, NYHS, reel 15. The best account of daily life at the Manor during the Revolution is William H. W. Sabine, ed., *The Memoirs of William Smith* . . . , 2 vols. (New York, 1958), vol. 2.

[77] Robert Livingston (1688–1775) to Gilbert Livingston, 30 Sept. 1744, Misc. MSS., Robert Livingston (1688–1775), NYHS; Robert R. Livingston to Robert Livingston (1688–1775), 21 July 1758, 2 June 1760, 24 Aug. 1765, 20 July 1768, Robert R. Livingston Papers, NYHS, reel 1; Thomas Streatfield Clarkson, *A Biographical History of Clermont* . . . (Clermont, N.Y., 1869), p. 48.

The Family Land

By the middle decades of the eighteenth century, Livingston Manor was a business enterprise, a family gathering place, and a symbolic representation of the ideals of the proprietary family. Robert and Alida Livingston had valued the Manor mainly for its commercial potential; their son Philip had regarded his estate as both market and supplier for his flourishing trade. During the lifetime of Philip's son Robert Livingston, Jr., the Manor continued to grow as a business enterprise, as its tenant population grew and the ironworks at Ancram thrived and expanded. At the same time, however, the family land was attaining a new social and emotional significance among members of proprietary family.

The grandchildren of Robert and Alida Livingston had become gentlefolk who cultivated the privileges and attributes of a provincial gentry even as they continued to work and to improve their family's landholdings. Like his father, Philip, Robert Livingston, Jr., had moved to the country more to exploit the land's industrial and commercial possibilities than to enjoy his rural leisure. Robert and Alida's entrepreneurial values persisted among their descendants, who struggled to reconcile the values of the work ethic with their emerging affinity for aristocratic ideals and genteel living.

[4]

Useful Gentlefolk

During the first half of the eighteenth century, the descendants of successful immigrants coalesced into a stable and entrenched provincial elite. Like the Livingstons, most of New York's leading families had made their fortunes in land and trade, and most also had benefited from the largesse of the colony's English governors. The descendants of the founders expanded and diversified their families' landed and commercial interests. Their success as merchants, landlords, and entrepreneurs brought them more wealth, which in turn enhanced and solidified their social status.[1]

Increased wealth and secure social status were reflected in the changing values and culture of New York's provincial elite. During the middle decades of the eighteenth century, affluent New Yorkers began to embrace the aristocratic values of honor, gentility, and noblesse oblige. At the same time, they began to develop an anglicized, class-specific culture that prized refinement, display, and luxury. One New Yorker observed in 1744, "We have in America for some time past made great progress in Aping the Luxury of our Mother Country." This new genteel material culture graphically accentuated the differences between elites and their social inferiors and visibly reinforced and legitimized the elite's growing power and authority. During this same period, the elite's increasing emphasis

---

[1] For an explanation of the process of elite formation in British America, see John M. Murrin, "Political Development," in Jack P. Greene and J. R. Pole, eds., *Colonial British America: Essays in the New History of the Early Modern Era* (Baltimore, 1984), pp. 416–41.

on learning and education also distinguished them culturally from their humbler neighbors and justified their claims to be a proper governing class, an American aristocracy.[2]

Yet America's eighteenth-century elites did not abandon their ancestors' commitment to the values of the Protestant ethic. Instead, colonial gentlefolk combined the character traits of the Protestant ethic with the external behavioral qualities of an emerging "high-style," or elite, culture.[3] Even when they had amassed enough wealth to live lives of leisure, colonial gentlefolk continued to labor in their callings and expected their children to do the same. Even as they adopted the new aristocratic values and genteel ways of living, they clung to the work ethic of their ancestors, whose main achievement had been the creation of their families' fortunes.

Over the course of the eighteenth century, a distinct elite ethos emerged throughout provincial America. That ethos sought to combine the ideals of the bourgeois and aristocratic traditions by valuing gentility and cultural refinement without devaluing work and Christian morality. Increased wealth led provincial elites to become genteel, educated, and public-spirited, but it did not make them tolerate idleness, dependence, or irresponsibility. The ideal American leader would combine the gentleman's refinement, education, and public spirit with his ancestors' commitment to work and individual usefulness.

[2] Cadwallader Colden to Peter Collinson, June 1744, *The Letters and Papers of Cadwallader Colden*, 9 vols. (New York, 1918–37), 3:61. On the social and political ramifications of the development of a distinct elite culture in eighteenth-century Virginia, see Rhys Isaac, *The Transformation of Virginia, 1740–1790* (Chapel Hill, N.C., 1982), chaps. 4–6. On western New England, see Robert Blair St. George, "Artifacts of Regional Consciousness in the Connecticut River Valley, 1700–1780," in Robert Blair St. George, ed., *Material Life in America, 1600–1860* (Boston, 1988), pp. 335–56. In general, see also Richard L. Bushman, "American High-Style and Vernacular Culture," in Greene and Pole, eds., *British Colonial America*, pp. 345–83.

[3] For evidence of the coexistence of aristocratic and bourgeois values among elites outside of New York, see T. H. Breen, *Tobacco Culture: The Mentality of the Great Tidewater Planters on the Eve of Revolution* (Princeton, 1985), pp. 17–23, 32–37; Jack P. Greene, *Landon Carter: An Inquiry into the Personal Values and Social Imperatives of the Eighteenth-Century Virginia Gentry* (Charlottesville, Va., 1965), esp. chap. 3; Randolph Shipley Klein, *Portrait of an Early American Family: The Shippens of Pennsylvania across Five Generations* (Philadelphia, 1975), esp. pp. 82–83. Frederick B. Tolles, *Meeting House and Counting House: The Quaker Merchants of Colonial Philadelphia, 1682–1763* (Chapel Hill, N.C., 1948), esp. chaps. 6–8; Kevin M. Sweeney, "Mansion People: Kinship, Class, and Architecture in Western Massachusetts in the Mid-Eighteenth Century," *Winterthur Portfolio*, 19 (1984): 231–34.

The gentrification of elite culture occurred as a result of decades of prosperity and economic growth both in England and in America. Once leading provincials became financially secure, they began to spend more to improve their standard of living. Some contemporaries noticed the rise both in living standards and in living costs over the course of the eighteenth century. For instance, although a salary of £200 sterling provided a handsome—and allegedly extravagant—maintenance for New York's chief justice in 1715, a half-century later this sum was not enough to support the incumbent justice in a style befitting his office. By the 1760s, inflation had decreased the chief justice's real income to roughly £152 sterling— still a substantial sum but not nearly enough to enable the chief justice to keep up with the increasingly elegant and expensive tastes of New York's provincial elites. In 1762, Chief Justice Benjamin Prat complained to the Board of Trade that he needed more income in order to live on a par with New York's leading citizens. "When [the current salary] was first granted," he noted, "it would better support a Ch[ief] Justice than £400 sterling would now; such had been *the difference in the mode of living,* & the augmentation of the Expence of supporting a Family with Decency."[4]

Colonial economic growth brought New York elites the wealth they needed to live genteelly, but England's contemporary economic revolutions supplied them with the stuff of which gentility was made. England's eighteenth-century commercial revolution introduced consumers to fashion plates, Wedgwood pottery, and Chippendale furniture, as well as to various forms of commercialized leisure, such as exhibitions, shows, and public gardens. In eighteenth-century England, prosperity and social competition encouraged the growth of a material culture that exalted fashion over function. Indeed, the use of the terms "fashion" and "fashionable" to denote current cultural preferences was largely an innovation of the seventeenth and eighteenth centuries.[5]

[4] Benjamin Prat to Board of Trade, 24 May 1762, *DRNY,* 7:500–502, emphasis added; Paul M. Hamlin and Charles E. Baker, *Supreme Court of Judicature of the Province of New York, 1691–1704,* 3 vols. (New York, 1959), 1:96–98; John J. McCusker, *Money and Exchange in Europe and America, 1660–1775: A Handbook* (Chapel Hill, N.C., 1978), pp. 163–65.

[5] Neil McKendrick et al., *Birth of a Consumer Society: The Commercialization of Eighteenth-Century England* (London, 1982); *Oxford English Dictionary,* 1971 ed., s.v., "fashion," "fashionable," "fashionableness."

England's consumer culture was exportable, and American prosperity enabled provincials to purchase what the English were able to export. The absolute value of English goods imported by the colonists rose markedly in the latter half of the eighteenth century. During the 1730s, the colonists imported an average of £646,193 sterling in English goods each year, but by the 1750s that figure had more than doubled, to £1,577,415. Population growth alone does not explain the expansion of the Anglo-American trade during this period; per capita colonial consumption of English goods also rose more than 36 percent during the prosperous 1750s, although it then declined somewhat during the postwar depression of the following decade.[6]

By the closing decades of the colonial era, provincials in New York and elsewhere were importing a wider variety of goods in greater quantities, and these items were being consumed by a larger proportion of an increasingly prosperous colonial population. By 1774, New York Governor William Tryon claimed, "More than Eleven Twelfths of the Inhabitants of this Province both in the necessary and ornamental parts of their Dress are cloathed in British Manufactures, excepting Linen from Ireland and Hats and Shoes manufactured here." Tryon also believed that the overwhelming majority of New Yorkers bought most of their household goods from Great Britain as well, and he informed the home government of the continual growth of colonial demand for English domestic furnishings, groceries "of all sorts," "large Quantities of all kinds of East India Goods," and assorted manufactured items.[7]

Other contemporaries noticed this increased demand for English goods and attributed it both to general prosperity and to the great profits that at least some leading New Yorkers had made provision-

---

[6] *Hist. Statistics of the U.S.*, 2:1168, 1176–77. Per capita calculations based on white population only. The average annual per capita consumption of English goods for 1731–40 was £0.86 sterling. This figure soared to £1.24 during the 1750s and then dropped to an annual average of £1.06 for the years 1760–70. These figures probably underestimate the full impact of America's commercial revolution, because by the 1750s the movement of population to the western frontiers would have skewed per capita consumption rates downward by including thousands of people living in remote places with limited access to the market economy.

[7] Tryon's report to Lord Dartmouth, June 1774, *DRNY*, 8:446–47. On colonial consumption of imported goods in general and of the "new groceries" in particular, see Carole Shammas, *The Pre-industrial Consumer in England and America* (Oxford, 1990), esp. chaps. 3–5.

ing and privateering during King George's War in the 1740s. Observers in New York also noted that luxury items seemed to account for most of the province's increased trade in English imports. William Livingston—youngest brother of Robert Livingston, Jr., and grandson of Robert and Alida—reported in 1753, "Our extraordinary Success during the late War, has given Rise to a Method of living unknown to our frugal Ancestors." William Smith, Jr., New York's colonial historian, concurred with this judgment. "In the city of New-York," Smith wrote, "through our intercourse with the Europeans, we follow the London fashions. . . . Our affluence during the late war, introduced a degree of luxury in tables, dress, and furniture, with which we were before unacquainted."[8] During the closing decades of the colonial era, affluent New Yorkers built country homes after the fashion of the English gentry; they also built town houses where they and their families could enjoy Manhattan's increasingly elaborate social season.

Constructed primarily during the prosperous years between King George's War and the economic depression of the 1760s, New York's colonial great houses were built by men who wanted their homes to convey images of wealth, security, and permanence. In other words, these elaborate homes were erected both to celebrate and to reinforce the social dominance of their owners, as well as to provide them with an appreciating asset that could be passed on to future generations. Mansion-building, in New York as elsewhere, betokened a mixture of both confidence and anxiety on the part of the mansion-builders. While the great houses signified their owners' consciousness of their own preeminence, they also implied the need to use elaborate displays of material wealth to maintain their exalted status. In mid-eighteenth-century New York, a healthy and rapidly growing economy must have made elites feel confident and optimistic about their future. But the mansion-builders must also have been keenly aware of the insecurity of wealth and status in America's relatively fluid social order. Indeed, many of them had made their

---

[8] William Livingston et al., *The Independent Reflector*, ed. Milton M. Klein (Cambridge, Mass., 1963), pp. 257–58. William Smith, Jr., *The History of the Province of New-York*, ed. Michael G. Kammen, 2 vols. (Cambridge, Mass., 1972), 1:226. On the development of an anglicized consumer culture in eighteenth-century America, see T. H. Breen, "Creative Adaptations: Peoples and Cultures," in Greene and Pole, eds., *British Colonial America*, pp. 222–23.

fortunes only recently, and the wartime activities that had made them rich had ruined many others.[9] Nevertheless, by mid-century affluent New Yorkers increasingly owned great houses both in the town and in the country. Many used these houses as seasonal residences, living in the city during the cooler months and in the country during the summer.

In the early colonial period, most New Yorkers had lived in one place only, and business considerations had dictated their place of residence. Although the province's great men had owned both urban and rural property even in the seventeenth century, if they owned two or more houses they did so for business or political reasons and resided where the practical demand for their presence was greatest. For instance, by 1700 the first Robert Livingston had owned five houses: two in New York City, two in Albany, and another, just recently completed, at his Hudson Valley manor. Livingston did stay at one of his Manhattan homes when he was in town to attend the assembly or conduct business; equipped with a wharf and storeroom, this house was, at the time, more of an office than a residence. He and his family resided permanently in Albany County and, in fact, moved out of the town of Albany only when business required their presence at the Manor. Alida Livingston, visited New York City only twice—both times without her husband—and their children's trips there were equally infrequent. Robert Livingston had accumulated houses in order to provide each of his children with a place to live when they married or, in the case of his sons, when they left home to begin their own businesses. City houses often were investments to be used as rental properties and later to be awarded as dowries or bequests.[10]

[9] On the significance of mansion-building in general, see Isaac, *Transformation of Virginia*, esp. pp. 35–42; Roger G. Kennedy, *Architecture, Men, Women, and Money in America* (New York, 1985), chap. 7; St. George, "Artifacts of Regional Consciousness"; Sweeney, "Mansion People," pp. 231–35, 249–54; Dell Upton, *Holy Things and Profane: Anglican Parish Churches in Colonial Virginia* (Cambridge, Mass., 1988), esp. part 2. On country estates as appreciating investments, see Elizabeth Blackmar, *Manhattan for Rent, 1785–1850* (Ithaca, N.Y., 1989), pp. 25–28.

[10] Will of Robert Livingston, 24 Jan. 1710, Livingston-Redmond MSS., reel 3; Samuel Vetch's account with Livingston, 1707–20, ibid., reel 2; Deed of the house & 2 Lotts . . . at N. York to . . . Joanna [Livingston] Van Horn[e], 9 Aug. 1722, ibid., reel 4; I. N. Phelps Stokes, *The Iconography of Manhattan Island, 1498–1909*, 6 vols. (New York, 1915–28), 4:396.

In early colonial New York, the country homes of the elite were usually simple structures built on isolated manors, used mainly by proprietors supervising their rural enterprises and not by gentlefolk seeking an elegant bucolic retreat. Rensselaerswyck's first manor house, Fort Crailo, was a barn-like Dutch-style building that did triple duty as residence, office, and fortress. In 1740, the Van Rensselaers renovated and expanded Fort Crailo, and in 1765 they built a much more stylish and elaborate house, relegating the old fort to nonresidential use. Frederick Philipse, New York's wealthiest resident in the 1690s, also built an austere stone "castle" at his Hudson Valley estate in the seventeenth century. Philipse lived and traded at New York and visited his manor only briefly to attend to his milling and agricultural interests, which were otherwise supervised by his hired overseers. By the late 1720s, however, Philipse's heir had built a Georgian house at the Manor. The Philipses expanded their manor house in 1745 and renovated and redecorated a decade later.[11]

Robert and Alida Livingston built their Manor house in 1699 on the north side of Roeloff Jansen's Kill on the banks of the Hudson River. Like its Philipse and Van Rensselaer counterparts, the first Livingston Manor house seems to have been relatively large but plain. One near-contemporary account described Robert and Alida's Manor home as a long, low stone house with thick walls and a heavy Dutch-style roof. This type of dwelling became unfashionable during the early decades of the eighteenth century, but both Philip Livingston and Robert Livingston, Jr., seemed content to reside in the old Manor house built by Robert and Alida. Other eighteenth-century Livingstons built more fashionable houses. In the 1730s, Robert Livingston of Clermont built his family's first Georgian mansion at his estate on the banks of the majestic Hudson River.[12]

By mid-century, not only had the manorial families begun to reside on their estates, but prominent merchants and lawyers also had

[11] Hugh Morrison, *Early American Architecture: From the First Colonial Settlements to the National Period* (New York, 1952), pp. 108–9, 557–60, 563–64. On Philipse's wealth, see Thomas J. Archdeacon, *New York City, 1664–1710: Conquest and Change* (Ithaca, N.Y., 1975), p. 40. The Van Rensselaers' Fort Crailo was named for a family estate in the Netherlands.

[12] Helen Wilkinson Reynolds, *Dutch Houses in the Hudson Valley before 1776* (New York, 1929), pp. 86–88. Peter R. Livingston did not look forward to living in the Manor house, which he inherited in 1790. Uncomfortable and unstylish, the Manor house was demolished by Peter's son and heir nine years later.

begun building country houses, where they could take refuge from the city during the sweltering summer. Unlike the earlier manor houses, these new country homes were built purely for social and recreational purposes. Most were easily accessible to lower Manhattan, where their owners conducted their business. For example, after making his fortune during King George's War, New York City merchant Philip Livingston—brother of Robert Livingston, Jr.—built an elegant country residence across the East River at Brooklyn Heights. Lieutenant Governor James DeLancey and lawyers James Duane and John Morin Scott had their country seats in Manhattan, outside the city limits, at present-day Greenwich Village, Gramercy Park, and midtown, respectively. After 1760, the Le Roy, Van Zandt, Lawrence, Marston, and Schermerhorn families also built their country houses in mid-Manhattan, on the shores of the East River. Colonel Roger Morris, a member of the governor's council, erected his "Mount Morris" at Harlem Heights in 1765, and in 1770 Supreme Court Justice and Assemblyman David Jones built "Tryon Hall" to replace his family's smaller summer home at Fort Neck in Queens County. Frederick Van Cortlandt built his mansion in the Bronx in 1748. Lawyer-historian William Smith, Jr., and Peter Van Brugh Livingston—another merchant brother of Robert Livingston, Jr.—situated their country homes farther outside of town, in Westchester County. Nearby New Jersey was also a rural retreat for affluent New Yorkers. William Bayard had a stately mansion at Hoboken, across the Hudson from lower Manhattan. In 1762, merchant William Alexander began building his seat at Basking Ridge in Somerset County, where his neighbors included prominent New Jerseyans who spent their winters in Elizabethtown and Perth Amboy.[13]

By the middle decades of the eighteenth century, affluent New

[13] Morrison, *Early American Architecture*, pp. 560–61; Esther Singleton, *Social New York under the Georges* (New York, 1902), pp. 40–48; Harold Donaldson Eberlein, *Manor Houses and Historic Homes of Long Island and Staten Island* (Philadelphia, 1928), p. 139, and *The Manors and Historic Homes of the Hudson Valley* (Philadelphia, 1924), pp. 134, 147; John Adams, *Diary and Autobiography of John Adams*, ed. L. H. Butterfield, 4 vols. (New York, 1964), 2:105; Edward P. Alexander, *A Revolutionary Conservative: James Duane of New York* (New York, 1938), pp. 53–54, 156; Carl Bridenbaugh, *Cities in Revolt: Urban Life in America, 1743–1776* (New York, 1955), p. 339; Virginia D. Harrington, *The New York Merchant on the Eve of the Revolution* (New York, 1935), p. 24; William Strickland, *Journal of a Tour in the United States of America*, ed. J. E. Strickland (New York, 1971), pp. 90–91; Alan Valentine, *Lord Stirling* (New York, 1969), p. 111.

Yorkers valued both country seats and town houses for the social advantages they offered. If a summer in the country let merchants and lawyers enjoy pastoral gentility, a season in the city allowed the landed gentry to display their finery and to mingle with the colony's most distinguished and influential citizens. In 1744, for example, Philip Livingston, the second lord of Livingston Manor, broke with tradition by bringing his entire family to New York City to take in the social life of the capital while he himself attended the meetings of the provincial council. Such family outings, unheard of in his parents' time, became common in the decades preceding the Revolution.[14]

During the eighteenth century, the elite's new interest in display and gentility transformed both their city and country homes from functional residences to grand showplaces. Elaborate homes had been uncommon in the early colonial period. In 1704, when Sarah Knight visited New York, she found the homes there remarkable only for their cleanliness. Forty years later, however, Peter Kalm—who found little to admire in New York—conceded that the provincial capital was an attractive city with many fine buildings. In 1775, John Adams criticized New Yorkers for their boisterous manners but admitted that the homes of the province's leading citizens were unusually gracious and elegant.[15]

Advertisements in New York newspapers also suggest that during the second half of the eighteenth century the homes of elites became increasingly elaborate, partly as a result of the increasing numbers of skilled craftsmen among the city's residents. During this period, a growing demand for luxury items had encouraged many young Englishmen to enter various fashionable skilled trades. Having served their apprenticeships in London, these craftsmen began to take their business to London's cultural provinces, which included the British colonies in America. There they fulfilled the rising de-

---

[14] Philip Livingston to Jacob Wendell, 4 Sept. 1744, Livingston Papers, MCNY, box 2. See also Bridenbaugh, *Cities in Revolt*, pp. 337–40.

[15] Sarah Knight, *The Private Journal Kept by Madam Knight on a Journey from Boston to New-York in the Year 1704* (Boston, 1920), pp. 52–53; Peter Kalm, *The America of 1750: Peter Kalm's Travels in North America*, ed. Adolph B. Benson, 2 vols. (New York, 1937), 1:130–32; Adams, *Diary*, 2:105–11. For explanations of this transformation in colonies other than New York, see Isaac, *Transformation of Virginia*, pp. 70–79; Bushman, "High-Style and Vernacular Cultures," pp. 349–52.

Table 5
Newspaper advertisers for domestic amenities,
1726–1776

	1726–36	1747–56	1757–66	1767–76
Carving and gilding	0	2	2	6
Clocks and watches	4	12	13	53
Engravings	1	1	1	6
Furniture	2	10	19	31
Glassware	0	3	1	6
Paintings	0	4	7	10
Pewter	0	7	3	10
Pottery and china	1	1	7	20
Silver	2	3	17	22
Upholstery	0	4	7	14
TOTALS	10	47	77	178

Source: Data based on material in Rita Susswein Gottesman, comp., *The Arts and Crafts in Colonial New York, 1726–1776: Advertisements and News Items from New York City Newspapers* (New York, 1938).

mands of an increasingly affluent and fashion-conscious provincial elite.[16]

Table 5 shows the growth of several skilled trades in New York in response to elite demands for fashionable domestic items. Carved and gilded woodwork, for instance, probably was not even available in New York until the late 1740s, but by the final decade of the colonial era at least six local craftsmen made and sold moldings, frames, and other carved or gilded items. The prosperity of the 1750s also brought several skilled furniture-makers to New York, as well as the city's first resident upholsterers. Two of the most successful upholsterers, George Richey and Joseph Cox, had plied their trade in London before coming to America. Most advertisers claimed that their goods were either imported from England or made in New York according to the latest London fashions.

Changing tastes in wall coverings were most strikingly emblematic of the elite's increased regard for fashion and display as barometers of individual prestige and refinement. In the early colonial period, walls were whitewashed, painted, or paneled, and even in the finest

[16] Bushman, "High-Style and Vernacular Cultures," esp. pp. 364–67.

homes, hangings and paintings were uncommon. In the 1720s, Alida Livingston asked her husband to hire a painter to paint a mural over their parlor fireplace at the manor house, but there is no evidence that Robert ever complied with this request. Alida also asked for two gilt-framed paintings, and because both she and Robert did have their portraits painted later in life, these two paintings were probably the only nonfunctional decorations adorning the walls of the manor house during their lifetimes.[17] By the 1750s, however, not only were portraits and portrait painters increasingly common in New York, but at least three local merchants imported prints and engravings from England to be hung in the homes of wealthy provincials. In addition, imported paper, fabric, and leather hangings transformed the surfaces of the walls themselves, so that it became possible to identify individual rooms chiefly by the color or composition of their wall coverings. By the middle of the eighteenth century, a typically fashionable home might contain a "green and gold room" and a "great tapestry room," besides "red rooms and green rooms and chintz rooms up stairs and down, furnished with damask hangings."[18]

Affluent New Yorkers filled their homes with ornaments and fine furniture in order to impress visitors with their status and gentility. Portraits, looking glasses, and cupboards decked with silver and china graced the public, or ceremonial, rooms of the elite, whose private living quarters often were simple by comparison. The upstairs furnishings at Clermont were worth $2,500 when Robert R. Livingston, Jr., died in 1813, but downstairs the family displayed china and plate that by itself was worth roughly $7,000. Clermont's downstairs entry hall alone contained eight paintings and prints, four mahogany tables, three lamps, and six chairs valued at $200. Six other paintings and five looking glasses hung in the dining room, drawing room, and parlor, all of which were heavily orna-

[17] Knight, *Journal*, pp. 52–53; Alida Livingston to Robert Livingston, 25 Oct. 1717, 5 Nov. 1720, 7 July 1721, Livingston-Redmond MSS., reel 4. See also Ruth Piwonka, *A Portrait of Livingston Manor, 1686–1850* (Germantown, N.Y., 1986), pp. 24–25, 163.

[18] Livingston Rutherfurd, *Family Record and Events, Compiled Originally from the Original MSS in the Rutherfurd Collection* (New York, 1894), p. 42; George B. Tatum, *Philadelphia Georgian: The City House of Samuel Powel and Some of Its Eighteenth-Century Neighbors* (Middletown, Conn., 1976), p. 38; Singleton, *Social New York under the Georges*, pp. 88–90; G. C. Groce, Jr., "New York Painting before 1800," *NY Hist.*, 19 (1938): 44–58.

mented and furnished with fifty chairs and three sofas to accommodate large but exclusive social gatherings.[19]

By the middle of the eighteenth century, entertaining guests at home was an important part of the social life of provincial elites. Half seriously, the struggling young lawyer William Livingston suggested that the inability to offer hospitality to friends was the most onerous burden of "poverty." Like the Virginia gentry, affluent New Yorkers took pride in their homes and appreciated due praise for the hospitality they offered. When Governor William Tryon and his wife toured the Hudson Valley in 1772, Robert Livingston, Jr., boasted that they "were highly delighted with . . . the kind reception they had met with where Ever they came ashore, and perticularly at my House," at Livingston Manor. The Livingstons appreciated their visitors' compliments, "for in truth we did all we could to make them welcome . . . but all great folks do not Chuse to acknowledge when they are treated in the best manner the house affords."[20]

Ritualized hospitality and an increasingly elaborate culture of leisure accentuated the social differences between New York's elites and their less genteel neighbors. Perhaps the growing popularity of carriage rides best illustrated the elite's new affinity for display and leisure during the late colonial era, when parading through the streets, with no particular destination, became a form of entertainment and social ritual. One contemporary noted that affluent New Yorkers—especially well-dressed women—customarily rode through the streets in order to display their finery. The elite's increased demand for carriages attracted a growing number of coach-makers to New York. While the city had no resident coach-makers before 1740, in the ensuing quarter-century at least thirteen opened shops there to serve the province's leading citizens. While some of these businesses presumably failed, others, like Elkanah and William Deane's Broad Street establishment, were notably successful. The Deanes

[19] Inventory of the estate of Robert R. Livingston, Jr., 30 Sept. 1813, Robert R. Livingston Papers, NYHS, reel 11. On the ownership of chairs—particularly in matched sets—as an index of social status, see Gloria L. Main, *Tobacco Colony: Life in Early Maryland, 1650–1720* (Princeton, 1982), pp. 249–51; Sweeney, "Mansion People," p. 246.

[20] William Livingston to Noah Welles, 7 Nov. 1747, Livingston-Welles Corres.; Robert Livingston, Jr., to James Duane, 28 Aug. 1772, Duane Papers, NYHS, box 2; Isaac, *Transformation of Virginia*, pp. 70–80; Bushman, "High-Style and Vernacular Culture," pp. 351–52, 358.

sold their plain coaches "with Livery Lace, and fringed Seat ... richly painted and finished" for £200. Despite the expense, at least sixty-nine New York City residents—or roughly 1.3 percent of the city's households—owned carriages in 1775.[21]

Owning or riding in a carriage therefore signified one's membership in an exclusive and visibly distinctive social elite. Pre-Revolutionary New York City's carriage-owning elite included at least five members of the Livingston family. The merchant brothers Peter Van Brugh, Philip, and John Livingston all owned carriages, as did their sister Sarah Livingston Alexander. Robert Gilbert Livingston, the successful eldest son of the disgraced Gilbert Livingston, was the fifth carriage-owner among the Manhattan Livingstons. Overall, members of the Livingston family accounted for more than 7 percent of New York City's carriage-owning population. That fact alone is impressive evidence of the family's wealth and status in the pre-Revolutionary era.[22]

In New York, as in other colonial cities, the privileged classes also formed exclusive clubs to plan their social agendas. Beginning in the 1740s, the New-York Dancing Assembly sponsored fortnightly balls during the fall and winter social season. Merchant Philip Livingston and lawyer Robert R. Livingston, Jr., were among the many prominent New Yorkers who took their turns serving as the Assembly's managers. During this same period, the New York Harmonic Society began organizing concerts and musical evenings. Another group, the Social Club, gathered many of the city's leading men for evenings of drinking and conversation. In 1751, after he took up residence at the Manor, Robert Livingston, Jr., joined the Social Club so that when he visited New York City he could enjoy "a Gentle Bac-

---

[21] Alexander Hamilton, *Itinerarium* . . . , ed. Albert Bushnell Hart (St. Louis, 1907), pp. 52, 108; Rita Susswein Gottesman, comp., *The Arts and Crafts in Colonial New York, 1726–1776: Advertisements and News Items from New York City Newspapers* (New York, 1938), pp. 356–61; List of carriage-owners in New York City, 1775, Rutherfurd Collection, NYHS, vol. 1; New York census, 1771, *DRNY*, 8:457. New York City had 5,363 white male residents over sixteen years of age in 1771; this figure has been used as an estimate of the number of households in the city.

[22] List of carriage-owners in New York City, 1775, Rutherfurd Collection, NYHS, vol. 1. Additional members of the Livingston family may have owned carriages—for instance, the May 1784 will of Robert Livingston, Jr., indicates that he owned both a "coach" and a "chariot" (Livingston Family Papers, NYHS, reel 3). Neither was included in the 1775 list because Livingston did not reside in Manhattan.

chanalion Engagement" with the friends he had left behind there. Later, the Social Club's membership also included Robert's two youngest sons, as well as their Clermont kinsman, Robert R. Livingston, Jr.[23]

Perhaps a similar organization was responsible for planning turtle barbecues, the elaborate picnic feasts that attracted the attention of virtually every traveler passing through the province in the late colonial period. "There are several houses, pleasantly situated on the East river," one eighteenth-century visitor reported, "where it is common to have turtle-feasts . . . once or twice in a week." On the appointed day, he explained, "thirty or forty gentlemen and ladies meet and dine together, drink tea in the afternoon, fish and amuse themselves till evening, and then return home in Italian chaises, . . . a gentleman and a lady in each chaise."[24]

The middle of the eighteenth century also saw the opening of several resorts that, like the turtle barbecues, provided entertainment for one-day excursions to the countryside but, unlike them, were run by entrepreneurs for private profit. Beginning in the late Stuart period, England's elite had flocked to the new spas and public gardens that opened near London to offer gentlefolk a stylish but less structured alternative to the metropolitan social season. By the middle of the eighteenth century, affluent New Yorkers added English-style spas and public gardens to their own increasingly commercialized culture of leisure. Recreational bathing had become fashionable in New York by 1760, when a bath house was constructed on the East River, adjacent to bathing tanks that were filled with fresh water by each new incoming tide. A similar establishment opened in nearby Perth Amboy, New Jersey, in 1772, promising "A New and Convenient Bath In which [there] is a Room properly constructed to undress and dress in, with a Stair-Case leading into the Bathing Room, where Persons of either Sex may bath[e] in Salt-

[23] Smith, *History*, 1:226; Richard B. Morris, ed., *John Jay: The Making of a Revolutionary, Unpublished Papers, 1745–1780* (New York, 1975), p. 116n.; List of Members of the Social Club, c. 1770, ibid., pp. 113–14; Gulian Verplanck to Robert Livingston, Jr., 3 Oct. 1751, Livingston-Redmond MSS., reel 7; Singleton, *Social New York under the Georges*, pp. 291–92, 301–5; *New-York Mercury*, 24 Oct. 1774.

[24] On the turtle feasts, see Hamilton, *Itinerarium*, pp. 107–8; and Andrew Burnaby, *Travels through the Middle Settlements in North America*, in *A General Collection of the Best and Most Interesting Voyages and Travels in All Parts of the World*, ed. John Pinkerton (London, 1812), pp. 738–39.

Water, in the greatest Privacy." Far more elegant were the public gardens that opened in New York's rural Out-Ward in the 1760s. Raneleigh and Vauxhall gardens were exclusive resorts after the fashion of their famous London namesakes. Both establishments featured spacious formal gardens "laid out, at a great Expence, in a very genteel, pleasing Manner," as well as evening balls and musical entertainment. Raneleigh Gardens offered summer band concerts on Tuesdays and Thursdays. Vauxhall was famous for its wax works and evening teas.[25]

By mid-century, the cultural world of the Livingstons and their social peers bore little resemblance to that of their ancestors. Riding a wave of prosperity and commercialization, New York was transformed, within the space of a generation, from a rustic colonial outpost to a mature provincial society offering the benefits of both city and country life to those who could afford them. New York City, in particular, offered luxuries and entertainments that had not been available in America as recently as the 1720s.[26] By 1757, the historian William Smith, Jr., was boasting that New York City had become "one of the most social places on the continent" of North America. Although Smith was somewhat of a booster, the Reverend Jonathan Boucher of Maryland concurred with that judgment when he suggested that George Washington send his stepson to New York for his education. "[New York] is inhabited by some People of the most considerable Rank and Fortune," wrote Boucher. "It is a Place of the greatest Resort for Strangers of Distinction . . . and . . . is, I am told, generally reckon'd the most fashionable and polite Place on the Continent. As a Situation, therefore, for a young Gentleman, who is to be educated a little in the World as well as in Books, it wou'd Seem, that it deserves the Preference."[27]

---

[25] *New-York Gazette,* 11 Aug. 1760; *New-York Post-Boy,* 6 June 1765, 3 July 1766; *New-York Mercury,* 5 July 1768, 9 Mar., 17 Aug. 1772, 17 May 1773. On early English spas and public gardens, see Peter Clark and Paul Slack, *English Towns in Transition, 1500–1700* (Oxford, 1976), p. 36.

[26] Theater and light opera also first came to New York—and to America—during the second third of the eighteenth century. See Dixon Ryan Fox, "The Development of the American Theatre," *NY Hist.,* 17 (1936): 24; and Joseph Borome, "The Origins of Grand Opera in New York," ibid., 27 (1946): 169–78.

[27] Smith, *History,* 1:226; Boucher to Washington, 1770, quoted in Philip J. Greven, *The Protestant Temperament: Patterns of Child-Rearing, Religious Experience, and the Self in Early America* (New York, 1977), p. 288. Most scholars agree that Philadelphia, not New York, was the most cosmopolitan colonial city. See Bridenbaugh, *Cities in Revolt;*

Some provincials, however, condemned the increased appeal of high society and the decadence that its diversions seemed to encourage. The spread of anglicized elegance in late colonial New York was symptomatic of a cultural transformation that had engulfed most of British North America and everywhere elicited the censure of moralists who equated luxury with corruption. Although the New England clergy and the Virginia Baptists were probably the foremost advocates of moral reformation, a vocal minority in every colony warned their countrymen against the baneful effects of pride, profanity, and dissipation.[28] For instance, the observations of John Watts, a prosperous New York merchant, completely contradicted Boucher's account of Manhattan's manifold advantages. Watts condemned his native city as "the worst School for Youth of any of his Majesty's Dominions," and he lamented that, for most New Yorkers, "Ignorance, Vanity, Dress, and Dissipation [were] the reigning Characteristics of their insipid Lives."[29]

New York's most vocal and persistent social critic was William Livingston, the lawyer grandson of Robert and Alida who attained renown both as a factional leader and as a public-spirited pamphleteer in the late colonial era. As early as 1746, William privately christened Manhattan a "second Sodom"; a few years later, he publicly warned New Yorkers that the "annihilating Amusements" currently in vogue engendered both moral and intellectual degeneration. Such diversions, wrote Livingston in 1753, "are now become the reigning Employments of the Age, and . . . of too many of my Fellow Citizens of both Sexes; among those especially who call themselves the Polite and Well-bred. Hours, Days and Months, are sordidly wasted in one continued Circle of such trifling Amusements," much to the consternation of those who, like Livingston, valued reason and virtue. Following the Anglo-American Radical Whig tradition, Livingston warned that idleness and frivolity also would lead to political corruption. "The Dangers flowing from Luxury are evi-

---

Eric Foner, *Tom Paine and Revolutionary America* (New York, 1976), chap. 2; Henry F. May, *The Enlightenment in America* (New York, 1976), pp. 80–86, 197–222.

[28] For evidence of elites' perception of corruption and moral decay, see Jack P. Greene, "Search for Identity: An Interpretation of the Meaning of Selected Patterns of Social Response in Eighteenth-Century America," *Journal of Social History*, 4(1970): 189–220.

[29] Quoted in Bridenbaugh, *Cities in Revolt*, p. 318.

dent," he insisted, "[and] all wise Legislators have considered public Prodigality as the Bane of Society, a Kind of political Cancer which corrodes and demolishes the best regulated Constitution." Others echoed Livingston's distaste for urban amenities and entertainments. For instance, a young John Adams found little to admire in New England's metropolis, "that noisy, dirty Town of Boston, where Parade, Pomp, Nonsense, Frippery, Folly, Foppery, Luxury, [and] Polliticks" made him appreciate the "Spirit, Taste, and Sense" of his life outside the city limits.[30]

Both the Radical Whig tradition and the Protestant ethic taught provincials that luxury caused moral, political, and social degeneration. Consequently, many colonial elites were ambivalent toward their own genteel style of living. They enjoyed their balls, concerts, and country homes, but they also worried about the baneful effects of luxury and ostentation. Like his grandparents Robert and Alida, William Livingston expected his children to work hard to become self-sufficient and successful. He, like other members of the third generation of American Livingstons, prepared his children for useful and productive vocations, though he also expected them to become gentlemen and ladies who could shine in polite society.

Robert and Alida's descendants knew their wealth and status enabled them to give their children many advantages, but they also expected their offspring to make the most of these opportunities. For example, when Philip Livingston sent his eldest son, Robert Livingston, Jr., to New Rochelle to learn French, he repeatedly instructed the boy to work diligently so "that I may not give my money for nothing." Philip later chastised his youngest son, William, for neglecting his legal studies. As adults, both William and Robert were equally vigilant of their own sons' behavior, expecting to be informed regularly of their progress in school and ready to admonish them for their lack of industry. As a child, William had practiced his penmanship by recopying moralistic adages extolling the virtues of industry and perseverance; as an adult, he sought to perpetuate these values among his descendants. William praised his young

---

[30] Livingston et al., *Independent Reflector*, pp. 257, 405; Livingston to Noah Welles, 17 Sept. 1746, Livingston-Welles Corres.; John Adams to Abigail Smith, 14 Feb. 1763, in L. H. Butterfield et al., eds., *The Book of Abigail and John: Selected Letters of the Adams Family, 1762–1784* (Cambridge, Mass., 1975), p. 18. For similar sentiments, see also Greene, *Landon Carter*, pp. 22–26, 76–79.

grandson, Peter Jay, for applying himself to his studies and "improving in learning and knowledge," while urging the boy to "make as great progress in virtue & religion for that is of still greater importance."[31]

The Livingstons believed that youth was a time "to prepare for future usefulness." The pursuit of "usefulness" shaped the lives and aspirations of four generations of the Livingston family.[32] Usefulness meant industry, self-reliance, and success in one's calling. Robert and Alida's children had been called to be merchants and merchants' wives; their grandchildren and great-grandchildren were expected not only to work in such practical occupations but also to act as gentlemen and ladies, leaders and ornaments of their society. Not content to live lazily on his large inheritance, one fourth-generation Livingston declared, "I never will live an Idle life when I can make a sufficiency to maintain myself [because] without money . . . very few people will care to trust you because you are of a good family." But the sons of late colonial elites also recognized the value of a genteel education. Parents increasingly taught their children that learning was a social asset, "the only Qualification and Step to Raise [them] to Honour in this World."[33]

In planning their sons' careers, even very wealthy parents considered the material advantages that a given profession offered. For instance, Philip Livingston refused to allow his son William to go to Italy to study painting because he believed that a career in art would be frivolous and financially unrewarding. Because William had already failed as a merchant's apprentice, his father decided in 1742 that he should become a lawyer. Even after a family's fortune was

[31] Philip Livingston to Robert Livingston, Jr., 20 May, 3 Aug., 1724, Livingston-Redmond MSS., reel 7; Robert Livingston, Jr., to Robert Livingston (1654–1728), 23 Sept. 1723, ibid., reel 4; Robert Livingston, Jr., to Philip Livingston (1734–56), 24 Jan. 1753, Livingston Papers, MCNY, box 1; William Livingston to Noah Welles, 14 Nov. 1743, Livingston-Welles Corres.; William Livingston to Philip Livingston, 4 Dec. 1744, William Livingston Papers, Mass. Hist. Soc., reel 2; William Livingston to William Livingston, Jr., 16 Mar. 1782, ibid., reel 7; William Livingston to Peter Jay, 23 Feb. 1787, ibid., reel 9.

[32] The phrase is from John Henry Livingston's letter to his young brother Henry, 4 Feb. 1766, Livingston Family Papers, NYPL.

[33] Hendrick R. Hansen to Robert Livingston, Jr., 1 Jan. 1744, Livingston-Redmond MSS., reel 7; John R. Livingston to Robert R. Livingston, Jr., 18 June 1781, Robert R. Livingston Papers, NYHS, reel 2.

secured, parents remained primarily concerned about their children's material well-being. At mid-century, one prominent New Yorker observed that among his countrymen "the only principle [of] Life propagated among Young People is to get Money."[34]

Young New Yorkers took this lesson to heart and, like Robert and Alida's sons and grandsons, they overwhelmingly chose careers in commerce. Throughout the colonial period, trade offered the brightest promise of wealth and status for young New Yorkers whose parents had the connections and financial resources to apprentice them to a reputable mercantile establishment. By contrast, early New York had few full-time lawyers, and those who did practice law in the province were either disreputable "pettyfoggers" or had been fortunate and prosperous enough to have received an English education. By the middle of the eighteenth century, however, the law was becoming an attractive alternative for affluent young men, as professional organization and higher educational standards gradually enhanced both the profits and the prestige of the New York bar. Unlike the law, medicine remained both crude and disreputable through the Revolutionary era. The ministry, though always an honorable profession, was a relatively unpopular career choice among elites because doing God's work brought few economic and social advantages.[35]

While they continued to seek and to value diligence and material success, these eighteenth-century New Yorkers also became increasingly preoccupied with the aristocratic concept of noblesse oblige. They came to see themselves as a distinct governing class, and consequently sent their sons to college to acquire the knowledge and the public demeanor that would set them apart from their social

[34] Cadwallader Colden to SPG, 12 Dec. 1748, SPG Archives, Letter Book B; Milton M. Klein, "The American Whig: William Livingston of New York," (Ph.D. diss., Columbia University, 1954), pp. 71–72, 141n.

[35] On the legal profession in colonial New York, see Paul Hamlin, *Legal Education in Colonial New York* (New York, 1939), pp. 1–4; Bellomont to Board of Trade, 15 Dec. 1698, *DRNY*, 4:442; Milton M. Klein, "From Community to Status: The Development of the Legal Profession in Colonial New York," *NY Hist.*, 60 (1979): 133–56. For parallel developments in Massachusetts, see John M. Murrin, "The Legal Transformation: The Bench and Bar in Eighteenth-Century Massachusetts," in Stanley N. Katz and John M. Murrin, eds., *Colonial America: Essays in Politics and Social Development* (New York, 1983), pp. 540–63. On the medical profession, see Livingston et al., *Independent Reflector*, no. 12; Smith, *History*, 2:243.

inferiors. Philip Livingston, who sent four of his six sons to Yale, compared New Yorkers unfavorably to New Englanders, noting, "We have not such a publick Spirit here as you have among you nor ever will unless we have Some of your Education." Philip's son William repeatedly extolled the virtues of a liberal education and argued that a knowledge of the classics, in particular, was conducive to good citizenship and public-spiritedness. William maintained that without educated leaders, the people were susceptible to "Tyranny, Barbarism, ecclesiastical Domination, Superstition, Enthusiasm, corrupt Manners, and an irresistible confederate Host of Evils, to [a Country's] utter Ruin and Destruction."[36]

During the second quarter of the eighteenth century, the education of young men and women alike also developed an ornamental aspect as a result of the gentrification of Anglo-American elite culture. As participation in polite society became increasingly equated with wealth and prestige, education acquired a new social dimension. By the 1750s, even William Livingston, who was prone to stressing the moral and political benefits of education, also admitted that learning was "growing into Fashion" and therefore was indispensable to "making a figure in Life." Livingston was not alone in recognizing the social usefulness of education. No less an authority than John Witherspoon, president of the College of New Jersey, contended that politeness and sociability were among the many advantages conferred by a liberal education.[37] Like provincial elites elsewhere, prominent New Yorkers responded to these new social imperatives. Believing that they needed to be both wealthy and refined, they taught their children to emulate their usefulness but to surpass them in polite accomplishments.[38]

[36] Philip Livingston to Jacob Wendell, 17 June 1746, Livingston Papers, MCNY, box 2; Livingston et al., *Independent Reflector,* pp. 419–20; William Livingston to Peter R. Livingston, 10 Nov. 1758, William Livingston Papers, Mass. Hist. Soc., reel 2. See also Michael Kammen, *Colonial New York: A History* (New York, 1975), pp. 250–52. Many provincials shared William Livingston's high regard for the classics. See Bernard Bailyn, *The Ideological Origins of the American Revolution* (Cambridge, Mass., 1973), pp. 23–26; Gordon S. Wood, *The Creation of the American Republic, 1776–1787* (Chapel Hill, N.C., 1969), pp. 48–52.

[37] William Livingston to Peter R. Livingston, 10 Nov. 1758, William Livingston Papers, Mass. Hist. Soc., reel 2; John Witherspoon, *A Series of Letters on Education* (1775; New York, 1797), esp. pp. 61–62.

[38] David C. Humphrey, *From King's College to Columbia, 1746–1800* (New York,

Innovations in the education of the daughters of the gentry were the more substantial because, during the eighteenth century, the roles and functions of women changed more dramatically. A woman's duties as wife and mother were constant, but her subsidiary responsibilities changed over time, and the education of young women evolved to accommodate these changes. In the seventeenth century, colonial women, especially in sparsely settled or demographically unstable areas, had played many economic or entrepreneurial roles that were normally reserved for men.[39] As we have seen, Alida Schuyler was well versed in the ways of trade when she wed Robert Livingston in 1679, and she played an integral role in the family business during their forty-seven-year marriage. Nevertheless, in New York and elsewhere, female entrepreneurs like Alida became increasingly uncommon over the course of the eighteenth century. The more widespread enforcement of the English common law doctrine of coverture hampered the economic activities of married women, the growth of the provincial bar prompted husbands to employ lawyers instead of their wives as attorneys, and the development of family networks replete with male relatives rendered superfluous the business activities of most upper-class women.[40] Alida Livingston was her husband's business partner, but her

---

1976), chap. 6. On the growing regard for education among elites elsewhere in British colonial America, see Greene, *Landon Carter*, pp. 1–2; Isaac, *Transformation of Virginia*, pp. 81, 130; Daniel Blake Smith, *Inside the Great House: Planter Family Life in Eighteenth-Century Chesapeake Society* (Ithaca, N.Y., 1980), pp. 62–68, 89; Louis B. Wright, *The First Gentlemen of Virginia: Intellectual Qualities of the Early Colonial Ruling Class* (San Marino, Calif., 1940), pp. 38–62; Carl and Jessica Bridenbaugh, *Rebels and Gentlemen: Philadelphia in the Age of Franklin* (New York, 1942), pp. 180–90; Tolles, *Meeting House and Counting House*, pp. 133–43.

[39] See, for instance, Edmund S. Morgan, *American Slavery, American Freedom: The Ordeal of Colonial Virginia* (New York, 1975), pp. 164–70; Lois Green Carr and Lorena S. Walsh, "The Planter's Wife: The Experience of White Women in Seventeenth-Century Maryland," *WMQ*, 3d ser., 34 (1977): 542–71; Laurel Thatcher Ulrich, *Good Wives: Image and Reality in the Lives of Women in Northern New England, 1650–1750* (New York, 1982), chap. 2; Linda Briggs Biemer, *Women and Property in Colonial New York: The Transition from Dutch to English Law, 1643–1727*, Studies in American History and Culture 38 (Ann Arbor, Mich., 1983).

[40] Biemer, *Women and Property*, esp. chap. 1; Linda K. Kerber, *Women of the Republic: Intellect and Ideology in Revolutionary America* (Chapel Hill, N.C., 1980), chap. 4. On the displacement of wives by hired attorneys, see Joan R. Gunderson and Gwen Victor Gampel, "Married Women's Legal Status in Eighteenth-Century New York and Virginia," *WMQ*, 3d ser., 39 (1982): 133–34.

son Philip shared his entrepreneurial chores mainly with his sons and brothers.

As later generations delegated their business responsibilities to various male relatives, the public duties of elite women became primarily social rather than economic, and hospitality and sociability became increasingly important female attributes.[41] Because Alida Livingston had supervised her family's growing enterprises at Livingston Manor, she could justifiably scold her husband for sending her unannounced guests. In 1722, when Robert sent an unexpected visitor to Alida at the Manor, she sought lodging for her guest elsewhere and carried on with her business.[42]

Such a response would have been unthinkable for later generations of female Livingstons, who were not overwhelmed with business responsibilities and who were expected to be gracious and hospitable. Mary Stevens Livingston, for instance, was by all accounts an exemplary wife to Robert R. Livingston, Jr., chancellor of New York and one of the state's most prominent men during the Revolutionary era. Yet all we know of Mary is that she was a "polite, wellbred, sensible woman, of one of the best families in the State, and who brought a great property into the family." While Alida had been highly regarded for her business and administrative skills, Mary was widely admired for her unassuming devotion as a wife and mother and for her grace as a hostess and an ornament of New York society. By the Revolutionary era, grace and gentility had become the American gentlewoman's most admirable qualities. In 1778, Henry Beekman Livingston rejoiced in the marriage of his cousin, Robert Cambridge Livingston, to Alice Swift because the bride was "an amiable young Lady who will be an ornament to our Neighborhood."[43]

The introduction of high tea, dinner parties, balls, and other social functions had enhanced the visibility of women in provincial society. By the middle of the eighteenth century, the education of the

[41] An excellent summary of the changing images of women during this period is Ruth H. Bloch, "American Feminine Ideals in Transition: The Rise of the Moral Mother, 1785–1815," *Feminist Studies*, 4 (1978): 103, 108–16.

[42] Alida Livingston to Robert Livingston, 23 July 1722, in Linda Biemer, ed., "Business Letters of Alida Schuyler Livingston, 1680–1726," *NY Hist.*, 63 (1982): 205.

[43] Henry Beekman Livingston to Robert R. Livingston, Jr., 20 Nov. 1778, Robert R. Livingston Papers, NYHS, reel 1. On Mary Stevens Livingston, see Alonzo Potter's manuscript biography of Chancellor Robert R. Livingston, ibid., reel 15; and Strickland, *Journal of a Tour in the United States*, p. 119.

daughters of the elite was diversifying in order to prepare them for their new roles as aspiring belles and genteel ladies. Although the Livingston daughters continued to learn traditional domestic skills, their parents now considered lessons in French, music, and dancing equally useful. Some parents regarded their daughters' education as a matter of special importance. Philip Livingston made a provision in his will for educating his unmarried daughters, Alida and Catharine, age twenty-one and sixteen, respectively, when he died in 1749. Thirty years later, not even the ravages of war and revolution disrupted the dancing lessons of the Livingston girls at Clermont.[44]

While most daughters learned their lessons from hired tutors in their homes, some went elsewhere to acquire their education. In the pre-Revolutionary era, Robert R. Livingston's daughters Margaret and Gertrude studied French at New Rochelle. Alida Livingston, youngest daughter of the third lord of the Manor, spent the winter of 1762 in New York City residing with a married sister. Alida's sojourn in the provincial capital was not a mere vacation; her father had sent her to Manhattan to "improve" herself, warning that she "must not Spend her time Idlely." Likewise, James Duane sent his daughter to Philadelphia in 1781 because "she wanted this opportunity of polite Company to give her the Accomplishments which tho' inferior to those of the Mind are essential to her Rank."[45]

While the educational opportunities of some young women thus expanded perceptibly by the Revolutionary era, they did so primarily to make women more agreeable companions for men. Both William Livingston and William Smith, Jr., complained that frivolous and insipid women made bad company; they applauded female education as a means to promote virtue, good conversation, and pleasant society. Similarly, Colonel Alexander Hamilton enjoined his fiancée, Elizabeth Schuyler of Albany, to spend all her leisure time reading, because as her husband he would take pride in her accomplishment and "it will be a fund too, to diversify our enjoyments and

[44] Will of Philip Livingston, 15 July 1748, Livingston-Redmond MSS., reel 6; Margaret Beekman Livingston to Robert R. Livingston, Jr., 4 June 1782, Robert R. Livingston Papers, NYHS, reel 2.

[45] Margaret Livingston to Robert Livingston (1688–1775), 27 Oct. 1761, Robert R. Livingston Papers, NYHS, reel 1; Robert Livingston, Jr., to James Duane, 16 Oct. 1762, Misc. MSS., Robert Livingston, Jr., NYHS; James Duane to Mary Livingston Duane, 20 Feb. [1781], Duane Papers, NYHS, box 4; Julia Delafield, *Biographies of Francis Lewis and Morgan Lewis,* 2 vols. (New York, 1877), 1:152–57, 224.

amusements and fill all our moments to advantage."[46] The prescriptive literature of the period echoed these sentiments, arguing that women should cultivate their minds in order to attract and entertain men, the best of whom admired "simplicity, softness, a sedate carriage, and rational conversation." Contemporary moralists upheld virtue and graciousness as the new feminine ideal: women should be accomplished but not assertive, ornamental but not vain.[47]

This new genteel code of feminine behavior did not automatically debase women or deprive them of personal fulfillment. The advent of high society and the gentility it fostered gave women new social authority as the arbiters of good taste and decorum. The elite's growing regard for learning and refinement also gave some women opportunities for genuine intellectual growth.

By the middle decades of the eighteenth century, the increased availability of books, along with a desire to excel in polite conversation, encouraged young women to read far more than had their mothers and grandmothers. Such serious tomes as Smollett's *History of England* and Alexander Pope's *Works* accompanied the daughters of Robert R. Livingston on a summer visit to Clermont. Their future sister-in-law, Nancy Shippen Livingston, was an equally enthusiastic reader, whose favorites included Milton's poetry and Goethe's *Sorrows of Young Werter*. William Livingston's daughters were familiar with their father's political writings and wrote and received letters that revealed a detailed understanding of contemporary politics. Susannah Livingston, who served as her father's personal secretary, counted *Don Quixote, Robinson Crusoe*, and Noel Antoine Pluche's *Nature Delineated* among her personal favorites; these books, along with the Bible, were some of the basic texts Susannah used when she tutored her nephew Peter Jay in the 1770s.[48] Some—but by no

---

46 William Livingston to [Susannah French], 4 Oct. 1744, William Livingston Papers, Mass. Hist. Soc., reel 2; Smith, *History*, 1:227; Alexander Hamilton to Elizabeth Schuyler, [2–4 July 1780], in *The Papers of Alexander Hamilton*, ed. Harold C. Syrett and Jacob E. Cooke, 26 vols. (New York, 1960–79), 2:351.

47 James Fordyce, *Character and Conduct of the Female Sex* . . . , 3d ed. (Boston, 1781), pp. 11, 27–28, 39–43; John Gregory, *A Father's Legacy to His Daughters* (New York, 1775), pp. 8, 14–24.

48 Robert R. Livingston to Robert Livingston (1688–1775), 24 Aug. 1765, Robert R. Livingston Papers, NYHS, reel 1; Ethel Armes, ed., *Nancy Shippen, Her Journal Book* . . . (Philadelphia, 1935), pp. 141, 185; Catharine Livingston to Sarah Livingston Jay, 21 Nov. 1777, in Morris, ed., *John Jay: The Making of a Revolutionary*, pp. 448–49;

means all—of these well-informed young women added disclaimers to their letters, apologizing for their interest in and knowledge of traditionally male-dominated matters. On the other hand, the fact that they had this knowledge at all indicated a significant broadening of the intellectual horizons of colonial gentlewomen.[49]

Like their sisters, young gentlemen also came to value ornamental learning during the closing decades of the colonial era. As we have seen, Robert and Alida's sons had received only practical vocational training. Their more prosperous descendants continued to serve mercantile or legal apprenticeships, but they did so after learning Latin and Greek and receiving a gentleman's university education. Philip Livingston sent four of his six sons to Yale; of Philip's twenty grandsons, at least thirteen attended college either in England or in America. Robert R. Livingston, only child of Philip's brother, Robert Livingston of Clermont, was trained as a lawyer but did not attend college; of his four sons, however, Robert R. Livingston, Jr., received his baccalaureate from King's College, while Edward graduated from the College of New Jersey.[50]

Formerly the bastions of studious ministerial candidates, colonial colleges in the eighteenth century became finishing schools for the

Sarah Livingston Jay to Catharine Livingston, 1 Dec. 1780, in Richard B. Morris, ed., *John Jay: The Winning of the Peace, Unpublished Papers, 1780–1784* (New York, 1980), p. 171; Catharine Livingston to John Jay, 30 Dec. 1783, ibid., p. 671; William Livingston to Sarah Livingston Jay, 21 Aug. 1781, ibid., pp. 199–200; William Livingston to Catharine Livingston, 16 Nov. 1779, quoted in Theodore Sedgwick, Jr., *A Memoir of the Life of William Livingston* (New York, 1833), p. 340. See also the many letters exchanged by Matthew Ridley and his future wife, Catharine Livingston (Matthew Ridley Papers, Mass. Hist. Soc.). On the increased availability of books in New York after 1740, see Edwin D. Hoffman, "The Bookshops of New York City, 1743–1948," *NY Hist.*, 30 (1949): 53–54.

[49] Kerber, *Women of the Republic*, pp. 35, 76–79. For a much drearier portrait of female education in the pre-Revolutionary era, see Mary Beth Norton, *Liberty's Daughters: The Revolutionary Experience of American Women, 1750–1800* (Boston, 1980), pp. 257–63.

[50] Based on material in *Columbia University Alumni Register, 1754–1931* (New York, 1932); Franklin Bowditch Dexter, *Biographical Sketches of the Graduates of Yale College with Annals of the College History*, 6 vols. (New York, 1885–1912); *Dictionary of American Biography*; Richard A. Harrison, *Princetonians, 1769–1775: A Biographical Dictionary* and *Princetonians, 1776–1783: A Biographical Dictionary* (Princeton, 1980, 1981); James McLachlan, *Princetonians, 1748–1768: A Biographical Dictionary* (Princeton, 1976); John Langdon Sibley and Clifford K. Shipton, *Sibley's Harvard Graduates: Biographical Sketches of Those Who Attended Harvard College* (Boston, 1873–).

sons of the provincial gentry. Robert Livingston, Jr., the third lord of the Manor and the first of his family to play the part of the country squire, wanted all his sons to attend college and required that their childhood tutor have not only a liberal education but also "Something of the Gentleman in his Behaviour." New Yorkers established King's College in 1754 partly in response to the elite's desire to give their sons fashionably genteel educations. Because most of the Livingstons belonged to Dutch Reformed or Presbyterian congregations, they avoided sending their sons to King's because of its affiliation with the Church of England. As Protestant Dissenters, they patronized first the Congregationalist New England schools and later the newer Presbyterian College of New Jersey.[51]

While some young men undoubtedly valued knowledge for its own sake, many saw their attendance at an institution of higher learning primarily as preparation for success in genteel society. At the universities and at London's Inns of Court, young gentlemen mingled with their social peers and made important social contacts. During their college years, they also acquired at least a veneer of knowledge and sophistication. One young New Yorker was content to be at London's Middle Temple because his friends there were "Gentlmen of considerable fortunes" whose society he enjoyed thoroughly. Colonists paid handsomely to send their sons in increasing numbers to the prestigious Inns of Court, though by the eighteenth century those institutions had ceased to serve any genuine educational function.[52]

Some youths educated at home in America took an equally superficial view of the overriding objectives of a college education. In 1756, after a disastrous three years at Harvard, Peter R.

---

[51] William Livingston to Noah Welles, 18 Feb. 1749, Livingston-Welles Corres.; William Livingston to [?], 6 Dec. 1787, William Livingston Papers, Mass. Hist. Soc., reel 9; Humphrey, *From King's College to Columbia*, esp. pp. 85–86. Efforts to raise money to establish a college in New York began as early as 1746, though the school did not open until eight years later. On the changing clientele of colonial colleges, see Samuel Eliot Morison, *Three Centuries of Harvard, 1636–1936* (Cambridge, Mass., 1946), pp. 59–60, 110–23; Isaac, *Transformation of Virginia*, p. 130. Judge Robert R. Livingston and his children were members of the Church of England, but Philip Livingston and his descendants attended either the Dutch Reformed church or the Presbyterian church.

[52] Philip Peter Livingston to William Alexander, 25 Oct. 1762, William Alexander Papers, NYHS, vol. 3; Hamlin, *Legal Education*, p. 17.

Livingston—son of the lord of the Manor—enrolled in the College of New Jersey "to get what Knowledge I can, see[ing] it['s] so vastly necessary for the forming of a Man." Peter judged colleges according to their external styles and rituals; he initially disliked the New Jersey school because he believed Harvard's commencement ceremonies were far more impressive. In the end, Peter probably got what he wanted from his college experience. When he left the college without his degree in 1758, his spelling and grammar remained substandard, but he could feign erudition by quoting phrases from Horace and Seneca. Peter's studious uncle William censured his nephew's neglect of his studies and his failure to earn his bachelor's degree. Although William Livingston certainly appreciated the intrinsic value of knowledge, he also believed that learning was becoming socially desirable and that it would be "a Scandalous Reflection on a Gentleman of Distinction not to have the best Education the Country can afford."[53]

Despite their growing regard for gentility and fashionable learning, affluent New Yorkers remained consistently intolerant of idleness and frivolity. If the increasing cultural distinctiveness of the provincial gentry required that a man possess at least the rudiments of polite learning, the elite's continued commitment to usefulness and material success dictated that he must pursue some profitable vocation. Philip Livingston had sent most of his sons to college, but he also expected them to become self-supporting. "I do not bring any of my sons up for Idleness," he informed a friend, "but to mind Some Imployment or other or Else youth are deluded & brought over to bad Company & begett All vices." A generation later, the Livingstons' belief in the importance of work and self-reliance remained unaltered. Robert Livingston, Jr., sent his son Walter to Cambridge but ordered him to return home when he thought it was "high time for him to be put in away of business."[54]

[53] Peter R. Livingston to Oliver Wendell, 12 Aug., 12 Oct. 1756, 7 Jan. 1760, Livingston Papers, MCNY, box 1; Sibley and Shipton, *Harvard Graduates*, 14:183–84; William Livingston to Peter R. Livingston, 10 Nov. 1758, William Livingston Papers, Mass. Hist. Soc., reel 2.

[54] Philip Livingston to Jacob Wendell, 23 May 1738, Livingston Papers, MCNY, box 2; Robert Livingston, Jr., to James Duane, 22 Nov. 1763, 9 Nov. 1764, Duane Papers, NYHS, box 1.

Like Virginia planters whose public reputations were tied to their abilities as farmers and plantation managers, New York elites continued to see dependence and occupational failure as sources of public embarrassment. When Peter R. Livingston's extravagance and poor business sense forced him to bankruptcy in 1771, his relations tried to keep the matter confidential while privately lamenting the family's disgrace. "Cousin Robert is quite unfortunate in his Children," noted Robert R. Livingston of Clermont. "His Eldest son goes up in the Spring to live at the Manor & his good & generous father will be obliged to advance eleven thousand Pounds for him after which [Peter] will not be worth one groat." Peter's father paid his debts and gave him a place to live in order to preserve the family's honor. His obvious irresponsibility, however, forced Robert Livingston, Jr., to break the entail on Livingston Manor in order to save the family land. Like his ancestor Gilbert Livingston, Peter was arrogant, incompetent, and "not worth one groat." Like Gilbert, he too fell into disfavor.[55]

Protestantism and its enduring social ethic reinforced the elite's commitment to the morality of work and individual usefulness. Robert R. Livingston of Clermont, who had condemned Peter's lack of initiative and self-reliance, was a notably pious man who at least rhetorically attributed both good fortune and adversity to the mysterious workings of divine providence. He surely viewed material prosperity as a sign of God's favor, but he also believed that a righteous man had to pursue some useful calling in order to be so rewarded. As a father, he encouraged his eldest son, Robert R. Livingston, Jr., to apply himself to his legal studies because, although he would inherit a vast estate, righteousness demanded that he use his God-given talents "to be at the head of his profession." The elder Robert R. Livingston also believed that man had no choice but to trust in God completely, noting that "Whoever places his

---

[55] Robert R. Livingston to Robert Livingston (1688–1775), 11 Jan. 1771, Robert R. Livingston Papers, NYHS, reel 1; Robert Cambridge Livingston to James Duane, 26 Dec. 1774, Duane Papers, NYHS, box 3; Codicil to the will of Robert Livingston, Jr., [1771], Livingston Papers, MCNY, box 3. On the relationship between vocational success and public reputation among Virginia's gentry, see T. H. Breen, "Back to Sweat and Toil: Suggestions for the Study of Agricultural Work in Early America," *Pennsylvania History,* 49 (1982): 248, 252; and Breen, *Tobacco Culture,* chap. 2; Charles S. Sydnor, *Gentlemen Freeholders* (Chapel Hill, N.C., 1959), pp. 15–17.

Happiness on the Enjoyments of this World will surely be disappointed." A good man could value worldly goods so long as he realized that wealth was a gift from God and accordingly made the divine benefactor—and not the gift itself—the object of his worship. Thus, the pious Robert R. Livingston could thank God for his beneficence while observing, with great satisfaction, that his expected inheritances from both the Livingston and Beekman fortunes would eventually make him the "Richest Man in the whole Government."[56]

Robert R. Livingston's attitudes toward wealth and religion placed him squarely within a Protestant tradition that included most of his fellow colonists. Philadelphia's Quaker merchants, Virginia's great planters, and even the businessmen of colonial New England espoused a similar world view that valued industry and perseverance as a means to wealth, and material prosperity as a sign of divine favor. James Logan, a Quaker fur trader and William Penn's erstwhile secretary, had attributed his great success to "God's Blessing [and] my own Industry and management." Similarly, Landon Carter of Virginia noted, "I do the best I can and relye on Superiour mercy for the success of my endeavours." Like Carter, John Hull, a seventeenth-century Boston merchant, routinely asked divine protection for his business transactions and gave credit to God's providence for his most successful ventures. Hull's work ethic was remarkably similar to that of Philip Livingston, the eighteenth-century Albany merchant and second lord of Livingston Manor. Philip hoped that "with Gods blessing & their honest just Endeavers" his sons would become successful merchants and "Distinguish themselves in the world." When his eldest son, Robert Livingston, Jr., suffered a series of commercial setbacks, Philip reminded him, "We ought not to murmur & grumble at the all wise dispensations of our Creator but

[56] Robert R. Livingston to Robert Livingston (1688–1775), 17 Mar. 1762, 26 Nov. 1764, Robert R. Livingston Papers, NYHS, reel 1; Robert R. Livingston to Margaret Beekman Livingston, 25 June 1765, Livingston Family Papers, NYPL, box 3; Catharine Livingston Garretson to George Bancroft, 22 Sept. 1843, Bancroft Transcripts, NYPL, 1:99–100. Significantly, Colin Campbell has found in Calvinism the roots of both the Weberian work ethic and the culture of consumption that emerged in England and America during the eighteenth century. His work helps explain the apparent contradiction within Anglo-American elite values and suggests that those values—combining work and gentility—were in fact similar to those of England's rising entrepreneurial class (Colin Campbell, *The Romantic Ethic and the Spirit of Modern Consumerism* [London, 1987]).

patiently Submitt to his will." Attempting to console his distraught son, Philip added his best wishes that "the Almighty will be pleased to Prosper and bless your Just Endeavours for the future that you may Soon Retrieve the Maney Losses you have mett with."[57]

Provincial elites throughout America shared the Livingstons' continuing commitment to work and individual usefulness. They also shared a growing regard for learning and self-improvement. Indeed, it was through their perception of the value of education that affluent provincials were best able to reconcile the contradictory components of their emerging elite ethos. On the one hand, laboring to improve one's mind reaffirmed the elite's commitment to the values of work and usefulness; on the other hand, education also served an ornamental purpose, enabling those who possessed it to be accepted and appreciated in polite society. But learning also acquired a wider social purpose during the late colonial period, as members of the elite formed clubs and associations dedicated to the promotion and discussion of "useful" knowledge. While Benjamin Franklin's Philadelphia-based American Philosophical Society, founded in 1743, was the most notable of these organizations, colonial elites elsewhere founded their own local societies to exchange ideas with their social and intellectual peers. A group of prominent New Yorkers established their Society for the Promotion of Useful Knowledge in 1744. The elder Robert R. Livingston was among the Society's charter members.[58]

The aristocratic ideal that wealthy provincials sought to emulate had two sides: one emphasizing gentility and cultural refinement for the pleasure of the individual, the other stressing noblesse oblige, or the idea that the most highly placed members of a society were responsible for the welfare of the community. Consequently, the closing decades of the colonial era were a time of increased voluntarism and civic-mindedness among provincial elites throughout

[57] Philip Livingston to Storke and Gainsborough, 13 Nov. 1735, Livingston Family Letters, AAS; Philip Livingston to Robert Livingston, Jr., 1 June 1745, Livingston-Redmond MSS., reel 7; Tolles, *Meeting House and Counting House*, p. 57; Greene, *Landon Carter*, p. 37; Samuel Eliot Morison, *Builders of the Bay Colony* (Boston, 1930), pp. 169–70. See also Michael Walzer, "Puritanism as a Revolutionary Ideology," *History and Theory*, 3 (1964–65): 59–90, and Greene, "Search for Identity," esp. pp. 193–95.

[58] Beverly McAnear, "Politics in Provincial New York, 1689–1761" (Ph.D. diss., Stanford University, 1935), p. 543; Robert R. Livingston to Cadwallader Colden, 16 Mar. 1744, Robert R. Livingston Papers, NYHS, reel 1.

America. For instance, during the middle decades of the eighteenth century, colonial elites founded the first American libraries. Philadelphians again led the way by establishing the Library Company of Philadelphia in 1731; Newport, Rhode Island, established its subscription library in 1747; and the citizens of Charleston, South Carolina, founded the South's first library the following year. In 1754, six prominent New Yorkers—William Alexander, Philip Livingston, Robert R. Livingston, William Livingston, John Morin Scott, and William Smith, Jr.—raised £600 to create their province's first circulating library. More than one hundred New York gentlemen were charter subscribers to the New York Society Library, an institution dedicated to promoting "a spirit of inquiry among the people" of the province.[59] In New York, the library movement was closely related to concurrent efforts to found the colony's first college. Of the twelve men elected to the Society Library's first board of trustees in 1755, eight had already been installed among the first governors of King's College.

While the founders of the colleges, libraries, and learned societies catered to the elite's growing taste for knowledge, they also hoped that these institutions would benefit all the inhabitants of their respective communities. William Livingston—founding member of the New York Society Library as well as a leader in the movement to found a college—also unsuccessfully sought to persuade the provincial assembly to establish two grammar schools in each of New York's counties in order to give talented youths easier access to a college preparatory education. Livingston believed that such a plan would benefit both the students and the community, whose taxes would subsidize their studies. "Knowledge among a People," he asserted, "makes them free, enterprizing and dauntless; but Ignorance enslaves, emasculates and depresses them."[60]

Elites undertook other, more successful, projects intended to alleviate existing social ills. Voluntary associations proliferated in pre-Revolutionary America, and some of these concerned themselves

---

[59] Austin Baker Keep, *History of the New York Society Library* (New York, 1908), pp. 5, 132–36; Thomas Bender, *New York Intellect: A History of Intellectual Life in New York City, from 1750 to the Beginnings of Our Own Time* (New York, 1987), pp. 18–25; Smith, *History*, 2:150; Tolles, *Meeting House and Counting House*, p. 155; Bridenbaugh, *Cities in Revolt*, pp. 181–82.

[60] Livingston et al., *Independent Reflector*, no. 50.

primarily with benevolent or philanthropic activities. New Yorkers again lagged far behind the Quakers of Philadelphia, though the rise of philanthropy in both cities was significant when compared to the virtual absence of such activities in the early colonial period. In New York, the Society for the Promotion of Arts, formed in 1764, purported to "advance husbandry, promote Manufactures, and suppress Luxury" but was most active in providing employment for the urban poor. In the 1760s, the Society's main project was raising money to encourage the manufacture of linen; after collecting £600, they saved "many penurious Persons . . . from Beggary, and great Expence to the [City] by relieving Numbers of distressed Women" who were forced to return to the poor house when the linen venture eventually failed.[61] Founded in 1756 as a drinking club for men of Scottish extraction, the St. Andrew's Society regularly collected money to relieve the city's poor and also employed "poor scots Women" to spin flax, wool, and cotton in 1762.[62] In 1773, a group of New York gentlemen formed the American Society for the Promoting of Religious Knowledge among the Poor and, in 1771, prominent New Yorkers followed the example of Philadelphia's Quaker humanitarians by establishing New York's first hospital to engage in medical research and improve public health.[63]

To be sure, increased philanthropy came only in response to the growth of poverty in America's urban communities. Moreover, the elites' desire to alleviate poverty owed as much to their desire to control the poor as it did to their newfound sense of social responsibility.[64] But the very notion of noblesse oblige implies both social responsibility and social control; late colonial elites sought to control the poor because they believed the poor were incapable of controlling themselves.

Aristocratic notions of social leadership and noblesse oblige were

---

[61] Circular of the Society for the Promotion of Arts, 10 Dec. 1764, *DHNY*, 4:344–45; *New-York Post-Boy*, 31 Dec. 1767.

[62] *New-York Post-Boy*, 18 Feb. 1762; *New-York Mercury*, 5 Dec. 1757, 15 Dec. 1760.

[63] Singleton, *Social New York under the Georges*, pp. 376–77; Harrington, *New York Merchant*, p. 376. The Pennsylvania Hospital had been established in 1751. On philanthropy and benevolence in colonial cities, in general, see Bridenbaugh, *Cities in Revolt*, pp. 319–25.

[64] Gary B. Nash, "Urban Wealth and Poverty in Pre-Revolutionary America," *Journal of American History*, 6 (1975–76): 547–76; and Gary B. Nash, "Poverty and Poor Relief in Pre-Revolutionary Philadelphia," *WMQ*, 3d ser., 33 (1976): 3–30.

most influential in shaping the changing attitudes of provincial elites toward politics and their own roles in the political process. As elites came to view themselves as a distinctly privileged and well-informed social group, they increasingly translated this perception to the political arena, where they presented themselves to their social inferiors as a class uniquely qualified to govern in the best interests of the community. Of course, New York's elite was divided into competing factions during the entire colonial era. But the political rhetoric of late colonial elites suggests that noblesse oblige and interest group politics were not necessarily incompatible.

Although the wealthy always had dominated provincial politics, this newly self-conscious colonial elite sought not only to exploit the political process for their own gain but also to instruct and influence their social inferiors on a plethora of current issues. The main vehicle they used to achieve this end was the political essay, or pamphlet—genres that the colonists produced in remarkable quantities in the closing decades of the colonial era. The colonists published more than 400 pamphlets on imperial issues alone between 1750 and 1776; other writers addressed less momentous issues both in pamphlets and in essays printed in colonial newspapers. These pamphleteers and essayists expected neither material profit nor popular acclaim for the polemics they wrote. As "Atticus" observed in 1758, "A Writer who would employ his Genius in the Service of the Public, must have Constancy enough to bear the severest Reproaches; and a Resolution to suffer the *Martyrdom* of his Reputation." Nearly thirty years later, John Adams echoed these sentiments, candidly—and correctly—predicting that his ponderous *Defence of the Constitution* "will make me unpopular."[65]

The men who wrote colonial pamphlets in the pre-Revolutionary era were trained not as writers but as merchants, lawyers, clergymen, and planters.[66] That such men should take the time to instruct their readers in the great issues of the Anglo-American conflict is not surprising, but the same men also spoke out passionately on numerous less momentous issues. Carl Bridenbaugh's early work

[65] The quotation from "Atticus" is reprinted in Klein, ed., *Independent Reflector,* pp. 86–87. For Adams, see Wood, *Creation of the American Republic,* p. 581. On pamphlets in eighteenth-century America, see Bailyn, *Ideological Origins of the American Revolution,* pp. 1–2, 8.

[66] Bailyn, *Ideological Origins of the American Revolution,* pp. 14–15.

on urban life in British America showed that the late colonial period was one of civic improvements and public-spiritedness in leading cities throughout the colonies. Urban leaders formed fire companies, improved water supplies, supported road-building and maintenance, and attempted to discourage crime by improving the security of city streets. Although Benjamin Franklin of Philadelphia was, perhaps, the most famous and energetic of these late colonial civic leaders, his contemporaries in other cities promoted similar projects designed to improve the quality of life in their respective communities.[67]

In New York, the best example of elite activism and civic-mindedness was *The Independent Reflector*, a series of essays that appeared in the *New-York Post-Boy* in the early 1750s. The authors of the *Reflector*—the so-called "triumvirate" of William Livingston, William Smith, Jr., and John Morin Scott—sought to use their pens to reform the vices they found pervasive in their community. In order to inspire their readers to act, they imitated the shrill and irreverent style of Trenchard and Gordon's *Independent Whig*, one of the most popular English publications in pre-Revolutionary America. Like *The Independent Whig*, the *Reflector* espoused Radical Whig principles and employed the republican idiom to acquaint its readers with a variety of issues worthy of public attention. In language laden with republican significance, the *Reflector* thus announced in 1752 its literary designs for "vindicating the *civil and religious RIGHTS* of [our] Fellow-Creatures . . . exposing the peculiar Deformity of publick *Vice*, and *Corruption;* and displaying the amiable Charms of *Liberty*, with the detestable Nature of *Slavery* and *Oppression*."[68]

While many of the *Reflector* essays denounced Anglican attempts to attain control of New York's proposed college, the three New Yorkers also stridently instructed their readers on other seemingly less momentous issues. Fire engines, physicians, funerals, immigration policy, the city-watch, and riparian land rights were all considered fair game for the city's leading polemicists, who treated such

---

[67] Bridenbaugh, *Cities in Revolt*, chap. 8.

[68] See Klein, intro. to Livingston et al., *Independent Reflector*, pp. 3, 20–21, and app. 3; Livingston et al., *Independent Reflector*, p. 56; Bailyn, *Ideological Origins of the American Revolution*, pp. 35–36. In general, see also Dorothy Rita Dillon, *The New York Triumvirate: A Study of the Legal and Political Careers of William Livingston, John Morin Scott, and William Smith, Jr.* (New York, 1949).

relatively mundane matters with the same vigor and vehemence they showed toward their community's most controversial political matters. The authors of the *Reflector*, for instance, praised New Yorkers' quick response to fire alarms as "a Glaring Attestation of their public Spirit and exemplary Devotion to their Country" but then urged the implementation of more efficient methods of fire-fighting, noting their "Reluctance, at sparing the Rod, where Correction is necessary." Urging the adoption of a law to regulate the practice of medicine, the *Reflector* inveighed against the city's unqualified physicians—"those merciless Butchers of Human Kind"—lamenting that "we are tenacious of our *Property,* and justly glory in Laws wisely calculated for the Preservation of our Possessions, [but] how preposterous is our Conduct, in trusting our *Persons* to murderous Quacks, and licens'd Assassins!" The authors used an essay on the "Extravagance of our Funerals" as a vehicle to attack luxury in general and to urge the elite's responsibility to set a virtuous example for the rest of society by "suppressing this fantastical and inconvenient piece of Luxury." They also deplored the immigration of "mendicant foreigners," who were "absolutely incapable of advancing the Interest of the Countries into which they are imported," and they proclaimed the city-watch "a Grievance of the first Magnitude" because the men it employed were often "idle, drunken, vigilant Snorers, who never quelled any nocturnal Tumult in their Lives." The *Reflector* also asserted that selling water-lots by private petition rather than at public vendue was "inexcusable and unjust" because such favoritism violated the property rights of the entire city. Comparing New York with Pennsylvania—"a Province renown'd for its public Spirit"—the authors also accused their countrymen of neglecting to inspect their meat and butter exports properly, to the great detriment of their commercial reputation. In addition, they extolled New York's natural advantages and sought to instill in its citizens a sense of civic pride and public spirit.[69]

Polemics dealing with matters small and great became voluminous during the decades preceding the Revolution; most of these tracts were written by the colonies' leading citizens. These men wrote more

---

[69] Livingston et al., *Independent Reflector,* pp. 73, 84, 96–97, 140, 155, 221, 259, 433–39. The authors also planned essays dealing with pollution, jailhouses, and lighthouses, among other topics of purely local interest (ibid., pp. 441–45).

than their ancestors had because printing presses were more accessible and aspiring writers had more leisure time and more great political issues on which to comment. But late colonial elites also wrote because they believed it was their duty, as the natural governors of their society, to instruct their less learned countrymen in the ongoing controversies of local, provincial, and imperial affairs. As William Livingston noted with regard to his defense of the rights of Moravians to live and worship unmolested, "The Town is not yet ripe for Seeing plain Truth; The Veil must be removed from their eyes by slow degrees."[70] Livingston and others like him believed it was their responsibility to expose the "plain Truth" and to inspire their readers to take proper public action.

Such men were also devoting more of their time to acting on the public's behalf as elected officials, church leaders, and members of voluntary associations. For instance, New York's local government increasingly drew its aldermen and councilmen from among the city's leading merchants, lawyers, and landowners.[71] While the growing elitism of municipal government might be viewed as predatory class rule, it should be seen, in the context of a broader political and cultural development, as evidence of the elite's increased interest in public service.

The public career of New York City merchant Philip Livingston (1716–78) exemplifies the elite's growing civic-mindedness in the closing decades of the colonial era. This fourth son of the second lord of Livingston Manor graduated from Yale in 1737, served his business apprenticeship in Albany, and made his fortune in trade and privateering during King George's War in the 1740s. By 1748, Philip was an elder in New York City's Dutch Reformed Church; he became a deacon the following year and seems to have retained both posts for the remainder of the colonial era. Between 1754 and 1762, Philip was a member of the city's board of aldermen, and from 1759 until 1769 he sat in the provincial legislature. A noted philanthropist, in 1746 he endowed a professorship of divinity at Yale College—the first of his many charitable endeavors. Philip financially supported the Anglican King's College and was among the original

---

70 William Livingston to Noah Welles, 17 Jan. 1753, Livingston-Welles Corres.
71 Bruce M. Wilkenfeld, "New York City Common Council, 1689–1800," *NY Hist.*, 52 (1971): 249–73.

trustees of Queen's College, the Dutch Reformed seminary founded in New Jersey. He also contributed money to both the Dutch and Methodist churches. In addition, Philip served as president of the St. Andrew's Society as well as co-founder of the New York Society Library and the city's Chamber of Commerce. During the pre-Revolutionary imperial crisis, he took part in the resistance movement, and in 1774 he wrote an important pamphlet in response to Tory criticism of the Continental Congress. Philip Livingston exemplified the late colonial elite's ideal of the gentleman-leader. As one contemporary observer noted, "Among the considerable merchants in [New York] no one is more esteemed for energy . . . and public spirit than Philip Livingston."[72]

By mid-century, Philip Livingston and his social peers were part of a provincial aristocracy, a corps of wealthy, educated, and intermarried families who believed it was both their duty and their privilege to exercise political authority on behalf of the rest of their society. To be sure, these colonial leaders were, at best, hybrid aristocrats whose quasi-bourgeois elite ethos would have been out of place among the more traditional aristocracies of Europe. New York's elite was an aristocracy of wealth, not blood; provincial elites remained true to their middling social origins by perpetuating their ancestors' values and ethics. Yet at the same time colonial gentlefolk were becoming increasingly conscious of their position at the head of their society. Together, the culture of gentility and the new civic-mindedness helped elites to accentuate the differences between themselves and their social inferiors. By the eve of the Revolution, New York had an entrenched and self-conscious governing class whose authority would be challenged during the imperial crisis and the ensuing Revolutionary upheaval.

[72] *Dictionary of American Biography*, s.v., "Livingston, Philip"; Edwin Brockholst Livingston, *The Livingstons of Livingston Manor* (New York, 1910), pp. 170–71; *Ecclesiastical Records of the State of New York*, ed. E. T. Corwin, 7 vols. (Albany, 1901–16), 4:2996, 3024, 3085, 3123, 5:3500, 3556, 6:4061; Virginia D. Harrington, "The Place of the Merchant in New York Colonial Life," *NY Hist.*, 13 (1932): 375; Keep, *History of the New York Society Library*, pp. 132–34; Philip Livingston, *The Other Side of the Question* (New York, 1774).

[5]

Politics and Principles

Although the Livingstons had never abandoned politics entirely, after the first Robert Livingston died in 1728 his descendants did not play leading roles in the political affairs of the colony. All that changed after 1750, however, when the King's College controversy and other religious, constitutional, and imperial issues heightened the stakes of factional politics and resulted in the formation of the so-called "Livingston party." Motivated by a combination of whiggish principles, noblesse oblige, and partisan self-interest, Robert and Alida's grandsons and their allies battled for nearly three decades the formidable political party led by the elder and then the younger James DeLancey. By the eve of the Revolution, the Livingstons were one of New York's two most politically influential families.

The Livingston party traced its political lineage to the Morrisites of the 1730s. Like the Morrisites, the Livingston party identified primarily with the landed interest; like the Morrisites, they also supported an aggressive imperial defense policy. Moreover, both factions were supported by prominent members of the legal profession, who jealously guarded the independence of the judiciary and the common law rights of individuals. Certain families—the Morrises, Alexanders, Smiths, and Livingstons—were connected to both the Morrisite and the Livingston factions. Finally, both factions expressed their whiggish hopes and fears in the language of classical republicanism.

In the closing decades of the colonial era, religious, constitutional, and imperial issues complicated New York's colonial politics and gave rise to a principled opposition party led by the Livingston family. The Livingstons' adherence to Dissenting churches led them to oppose the spread of Anglican power and to look on religious establishments as threats to political liberty. Their knowledge of and interest in the bench and bar led them to condemn encroachments of the royal prerogative on the powers of the provincial judiciary. Finally, after 1765, the Livingstons condemned Britain's new imperial policies and ultimately emerged as the aristocratic leaders of New York's resistance coalition. The Livingstons were reluctant revolutionaries, who feared popular upheaval. But a combination of whiggish principles and political ambition persuaded them to cast their lot with the forces of resistance and rebellion.

Late colonial elites certainly hoped to profit by their political activities, but unlike their grandfathers they rarely admitted that their political objectives often were self-interested. Indeed, William Livingston, Robert and Alida's grandson and a pre-Revolutionary factional leader, reviled self-interest as "the sole Cause of . . . erroneous Judgment . . . [and] Injustice." William argued that only men like himself, of independent means, could afford to be disinterested leaders, "influenced . . . by a sincere Love of Mankind, and activated by no private views whatever." He maintained that disinterested leaders alone could preserve liberty and virtue, asserting that such men were responsible for "correcting the taste & improving the minds of our fellow Citizens" who were less knowledgeable and therefore in dire need of elite political guidance.[1]

In provincial New York, the rhetoric of public-spiritedness and the reality of party conflict developed simultaneously over the course of the eighteenth century. Philosophically minded, self-conscious political elites sought to reconcile their province's chronic factionalism with their own professed commitment to disinterested public service. William Livingston and his contemporaries knew that New York's political history was one of continual factional conflict. They also knew that, in their own time, political divisions persisted and showed little prospect of disappearing. Nevertheless, like most

---

[1] William Livingston to Noah Welles, 18 Feb. 1749, Livingston-Welles Corres.; William Livingston et al., *The Independent Reflector; or, Weekly Essays on Sundry Important Subjects More Particularly Adapted to the Province of New-York*, ed. Milton M. Klein (Cambridge, Mass., 1963), pp. 59, 118.

Britons, they looked upon political factions with profound distrust. Like the English Radical Whigs, whose ideas were so influential in America, many New Yorkers saw factionalism as the antithesis of civic virtue and generally attributed party divisions to corrupt self-interest, which they deemed injurious to the welfare of civil society.

In the Anglo-American tradition, however, this visceral abhorrence of party spirit was occasionally tempered by a grudging recognition that parties, when based on altruism or principle, were often desirable or even necessary to thwart the agents of corruption.[2] Because contemporary political culture did not explicitly accept the notion of a loyal opposition, opposition spokesmen were the most frequent defenders of partisan activity.[3] Consequently, the Morrisites and later the Livingstons penned New York's most articulate defenses of party politics. Both groups employed the concept of public jealousy to justify their partisanship, maintaining that an opposition party's distrust of the power of the ruling party acted to preserve the people's liberties. The jealousy, or vigilance, of an opposition party obviously arose from competition between ins and outs, but, far from being the equivalent of a mere lust for power, its persistent sensitivity toward the authoritarian pretensions of the ruling party also complemented the antiauthoritarianism of the Anglo-American republican tradition. Thus, both the Morrisites and the Livingstons were able to participate in factional politics, but as relatively powerless minorities during key political crises they could also be the most vociferous critics of government policy.[4]

Both the Morrisites and the Livingstons explicitly invoked public jealousy to justify their partisan activities. In 1734, an anonymous commentator in Zenger's *New-York Weekly Journal* explained the concept of public jealousy clearly and emphatically. "Political jeal-

---

[2] See, for instance, Bernard Bailyn, *The Origins of American Politics* (New York, 1968), pp. 126–31, and Caroline Robbins, *The Eighteenth-Century Commonwealthman: Studies in the Transmission, Development, and Circumstance of English Liberal Thought from the Restoration of Charles II to the War with the Thirteen Colonies* (Cambridge, Mass., 1959), pp. 34–35, 321–23, 382–83.

[3] Richard Hofstadter, *The Idea of a Party System: The Rise of Legitimate Opposition in the United States, 1780–1840* (Berkeley, Calif., 1972), esp. chap. 1.

[4] James H. Hutson, "The Origins of the Paranoid Style in American Politics: Public Jealousy from the Age of Walpole to the Age of Jackson," in David Hall et al., eds., *Saints and Revolutionaries: Essays in Early American History* (New York, 1984), pp. 336–42.

ousy . . . in the People is a necessary and laudable Passion," wrote this opposition supporter, "because Liberty chastises and shortens Power, therefore Power would extinguish Liberty; and consequently Liberty has too much cause to be exceeding jealous, and always upon her Defence." William Livingston's *Independent Reflector* revived this idea twenty years later, contending that a public-spirited faction could enhance the cause of liberty by opposing tyrants.[5]

The Morrisites had inveighed against Governor William Cosby's arbitrary pretensions and called themselves a "country" party formed to oppose the tyrannous ambitions of the governor's "court" faction. They employed the republican idiom and interpreted their struggle with Cosby in apocalyptic terms, contending that his manipulation of the judiciary, violation of the right to trial by jury, and suppression of the free press would ultimately lead to the extinction of liberty. But as we have seen, the Livingstons were ambivalent toward the Morrisites and had played no public role in the Morris-Cosby controversy. Philip Livingston, the second lord of Livingston Manor, had privately encouraged the Morrisite opposition while he publicly avoided antagonizing Cosby in order to protect his land titles and his seat on the provincial council. Philip's eldest son, Robert Livingston, Jr., who represented the Manor in the assembly, wholeheartedly supported the Cosbyite leader Adolph Philipse in his 1737 disputed election against Cornelius Van Horne, possibly because, as a New York City merchant, he shared Philipse's commercial interests. Later that year, however, Robert Livingston, Jr., voted with the Morrisite leaders to deprive acting governor George Clarke of the additional salary he claimed.[6] Robert's brother, Peter Van Brugh Livingston, also was initially cool toward Morris's cause, but by 1735 he had agreed to help circulate petitions on the opposition leader's behalf. Robert Livingston of Clermont made a donation to help defray the costs of Morris's trip to London, but neither he nor any of his kin were among the leaders of the opposition party.[7]

---

[5] *New-York Weekly Journal*, 11 Mar. 1733/4; Livingston et al., *Independent Reflector*, nos. 13, 18–22, 36–37.

[6] *Assem. J.*, 1:711–17, 724. The disputed election resulted in nine divisions; six roll-call votes were taken concerning Clarke's claims. Cornelius Van Horne had married Joanna Livingston and was therefore Robert's uncle by marriage. Joanna had died in childbirth in 1733, and Van Horne had since remarried (C. S. Williams, *Jan Cornelis Van Horne and His Descendants* [New York, 1912], p. 61).

[7] Names of those agreeing to sustain Col. Morris, [1734], Rutherfurd Collections,

When Morris's leading supporters allied with Governor George Clinton (1743–53) to oppose the increasingly powerful Chief Justice James DeLancey, the Livingstons once again remained ambivalent and relatively inactive. In the 1740s, King George's War and the distribution of patronage complicated the Livingstons' relations with Governor Clinton and his supporters. Because of their Morrisite leanings and frontier interests, the Livingstons were at first well disposed toward both Clinton and his aggressive military policies. Both Philip Livingston and his son Robert Livingston, Jr., supported the governor's war policies in the 1740s. In the assembly, Robert Livingston, Jr., was among those most consistently willing to vote both men and money to improve the war effort; his father lamented Clinton's inability to procure funding for an expedition to Crown Point and in 1745 applauded the governor's decision to dissolve the assembly in hopes of securing a more cooperative legislature.[8]

Although he supported Clinton's military policies, Philip did condemn as petty and impolitic the vengeful behavior that prevented their implementation. During this time, Cadwallader Colden was Clinton's closest adviser, and the governor attempted to reward Colden's loyalty by making him lieutenant governor. But James DeLancey—chief justice, leader of the majority faction, and Clinton and Colden's archenemy—had influential patrons in England who managed to get him the lieutenant governorship despite Clinton's protests. After DeLancey received his commission, Clinton snubbed his new lieutenant governor and continued to rely on Colden as his chief adviser. Philip Livingston blamed Clinton's slavish reliance on his "darling" Colden and his inability to come to terms with DeLancey for perpetuating the factional bickering that paralyzed the government in the midst of a wartime crisis. Clinton's disdain for all advisers save Colden, coupled with his unwillingness to come to

NYHS, vol. 2; Philip Livingston to James Alexander, 14 Aug. 1736, ibid.; Lewis Morris, Jr., to Robert Hunter Morris, 3 June 1735, Morris Papers, Rutgers University, box 2.

[8] *Assem. J.*, 2:33, 37, 54, 60, 108, 111–12; Philip Livingston to Robert Livingston, Jr., 29 Oct. 1745, Livingston-Redmond MSS., reel 7; Marc Egnal, *A Mighty Empire: The Origins of the American Revolution* (Ithaca, N.Y., 1988), chap. 3. On DeLancey's growing power and influence, see Stanley N. Katz, *Newcastle's New York: Anglo-American Politics, 1732–1753* (Cambridge, Mass., 1968), chaps. 7–8. On Clinton's use of patronage to build his own rival party, see Patricia U. Bonomi, *A Factious People: Politics and Society in Colonial New York* (New York, 1971), pp. 158–65.

terms with the assembly, led Philip to join the majority of his colleagues on the council in breaking openly with the governor in December 1746. By 1747, Philip feared the fall of Albany and the eventual loss of all New York if effective military action was not taken.[9]

Clinton's attempts to purge unfriendly officeholders and his subsequent manipulation of the patronage further enraged Philip Livingston and his sons. Cognizant of Philip's increasing disdain for his administration, the governor had recommended his removal from the secretaryship for Indian affairs as early as July 1746. Within a year, however, Clinton urged the home government to suspend Philip from all his offices, including his place on the provincial council, on the grounds that he had allegedly "abandoned his Country, neglects his Office and supports the neutrality." Philip managed to keep his offices, but when he died in 1749, Clinton purposefully excluded his sons from the vacated positions. The council seat and Albany clerkships were not, strictly speaking, hereditary offices, though for decades they had been held by the head of the Livingston family. Anticipating a dissolution of the assembly, Philip's sons Robert and John and some of their sympathetic cousins had already begun campaigning against Clinton within five days of their father's death in February 1749.[10]

Clinton's attachment to Cadwallader Colden undermined his own authority and influence and was instrumental in pushing Philip Livingston and his sons, at least temporarily, into an uneasy alliance with DeLancey's anti-Clintonian faction. Philip certainly blamed Colden for Clinton's inability to carry out an effective war policy, and quite possibly he harbored additional misgivings toward Colden as a longtime critic of New York's large manorial grants. Colden also was intimately involved in devising the governor's patronage strategies that eroded the Livingstons' influence at both the local level and the provincial level. Colden himself coveted Philip's council seat, and he

[9] Bonomi, *Factious People,* pp. 149–58; Philip Livingston to Jacob Wendell, 17 June, 24 Nov., 16 Dec. 1746, 26 Feb., 27 July, 30 July, 2 Nov., 21 Dec. 1747, Livingston Papers, MCNY, box 2; Representation of seven members of the council, 16 Dec. 1747, in *The Letters and Papers of Cadwallader Colden,* 9 vols. (New York, 1918–37), 3:294.

[10] Clinton to Colden, 9 Feb. 1749, *Colden Papers,* 4:189; Clinton to Board of Trade, 30 Nov. 1747, *DRNY,* 6:413; Clinton to Duke of Newcastle, 30 Nov. 1747, ibid., 6:414.

expected his own son John to be given the Albany clerkships.[11] Finally, Colden himself was personally unpopular; even some of Clinton's supporters came to see him as a political liability. As William Smith, Jr., a leading Clintonian, later recalled, Colden "was violent & obstinate & ruined Clinton by his Councils. . . . He never thought of raising himself by New Greatness but valued himself more upon a Cunning Device than for a courageous Effort."[12] Thus, Colden's influence alienated some who, like Philip Livingston, may have been predisposed to support Clinton and his policies.

The Clintonians' inability to win elections bore testimony to their unpalatable public image, due partly to Colden's vast influence. Their desire to rehabilitate their image by revamping their personnel probably led to the political bargain, struck in 1751–52, that brought the Clermont Livingstons into an alliance with Clinton and his partisans. In December 1751, Robert Livingston of Clermont, Philip's younger brother, approached James Alexander, a leading Clintonian, and offered the support of himself and his son, Robert R. Livingston, in exchange for political preferment. The proprietor of Clermont argued that James DeLancey's great influence came mainly from his power as chief justice and that "as that power cannot be absolutely taken from him the only thing that can be done is to Lessen that power" by appointing a third justice "of good Sense, Spirit and independent Estate" who could in turn lessen DeLancey's control of the high court. Robert Livingston of Clermont recommended his own son for the position and offered himself as the Clintonians' candidate for the Manor's seat in the provincial legislature. As the Clintonians' allies, the Clermont Livingstons could provide the faction with new personnel and connections, while the governor could in return give them access to political office.[13]

[11] Colden to Clinton, 9 Feb., 19 Feb. 1749, *Colden Papers*, 4:94, 102. John Colden did serve as Albany's town clerk in 1749, but Clinton appointed Harme Gansevoort town clerk and clerk of the peace and common pleas in 1750. See Joel Munsell, ed., *The Annals of Albany*, 10 vols. (Albany, N.Y., 1850–59), 10:139; Peter Wraxall, *An Abridgement of the Indian Affairs . . .*, ed. Charles Howard McIlwain (Cambridge, Mass., 1915), pp. 5–6.

[12] William H. W. Sabine, ed., *Historical Memoirs of William Smith . . .*, 2 vols. (New York, 1958), 1:147. Few contemporaries remarked favorably on Colden's personal or political qualities.

[13] James Alexander to Cadwallader Colden, 5 Dec. 1751, *Colden Papers*, 4:303–4.

The proposed bargain soon foundered on the refusal of Robert Livingston, Jr., to allow his uncle to represent the Manor in the upcoming assembly. The new lord of the Manor and his brothers still blamed Clinton and Colden for the loss of their late father's offices. Consequently, they continued to favor DeLancey over Clinton, at least for the time being, and Robert Livingston, Jr., continued to represent his own Manor in the provincial legislature.[14]

This incident suggests that a certain amount of caution is called for in discussing the relationship between family and politics in colonial New York. Unlike their cousins, the Clermont Livingstons were willing to align themselves with the Clintonians in 1751 both to gain access to the governor's patronage and to fight the imposition of a tax on unimproved land, a measure that was fast becoming a pet project of DeLancey and his partisans.[15] Although Philip's sons also would have opposed the land tax, Colden's manipulation of the patronage made them unwilling either to ally with Clinton themselves or to give the Manor's assembly seat to a pro-Clintonian relative. Moreover, during this period the Manor Livingstons were the political enemies of James Alexander, the father-in-law of two of Philip Livingston's children and the intermediary that Robert Livingston of Clermont—who was not related to the Alexanders— had used in proposing his unsuccessful bargain. On the other hand, Henry Beekman of Dutchess County, the powerful father-in-law of Robert R. Livingston, was a prominent anti-Clintonian who must have bitterly opposed his son-in-law's defection to the governor's party.[16]

[14] John Livingston (1714–86) to Robert Livingston, Jr., 25 Nov. 1751, 25 Mar. 1752, Livingston-Redmond MSS., reel 7; Philip Livingston (1716–78) to Robert Livingston, Jr., 29 Nov. 1751, 15 Feb. 1752, ibid.; James Alexander to Cadwallader Colden, 21 Jan. 1752, *Colden Papers*, 4:307–8.

[15] *Assem. J.*, 2:237–38; *New-York Post-Boy*, 11 Nov. 1751; Beverly McAnear, ed., "Mr. Robert R. Livingston's Reasons against a Land Tax," *Journal of Political Economy*, 48 (1940): 63–90.

[16] Nevertheless, the "family politics" interpretation has remained influential. See Roger Champagne, "Family Politics versus Constitutional Principles: The New York Assembly Elections of 1768 and 1769," *WMQ*, 3d ser., 20 (1963): 57–79; and Leopold S. Launitz-Schürer, *Loyal Whigs and Revolutionaries: The Making of the Revolution in New York* (New York, 1980), esp. pp. 1–2. Two penetrating critiques of this interpretation of New York's colonial politics are Bonomi, *Factious People*, esp. pp. 237–39; and Milton M. Klein, "Democracy and Politics in Colonial New York," *NY Hist.*, 40 (1959): 225–28.

Although Robert Livingston of Clermont was unable to cement his alliance with the Clintonians, the entire Livingston family soon would join together to oppose James DeLancey and his partisans. Like most articulate New Yorkers, the Livingstons accepted the inevitability of factional divisions, though they remained somewhat ambivalent about the effects of party rivalries.[17] In 1753, William Livingston penned an essay that captured the essence of their ambivalence. He denounced party spirit and self-interested "enthusiasm" as injurious to the public good. In particular, he attacked the "court" faction that sought to impose an Anglican college on New York's Dissenting majority, attempting to rally public opinion to create a new "country" party to oppose the overmighty "court." Livingston assumed that his own party would be both disinterested and patriotic, unlike that of his political adversaries. Although he had begun his essay by condemning party divisions in general, Livingston thus concluded that parties, when they were not motivated by self-interest, could be both necessary and useful. An absence of factionalism, he admitted, "may be the Result of a Confederacy in Guilt, and an Agreement between Rulers to advance their private Interest, at the Expence of the People." Far from urging a complete abjuration of party politics, Livingston ultimately decided that virtuous citizens were obliged to form a party to oppose "Measures subversive of our Liberties."[18]

For most of the quarter-century preceding the Revolution, William Livingston led a party committed to preserving New Yorkers' religious and political liberties. Along with his associates, William Smith, Jr., and John Morin Scott, he used his pen to create and promote the political faction that came to be known as the "Livingston party." Led by a triumvirate of Presbyterian lawyers, that party revived the Morrisites' opposition to the expansion of prerogative power while mounting a new offensive against the growing ambitions of New York's religious establishment.

At mid-century, the imposing figure of James DeLancey dominated New York's provincial politics. DeLancey's supporters consis-

---

[17] Two assertions of the inevitability of factional divisions are Cadwallader Colden to Lord Hillsborough, 7 July 1770, *DRNY*, 8:217; and McAnear, ed., "Mr. Robert R. Livingston's Reasons against a Land Tax," p. 82.

[18] Livingston et al., *Independent Reflector*, no. 13.

tently held majorities both in the assembly and on the governor's council, while DeLancey himself was chief justice of the provincial Supreme Court and, after 1747, lieutentant governor. In 1753, the home government recalled the ineffectual Clinton, replacing him with Sir Danvers Osborne, who committed suicide within two days of his arrival in the colony. Upon Osborne's death, Lieutenant Governor James DeLancey became New York's acting governor. DeLancey would act as the colony's chief executive during most of the period between 1753 and his death in 1760.[19]

Virtually all the issues that had previously divided New Yorkers resurfaced during the DeLancey years, giving rise to two great rival factions known as the Livingstons and the DeLanceys. The King's College controversy pitted the colony's Anglican minority against Protestant Dissenters, who wanted a nonsectarian college. Conflicts over tax policy pitted the DeLancey-led merchants who favored a land tax against the great landowners who supported the current system of raising revenue by means of commercial duties. Financing military expeditions and awarding wartime supply contracts involved not only the revenue issue but also the problems of patronage and perquisites. Indeed, DeLancey's manipulation of the patronage—especially his replacement of the provisioners Peter Van Brugh Livingston and William Alexander in 1756 with his own brother Oliver—contributed to the Livingstons' growing dissatisfaction with his government.[20] At the same time, DeLancey's slowness to act to protect the province's eastern boundary also angered the Livingstons and other landowners whose estates the border dispute endangered.[21]

DeLancey's opponents had little success against him, though the Livingstons' political fortunes did improve somewhat after the lieutenant governor's death in 1760. The 1761 election brought them a

[19] On the DeLancey era, see Bonomi, *Factious People*, chap. 5.

[20] See Robert Livingston, Jr., to [Peter Van Brugh Livingston], 26 Nov. 1756, Misc. MSS., Robert Livingston, Jr., NYHS.

[21] William Livingston to Robert Livingston, Jr., 4 Feb. 1754, Livingston-Redmond MSS., reel 7; William Smith, Jr., *The History of the Province of New-York*, ed. Michael G. Kammen, 2 vols. (Cambridge, Mass., 1972), 2:220–21. William complained to his brother that DeLancey "cares not a Groat for you nor your Manor nor for any Man living," but there is no evidence that Robert himself ever openly condemned the lieutenant governor's conduct. See also [William Livingston], *A Review of the Military Operations in North-America . . .* (New York, 1770).

plurality of seats in the provincial assembly, where their party was represented by four Livingston cousins and eight staunch supporters—mostly assemblymen from the Hudson Valley. Although twelve of twenty-seven seats did not constitute a legislative majority, over the next seven years the Livingston cousins were able to be on the winning side in seventeen of forty-three legislative divisions.[22] Unlike their opponents, the Livingston party never captured a majority of seats either in the assembly or on the governor's council.

Although informed contemporaries often identified rival factions with the Livingston and DeLancey surnames, they also believed that the parties represented more than the interests of one particular family. It is significant that religious labels appeared nearly as frequently as family names in New York's political nomenclature. While the parties divided over a succession of economic, political, and constitutional issues during the quarter-century before independence, religious concerns—pitting Anglican privileges against the rights of Protestant Dissenters—were both the initial raison d'être of the Livingston party and a source of recurring political controversy.

The King's College controversy and the rise of the Presbyterian triumvirate marked the reemergence of the Livingston family as a political force in New York. At least one member of the triumvirate—William Smith, Jr.—believed that New York's late colonial factional alignments arose from the battles between Anglicans and Dissenters over the creation of a church-affiliated college. Specifically, Smith traced the genesis of New York's late colonial political rivalries to the election of 1758, in which the fledgling opposition party made Anglican authoritarianism their main campaign issue. "From this time," wrote Smith, "we shall distinguish the opposition under the name of the Livingston party, though it did not always proceed from motives approved of by that family." In his diary, however, the historian continued to use family and religious labels almost interchangeably as late as the 1770s.[23]

Thomas Jones, a DeLancey supporter, also saw factional divisions

---

[22] Bonomi, *Factious People,* pp. 232–33. Bonomi's research is important, because earlier scholars had assumed the Livingstons controlled the assembly that sat from 1761 until 1768. Leopold S. Launitz-Schürer is the most recent proponent of this erroneous view. See his *Loyal Whigs and Revolutionaries,* p. 15.

[23] Smith, *History,* 2:237; Sabine, ed., *Memoirs of William Smith,* vol. 1, esp. pp. 146–47.

in a primarily religious light. Jones opened his narrative *History of New York during the Revolutionary War* in 1752, at the conclusion of what he considered a "Golden Age" of domestic peace and unity. Writing in exile in the 1780s, he argued that the King's College controversy had divided New Yorkers into religious and political factions that presaged the subsequent division between patriots and loyalists. Jones's hindsight led him to portray the Livingstons and Dissenters as "republicans" and "enemies of monarchy" as early as the 1750s. Nevertheless, he described New York politics between 1752 and 1776 mainly in terms of its religious factionalism. "The contending parties in New York," he claimed, "were those of the DeLanceys and the Livingstons, the former supported by the Episcopalians, the latter by the Presbyterians."[24]

The Livingstons themselves also were prone to equate political divisions with religious differences. William Livingston's hostility toward the Anglican establishment was well known. A son of the Enlightenment, committed to free inquiry and distrustful of all orthodoxies, William spent most of his public career denouncing the political ambitions of predatory Churchmen and authoritarian bishops. But William's nephew Peter R. Livingston also believed that two parties, "Church & Discenters," vied for control of the New York assembly, and as late as 1770, Robert Livingston, Jr., the lord of Livingston Manor, maintained that the central issue in provincial politics was "whether the Church or Meeting shall rule."[25]

James DeLancey, himself a Churchman, supported the plan to create an Anglican college, which received its royal charter in 1754, though religious Dissenters from both legislative factions prevented the college from receiving public funding. This compromise amounted to a half-victory for the triumvirate and a rare near-defeat for the lieutenant governor. Ordinarily, DeLancey's power, popularity, and British connections made him virtually invincible. As William Livingston himself observed, even when DeLancey was not

[24] Thomas Jones, *History of New York during the Revolutionary War*, ed. Edwin Floyd DeLancey, 2 vols. (New York, 1869), esp. 1:1–33, 229, 2:291n.

[25] Peter R. Livingston to Oliver Wendell, 19 Jan. 1769, Livingston Papers, MCNY, box 1; Peter R. Livingston to Robert Livingston, Jr., 20 Apr. 1770, Livingston-Redmond MSS., reel 8. On William Livingston's position on the relationship between church and state, see Milton M. Klein, "The American Whig: William Livingston of New York" (Ph.D. diss., Columbia University, 1955), esp. pp. 275–85, 624–34, 641.

acting governor, "as Chief justice great is his interest in the counties; with that interest he commands elections: with his sway in elections he rules the assembly: and with his sovereignty over the house controls a governor." William Smith, Jr., like Livingston, conceded DeLancey's skill as a master politician and admitted that he had "laid deep Foundations for Power in his Popularity" and had reconciled most New Yorkers to his leadership by his willingness to compromise to accommodate factional differences.[26]

Because DeLancey's own party was a coalition of Anglicans and Dissenters, the King's College controversy had put him in a delicate position. Anglicans accounted for roughly 10 percent of New York's population, and the lieutenant governor hoped to avoid alienating the Dissenting majority, who already resented the practical disadvantages of nonconformity. Royal governors and imperial authorities had repeatedly rejected the petitions of Dissenting churches for charters of incorporation, thus making it impossible for their congregations to raise money or own property. William Livingston's own New York City Presbyterian church was denied a charter in 1759 and 1767; the latter request marked the fifth time since the creation of the congregation in the 1720s that their petition for incorporation had been rejected. Lieutenant Governor DeLancey also refused to grant a charter to the New York City Lutherans in 1759; four years later, his successor persuaded the Board of Trade to disallow the petitions of the Lutherans and two other Dissenting churches because he believed it unwise to grant them the corporate privileges normally reserved for Anglican congregations.[27]

The ecclesiastical establishment also penalized the Dissenting majority by forcing them to pay taxes to maintain an Anglican ministry. Although the Ministry Act of 1693 obliged the inhabitants of the counties of New York, Westchester, Queens, and Richmond to support a "good, sufficient Protestant Minister," in practice, the governors and their supporters had made sure that only Anglican cler-

[26] [Livingston], *Review of Military Operations,* esp. p. 36; Sabine, ed., *Memoirs of William Smith,* 1:147; Bonomi, *Factious People,* pp. 176–77.

[27] Colden to Board of Trade, 7 Dec. 1763, and Board to Colden, 13 July 1764, *DRNY,* 7:585, 642; Petition of the New York City Presbyterians, 18 Mar. 1766, and pertinent letters of Sir Henry Moore, Board of Trade, and Privy Council, 29 July 1766–26 Aug. 1767, *DHNY,* 3:497–508. See also Carl Bridenbaugh, *Mitre and Sceptre: Transatlantic Faiths, Ideas, Personalities, and Politics* (New York, 1962), pp. 127–28, 253.

gymen served the six tax-supported parishes created by that legislation. Dissenters always had resented the taxes imposed by the Ministry Act, but these levies, like the charter controversies, became particularly objectionable in the late colonial era. In 1764, Churchmen sought to expand the scope of the Ministry Act by creating a new tax-supported Anglican parish on the manor of Philipsburgh in Westchester County. Dissenters defeated this proposal in the assembly, where some DeLancey supporters crossed party lines and voted with the non-Anglican legislators in the Livingston party.[28] Over the course of the next decade, however, religion would become a party issue; as factional divisions grew more rigid during the imperial crisis, defending the rights of religious dissenters became the exclusive domain of the Livingston party.

Religious issues revived the republican language and the whiggish concerns that the Morrisites had expressed in the 1730s, but legal and constitutional issues, more reminiscent of the Morrisites' immediate concerns, also reemerged in New York in the pre-Revolutionary era. Imperial threats to the right to trial by jury and the independence of the judiciary were important issues throughout British America in the late colonial era.[29] New Yorkers in particular passed through two local legal crises en route to revolution. In both cases, the Livingston party led the province's crusade against the expansion of prerogative power.

The legal controversies of the 1760s, concerning judicial tenure and the right to trial by jury, further heightened the Livingstons' whiggish sensitivities toward encroaching power and solidified their intellectual links with the old Morrisite opposition. Like the leading Morrisites of the 1730s—for whom an independent judiciary and the primacy of jury trials were transcendent issues—the most prominent and vocal opposition leaders of the 1760s were members of the legal profession. These men, again led by the Presbyterian triumvirate, were acutely sensitive to executive attempts to control the judicial process and, like the Morrisites, they used their pens to turn the issues at hand into major political controversies.

[28] *NY Col. Laws*, 1:328–31; *Assem. J.*, 2:768. The Dissenters' counteroffensive in the house was led by Speaker Philip Livingston, a member of the Dutch Reformed church.

[29] Bernard Bailyn, *Ideological Origins of the American Revolution* (Cambridge, Mass., 1973), pp. 105–8.

In the 1760s, for both personal and political reasons, Lieutenant Governor Cadwallader Colden sought to expand the executive's control of the judiciary. Colden's enmity toward Chief Justice James DeLancey, born of years of political warfare, had persuaded him that judicial appointments during good behavior made judges too powerful and unresponsive to the Crown's interests; his general disdain for the members of the New York bar and their personal and political connections with his own political enemies led him to believe that the colony's judges should be "disinterested" outsiders without family or friends in New York. In 1760, both DeLancey and King George II died, and as the new acting governor Colden was able to implement the reforms he desired. The remaining judges resigned their commissions, as was customary upon the death of a monarch, but their new commissions, issued by Colden in the name of George III, stipulated that they were to serve only at the Crown's pleasure. All the judges refused to serve under these circumstances, except for the new chief justice, Benjamin Prat, whom Colden had brought in from Boston to assume the post vacated by DeLancey's death. In England, the Board of Trade approved Colden's conduct. In fact, the King-in-Council recently had disallowed a 1759 Pennsylvania law stipulating that all judges would serve during good behavior; in the wake of this disallowance, the new king, George III, issued an order-in-council requiring that judges in all colonies be commissioned to serve at pleasure. Late in 1761, the Board of Trade informed colonial governors of the king's directive. In other words, Colden's actions simply anticipated a change in British imperial judicial policy.[30] In New York, however, no one supported the lieutenant governor's judicial policy, which threatened the courts' independence and responsiveness to local needs and interests.

Four years later, Colden again attempted to enhance the executive's control of the courts by allowing an appeal to the governor and council in the absence of legal error. On 31 October 1764, Colden issued a writ granting the convicted defendant in an assault case, *Forsey v. Cunningham,* an appeal to the executive to reconsider the jury's verdict. *Forsey v. Cunningham* was the first common law case heard by the New York Supreme Court to be granted such an appeal. Previously, appeals to the governor and council were possible

---

[30] Board of Trade to George III, 2 Dec. 1761, *DRNY*, 7:477–80.

only in civil cases on the basis of an error in law. In such cases, the governor could issue a writ of error to review questions of law only. Colden, however, defied custom and allowed the appeal, though he himself admitted that no legal error had been made. Instead, he argued that the custom he violated was a specious one, used only by lawyers, judges, and landowners to protect fraudulent land titles and thereby usurp the king's proprietary rights. New Yorkers, of course, saw the matter differently: Colden's designs jeopardized the citizen's customary right to trial by jury.[31]

Colden ultimately emerged as the loser in the appeals controversy when, in November 1765, the home government ruled that appeals to the governor and council were permissible only by a writ of error in civil cases involving more than £300.[32] The judicial tenure question, on which both sides could find precedents to support their positions, was resolved in 1763 when Governor Robert Monckton chose Robert R. Livingston and William Smith, Sr., to be judges of the provincial Supreme Court. In principle, Colden had won this battle; in accordance with the royal order-in-council, the new judges were commissioned to serve at pleasure. Nevertheless, both Livingston and Smith were insiders, and the favored candidates of the lawyer-landlord-opposition coalition. Robert R. Livingston, son of Robert Livingston of Clermont, was destined to inherit a vast landed estate; William Smith, Sr., was one of the province's leading attorneys, as well as the mentor and ally of all three members of the troublesome triumvirate. William Livingston, William Smith, Jr., and John Morin Scott all had studied law in the office of William Smith, Sr., one of New York's most prominent lawyers. Both these new judges were precisely the sort of men that Colden had wanted to exclude from the judiciary because they seemed hostile toward the royal prerogative and dangerous to the Crown's material interests.

[31] The best analysis of the legal controversies of the 1760s is Milton M. Klein, "Prelude to Revolution in New York: Jury Trials and Judicial Tenure," *WMQ*, 3d ser., 17 (1960): 439–62. See also Herbert A. Johnson, "George Harison's Protest: New Light on *Forsey v.Cunningham*," *NY Hist.*, 50 (1969): 61–82. Colden often complained of an alliance between lawyers and landowners. See his letters to the Earl of Egremont, 14 Sept. 1763, to the Board of Trade, 22 Jan. 1765, and to Lord Halifax, 22 Feb. 1765, *DRNY*, 7:549, 695–700, 705–6.

[32] Representation of the Board of Trade, 24 Sept. 1765, *DRNY*, 7:762–63; Report of Attorney and Solicitor Generals, 2 Nov. 1765, ibid., 7:815–16.

Although Colden's attack on the judiciary had found virtually no support in New York, for professional, personal, and ideological reasons members of the Livingston faction led the local opposition to the lieutenant governor's judicial policies. As lawyers, these men had a proprietary interest in the integrity of the courts and the credibility of their own role in the judicial process.[33] Moreover, although Colden exaggerated the extent to which lawyers, judges, and landlords conspired to defraud the Crown of valuable acreage, friendly courts free of hostile executive interference were crucial to the interests of New York's great landowners, whose titles often were questionable. But the constitutional implications of the legal controversies of the 1760s were far more important than the individual interests at stake. Colden's policies alerted New York's lawyers to the potential abuses of executive power and accustomed them to leading colonial opposition to the seemingly gratuitous expansion of the royal prerogative.

Throughout British America, lawyers provided the intellectual leadership for the defense of colonial rights.[34] In New York, the lawyers who led the crusade against Colden's policies were drawn overwhelmingly from the Livingston party. Judge Robert R. Livingston, assemblyman for Dutchess County, guided a bill through the legislature which, if enacted, would have given all judges tenure during good behavior. Later, as a member of the Supreme Court during the appeals controversy, Judge Livingston was among Colden's most outspoken critics, singled out by the lieutenant governor to be removed from office for his imprudence.[35] Meanwhile, the judge's cousin, William Livingston, led the opposition in the public press, devoting his first five "Sentinel" essays entirely to a discussion

[33] On the professionalization of the provincial bar, see Milton M. Klein, "From Community to Status: The Development of the Legal Profession in Colonial New York," *NY Hist.*, 60 (1979): 133–56; John M. Murrin, "The Legal Transformation: The Bench and Bar in Eighteenth-Century Massachusetts," in Stanley N. Katz and John M. Murrin, eds., *Colonial America: Essays in Politics and Social Development*, 3d ed. (New York, 1983), pp. 540–63.

[34] Murrin, "Legal Transformation," in Katz and Murrin, eds., *Colonial America*, pp. 565–68; Klein, "Prelude to Revolution," esp. pp. 439–42; Milton M. Klein, "New York Lawyers and the Coming of the American Revolution," *NY Hist.*, 55 (1974): 383–407.

[35] *Assem. J.*, 2:671; Colden to Board of Trade, 27 Jan. 1765, *DRNY*, 7:703; *New-York Post-Boy*, 31 Jan. 1765; Colden to Earl of Shelburne, 23 Nov. 1767, 21 Jan. 1768, *DRNY*, 7:995–97, 8:5. Livingston, however, retained his post.

of the inviolability of the right to trial by jury and the grave threat to liberty posed by encroaching prerogative power. William Livingston and his associates reprinted these essays in pamphlet form and sent them to England in hopes of influencing the home government. Livingston also penned a petition to Parliament, begging its support on the appeals issue; the other two-thirds of the Presbyterian triumvirate, John Morin Scott and William Smith, Jr., addressed similar statements to the king and former governor Robert Monckton, respectively.[36]

By February 1765, Colden reported that the city was in an uproar; he correctly blamed the lawyers and their associates for fomenting what he called the "artificial clamour" on behalf of the judges' defense of the right to trial by jury.[37] By the end of the year, the Stamp Act had supplanted the appeals issue as New Yorkers' main political concern, but Colden still blamed the lawyers and judges for all his problems. Characteristically insensitive to popular grievances and changing political circumstances, as late as December 1765 he also mistakenly continued to believe that his judicial policy, and not the Stamp Act, was the main cause of local unrest.[38]

Colden's response to the Stamp Act had been predictable. Determined to uphold imperial authority and the royal prerogative, he insisted on its enforcement. The people out-of-doors responded by making the lieutenant governor the target of their most violent protests. In 1765, the rioting in New York reached a crescendo on 1 November, when the crowd, protesting the Stamp Act, stormed Colden's carriage house and stole his chariot, which they used to parade his effigy through the city's streets. Colden and Satan were hanged and burnt in effigy; the lieutenant governor was the only public official the rioters thought deserving of this most dubious honor.[39]

---

[36] *New-York Post-Boy*, 28 Feb.–28 Mar. 1765; Colden to Board of Trade, 14 Apr. 1765, *DRNY*, 7:709–10; Sabine, ed., *Memoirs of William Smith*, 1:24.

[37] Sabine, ed., *Memoirs of William Smith*, 1:27–28; Colden to Board of Trade, 22 Feb. 1765, *DRNY*, 7:707.

[38] Colden to Secretary Conway, 23 Sept., 9 Nov. 1765, *DRNY*, 7:759, 773–74; Colden to Board of Trade, 6 Dec. 1765, ibid., 7:792.

[39] The best contemporary descriptions of the 1 November riot are Colden's letter to Secretary Conway, 5 Nov. 1765, ibid., 7:771, and Sabine, ed., *Memoirs of William Smith*, 1:31. See also Philip Ranlet, *The New York Loyalists* (Knoxville, Tenn., 1986), chap. 2, and Paul A. Gilje, *The Road to Mobocracy: Popular Disorder in New York City, 1763–1834* (Chapel Hill, N.C., 1987), chap. 2. On Colden's political ideology, see Carole Sham-

The Stamp Act crisis was a transforming event that politicized many ordinary people who were accustomed to deferring to their social superiors. Before 1765, New York politics had been "popular" only to the extent that political leaders were accustomed to soliciting the support of the voters. Treating—the ritual wooing of voters with food and drink—was common enough to merit a disapproving lecture from the *Independent Reflector,* and the opposition press, first established during the Morris-Cosby dispute, had become a permanent feature of New York's political environment. Beginning in 1739, candidates for the provincial assembly routinely advertised in New York newspapers, and the city's presses also increasingly published more substantive campaign propaganda in the form of broadsides and pamphlets. By 1750, a provincial election prompted the publication of forty pamphlets addressing campaign issues, and polemicists became more prolific with each subsequent contest. By 1769, when New Yorkers elected their last colonial assembly, 135 pamphlets on sundry political topics competed for the voters' attention.[40]

Electioneering was a social ritual that legitimized government by the few in a polity purportedly based on the notion of popular sovereignty. At election time, political elites asked the voters to think about issues, to give their opinions, and then to choose between the candidates who competed for their support. Once the election was over, leaders expected to do the actual governing themselves, by their own lights, without advice from ordinary people.[41]

In the context of eighteenth-century Anglo-American political theory and practice, there was nothing paradoxical in the elite's expectation that they would receive the deference and respect of their social inferiors.[42] But in 1765, for the first time, a significant

mas, "Cadwallader Colden and the Role of the King's Prerogative," *New-York Historical Society Quarterly,* 53 (1969): 102–26.

[40] Michael Kammen, *Colonial New York: A History* (New York, 1975), p. 245; Beverly McAnear, "Politics in Provincial New York, 1689–1761" (Ph.D. diss., Stanford University, 1935), pp. 559–60, 740; Livingston et al., *Independent Reflector,* no. 32. On treating and electioneering, see also Nicholas Varga, "Election Procedures and Practices in Colonial New York," *NY Hist.,* 41 (1960): 264–65.

[41] See Edmund S. Morgan, *Inventing the People: The Rise of Popular Sovereignty in England and America* (New York, 1988), esp. chap. 8.

[42] J. G. A. Pocock, "The Classical Theory of Deference," *American Historical Review,* 81 (1976): 516–23. For a different view, see Edward Countryman, *A People in Revolution: The American Revolution in New York, 1760–1790* (Baltimore, 1981), p. 76.

number of New York's middling folk refused to defer to their traditional leaders. During the Stamp Act crisis, they rejected outright the moderate policies put forward by elites in the legislature and took to the streets demanding a more aggressive defense of colonial liberties.

New York's governing class had reacted cautiously to George Grenville's imperial reform program. The Sugar Act of 1764 had angered the merchants of New York, who petitioned Parliament for its repeal on both economic and constitutional grounds, but both the merchants and the city remained calm after its enactment.[43] When news of the Stamp Act reached New York, the assembly sent another petition to London, emphasizing the impropriety of taxation without representation. Unlike the Sugar Act, the Stamp Act affected virtually everyone; even the cautious assemblymen had characterized the new law not as an economic burden but as an abridgement of "the Natural Right of Mankind" to "an Exemption from . . . ungranted, involuntary Taxes."[44]

The members of the assembly drafted their petition in October 1764, when they had first heard of Grenville's proposed innovations. Thereafter, with the exception of attending the Stamp Act Congress in October 1765, the province's political leaders did nothing officially to indicate that they were taking a decisive stand against this most objectionable law. Their inactivity allowed the people out-of-doors to seize the initiative.

Buoyed by the news of the Boston riots and impatient with the inactivity of their own leaders, the artisans and mechanics of New York were not content to wait calmly for Parliament to respond to their grievances. By late August, they had taken to the streets in protest. Popular unrest culminated on 1 November, the day on which the Stamp Act was scheduled to go into effect. As many as 2,000 angry New Yorkers protested the Stamp Act and Colden's

[43] Memorial of the New-York merchants, 20 Apr. 1764, *Assem. J.*, 2:740–44; Edmund S. Morgan and Helen M. Morgan, *The Stamp Act Crisis: Prologue to Revolution* (Chapel Hill, N.C., 1953), pp. 33–38. As the Morgans point out, only New Yorkers and North Carolinians challenged the Sugar Act on the grounds that it was a revenue measure and therefore violated the colonists' right to be taxed exclusively by their own representatives.

[44] New York petition to the House of Commons, 18 Oct. 1764, in Edmund S. Morgan, ed., *Prologue to Revolution: Sources and Documents on the Stamp Act Crisis, 1764–1766* (Chapel Hill, N.C., 1959), pp. 8–14.

willingness to enforce it; the crowd began rioting early that evening and did not cease until four o'clock the following morning. Meanwhile, in the fall of 1765, New York's popular leaders had begun to develop the organizational apparatus that came to be known as the Sons of Liberty. Founded to promote intercolonial cooperation in resisting imperial policies, the Sons of Liberty ultimately became the popular arm of New York's Revolutionary coalition.[45]

The Livingstons, with their strong ties to the bench and bar, fought the battle against the Stamp Act in pamphlets and essays couched in legal and constitutional terms, but they remained aloof from the rioters in the city's streets. William Livingston, as usual, led New York's literary barrage in defense of liberty, but he actually stopped writing his "Sentinel" essays in August 1765 because he was increasingly distressed by the inability of men of quality to control popular unrest. William Smith, Jr., and Judge Robert R. Livingston were equally worried by the increasing assertiveness of the people out-of-doors. By May 1766, the combined impact of the Stamp Act riots and the agrarian unrest in the Hudson Valley caused Judge Livingston to hope for "some little time of calm" so that the "government can regain its authority & the lower sort can be reduced to a due submission." With unwitting foresight, he added that "whatever jealousy may have obtained at our aiming at an Independence nothing is more foreign from the thoughts of every man of property amongst us, for the confusions & disorders which would arise if this was the case would render this country the most disagreeable of any in the universe."[46]

The DeLanceys were no more egalitarian than the Livingstons, but they were more politically astute and opportunistic. Indeed, the Livingstons' political opponents were able to use the Stamp Act crisis to mount a new political offensive, and the unrest in the provincial capital ultimately served as a springboard for the emergence of

[45] Pauline Maier, *From Resistance to Revolution: Colonial Radicals and the Development of American Opposition to Britain, 1765–1776* (New York, 1972), pp. 67–70, 77–81; James and John Montressor, *The Montressor Journals*, ed. G. D. Scull (New York, 1882), pp. 336–37; Colden to Secretary Conway, 5 Nov. 1765, *DRNY*, 7:771.
[46] Colden to Secretary Conway, 9 Nov. 1765, *DRNY*, 7:773–74; Klein, "American Whig," pp. 550–54, 558–68; Sabine, ed., *Memoirs of William Smith*, 1:95; Robert R. Livingston to Robert Livingston (1688–1775), 2 Nov. 1765, Bancroft Transcripts, NYPL, 1:25–27; Robert R. Livingston to John Sargent, 2 May 1766, ibid., 2:56–57. See also Egnal, *Mighty Empire*, pp. 170–76.

James DeLancey, Jr., as a charismatic and popular leader. Unlike the Livingstons, DeLancey could afford to court the common people. For one thing, his party was not identified with the city's lawyers, who became targets of popular criticism for ceasing to do business rather than defy the Stamp Act openly. Nor was DeLancey's party associated with the great landlords of the Hudson Valley; consequently, he was free to appeal to the people by condemning the landlords, while the Livingstons took a more moderate tack, hoping for government assistance in suppressing the agrarian rioters. Finally, the Livingstons were on good terms with Sir Henry Moore and did not want to jeopardize their relationship with the governor. DeLancey, on the other hand, risked nothing by posing as an anti-government rabble-rouser because the governor disliked him and favored his political adversaries.

DeLancey used his new popularity to great effect in 1768, when the Septennial Act forced Governor Moore to dissolve the assembly and hold new elections. In 1768, DeLancey's campaign capitalized on the popular distrust of lawyers and landlords. In the wake of the Stamp Act crisis and the violent suppression of the Hudson Valley revolts, the slogan "No Lawyer in the Assembly!" was a political masterstroke admirably befitting the popular mood. DeLancey's strategy put his opponents on the defensive and forced them to wage an uninspiring campaign stressing the sterling qualities of an unpopular legal profession. When the election was over, the DeLanceys did not have a majority, but they had managed to unseat both Judge Robert R. Livingston and his cousin Henry. They also defeated candidate John Morin Scott, a member of the triumvirate and one of the extralegislative leaders of the Livingston party.[47] The election of 1768 left the parties roughly equal in strength, with New York merchant Philip Livingston winning the speakership but the DeLanceys winning nine of sixteen votes in the short-lived assembly that followed.[48]

After the election, the Livingstons' response to the deepening imperial crisis did nothing to redeem their popular image. In February

[47] On the campaign of 1768, see Colden to Lord Hillsborough, 25 Apr. 1768, *DRNY*, 8:60–62, and Bonomi, *Factious People*, pp. 239–46. For examples of the Livingston party's campaign literature, see the "Mirror" and "American Whig" essays printed in the *New-York Post-Boy*.

[48] *Assem. J., 1766–1776*, 27 Oct. 1768–2 Jan. 1769.

1768, the Massachusetts assembly had dispatched a circular letter to the twelve other colonies, urging intercolonial cooperation to secure the repeal of the Townshend Revenue Act and other offensive imperial legislation. In March, the merchants of New York adopted a nonimportation agreement, which would become effective on 1 October if Parliament did not repeal the Townshend duties. Although the assembly was not then in session, DeLancey's supporters on the council upheld the merchants' right to make such an agreement, despite Governor Moore's opposition. New York City remained calm until 14 November, when a riot occurred in support of nonimportation and the Massachusetts Circular Letter. When Moore issued a proclamation against the rioters, William Smith, Jr., supported it, while all of DeLancey's partisans on the council denounced the governor's actions. Councillors Watts, Cruger, and Oliver DeLancey not only opposed Moore's proclamation but also gleefully admitted their party's complicity with the Sons of Liberty in encouraging popular unrest. In the assembly, James DeLancey, supremely confident of his popular support and heedless of a governor who showed preference toward his adversaries, took an aggressive stance against the latest Parliamentary offenses. Under DeLancey's leadership, the house withheld a revenue bill, proposed the rejection of an address supporting Moore's denunciation of the rioters, and, by forcing a discussion of the Massachusetts Circular Letter, brought about a speedy dissolution of the thirtieth assembly. Aware that a dissolution was unavoidable, the Livingstons did offer their own set of resolutions against the duties and in support of the Massachusetts letter, but their belated action seemed insincere. Consequently, the election of 1769 was a disaster for the Livingston party.[49]

In January 1769, Cadwallader Colden, who at that time had little sympathy for either party, reported that New York was "divided into two parties, which violently oppose each other. One consisting of the new Members chosen into the [1768] Assembly, and the other supposed to be favoured by the Gov[erno]r; both sides had the preserving of their popularity in view [in the late assembly]. It is supposed this opposition will continue at the ensuing election."[50] In the elec-

---

[49] Moore to Lord Hillsborough, 12 May, 17 July, 18 Aug. 1768, 4 Jan. 1769, *DRNY*, 8:69, 80, 96–97, 143–44; Sabine, ed., *Memoirs of William Smith*, 1:46–50; *Assem. J., 1766–1776*, 27 Oct. 1768–2 Jan. 1769.

[50] Colden to Lord Hillsborough, 7 Jan. 1769, *DRNY*, 8:146.

tion of 1769, DeLancey's party vigorously cultivated their identification with the Sons of Liberty, a strategy that enabled them to win a substantial legislative majority. Meanwhile, the Livingston party waged a venomous campaign against their old nemesis, the Church of England, focusing on the tyrannous portents of current plans to bring a bishop to the colonies.[51] While both parties directed their rhetoric against threats to popular liberties, the DeLanceys' campaign was far more successful. When the new legislature convened in April 1769, the Livingstons controlled only ten of twenty-seven seats, giving the DeLanceys a commanding majority.

The Livingstons' electoral defeat notwithstanding, their anti-episcopacy campaign had focused on a timely issue that concerned many Americans. Indeed, religious issues acquired heightened political significance in the late 1760s when, while Parliament was enraging the colonists with the Stamp Act, the Declaratory Act, admiralty courts, standing armies, and the Townshend duties, prominent Anglicans in both England and America redoubled their efforts to create a colonial episcopate. William Livingston considered this latest Anglican offensive an "ecclesiastical stamp-act, which, if submitted to will at length grind us to a powder." His "American Whig" essays, published in the *New-York Post-Boy* in 1768, undertook to expose the tyranny of Anglican designs and to defend "the liberties of [the] Country against every other project calculated to ruin and enslave it." Livingston believed that the creation of American bishops would result in "Spiritual Thraldom." In his famous *Letter to the Bishop of Landaff*, he again explicitly connected the religious issue with the general pattern of English tyranny.[52]

Like New Englanders who opposed the episcopacy scheme, and Virginians who reacted so vigorously to the Two-Penny Act and the Parsons' Cause, William Livingston and his partisans regarded Anglican authoritarianism as part of a much broader conspiracy against

[51] Sabine, ed., *Memoirs of William Smith*, 1:47–49, 60. The best account of the 1769 campaign is Bonomi, *Factious People*, pp. 248–57.

[52] *New-York Post-Boy*, 14 Mar. 1768; William Livingston to Samuel Cooper, 28 Mar. 1768, in *Ecclesiastical Records of the State of New York*, ed. E. T. Corwin, 7 vols. (Albany, N.Y., 1901–16), 6:4114; William Livingston, *A Letter to the Right Reverend Father in God, John, Lord Bishop of Landaff . . .* (New York, 1768). The best account of the episcopacy controversy in New York is Klein, "American Whig," pp. 588–643. For a more general account, see Bridenbaugh, *Mitre and Sceptre*, part 2.

colonial liberty.[53] Thus, William Livingston could find parallels between the Stamp Act and the episcopacy project and like-minded
New Yorkers could establish the New York Society of Dissenters, an
organization dedicated to preserving the "Civil and Religious Rights
and Privileges" of non-Anglicans by forging an intercolonial alliance
against ecclesiastical tyranny. This short-lived society planned to
adopt recently successful methods of political protest—committees
of correspondence and the like—to resolve the current religious
crisis.[54] So too did the Livingston party use the election campaign of
1769 to publicize their fears of ecclesiastical tyranny.

In 1769 and after, more than ever before, religion became a party
issue in New York's provincial politics. The members of the
Livingston party—Dissenters all—supported the rights of Dissenting Protestants and opposed the expansion of Anglican power and
privilege. On the other hand, DeLancey and his partisans—a coalition of Anglicans and members of conservative Dutch Reformed
congregations—increasingly united in support of the colony's religious establishment. Whereas earlier religious issues had pitted
Dissenters against Anglicans, now such legislative divisions arrayed
the Livingstons against the DeLanceys.[55]

Not mere opportunists, the leaders of the Livingston party sought
to preserve and expand the rights of Dissenters even once the election was over. In the spring of 1769, during the first session of the
thirty-first assembly, opposition leaders launched an abortive attack
on the privileged position of the Church of England. They introduced two bills addressing the Dissenters' main local grievances:
their inability to obtain corporate charters and their obligation to
pay taxes to maintain the Anglican clergy. Although both bills ultimately failed, the pertinent roll-call votes illustrate the extent to
which religion had become a party issue. One division, concerning a

[53] See Patricia U. Bonomi, *Under the Cope of Heaven: Religion, Society, and Politics in
Colonial America* (New York, 1986), chaps. 6–7; Bailyn, *Ideological Origins of the American Revolution,* pp. 251–61.

[54] Herbert Levi Osgood, ed., "The Society of Dissenters Founded at New York in
1769," *American Historical Review,* 6 (1901): 498–508; Bridenbaugh, *Mitre and Sceptre,*
pp. 277–79.

[55] On the religious composition of New York's late colonial legislative factions, see
James S. Olson, "The New York Assembly, the Politics of Religion, and the Origins of
the American Revolution," *Historical Magazine of the Protestant Episcopal Church,* 43
(1974): 22–23n.

bill allowing all churches in Albany County to own property—and thus circumventing their need to obtain individual corporate charters—pitted James DeLancey, Jr., and seven of his partisans against all of the voting opposition members, plus three men who normally voted with DeLancey. In the only division concerning Lewis Morris III's bill to exempt all New Yorkers from taxes to support clergymen of denominations other than their own, party unity was even more striking. All the members of the Livingston party, save one absentee, took the antiestablishmentarian position; all but one of the voting members of DeLancey's party supported the ecclesiastical status quo.[56]

The Livingston party's explicitly antiauthoritarian ideology of dissent enabled them to connect religious issues to imperial ones, weaving them together into a grand design of British tyranny. All ten of the party's assemblymen ultimately supported the Revolution; all but one of the DeLancey party's Anglican members remained loyal to the Crown, as did several of their dissenting allies.[57]

But constitutional issues overshadowed religious ones after September 1769, when Sir Henry Moore died and Cadwallader Colden once again became New York's acting governor. Once in office, Colden's top priority was to prevail on the legislature to pass the quartering bill demanded by British imperial authorities. Since 1760, Colden had stood alone as the champion of prerogative and the villain of the judicial tenure, appeals, and Stamp Act episodes. New Yorkers of both parties disdained Colden. Yet shortly after Colden's return to power, DeLancey and his partisans made a political alliance with the lieutenant governor.

The DeLancey-Colden alliance resulted in the most consequential political realignment in New York's colonial history, a realignment that for both ideological and political reasons largely determined the

---

[56] *Assem. J., 1766–1776*, 9 May 1769 and 25 Jan. 1770. Historians often accuse the opposition leaders of opportunistically exploiting the religious issue, despite their later actions in the legislature. See Champagne, "Family Politics Versus Constitutional Principles"; Carl Becker, *History of Political Parties in the Province of New York* (Madison, Wis., 1909), pp. 74–75; Bonomi, *Factious People*, pp. 248–57.

[57] Olson, "The New York Assembly," pp. 22–23n.; Bonomi, *Under the Cope of Heaven*, chap. 7. On the relationship between opposition ideology and religious dissent in England, see Robbins, *Eighteenth-Century Commonwealthman*, chap. 7.

subsequent division between loyalists and revolutionaries. After 1769, executive favor preserved DeLancey's legislative majority, and indeed his party's complete dominance of the provincial government, but destroyed his credibility as a popular leader. Conversely, the realignment of 1769–70 reinforced the political impotence of the Livingston-led opposition but enabled them to supplant their adversaries as the elite representatives of popular grievances.

The realignment of 1769–70 did not make the Livingstons more radical, but it did make them more palatable as extralegislative political leaders. DeLancey, Colden, and their partisans seemed to become part of a conspiratorial design to undermine colonial liberties. By contrast, in the 1770s, the Livingstons' whiggish world view served them well en route to rebellion, as they joined forces with the Sons of Liberty to fight the new and seemingly omnipotent court faction created by DeLancey and Colden.

Colden had allied himself with DeLancey's party in order to ensure the passage of a quartering bill, and the ensuing controversy over the quartering of troops in New York provided the first indication of the overall impact of factional realignment. Although the abhorrence of standing armies was a hallmark of the Anglo-American libertarian tradition, New Yorkers had found the Stamp Act so repulsive that they virtually ignored Parliament's passage of the Quartering Act of 1765, which required colonial legislatures to maintain a peacetime force of British regulars stationed in America.[58] The New York assembly did pass a quartering bill in July 1766, partly because the Livingstons and their allies hoped the troops could be used to suppress the riots in the Hudson Valley. But the landlords and their allies probably did not view this quartering bill as the basis of a peacetime standing army because the Hudson Valley rioters were anything but peaceable. Furthermore, there is no evidence that these men advocated the use of British troops to maintain order in New York City. Although this distinction seems specious, those landlords under siege did draw parallels between oppressive

---

[58] The assembly that met in November 1765 to adopt resolutions against the Stamp Act did not discuss the Quartering Act. See *Assem. J.*, 12 Nov. 1765–23 Dec. 1765; and Launitz-Schürer, *Loyal Whigs and Revolutionaries*, pp. 49–51. On Anglo-American distaste for standing armies, see John Philip Reid, *The Standing Army Controversy, The Two Constitutions, and the Coming of the American Revolution* (Chapel Hill, N.C., 1981), esp. chaps. 1, 9–10.

imperial policies and lawless agrarian unrest, both of which they believed threatened their property rights and civil liberties. Moreover, in 1766 they worded the legislation so as to indicate that the support provided was given freely as a gift to the king rather than in humble submission to Parliamentary dictates.[59]

In 1769, however, the quartering act desired by Colden and demanded by the home government was intended primarily for the maintenance of a standing army in the city of New York, where it could police the activities of ordinary citizens. In the assembly, DeLancey kept his part of the bargain: in seven of nine legislative divisions concerning the quartering bill, his party voted unanimously in favor of Colden's legislation, while in the remaining two votes only one member of the majority party voted with the Livingston party in opposition. The Livingstons unanimously opposed the quartering bill in all nine roll-call votes.[60]

The DeLanceys' overwhelming support for Colden's quartering bill was so crucial a turning point in New York's pre-Revolutionary politics because it aggravated existing antiarmy sentiment and, more important, precipitated a rapprochement between the Sons of Liberty and the Livingston-led opposition. Ever since the Livingstons' cautious response to the Stamp Act crisis, the vast majority of the Sons of Liberty had allied themselves with DeLancey's party. They had supported the DeLanceys in the elections of 1768 and 1769, though by 1769 the alliance showed signs of weakening, as DeLancey's merchant supporters grew weary of nonimportation despite the continued enthusiasm of the Sons of Liberty.[61]

Consequently, even before the quartering bill received its final reading in the assembly, Alexander McDougall was laying the groundwork to reunite the Sons of Liberty and ally them with the Livingston party. McDougall was a prominent member of the minority faction within the Sons of Liberty who had remained loyal to the Livingstons, despite their lack of flamboyance in resisting imperial policies. As a member of the Presbyterian church, McDougall had learned his whiggish politics from the triumvirate and shared their

[59] See the letters exchanged by Governor Moore and his English superiors, *DRNY*, 7:831, 848, 867–68, 945, 948–49, 994, 8:63–64, 87–88, 89–91.

[60] *Assem. J., 1766–1776*, 15–30 Dec. 1769.

[61] Roger J. Champagne, *Alexander McDougall and the American Revolution in New York* (Schenectady, N.Y., 1975), pp. 13–19; Becker, *History of Political Parties*, chap. 2.

interest in religious issues. With Livingston, Smith, and Scott, he was a founding member of the Society of Dissenters in 1769.[62] On 16 December, McDougall published his famous broadside, *To the Betrayed Inhabitants of the City and Colony of New-York,* under the pseudonym "A Son of Liberty."

McDougall's tract was a vicious indictment of "the DeLancey family," who by virtue of their corrupt bargain with Colden had "trampled upon the liberties of the people . . . in order to secure them the Sovereign Lordship of this colony." The DeLanceys had betrayed the people because, McDougall argued, "Our granting Money to the Troops is implicitly acknowledging the [Parliamentary] Authority that enacted the Revenue-Acts . . . for the express Purpose of taking Money out of our Pockets, without our Consent." To make matters worse, the illegal taxes had been raised for "the Support of Troops kept here, not to protect, but to enslave us."[63]

McDougall himself was the indispensable link between the Sons of Liberty and the Livingston party, and the publication of *To the Betrayed Inhabitants,* by specifically denouncing the DeLanceys as the enemies of liberty, paved the way for the creation of a new popular coalition. McDougall's use of the pseudonym "A Son of Liberty" advertised his own impeccable credentials as a popular leader; his reputation as a leading Presbyterian gave him important personal connections within the opposition's inner circle, as well as a respectability that made him an appealing ally for the minority faction within New York's political elite. Most important, McDougall's subsequent imprisonment for seditious libel gave the Livingstons a popular issue that they could use to rehabilitate their public image. While the government inflamed public opinion by continuing its libel proceedings against McDougall, opposition leaders embraced his cause as their own, using their legal skills to urge his innocence and their polemical talents to turn him into a popular martyr for the cause of colonial liberty.

The Livingstons' leadership during the McDougall affair stands in

---

[62] Champagne, *Alexander McDougall,* pp. 13–17; Osgood, ed., "Society of Dissenters," pp. 500–501.

[63] [McDougall], *To the Betrayed Inhabitants,* in Jones, *History of New York,* 1:426–30. On popular antiarmy sentiment in New York, see Sir Henry Moore to Duke of Richmond, 21 Feb. 1766, *DRNY,* 7:867–68; Colden to Lord Hillsborough, 21 Feb. 1770, ibid., 8:208.

marked contrast to their fathers' quiescence during the Morris-Cosby controversy. In 1770, William Livingston and John Morin Scott served as McDougall's legal counsel, thus identifying themselves publicly with the defendant and his cause. The *Watchman* pamphlets, largely the work of William Livingston, vilified Colden and De-Lancey and defended the freedom of the press. Meanwhile, William Smith, Jr., published a ponderous history of libel law and, using the truth as his defense, argued eloquently for McDougall's acquittal. Smith also wrote letters to newspapers in other cities, denouncing McDougall's unjust imprisonment and praising him as a man of conviction and good character. Peter R. Livingston—William's nephew and the son of Robert Livingston, Jr.—sent copies of essays and articles concerning the McDougall affair to friends in Boston and Philadelphia, requesting that they be placed in leading local papers. As he explained to Oliver Wendell of Boston, the opposition party sought "to make Capt. McDugalls Cause as popular as possible that in case he should be Convicted the fires may be light[ed], and the more we git the other Colonies to take Alarm the greater the probability to git him Cleared."[64]

The government ultimately dropped its case against McDougall, who stayed in jail for eighty days but was released on bail in April 1770. By then, the debate over nonimportation dominated New York politics, as the Sons of Liberty struggled to keep the city's merchants faithful to the Nonimportation Association adopted in 1768 to protest the Townshend duties. In 1768, the merchants had supported nonimportation as a financially advantageous form of patriotic protest; enforcing the Association would result in a scarcity of imported goods, thus creating a seller's market for merchants who had bulging inventories during a period of economic stagnation. By 1770, however, the merchants' stocks were depleted, and the Association prevented them from resuming business as usual. Moreover, they argued that because Parliament had repealed all but

[64] Peter R. Livingston to Oliver Wendell, 15 Feb., 19 Feb., 9 Apr. 1770, Livingston Papers, MCNY, box 1; "Letter concerning Capt McDougel," [1770], Smith Papers, NYPL, box 2; Klein, "American Whig," pp. 671–72; Champagne, *Alexander McDougall*, chap. 3; Launitz-Schürer, *Loyal Whigs and Revolutionaries*, p. 85; Sabine, ed., *Memoirs of William Smith*, 1:75–76; *New-York Post-Boy*, 19 Mar. 1770. The public declaration of the alliance between the Livingstons and the Sons of Liberty appeared in the *New-York Journal*, 10 May 1770.

the tea duty, the Nonimportation Association had done its job and now could be rescinded. By mid-June, the merchants had collected 1,200 signatures in support of their position. In July, they voted to resume importation of everything but tea, despite the protests of the Sons of Liberty and the initial refusal of Boston and Philadelphia to abandon the Association. The nonimportation controversy completed the break between the Sons of Liberty and the DeLancey party.[65]

Meanwhile, DeLancey's manipulation of New York's election laws further alienated the Sons of Liberty and strengthened their new alliance with the Livingston party. Indeed, the majority leader's attempts to purge the legislature of his most influential adversaries lent credence to McDougall's charge that he and his partisans had traded the people's liberties for lordly powers. In the first session of the thirty-first assembly, DeLancey's partisans expelled two opposition members, Lewis Morris III and former speaker Philip Livingston, for nonresidence. In the second session, their attempt to oust Abraham Ten Broeck of Rensselaerswyck on the same grounds failed by a narrow margin. Although the majority's proceedings against the nonresident assemblymen complied with the provisions of the 1699 election law, their motives for enforcing that law were clearly political. Before 1769, the assembly habitually ignored the residency requirement; since 1699, the legislators had expelled only three nonresidents, while allowing twenty-one nonresident representatives to retain their seats. Moreover, in 1769 DeLancey's party removed Morris from his Westchester borough seat and replaced him with another nonresident, John DeLancey, the majority leader's cousin.[66]

---

[65] Champagne, *Alexander McDougall*, pp. 34–39; Becker, *History of Political Parties*, pp. 61–63, 83–93.

[66] *Assem. J., 1766–1776*, 12, 14, and 20 Apr., 12 May 1769, 29 Dec. 1770; Lawrence H. Leder, "The New York Elections of 1769: An Assault on Privilege," *Mississippi Valley Historical Review*, 49 (1963): 676–77. Although he resided in New York City, in 1769 Philip Livingston represented Livingston Manor in the provincial legislature. Philip presumably believed that standing for the Manor seat would ensure his presence in the assembly by enabling him to avoid stiff electoral competition from DeLancey's partisans. In an ironic turn of events, the assembly disqualified John DeLancey for nonresidence in January 1772. Only four assemblymen, all opposition members, voted for him to retain his seat, as DeLancey's own party sacrificed him to strengthen their case against nonresidents elsewhere.

Because nonresident assemblymen usually were wealthy men who owned property in more than one county, the majority's enforcement of the residency requirement in 1769 might have been viewed as an attempt to diminish elite dominance in the provincial legislature. It was not. Instead, in the context of the ongoing imperial crisis, the exclusion of Livingston and Morris raised fundamental constitutional questions concerning the people's right to representation. The majority's proceedings against the nonresident members seemed a gratuitous violation of the right of electors to choose their own representatives. As the freeholders of Livingston Manor observed, the attack on Morris and Livingston "originated in party Spirit"; the assembly's cavalier dismissal of the freeholders' petition seemed to typify the majority's authoritarian tactics.[67]

Yet even after the expulsion of the nonresidents, DeLancey and his partisans continued to attack the weakened remains of the Livingston party. DeLancey correctly anticipated that Judge Robert R. Livingston, another influential and experienced legislator, would replace his ousted cousin Philip as the Manor's representative. At the beginning of the second legislative session, DeLancey's party therefore passed a bill excluding Supreme Court justices from the provincial assembly. When Judge Livingston appeared in the house on 24 November 1769, he was disqualified by a vote of 15 to 7 in which members divided strictly along party lines. On 6 December, the judge was unanimously reelected to the Manor seat, but the majority again refused to seat him. Despite Colden's protests, the Crown disallowed the bill barring judges from the assembly in June 1770. Nonetheless, DeLancey ignored the Crown's decision, as did his partisans in the council and assembly. Fearing the loss of DeLancey's support, neither Colden—who despised the Livingstons anyway—nor his successor, William Tryon, intervened on Judge Livingston's behalf. The judge was reelected again in 1771, 1772, and 1774, but each time the majority refused to admit him to the house. Meanwhile, DeLancey also proposed to exclude lawyers from the provincial council, a strategy designed to unseat William Smith, Jr., the only councillor not affiliated with the majority party. DeLancey also unsuccessfully attempted to pass a bill abolishing the three manorial assembly seats, all of which were held by his political adversaries.[68]

---

[67] *Assem. J., 1766–1776*, 14 and 20 Apr., 12 May 1769.

[68] Ibid., 24 Nov., 21 Dec. 1769, 25 Jan. 1771, 5 Feb. 1772, 26 Jan. 1774; Colden to

The party politics of 1769–75 outraged the libertarian sensibilities of the Livingstons and their allies. In the assembly, Judge Livingston's supporters were the same men who had fought the quartering bill in 1769 and decried the unjust taxation of religious Dissenters in 1770. In 1773, they would oppose the Tea Act and defend the actions of those involved in the Boston Tea Party. Finally, in the last session of New York's last colonial assembly, they would condemn the Intolerable Acts of 1774 and support the creation of a Continental Congress.

Ever since the King's College controversy, the Livingstons had been constructing a libertarian world view that proved far more durable than the DeLancey party's momentary pursuit of popularity. The Livingstons and their associates, even in the 1760s, were "moderates" only insofar as they sought to reverse imperial violations of colonial liberties by rational and peaceable means. Like their opponents, they were not above politicking, but their response to the imperial crisis was legalistic, intellectual, and largely decorous. Their preference for reasoned and cautious argumentation over decisive action made for comparatively uninspiring political campaigns in the 1760s. Nevertheless, in the 1770s, legalism and constitutionalism enabled them to choose rebellion and revolution, while their adversaries opted for loyalism. New York's opposition leaders articulated their libertarian fears within a classical republican framework and provided intellectual guidance for the Revolutionary generation.

The Livingstons' world view predisposed them to take libertarian positions on the key issues of the late colonial era, but the dynamics of party politics made them even more acutely sensitive to both imperial and local threats to their liberties. To a man, the members of the assembly's embattled opposition supported the Revolution because they feared tyranny. Most of DeLancey's supporters remained loyal to the Crown, in part because they enjoyed power. Outside the assembly, however, there were several noteworthy deviations from this pattern. John Jay and James Duane, both prominent

---

Lord Hillsborough, 21 Feb., 18 Aug. 1770, *DRNY*, 8:209–10, 245; Robert R. Livingston to Lord Hillsborough, 4 Dec. 1769, ibid., 8:192; Lord Dunmore to Lord Hillsborough, 9 Mar. 1771, ibid., 8:265; William Tryon to Lord Hillsborough, 4 June 1772, ibid., 8:299; Robert R. Livingston to Lord Dartmouth, 5 Nov. 1772, ibid., 8:319–20; Sabine, ed., *Memoirs of William Smith*, 1:82, 92–94, 97, 100.

Anglicans associated with the majority party, ultimately chose to support the Revolution. Both men were lawyers who had married into the Livingston family. Conversely, after months of torturous self-examination, William Smith, Jr., erstwhile member of the triumvirate and longtime opposition leader—also a lawyer and husband of a Livingston—decided that American liberty could best be preserved within the confines of the British Empire.[69]

In the 1770s, the Livingston family had been the target of De-Lancey's most predatory designs and, as a result, their political fortunes within the government had declined precipitously. In time, they came to believe that their family's political difficulties in New York were related to the more general conspiracy against colonial rights and liberties. When the majority party disqualified Judge Robert R. Livingston for the fourth time in 1772, his cousin, the lord of Livingston Manor, concluded that DeLancey and his supporters "would ruin me & my family with all their hearts." By 1774, the judge's eldest son also complained of a personal vendetta against his family that was typified by his father's difficulties. The tyrannous majority "will pursue him without doubt through Life," wrote Robert R. Livingston, Jr., "and no doubt after death if any of his posterity of his Name should survive."[70]

The Livingstons also interpreted their personal difficulties within the broader context of the Anglo-American crisis. Judge Livingston repeatedly asserted that his exclusion from the assembly was a tyrannical violation of the people's right to representation, which the voters of Livingston Manor righteously opposed by reelecting him in defiance of the dictates of DeLancey's party. Similarly, Robert R. Livingston, Jr., portrayed his father as "a true Friend to Liberties," unlike the "tyrants" whose partisan ambitions led them to persecute the judge and in so doing abridge the rights of a free people. Robert Livingston, Jr., the lord of Livingston Manor, saw in DeLancey's

---

[69] Loyalist members of the assembly have been identified in Gregory Palmer, *Biographical Sketches of the Loyalists of the American Revolution* (Westport, Conn., 1984). Smith's deliberations are recorded in Sabine, ed., *Memoirs of William Smith*, vol. 2. See also L. F. S. Upton, *The Loyal Whig, William Smith of New York and Quebec* (Toronto, 1969), chaps. 8–9.

[70] Robert Livingston, Jr., to James Duane, 6 Apr. 1772, Duane Papers, NYHS, box 2; Robert R. Livingston, Jr., "Livingston and Liberty," [c. 1774], Robert R. Livingston Papers, NYHS, reel 1.

enforcement of the residency rule, and his subsequent exclusion of the judge, a conspiratorial design whereby the majority leader could control elections even in districts where his party commanded little support. By 1772, the lord of the Manor was ominously predicting that "the next Vote . . . will be that none Shall Sitt in that respectable House that has a Furnace or uses a plough & so on untill no one has the Liberty but the Gentlemen in New York or at most a few tools with them." He concluded, therefore, that "men of more Sence & honour"—or, more specifically, men who opposed DeLancey's domination—must band together so "that the Constitution be not over-turnd, & the Liberties of the People [are] kep[t] Sacred."[71]

In the 1770s, the Livingstons' escalating rhetoric aptly described their political reality. In the final years of the colonial era, Colden, DeLancey, and the imperial authorities simultaneously attempted to change the political rules in ways that undermined the liberties of both ordinary people and elites within the minority party. Imperial authorities sought to tax the colonists without their consent and force them to maintain both a standing army and an Anglican bishop. In New York, DeLancey's simultaneous attack on an already weakened minority party threatened to obliterate political dissent within the government, though New Yorkers had accepted the legitimacy of such dissent—at least implicitly—since the resolution of the Leislerian controversy. The Livingstons' fears of tyranny were genuine and well founded. Ultimately, these fears led the cautious and legalistic Livingstons to take part in America's republican revolution.

Shut out of the politics of their own colony, by 1774, members of the Livingston-led opposition were forced to content themselves with electing delegates to the Continental Congress, where they could vent their individual and collective grievances. New York's congressional delegates were an extraordinarily conservative lot. Established elites like the Livingstons, who tried to lead New York's Revolutionary movement, remained wedded to the assumption that only men of quality were fit to govern. In their uneasy alliance with

[71] Robert R. Livingston, Jr., "Livingston and Liberty," [c. 1774], Robert R. Livingston Papers, NYHS, reel 1; Robert R. Livingston to Robert R. Livingston, Jr., 17 Feb. 1771, ibid.; Robert R. Livingston to the freeholders of Livingston Manor, 22 Feb. 1772, ibid.; Robert Livingston, Jr., to James Duane, 17 Feb., 6 Apr. 1772, Duane Papers, NYHS, box 2.

the "common sort," these men infiltrated and attempted to control the proceedings of New York's local committees in the years immediately preceding the Revolution. When, in May 1775, the New York committee agreed to submit to the authority of the provincial and continental congresses, Judge Robert R. Livingston rejoiced, "We are got now into a regular kind of Government and the Power of our Demagogs are at End."[72] Had he not died the following December, Judge Livingston would have learned that the threats to his familiar, privileged world had only just begun.

[72] Robert R. Livingston to Margaret Beekman Livingston, 3 May 1775, Livingston Family Papers, NYPL, box 3.

[6]

Aristocratic Republicans

The assumption that only men of quality were fit to govern was implicit in the colonial system of politics: elites formulated the issues, and ordinary people merely responded to the rhetoric of contending elite factions. Beginning with the Stamp Act crisis of 1765–66, however, imperial issues and declining economic circumstances made activists of mechanics and artisans who for the first time took the political initiative away from their more cautious leaders. The increasing assertiveness of the "common sort" deeply distressed many prominent New Yorkers who, in 1766, applauded the use of military force to suppress the Hudson Valley rioters and later tried to dominate the proceedings of New York City's pre-Revolutionary committees.

The political and social ferment that accompanied New York's War of Independence fundamentally altered the conduct of popular politics. During the Revolutionary era, elected officials became responsible to the people, who now held supreme political power. At the same time, many politically inexperienced men of middling origins emerged as popular leaders, supplanted traditional elites, and occupied positions of political authority. While New York's colonial politics had given the common sort opportunities to support or condemn rival elite-led factions, the Revolutionary regime encouraged widespread direct involvement in the affairs of the new state government.

After reluctantly renouncing their king in 1776, the Livingstons had hoped to reestablish New York's old political order—minus the king, his governor, and the tyrannous majority party led by James DeLancey. The Livingstons had followed their fellow colonists into rebellion primarily to protect their liberties from imperial and local predators. They did not expect to relinquish political authority, but rather to exercise their authority wisely and beneficently on behalf of their social inferiors. In time, however, the Revolution appeared to jeopardize their most cherished rights and privileges. During the war, a new government arbitrarily levied excessive taxes and commandeered supplies at will. At the same time, an increasingly undeferential citizenry openly denigrated New York's great families and challenged their property rights, their public spirit, and their capacity to govern.

Throughout the Revolutionary era, the Livingstons and their social peers clung to the principles of Whig constitutionalism that had led them to rebellion. In the context of the political and social changes that confronted them during the Revolutionary era, New York's rebellious aristocrats can best be described as conservative Whigs. Like future Federalists throughout America, they distrusted both the new state governments and the policies they pursued, and they saw in the contentious politics of the times a threat that undermined the people's civic virtue and thus endangered the future of republican government.[1]

The Tea Act of 1773, the raid on the tea ship in Boston harbor, and Parliament's subsequent attempts to punish Massachusetts began the last phase of the imperial crisis and resulted in the formation of a succession of extralegal committees that ultimately led most New Yorkers to rebellion. The committees represented a coalition of established political elites and increasingly radical middling folk. The formation of the extralegal committees of the 1770s thus began the entry of new classes and new men into the previously narrow circles of political power.[2]

William Livingston moved to New Jersey in 1773, but his brothers Philip and Peter Van Brugh Livingston represented their family in New York's pre-Revolutionary committees. The Livingston brothers

[1] See Gordon S. Wood, *The Creation of the American Republic, 1776–1787* (Chapel Hill, N.C., 1969), esp. chap. 10.

[2] Edward Countryman, *A People in Revolution: The American Revolution in New York, 1760–1790* (Baltimore, 1981), pp. 124–29.

were members of the Committee of Fifty-One, elected in May 1774 to enforce the Sons of Liberty's boycott of all dutied tea. They also served on the more radical Committee of Sixty, formed in November 1774 to implement the new economic sanctions adopted by the Continental Congress. In 1775, both Philip and Peter also were included in the Committee of One Hundred—the last of New York's pre-Revolutionary committees—which called for the election of a provincial congress. Meanwhile, their nephews Walter and Peter R. Livingston, sons of the Manor's proprietor, were among the leading members of Albany County's committee, which first convened that January.[3]

Between 1773 and 1776, the DeLancey-led assembly, the old political factions, and indeed the entire provincial government became increasingly irrelevant. Extralegal committees and congresses proliferated in part because the government and the governing party were completely unattuned to the public's response to the escalating Anglo-American crisis. The governor and his council reacted cautiously to each new development, fearful lest any attempt to act decisively would expose the weakness of the imperial government. In the assembly, DeLancey's majority refused to recognize the Continental Congress and condemned its proceedings, but continued to address their own petitions to the king, listing the colonists' manifold grievances.[4] Meanwhile, de facto political authority passed gradually from the provincial government to New York City's extralegal committees. Ever mindful of their responsibility to lead and their desire to maintain order and decorum, elites of both parties sought to dominate the proceedings of those committees and to thwart the exuberant rebelliousness of the people out-of-doors.

New Yorkers' response to the Tea Act of 1773 had solidified the alliance between the Sons of Liberty and the Livingston party that had been forged during the McDougall controversy. From the outset, however, the allies disagreed on how far they should go beyond

[3] Lists of the New York City committees of 51, 60, and 100 appear in Leopold S. Launitz-Schürer, *Loyal Whigs and Revolutionaries: The Making of the Revolution in New York, 1765–1776* (New York, 1980), pp. 125, 127, 167. For the Albany County committee, see *Minutes of the Albany Committee of Correspondence*, comp. James Sullivan, 2 vols. (Albany, N.Y., 1923).

[4] Cadwallader Colden to Lord Dartmouth, 6 July 1774, *DRNY*, 8:469–70; William Tryon to Dartmouth, 4 July 1775, ibid., 8:589–90; *Assem. J.*, *1766–1776*, 26 Jan.–31 Mar. 1775.

the boycott to oppose the new tax on tea. In order to avoid popular unrest, Governor William Tryon had suggested privately that when the tea ship arrived in New York he would allow its cargo to be landed, but then stored in a warehouse rather than distributed among the city's merchants. As a member of Tryon's council, William Smith, Jr., was aware of the governor's plan, and on 13 December 1773 he met with four key signers of the Association in hopes of enlisting their cooperation in preserving the city's peace. Smith found that merchants Philip Livingston and Isaac Low hoped to avoid violence at all costs, but that the prospect of popular unrest alarmed neither Alexander McDougall nor Isaac Sears, both of whom represented the Sons of Liberty. Indeed, McDougall and Sears intimated that they could organize "10,000 People on the Wharf" to prevent the landing of the tea. Smith stressed the need to avoid bloodshed, and Livingston and Low agreed, but according to Smith, "Sears remained unaltered, & McDougal . . . put the Question What if we prevent the Landing, & kill [the] Gov[erno]r & all the Council?"—to which a shocked Philip Livingston replied, "I won't think half so far."[5]

The opinions expressed during this informal meeting epitomized the fundamental and persistent divisions within New York's Revolutionary coalition. As Smith noted in 1774, "Many People of Property dread the Violence of the lower Sort," not only because they stood to lose more by acting rashly, but also because they were horrified by the political and social implications of mass organization and popular initiative.[6]

Throughout the Revolutionary era, New York's political elites sought to restrain popular radicalism and to protect their own interests. Even James DeLancey's merchant allies, who had remained aloof from the tea-boycotting Association of the Sons of Liberty, were well represented in New York City's Committee of Fifty-One, established in May 1774 to enforce the boycott in the wake of the passage of the Boston Port Act. These New York merchants feared

[5] William H. W. Sabine, ed., *Historical Memoirs of William Smith*, 2 vols. (New York, 1958), 1:157–58. New Yorkers did stage their own "tea party" on 23 April 1774, but earlier that month Tryon had left for England.

[6] Ibid., 1:186. See also Colden to Dartmouth, 7 Sept. 1774, *DRNY*, 8:488, in which Colden reported that men "who have much at stake" were trying to erode the influence of New York's "Demagogues."

that the city's "hot headed Men" would either adopt a general plan of nonimportation or do something else to offend the home government, which in turn could result in the closing of the port of New York. Either way, trade would suffer. In 1774, the merchants thus sought to protect their trade by taking control of the new extralegal committee. As Colden noted in his report to Lord Dartmouth, the merchants "were induced to appear in what they are sensible is an illegal character, from a Consideration that if they did not the Business would be left in the same rash Hands as Before."[7]

These pro-DeLancey merchants did succeed in postponing the implementation of a nonimportation agreement until November 1774, and they also made sure that New York sent a thoroughly conservative delegation to the first Continental Congress. Nevertheless, the high-handed tactics and unsavory maneuvers they used to influence the committee's policies outraged both the Sons of Liberty and their Livingston party allies. As a result, the voters virtually excluded DeLancey's merchant supporters from the new Committee of Sixty formed in November to enforce the resolves of the Continental Congress.[8]

Even so conservative and cautious an observer as William Smith, Jr., had condemned the merchants' attempts to prevent the Committee of Fifty-One from taking any decisive action. He and his opposition party allies believed that intercolonial congresses and nonimportation agreements could provide legalistic, decorous, and effective solutions to the Empire's increasingly serious problems. In July 1774, Smith lamented the committee's slowness to send delegates to the Congress at Philadelphia, noting that New York lagged "behind all the Rest" of the colonies in opposing British violations of American liberties. At the same time, Smith disapproved of the rising "Spirit of the lower Classes," whose incendiary speeches calling the king "*a Knave* or *a Fool*" were lacking in deference and thus clearly challenged the existing social and political orders. Smith later rejoiced at the creation of the Committee of Sixty, noting that under its leadership New York would "concur in the same Spirit with the

---

[7] Colden to Dartmouth, 1 June 1774, *DRNY*, 8:433–34.

[8] The best summary is Carl Becker, *History of Political Parties in the Province of New York* (Madison, Wis., 1909), chap. 5, pp. 164–69. See also Bernard Mason, *The Road to Independence: The Revolutionary Movement in New York, 1773–1777* (Lexington, Ky., 1966), pp. 22–40.

other Colonies . . . [and will be] now no longer imbarrassed by the Hesitation of the Merchants who were opposed to the Non Importing Scheme for the Relief of Boston." Like other conservative Whigs, he believed the committee was a safer and more controlled alterative to the potentially incendiary protests of the people out-of-doors.[9]

Philip Livingston shared Smith's fear of social upheaval as well as his faith in legalistic forms of resistance to imperial tyranny. In an important 1774 pamphlet, Philip used historical precedents and Lockean political theory to justify the colonists' opposition to Parliamentary taxation and defended the Congress's adoption of nonimportation as an effective form of collective action. Like Smith, however, he continued to hope for reconciliation with Great Britain. Independence, he claimed, was "the most vain, empty, shallow, and ridiculous project." Philip believed independence would bring chaos. "If England should turn us adrift," he asserted, "we should instantly go to civil Wars among ourselves." He also dreaded the rise of "the Levelling Spirit," which he believed would accompany America's withdrawal from the British Empire.[10]

This faith in political institutions guided by the moderate influence of experienced leaders typified the Livingstons' response to the imperial crisis. In January 1775, DeLancey's majority party returned to the newly reconvened assembly and proceeded to ignore the resolutions of the Continental Congress. For political and ideological reasons, the opposition party supported the Congress and, deprived of power within the provincial govern, exercised political authority through the institutions created during the imperial crisis. In addition to their activities in the extralegal committees, the Livingstons were well represented in the Continental Congress. New York's delegation included Philip Livingston and Judge Livingston's son, Robert R. Livingston, Jr. Also present were James Duane, son-in-law of the lord of the Manor, and John Jay, son-in-law of William Livingston. William himself represented New Jersey in the Continental Congress until 1776, when he became that state's first governor.

---

[9] Sabine, ed., *Memoirs of William Smith*, 1:188, 190, 192, 203.
[10] Philip Livingston, *The Other Side of the Question* (New York, 1774), esp. pp. 25–29; John Adams, *Diary and Autobiography of John Adams*, ed. L. H. Butterfield, 4 vols. (New York, 1964), 2:107.

Even more significant was the prominence of the Livingston family in New York's provincial congress. Elected in May 1775 in response to the alarming news from Lexington and Concord, that congress was New York's de facto government from that time until the ratification of the first state constitution in 1777. On 3 April 1775, Lieutenant Governor Cadwallader Colden had adjourned the provincial assembly until 3 May, but because of the ongoing tumult in the city the assembly never reconvened. Meanwhile, the provincial congress organized the colony's defenses, formulated grievances, and attempted to keep order in the capital. As early as 7 June 1775, Colden reported that the congress and its subordinate county committees "are acting with all the confidence and authority of a legal Government." Judge Robert R. Livingston considered the congress a legitimate and "regular kind of Government" that could resolve American grievances without undue popular disorder.[11]

The judge might well have rejoiced at the election of a provincial congress, for that body became a vehicle for reviving his family's political fortunes. A member of the Livingston family presided over the deliberations of the congress throughout most of its brief life: Peter Van Brugh Livingston was president of the New York provincial congress in 1775, and his nephew Peter R. Livingston held that post in 1776 and 1777. Philip, Walter, Gilbert, and the younger Robert R. Livingston also were delegates, as were Jay, Duane, and Judge Livingston's son-in-law Richard Montgomery.[12]

The response of the provincial congress to the deepening crisis was firm but moderate. Moderate leaders, including the Livingstons, opposed the new imperial policies and raised five battalions to de-

---

[11] Colden to Dartmouth, 3 May, 7 June 1775, *DRNY*, 8:571–72, 579–80; Robert R. Livingston to Margaret Beekman Livingston, 3 May 1775, Livingston Family Papers, NYPL, box 3.

[12] Terms of Livingston family members in the provincial congress were as follows: Peter Van Brugh Livingston (1775–76), Peter R. Livingston (1775–77), Philip (1776–77), Walter (1775–76), Gilbert (1775–77), Robert R. (1776–77), Jay (1775–77), Duane (1775–77), Montgomery (1775). This Gilbert Livingston (1742–1806) was the grandson of the original Gilbert Livingston, and the son of Henry Livingston, a former member of the colonial assembly for Dutchess County. Richard Montgomery had married Janet Livingston, the eldest daughter of Judge Robert R. and Margaret Beekman Livingston in 1773. For lists of members of New York's four provincial congresses, see *Journals of the Provincial Congress, Provincial Convention and Council of Safety of the State of New York*, 2 vols. (Albany, N.Y., 1842), 1:1, 205, 445, 515.

fend their province against an expected British offensive. Nevertheless, their stance was basically defensive, and they viewed independence as the least desirable of colonial options. In May 1775, the lord of Livingston Manor still hoped that the new congress would restore the peace "least we both be Ruined, & become a pray to any dareing aspiring Prince in Europe." As late as October 1775, James Duane dreaded "a Separation from Great Britain," which, he maintained, "can be acceptable to very few." Even in 1776, both Duane and William Smith, Jr., were promoting plans for imperial reorganization in hopes of averting a complete break with the mother country.[13] New York's provincial congress did not instruct its delegates in Philadelphia to vote for independence until August 1776, thus making New York the last province to officially sever the imperial connection.

Having accepted independence, New York's reluctant revolutionaries next attempted to contain the enthusiasm of their more radical political allies. On 15 May 1776, the Continental Congress urged each colony to adopt a new frame of government to replace both their provisional congresses and the defunct imperial regime. In response to the recommendations from Philadelphia, New York's provincial congress resolved, on 31 May 1776, to "institute and establish such a government as [its members] shall deem best . . . to continue in force until a future peace with Great Britain." In June 1776, a new congress, or convention, was elected to draft New York's first constitution, but the delegates did not complete their work until April 1777.[14] In the meantime, the colonies had declared independence, New York's southern counties had succumbed to British forces, the loyalists had withdrawn from politics, and the Livingstons and their friends had emerged as the leaders of a conservative Revolutionary republican faction.

By the autumn of 1776, these conservatives were committed to independence, but they opposed most internal political changes, with the exception of getting rid of the imperial administration. The members of New York's conservative core—Robert R. Livingston,

[13] Robert Livingston, Jr., to Mary Livingston Duane, 9 May 1775, Duane Papers, NYHS, box 3; James Duane to Robert Livingston, Jr., 23 Oct. 1775, Livingston-Redmond MSS., reel 8; Robert Livingston, Jr., to Richard Montgomery, 15 Nov. 1775, ibid. See also Colden to Dartmouth, 7 June 1775, *DRNY*, 8:579–83, and William Smith, Jr., to William Tryon, 17 Dec. 1775, ibid., 8:653–54.

[14] *Journals of the Provincial Congress*, 1:460, 469.

Jr., John Jay, James Duane, Philip Schuyler, and Gouverneur Morris—believed it was their duty, and well as in their interest, to direct the formation of New York's new government. Robert R. Livingston, Jr., sincerely believed that the experience and influence of "old families of wealth and age" could offset the vengeful partiality of radical demagogues who, he contended, were ill-equipped to undertake the difficult business of statecraft. He and his associates correctly perceived the long-term significance of the state constitutions. As Livingston reported to Edward Rutledge, an equally conservative South Carolinian, "Everything is at stake here—*two thirds of our gentlemen fell off early in this controversy,* [and] the stagnation of our trade, and large openings to wealth in the Eastern States have taken from us the few merchants who have been hitherto supports of the cause of Liberty."[15] Unlike the "gentlemen" who had adhered to the Crown and the few patriot merchants who moved to New England during the British occupation, these conservative statesmen worked toward molding New York's Revolutionary regime in their own pre-Revolutionary image.

The conservatives' task was made easier by the British occupation of Manhattan in August and September of 1776, which left the city's radicals disorganized and dispersed, as well as by the early departure of leading radicals to take up commissions in the patriot army.[16] At the constitutional convention that met at White Plains, Fishkill, and Kingston, successively, the conservatives' adversaries were mainly farmers and other middling men who wanted substantive democratic reforms but were both less organized and less radical than the mechanics of Manhattan.[17] Still, the conservatives were a minority, and wisely their approach to the convention was both cautious and conciliatory. Robert R. Livingston, Jr., for instance, emphasized "the propriety of Swimming with a Stream which it is impossible to Stem," suggesting that his like-minded colleagues should "yield to the torrent if they hoped to direct its Course."[18]

[15] Robert R. Livingston, Jr., to Edward Rutledge, 10 Oct. 1776, Bancroft Transcripts, NYPL, 2:229–35.

[16] On this point, see Roger Champagne, "New York's Radicals and the Coming of Independence," *Journal of American History,* 5 (1964): 21–40, and Countryman, *People in Revolution,* pp. 163–66.

[17] See Alfred F. Young, *The Democratic Republicans of New York: The Origins, 1763–1797* (Chapel Hill, N.C., 1967), pp. 12, 16–22, chap. 2.

[18] Robert R. Livingston, Jr., to William Duer, 12 June 1777, Robert R. Livingston Papers, NYHS, reel 1.

Because New Yorkers wanted to present a united front against the British invaders, the constitution of 1777 was by necessity a compromise measure acceptable to both wings of the state's truncated Whig coalition. Nevertheless, the document was largely the work of Jay and Livingston, two college-educated conservative lawyers. The conservatives made the new constitution their top priority, and they were willing and able to devote most of their time to drawing up the new frame of government. Although they may have been more influential than their minority status warranted, all but one of the convention's delegates ultimately approved the new constitution. Peter R. Livingston, eldest son of the lord of the Manor, cast the lone dissenting vote. He undoubtedly shared his father's outrage over the constitution's abolition of all colonial pocket boroughs, which of course included his family's assembly seat representing Livingston Manor.[19]

The constitution of 1777 preserved some aspects of the old order, but the conservatives compromised on several key issues to maintain unity and avoid discrediting themselves in the eyes of their more democratic colleagues.[20] For example, the conservative delegates were willing to abolish the manorial assembly seats, but the constitution explicitly protected all land titles bestowed by royal patent, including the great manorial grants. As for the structure of the new state government, conservatives and radicals alike accepted the traditional arrangement of governor, lieutenant governor, and a bicameral legislature, and the conservatives agreed to have the executive and upper house popularly elected, though in both cases they would have preferred indirect election by the state assembly. Radicals and conservatives also compromised on the issues of executive powers, the frequency of elections, and the introduction of the written ballot. The delegates also reached an accommodation on the issue of property qualifications for the suffrage, ultimately lowering the requirement for voting in assembly elections from £40 to £20, but imposing a £100 minimum on elections for the governor and senators.

[19] Sabine, ed., *Memoirs of William Smith*, 2:136–37.

[20] The best summary of the convention's proceedings is Young, *Democratic Republicans*, pp. 17–22. New York's state constitution appears in its entirety in Francis Newton Thorpe, comp., *The Federal and State Constitutions, Colonial Charters and Other Organic Laws of the States, Territories and Colonies now or heretofore forming the United States of America*, 7 vols. (Washington, D.C., 1909), 5:2623–38.

The creation of an extraordinarily powerful state judiciary was the single unequivocal conservative triumph. The new constitution stipulated that New York's chancellor and supreme court justices would serve during good behavior. With the governor, they also would act as a Council of Revision, a body proposed by Robert R. Livingston, Jr., as a compromise measure to weaken the governor's veto power without eliminating it entirely. The council's veto could be overridden only by a two-thirds majority in both houses of the state legislature. Livingston's proposal seems to have elicited no serious protests, even though the creation of the council gave the traditionally conservative judiciary unprecedented legislative and political powers.[21]

The convention filled the top judicial offices with conservatives and moderates, possibly out of deference to their education and legal experience. In two close votes, the delegates chose John Jay and Robert R. Livingston, Jr., as chief justice and chancellor, respectively. The two remaining places on the supreme court went to John Sloss Hobart, a conservative landowner from Suffolk County, and Robert Yates, a moderate Whig and future Anti-Federalist from Albany. Jay and Livingston's friend and political ally, Egbert Benson, became the state's first attorney general.

The results of the elections of June 1777 offset the conservatives' domination of the judiciary by giving the radicals control of the legislature. In New York, as in the other newly independent states, the Revolution democratized officeholding by bringing many new men into the circles of political power. The departure of the loyalists, who had accounted for roughly half of New York's colonial elite, had left some political vacancies at the state level, while the new constitution had created more elective offices by increasing the membership of the assembly from thirty-one to sixty-five and by adding an elective senate with twenty-four members. The democratizing spirit of the Revolution encouraged New Yorkers to choose obscure men, like themselves, to fill these political offices. The result was that of the 290 assemblymen who served during the Revolutionary and Confederation periods, only six had sat in the colonial assembly; likewise, only six of fifty-five senators had sat in the provincial legislature. Many of these new men had received their political education as members of the Revolutionary committees. Although

21 *Journals of the Provincial Congress*, 1:860, 910; Young, *Democratic Republicans*, p. 22.

New York's assemblymen did choose Walter Livingston as their first speaker, their choice was more a conciliatory gesture than a portent of the state's political future.[22]

Conservative Whigs continued to take pride in their constitution, but they resented the rise of middling men to positions of authority traditionally held by members of New York's leading families. Most conservatives could accept the election of George Clinton to the governorship because he was a military hero and a former member of the colonial assembly; nevertheless, many shared Philip Schuyler's opinion that Clinton's "family and connections do not entitle him to so distinguished a predominance."[23] The old elites found the types of men elected to the new legislature far more offensive. As early as January 1778, Chancellor Robert R. Livingston was begging his friend Gouverneur Morris to absent himself from the Continental Congress in order to attend the state legislature, reminding him, "You know too much of Some People in power here to think the State safe in their hands." Philip Livingston claimed that no more than four assemblymen and three senators were capable of drawing up legislation; Walter Livingston, the speaker of the new assembly, doubted that even that many of the new men had enough education or experience to govern effectively. Walter lamented, "The little aristocracy which [was] formerly enjoyed in this State is torn up by the root." New York's new governors, he asserted, did not show due regard for the learning and experience of their social superiors.[24]

The decline of deference occasioned by the Revolution had turned New York politics upside down. Philip Schuyler exaggerated the democratization of officeholding somewhat when he observed in 1778 that "Abraham Yates, I mean the Honorable Abraham Yates Esq. one of the Senate of this State . . . [and] late Cobler of Laws and Old Shoes, is to be put in Nomination for Lieut[enant] Governor." Yates was no shoemaker, but he was an Albany attorney of decidedly

[22] Countryman, *People in Revolution*, pp. 196–202, app. 2; Jackson Turner Main, "Government by the People: The American Revolution and the Democratization of the Legislatures," *WMQ*, 3d ser., 23 (1966): 394, 399–400, and *Political Parties Before the Constitution* (Chapel Hill, N.C., 1973), chap. 5.

[23] Philip Schuyler to John Jay, 14 July 1777, in Henry P. Johnston, ed., *The Correspondence and Public Papers of John Jay*, 4 vols. (New York, 1890), 1:147.

[24] Robert R. Livingston, Jr., to Gouverneur Morris, Jan. 1778, Robert R. Livingston Papers, NYHS, reel 1; Walter Livingston to John Carter, 11 Aug. 1777, Livingston Family Papers, NYHS, reel 15; Sabine, ed., *Memoirs of William Smith*, 2:159–160.

middling origins. As William Smith, Jr., sardonically noted, "the great Offices go to meaner Hands . . . [Senator Dirck] Ten Broeck was a Justice of the Peace who would not be perswaded formerly to act until Mr. [Robert] L[ivingston] promised to assist him." By 1777, however, Ten Broeck and Yates, as well as many other men of even more obscure origins, were exercising political authority, while men like Livingston, Smith, and Schuyler wondered what had gone wrong.[25]

As they became increasingly disillusioned with the politics of their state, New York's old elites either withdrew from the Revolutionary movement or attempted to reaffirm their political authority at the national level. In 1779, John Jay gave up the chief justiceship to become president of the Continental Congress. By 1780, Gouverneur Morris, William Duer, and Egbert Benson also had abandoned their New York offices for congressional seats. James Duane and Robert R. Livingston retained their offices as state senator and chancellor, respectively, but both devoted progressively more time to politics at the national level. Walter Livingston gave up politics entirely in 1779, though his elder brother Peter R. Livingston took his place briefly in the state assembly. Both Peter and Walter, however, had stopped attending the meetings of the Albany County committee long before it disbanded in 1778, and the Livingston family did not participate in the revived committees of 1779.[26]

Elites who had taken up military posts also found themselves at odds with the Revolution's decidedly popular spirit. During the early years of the Revolution, the Livingston family produced two military heroes, both of whom criticized the relative lack of deference and social hierarchy within the Continental Army. Richard Montgomery—Judge Livingston's son-in-law—had received his commission as brigadier general in June 1775; in December he died leading the siege of Quebec, thus becoming a national hero. Nevertheless, as early as October 1775, Montgomery at least rhetorically regretted his association with so untraditional a fighting force, claiming that

[25] Sabine, ed., *Memoirs of William Smith*, 2:159–60; Philip Schuyler to Gouverneur Morris, 3 Feb. 1778, quoted in Staughton Lynd, "Abraham Yates's History of the Movement for the United States Constitution," *WMQ*, 3d ser., 20 (1963): 225.

[26] Peter last attended the committee on 15 June 1776. Walter attended frequently until October 1776; he made only three subsequent appearances, the last in June 1777 (*Minutes of the Albany Committee*, passim).

he intended to retire from the army after the Canadian expedition. In a letter to his brother-in-law, the future chancellor, Montgomery complained, "Nothing shall ever tempt me again to hazard my reputation at the head of such ragamuffins; Honor[,] the very soul of the soldier has no existence among us."[27]

Colonel Henry Beekman Livingston—Montgomery's brother-in-law and the chancellor's younger brother—also criticized the demeanor of soldiers and officers alike and complained bitterly that the Continental Army made officers of men of inferior social status. Henry had been with Montgomery in Quebec and later served with distinction at Brooklyn Heights, Monmouth, and Rhode Island. By 1777, however, he was lamenting the fact that he could not "find in the whole Army a Sett of Gentlemen to associate with." Meanwhile, Henry unsuccessfully attempted to use both his military record and his personal connections to secure a promotion. With some justification, he worried that New Englanders in Congress conspired against the advancement of New Yorkers. Less justifiably, he concluded that the members of Congress discriminated against all gentlemen, regardless of their military abilities or political connections. Though haughty and difficult, Henry Beekman Livingston was a courageous and dedicated soldier who spent the winter at Valley Forge in 1777–78. But by January 1779, he had resigned his commission, protesting the unwillingness of Congress to reward him with the rank to which he believed he was entitled.[28]

Most gentlemen scorned the Revolutionary changes that undermined the importance of connections and social status and made officeholders public servants, in the most literal sense. Conservative Whigs increasingly regarded state politics, in particular, as a dirty and even disreputable avocation. After a particularly contentious meeting of the state legislature, Chancellor Robert R. Livingston felt

[27] Richard Montgomery to Robert R. Livingston, Jr., 5 Oct. 1775, Bancroft Transcripts, NYPL, 2:59; Charles Royster, *A Revolutionary People at War: The Continental Army and the American Character, 1775–1783* (Chapel Hill, N.C., 1979), pp. 120–26.
[28] Mark Mayo Boatner III, *Encyclopedia of the American Revolution* (New York, 1966), p. 639; George Dangerfield, *Chancellor Robert R. Livingston of New York, 1746–1813* (New York, 1960), pp. 110–13; Sabine, ed., *Memoirs of William Smith*, 2:222; Robert R. Livingston, Jr., to Gouverneur Morris, Jan. 1778, Robert R. Livingston Papers, reel 1; Robert R. Livingston, Jr., to George Washington, 12 Jan. 1778, ibid.; Gouverneur Morris to Robert R. Livingston, Jr., 21 Jan. 1779, ibid.

a need to retire to Clermont to "rub off the rust of Politicks," noting that he had recently "engaged in a round of little politicks to which *I feel myself superior.*" Livingston disdained the "paltry party politics" of the Revolutionary era which quickly undermined the cooperative spirit that had prevailed within New York's early Revolutionary coalition. Under the new constitution, frequent elections and an assertive electorate meant that officeholders had to be responsive to the popular will. Because the old elites were accustomed to leading the people—not following their orders—they resented this newly obligatory "pursuit of popularity."[29]

Under these circumstances, many conservative Whigs found public service a dubious honor, at least at the state level. In 1781, Walter Livingston concluded, "There is not an office in the gift of the people that I would accept of from the highest to the lowest." Yet despite his own withdrawal from politics, Walter believed New York needed enlightened gentlemen-leaders to preserve both good government and social order. Commenting on the resignation of yet another disillusioned gentleman, he wondered, "Who can we expect will [hold office]? . . . If every man says let others do it, our misfortunes are only beginning . . . & the distinction between men will cease in the place of which anarchy will rise—If he resigns other gentlemen may follow his example." Paradoxically, others echoed Walter's sentiments, calling for wise and experienced leadership while they themselves withdrew from the arena of state politics.[30]

During the Revolutionary era, New York's conservative Whigs were torn between their desire to protect the remnants of their private, privileged world and their urge to maintain their class's tradition of public service. Those who remained active in public affairs believed it was their patriotic duty to lead—and also to restrain—their countrymen in a time of national crisis. Their private correspondence indicates that they did not enjoy their public responsibilities, which took them away from their homes and families and nearly ruined their personal fortunes. As Chancellor Robert R.

---

[29] Robert R. Livingston, Jr., to John Jay, 2 Feb., 4 Mar. 1779, Robert R. Livingston Papers, NYHS, reel 1; Robert R. Livingston, Jr., to Gouverneur Morris, 9 Feb. 1779, ibid., emphasis added; Countryman, *People in Revolution*, esp. pp. 189–90, 193–200.

[30] Walter Livingston to Robert R. Livingston, Jr., 7 Jan. 1781, Livingston Family Papers, NYHS, reel 15; Walter Livingston to Robert G. Livingston, 10 Jan. 1781, ibid.; Walter Livingston to John Carter, 11 Aug. 1777, ibid.

Livingston observed upon his reelection to the Continental Congress in 1779, "I am to have the supreme felicity of making them a second Sacrifice of my health, fortune, & enjoyments . . . To this I submit, but with the reluctance of the shipwrecked wretch who embarks again after having once safely landed." James Duane protested that he "never sought publick Employment [but] when called upon by the Voice of my Country could I refuse in a Cause in which my Conscience approved?" Duane, who was deeply interested in the Vermont land disputes Congress was currently resolving, feigned the disinterested noblesse oblige appropriate to the most public-spirited of aristocrats. "Do not," he urged his distraught family, "repine at what cannot be prevented, but submit as chearfully as possible to our present lot."[31]

Most of the New York's conservative leaders were young men who, because of their age or their earlier membership in the Livingston-led opposition, had been denied access to political office during the colonial era.[32] While many among New York's older generation of conservative Whigs—most notably Philip and Peter Van Brugh Livingston—withdrew from politics as the implications of the Revolution became increasingly apparent, a new younger generation emerged to take their places, especially at the national level. Chancellor Robert R. Livingston was only thirty years old when the colonies declared their independence; John Jay was a year younger. At forty-three, James Duane was considerably older, but in 1776 Gouverneur Morris and the increasingly influential Alexander Hamilton were only twenty-four and twenty-one years old, respectively.[33]

---

[31] Robert R. Livingston, Jr., to John R. Livingston, 8 Nov. 1779, Robert R. Livingston Papers, NYHS, reel 1; James Duane to Mary Livingston Duane, 6 Mar. 1781, Duane Papers, NYHS, box 4. On Duane's landholdings in Vermont, see Edward P. Alexander, *A Revolutionary Conservative: James Duane of New York* (New York, 1938), chap. 7.

[32] See Stanley Elkins and Eric McKitrick, "The Founding Fathers: Young Men of the Revolution," *Political Science Quarterly*, 76 (1961): 202–6, on the relative youth and lack of prior political experience among future Federalists in general. Nevertheless, the Elkins-McKitrick thesis—that these men simply exceeded their opponents in energy and optimism—does not hold, at least in the case of New York, where the "young men of the Revolution" were conservatives profoundly alarmed by the increasingly democratic direction of the politics of their state.

[33] Despite his deepening conservatism, Philip Livingston remained a member of the Continental Congress until his death in 1778, though he was not active in state politics. After 1776, Peter Van Brugh Livingston withdrew from politics entirely and

Despite their increasing disillusion and discomfort, these men continued to hold public office, kept abreast of current affairs, and still tried to shape the Revolution's ultimate outcome. They played a vital role in public affairs and never regretted America's declaration of independence; nor did they doubt the ability of the new nation to win its war with Britain. Just as the Revolution had energized the people at large, it had strengthened both the sense of duty and the conservative fears of New York's most public-spirited young gentlemen. If the popular spirit of the Revolution forced these men to adopt a defensive stance, it did not diminish their determination to preserve the new Republic by opposing popular licentiousness.

While politically active members of the old elite sought to limit the impact of popular government, their social peers who remained at home grappled with wartime dislocations, uncertainties, and hardships. From the commencement of hostilities in southern New York in 1776, Livingston Manor became an aristocratic island in the midst of an increasingly popular upheaval. In the Revolutionary era, members of the Livingston family gathered at the Manor and at Clermont, where they sought to escape both the enemy and the depredations of New York's new state government.

The war and the British occupation of New York City had dispersed the Livingston family. Judge Livingston's widow, Margaret Beekman Livingston, remained at Clermont with her six daughters during the war years, but her sons went elsewhere to exploit the political, military, and commercial opportunities that the times offered. Robert R. Livingston, Jr., the eldest, divided his time between the chancery and the Continental Congress. Henry Beekman Livingston was with the army. John R. Livingston spent the war years in Boston, where he invested in privateers and illicit trade. Edward, the youngest Livingston brother, attended school at Albany, Kingston, and Princeton, successively.[34]

---

spent the war years in New Jersey, New York City, and Europe, attempting to remain neutral.

[34] On John R. Livingston's wartime career, see his letters to his brother Robert R. Livingston, Jr., 2 Feb. 1777, 29 Mar. 1780, 18 June 1781, 6 Mar. 1782, 17 July 1782, Robert R. Livingston Papers, NYHS, reels 1–2. On Edward Livingston, see William B. Hatcher, *Edward Livingston: Jeffersonian Republican and Jacksonian Democrat* (University, La., 1940), p. 4. Edward Livingston, who was born in 1764, entered Princeton in 1779 and graduated two years later.

The war also scattered Robert Livingston, Jr., and his brothers, the third generation of the Manor branch of the Livingston family. The British occupation of Manhattan caused both Peter Van Brugh and Philip Livingston to flee the city, though Peter returned after retiring from politics shortly after Congress declared independence. Brother John Livingston, a Tory, remained in Manhattan throughout the war. Robert Livingston, Jr., continued to reside at his Manor, unable to visit his city-dwelling brothers. Meanwhile, William Livingston governed New Jersey, fled British forces, and desperately tried to keep his own family safe and solvent. As governor, his most difficult task was refusing his relatives' repeated petitions for passes to visit Tory kin in nearby New York City.[35]

The British occupation of Manhattan also resulted in the relocation of the merchant sons of Robert Livingston, Jr. All Robert's sons spent at least part of the war at Livingston Manor, as did one of his married daughters. At Livingston Manor, ties of kinship and friendship were more important than political loyalties. Robert Livingston, Jr., graciously extended his hospitality to the prominent Tory William Smith, Jr., as well as to his daughter Catharine and her loyalist husband John Patterson. Both the Pattersons and the Smiths continued to reside at the Manor until 1778, when the state government banished them by act of attainder. Friends and relatives who either supported the Revolution or did not actively oppose it partook of the Livingstons' hospitality throughout the war. As late as 1782, when peace had long since returned to the Hudson Valley, Robert Livingston, Jr., reported that there was "not one Spare bed left" in his mansion at the Manor.[36]

[35] See, for instance, Mary Alexander Watts to William Livingston, 5 Aug. 1777, William Livingston Papers, Mass. Hist. Soc., reel 1; William Livingston to Philip Hoffman, 15 Sept. 1781, ibid., reel 7; William Livingston to Robert Livingston, Jr., 22 Apr. 1782, ibid.; William Livingston to Alida Livingston Hoffman, 29 Oct. 1782, ibid. John Livingston (1714–86), the Manor lord's brother, remained loyal to the Crown but stayed in New York after the war was over. He was never active politically and in 1776 probably followed the lead of his in-laws, the DePeysters, a prominent loyalist family.

[36] Robert Livingston, Jr., to Peter Van Brugh Livingston, 28 Jan. 1782, Welch-Livingston Collection, NYHS. See Sabine, ed., *Memoirs of William Smith*, vol. 2, for accounts of various Manor residents and guests. Smith was doubly related to the Manor family; he had married one of their distant cousins, and his sister had married Peter R. Livingston.

Robert Livingston, Jr., played no active role in the politics of the Revolutionary era. His case suggests that conservatives who were not active in public affairs often wavered in their support for the Revolution, as well as in their confidence in America's future. In 1776, Robert reluctantly had accepted independence, but by April 1777 he regretted his countrymen's earlier boldness and wished "that the Congress would bargain away their Independency for Peace." By August, as British forces marched toward Livingston Manor, Robert was claiming that he had always opposed the colonists' break with England. After the patriots' stunning victory that October at Saratoga, however, he changed his mind again because upstate New York was out of danger and the tide had seemed to turn in America's favor. As the war moved southward and out of the Hudson Valley, and as the French began to aid the Continental Army, Livingston became more optimistic and once again declared that he favored independence, though he continued to hope for a speedy peace and a return to the prewar politics of deference and decorum.[37]

Livingston's vacillation was symptomatic of the garrison mentality that developed quickly among Manor house residents, who had few reliable sources of political and military information. Visitors to the Manor were varied and frequent. Each claimed to bring the latest news, but often their information was erroneous. In December 1776, the Livingstons and their guests heard that King George had died, but, as Smith wisely concluded two months earlier, "one knows not what to believe in these days of false Rumour." With the British army in upstate New York in 1777, Manor residents lived in constant fear of an attack, receiving often contradictory reports of the enemy's current location.[38]

When the British did arrive in October 1777, they burned the Clermont homes of Margaret Beekman Livingston and her son the chancellor, as well as the houses of several Manor tenants on the north side of Roeloff Jansen's Kill. The invaders spared the Manor house and outbuildings of Robert Livingston, Jr., but the lord of the Manor nevertheless moved his family to Ancram for safety. Mar-

---

[37] Sabine, ed., *Memoirs of William Smith*, esp. 2:16, 54, 57, 123–24, 180–90, 202, 214, 240, 319, 371, 375; Robert Livingston, Jr., to James Duane, 12 June 1778, Duane Papers, NYHS, box 3; Robert Livingston, Jr., to Peter Van Brugh Livingston, 4 Apr. 1780, Welch-Livingston Collection, NYHS.

[38] Sabine, ed., *Memoirs of William Smith*, esp. 2:29, 53, 106, 178, 221.

garet Beekman Livingston and her daughters left Clermont for nearby Salisbury, Connecticut, until part of their house could be renovated and made fit for habitation. By the summer of 1778, one of the chancellor's sisters reported, "Mama is at her little Chateau . . . where she has had a visit from a gang of robbers; we are in daily expection of them, & we have not one white man in the house" for protection.[39]

Like most Americans, the Livingstons who remained at home also suffered the ill effects of chronic wartime shortages. Peter R. Livingston's children went without shoes in 1777 because local shoe-makers would not accept inflated paper currency. That winter, Peter, then attending the provincial congress at Fishkill, never received his newspapers, which when they arrived at the Manor had been "cut up in Patterns for the Ladies" to make winter clothing. As late as 1781, Robert Livingston, Jr., complained that his family still needed winter clothes, though without hard money or access to the port of New York they had little hope of obtaining dry goods and other necessities.[40] The Manor's wartime residents occasionally ordered clothing and other items from Philadelphia through their friends and relatives who were there serving in the Continental Congress. But their morale suffered and their patriotism wavered when they heard of Tories in occupied New York City living in comfort, ease, and luxury.[41]

Fear of British raids and dissatisfaction with wartime shortages made Manor residents anxious, but anxiety turned to outrage as the egalitarian implications of New York's state politics became increasingly apparent. It was one thing to be victimized by enemy armies or to suffer the material inconveniences that generally accompanied war; it was quite another matter when one's own government seemed to jeopardize the very rights and liberties it was sup-

---

[39] Ibid., 2:237–38; Margaret Livingston to Susannah Livingston, July [1778], William Livingston Papers, Mass. Hist. Soc., reel 3.

[40] Sabine, ed., *Memoirs of William Smith*, 2:68, 185–86; Robert Livingston, Jr., to Peter Van Brugh Livingston, 1 Oct. 1781, Welch-Livingston Collection, NYHS.

[41] Robert R. Livingston, Jr., to John Jay, 4 Mar. 1779, Robert R. Livingston Papers, NYHS, reel 1; Jay to Robert R. Livingston, Jr., 14 Mar. 1779, ibid.; Catharine Livingston to Robert R. Livingston, Jr., 16 Feb. 1780, ibid.; Robert Livingston, Jr., to Peter Van Brugh Livingston, 4 Apr. 1780, Welch-Livingston Collection, NYHS; John Livingston (1714–86) to Robert Livingston, Jr., 27 Sept. 1781, Livingston-Redmond MSS., reel 8.

posed to be protecting. Chief among those rights and liberties were the rights to property and to representation, both of which conservative Whigs believed were endangered in New York during the Revolutionary era.

The Livingstons and their peers in New York who supported the Revolution did so in order to protect these rights and liberties. They believed their right to representation had been violated by imperial taxation and, closer to home, by the majority party's repeated expulsion of Judge Livingston from the assembly. London's taxes and disciplinary measures, as well as Colden's attack on the judiciary, also had threatened colonial property rights. Yet from the Livingstons' perspective these rights seemed no safer under the new state government. Robert Livingston, Jr., and his sons believed that the state convention's abolition of the Manor's legislative seat violated their rights both to property and to representation and gave them an inkling of the hard times ahead for the proponents of conservative whiggery. As Walter Livingston shrewdly observed in August 1777, his own family, as the most prominent remnant of New York's aristocratic past, would be the object of the new legislators' most rigorous scrutiny. Walter noted that the new popular party "dont want to see a Gentleman have influence in the Country." As a result, they deprived his family of "our leading Representative to the house of Assembly which [is an] *unalienable right* we hold by Law, usuage, & Pattent."[42]

In the ensuing years, the Livingstons came to fear the tyranny of both the state and its people. Most of all, they resented the state's new system of taxation. The Revolution brought several significant changes to New York's tax system, all of which undermined the interests of the great landed families by making taxation more equitable and democratic. First, in March 1778, the state government imposed an *ad valorum* tax on both improved and unimproved land and stipulated that land values would be decided by popularly elected assessors. The government then enacted an excess profits tax of 5 percent on all war profits of more than £1,000 per year. Taken together, these two laws saddled speculators, landed magnates, and profiteers with the lion's share of the tax burden. At the other end of

[42] Walter Livingston to John Carter, 11 Aug. 1777, Livingston Family Papers, NYHS, reel 15.

the social spectrum, the new system gave tax exemptions to soldiers and to men with families having personal estates worth less than £300. The government discontinued the *ad valorum* land tax in 1779, but the elected assessors retained virtually absolute authority to assess taxes according to their own sense of an individual's ability to pay.[43]

Conservative elites repeatedly tried to make the new system more responsive to their interests by making the assessors appointive; they also tried to lessen the tax burden of wealthy New Yorkers by doing away with the "ability to pay" criterion. As a member of the Council of Revision, Chancellor Robert R. Livingston was among the leading critics of the new system. Nevertheless, the legislature consistently overrode the council's vetoes of its tax legislation.[44]

Tax reform was the state government's greatest democratic achievement as well as the old elite's greatest Revolutionary grievance. The Livingstons considered the new taxes both an imposition and a personal affront. While they did expect to pay taxes to support the war effort, the financial costs of rebellion far exceeded their expectations. Furthermore, the Livingstons correctly saw the new tax system as an attempt to revoke some of the special privileges they had enjoyed during the colonial era. In 1780, Robert Livingston, Jr., lord of the Manor, aptly summarized his family's position on the matter of taxation: "I well know it is necessary in time of war that Taxes Should be laid, to carry it on," he wrote, "but more time [between levies] ought to be given, & the burdens made more Equal; this might be done by our Legislature but alas I fear they have but little Judgment in those Matters, they are all new raw hands."[45]

The government collected new taxes every few months, and sometimes the Livingstons were hard-pressed to meet their financial obligations. The tax burden was heaviest for men who continued to hold public office. Chancellor Robert R. Livingston, for instance, had his estate valued at more than £3,600 in 1779 and thus found himself among the most highly taxed residents of Albany County.[46] Yet,

[43] Robert A. Becker, *Revolution, Reform, and the Politics of American Taxation, 1763–1783* (Baton Rouge, La., 1980), pp. 157–63.

[44] Ibid.; Dangerfield, *Chancellor Robert R. Livingston*, pp. 106–8.

[45] Robert Livingston, Jr., to Peter Van Brugh Livingston, 4 Apr. 1780, Welch-Livingston Collection, NYHS.

[46] His real and personal estates were valued at £1,000 and £2,606, respectively. See Albany County tax lists, March 1779, New York State Library.

unlike his cousins at the Manor who traded throughout the war, he divided his time between the chancery, the Congress, and later the secretaryship of foreign affairs. The financial benefits of officeholding were negligible, and the chancellor's private affairs deteriorated as a result of his prolonged absences.

In 1780, the chancellor's mother informed him, "We are a good deal puzled how to get money to pay your Tax." Margaret Beekman Livingston, whose wheat had been seized by the assessors the previous year to pay her own taxes, told her son John to sell his brother Robert's horses in order to pay his taxes, "for if [his] Cattle should be distrained they would sell for a triffle." Chancellor Livingston later considered appealing to the legislature for a reduction of his taxes, but Governor Clinton wisely urged him to drop the matter, warning that requesting special treatment would "incur blame and effect your influence in the State." The chancellor sensibly heeded Clinton's advice, though he had to borrow £2,000 to pay his taxes at home and his living expenses in Philadelphia.[47]

Both Margaret Beekman Livingston, a stalwart supporter of the Revolution, and Robert Livingston, Jr., a far more lukewarm patriot, bitterly resented the "arbitrary" assessors who imposed these "monstrous" taxes.[48] Their outrage arose partly from an aristocratic revulsion toward the legislators and assessors—men who, though previously subservient to the Livingstons and their peers, now had the authority to lord over them. Attorney General Egbert Benson attributed the tax system's alleged deficiencies to the stupidity of legislators and assessors. In 1780, the conservative Benson proposed "at least twenty different schemes for a more equitable and certain System of Taxation," but the legislators resolutely implemented their own more progressive plan. Once the tax laws were passed, Benson complained, the people elected assessors who were too inept to un-

[47] Margaret Beekman Livingston to Robert R. Livingston, Jr., 30 Dec. 1779, 4 Apr. 1780, Robert R. Livingston Papers, NYHS, reel 1; Robert R. Livingston, Jr., to George Clinton, 21 May 1780, ibid.; Ezra L'Hommedieu to Robert R. Livingston, Jr., 7 June 1780, ibid.; John Morin Scott to George Clinton, 26 Sept. 1780, in Hugh Hastings, ed., *The Public Papers of George Clinton*, 10 vols. (New York and Albany, 1899–1914), 6:255.

[48] On Margaret's Revolutionary fervor, see Sabine, ed., *Memoirs of William Smith*, 2:115. Smith reported: "Upon other Subjects I scarce know a more reasonable Woman . . . [but] She verily believes that it is God's Will to seperate the Colonies from the Mother Country and that the Work has been already countenanced and advanced by the most signal Interpositions of his Providence."

derstand them and too vengeful and jealous of their social superiors to make impartial assessments. The attorney general suggested that New York's embattled elite must "wait patiently for a Change of Spirit and Sentiment" in order to make the system more responsive to their interests.[49]

The Livingstons complained bitterly of the tyranny of popular government. Chancellor Robert R. Livingston believed that power had corrupted popular virtue, making the people domineering agents of tyranny and oppression. His mother, Margaret Beekman Livingston, feared "the persecutions of the Lower Class who I foresee will be as dispotic as any Prince . . . in Europe."[50] The lord of the Manor, for his part, accused the assessors of bearing a special enmity toward his family and complained that the Manor's taxes were nearly three times those levied on all of Rensselaerswyck. Robert Livingston, Jr., went so far as to contest the Manor's 1781 assessment, but he lost his case and was ordered to pay approximately £1,620 in back taxes.[51]

In colonial New York, an entrepreneur's profits from military contracts and privateering had easily offset his expenditures for wartime taxes. In Revolutionary New York, however, not only did the entrepreneurial class pay a greater share of the state's taxes, but the government imposed price ceilings and trade regulations in an attempt to curb profiteering and soften the impact of wartime inflation. The less public-spirited members of the Livingston family viewed the War of Independence as a typical war, a situation they could exploit for their own financial benefit. During the Revolution, however, when the success of America's entire republican experi-

---

[49] Egbert Benson to Robert R. Livingston, Jr., 20 Feb. 1780, Robert R. Livingston Papers, NYHS, reel 1. On Benson's importance as a conservative leader at the state level, see Countryman, *People in Revolution*, pp. 204–9.

[50] Robert R. Livingston, Jr., to Gouverneur Morris, 13 June 1778, Robert R. Livingston Papers, NYHS, reel 1; Margaret Beekman Livingston to Robert R. Livingston, Jr., 30 Dec. 1779, ibid. For similar sentiments among conservative Whigs elsewhere, see Wood, *Creation of the American Republic*, chap. 10.

[51] Teunis Van Vechten to Robert Livingston, Jr., 4 Sept. 1781, Livingston-Redmond MSS., reel 8; Cornelius Bradford to Robert Livingston, Jr., 6 Feb. 1782, ibid.; Robert Livingston, Jr., to Peter Van Brugh Livingston, 28 Jan. 1782, Welch-Livingston Collection, NYHS. In 1779, the assessors valued his real and personal estates at £30,000 and £80,000, respectively. See Albany County tax lists, March 1779, New York State Library.

ment was believed to depend on the virtue of its citizens, such men were denounced as rogues and Tories.[52]

The Livingstons' commitment to continuing their business as usual did irreparable harm to the family's reputation and further estranged them from New York's Revolutionary government. For instance, Robert Livingston, Jr., was eager to supply iron and foodstuffs to the patriot forces, but his own support for the Revolution did not diminish his businessman's concern for profits. To some extent, Livingston was obliged to run his business according to economic rather than political rules. In June 1777, for example, he found himself forced to raise the price of his iron in order to satisfy his workers' demands for higher wages. Livingston had two options: he could either appease the workers or close the ironworks, which were essential to New York's war effort. "In either Case," as William Smith, Jr., astutely predicted, "he will be called a Tory." Since Livingston considered himself first and foremost a businessman, it never occurred to him to continue running his ironworks at a financial loss. Instead, he haggled with the quartermaster general over the price of his iron, and in 1778 he demanded more than the congressionally sanctioned price for a shipment of Manor flour.[53]

Livingston's behavior enraged government officials and added to his family's already unsavory public reputation. He and his sons also compounded their offenses by shipping flour to Boston in defiance of New York's ban on the export of all commodities that were essential to the state's war effort. During the war, Robert's son Henry was trading in Boston because the British occupation had closed New York's own ports to all nonloyalist trade. Henry had formed a partnership with his brother Walter whereby he would buy rum in Boston to be sold by Walter in New York, where the liquor was in great demand for provisioning patriot forces. Walter himself was involved in provisioning throughout the war, and access to depend-

---

[52] For the debate over the propriety of wartime profit-making in Revolutionary America, see Cathy Matson, "Public Vices, Private Benefit: William Duer and His Circle," in William Pencak and Conrad Edick Wright, eds., *New York and the Rise of American Capitalism: Economic Development and the Social and Political History of an American State, 1780–1870* (New York, 1989), esp. pp. 72–76, 83–92.

[53] Sabine, ed., *Memoirs of William Smith*, 2:168–69, 317, 319; Morgan Lewis to Robert Livingston, Jr., 2 June 1777, Livingston-Redmond MSS., reel 8; Elias Boudinot to Robert Livingston, Jr., 20 Apr. 1778, ibid.

able supplies of rum and other necessities made his business especially lucrative. While in Boston, Henry also acted as his father's agent, smuggling his flour into New England to exchange it for rum and other items that were scarce at home. Henry also may have sold some of Robert's iron in Boston, where the prices were far higher.[54]

The Livingstons' wartime trade was immensely profitable. By his own account, between his legitimate military contracts and his illicit New England trade, Robert Livingston, Jr., cleared £10,000 in the summer of 1778 alone, besides what his sons gained from their own business. Well might Peter R. Livingston caution that "the Family will create Enemies by exposing themselves to the Charge of acting only upon Motives of private Gain."[55]

Robert Livingston, Jr., did not trade with the enemy, but he did put his interests as a merchant-entrepreneur ahead of his responsibilities as a citizen of a virtuous republic.[56] In any previous war, Livingston's conduct would have been unexceptionable. During the Revolution, however, his business practices did "create Enemies" for himself and his family, and many of those enemies wielded power in the new Revolutionary government.

In December 1777, the New York Council of Safety unanimously accused Livingston of charging extortionate prices for his iron, on the basis of a complaint lodged by the yeomen farmers of the Rhinebeck district committee. The council summoned Livingston to answer the charges of the farmers, who complained that the lord of the Manor, as the owner of New York's only operating ironworks, would single-handedly cause a famine by making it impossible for local

[54] Articles of agreement between Henry Livingston and Walter Livingston, 19 Nov. 1776, Robert R. Livingston Papers, NYHS, reel 1; Henry Livingston to Walter Livingston, 31 May, 10 June 1777, ibid.; Profits on rum, 1776–79, Walter Livingston's account book, Livingston Family Papers, NYHS, reel 15; Walter Livingston to John Carter, 21 July 1777, ibid.; Henry Livingston to Walter Livingston, 6 June 1777, ibid., reel 18; Henry Livingston to Robert Livingston, Jr., 8 Jan., 5 June, 20 Aug. 1778, Livingston-Redmond MSS., reel 8; Matson, "Public Vices, Private Benefit," in Pencak and Wright, eds., *New York and the Rise of American Capitalism*, pp. 78–79, 85–92.

[55] Peter R. Livingston to Robert Livingston, Jr., 4 Sept. 1778, Livingston-Redmond MSS., reel 8; Sabine, ed., *Memoirs of William Smith*, 2:214, 256, 294, 309.

[56] Robert's son Walter and the chancellor's brother John did trade illegally with British merchants via Amsterdam and Sweden. See Walter Livingston to Harrison & Ansley, 22 Oct. 1780, Livingston Family Papers, NYHS, reel 15; Walter Livingston to John R. Livingston, 22 Oct. 1780, ibid.; John R. Livingston to Robert R. Livingston, 6 Mar. 1782, Robert R. Livingston Papers, NYHS, reel 2.

husbandmen to purchase the iron they needed for plows and other farming implements. By 1777, popular outrage against the Livingstons was increasing daily. Walter's business partner in Albany reported, "People censure the conduct of your Family in [a] free Manner . . . [and] they declare that not one of you takes a single Step to assist to save your Country, which they say you certainly would do if you intended to oppose the common Enemy." The people of Albany believed the Livingstons would make their peace with Britain, and they were unmoved by the attempts of Walter's friend to defend the manorial family. Accordingly, Attorney General Egbert Benson warned that the lord of the Manor should cooperate with the Council of Safety because "People are exceedingly clamourous and he is rendering both himself and [his] Family very odious" to the government and its constituents. In March 1778, William Smith, Jr., reported, "All the Livingstons grow into Disesteem, & they consequently [are] more and more disgusted."[57]

In January 1778, Robert Livingston, Jr., had responded angrily to the summons of the Council of Safety, asserting that they must wait on him—and not the other way around—to investigate the farmers' accusations more fully. He believed he was being singled out unjustly for allegedly exorbitant pricing in a time of general inflation. Robert answered the extortion charge ambiguously, urging Governor Clinton to examine his ledgers to prove his innocence and then complaining that the high costs of labor and cartage made it nearly impossible to comply with the state's price ceilings. John Morin Scott had advised Livingston to adhere to the state's guidelines and "set an Example of Patriotism by a Sacrifice of his Wealth." This Robert refused to do, but he instead offered to let the state assume full responsibility for the operation of the ironworks. Although the Council of Safety eventually let the matter drop, in 1780 Livingston again suggested that the state take over the works at Ancram. Owning New York's only productive ironworks put him in a delicate position, "[e]qually afraid," in the words of his son-in-law, "to decline or to carry them on." To close the works would be viewed as treasonous, but to operate them wholly in compliance with the state's

[57] John Carter to Walter Livingston, 10 Aug. 1777, Robert R. Livingston Papers, NYHS, reel 1; Egbert Benson to Robert R. Livingston, Jr., 3 Dec. 1777, ibid.; Sabine, ed., *Memoirs of William Smith*, 2:315.

regulations, Livingston believed, would be ruinous. He therefore kept the ironworks functioning, bent the rules occasionally, and repeatedly requested special exemptions and favors to ease his financial burdens.[58]

William Smith, Jr., recognized that the government's economic controls, the people's decreasing deference, and the escalating demands of wartime taxes frightened and embittered men like Robert Livingston, Jr., who were accustomed to running their own affairs. Smith argued—and Livingston would have agreed—that America needed the political and economic leadership of the old elite to ensure an orderly and prosperous future. "These People have had no Foresight of the natural Consequences of a republican Spirit in a poor Country, where Gentlemen of Fortune are but few," Smith lamented. Yet, far from deferring to the wise and the wealthy, the powers ascendant in Revolutionary New York seemed determined to harass them to the point that they "will be happy if they can save their Estates."[59]

Indeed, during the Revolution, Robert Livingston, Jr., believed that his estate was threatened doubly. On the one hand, the interference of the state government abridged his right to property and harmed his family's reputation; on the other, tenants and interlopers rioted and raided at the Manor and jeopardized Livingston's title to and enjoyment of his family's landed legacy. Given the Manor's recent history of riot and disorder, its proprietor was sensitive to even the slightest hint of popular unrest. Under Revolutionary conditions, he believed the combined tyranny of the people and the state could easily result in the loss of the family land.

From the spring of 1776 through the fall of 1777, riots occurred intermittently at Livingston Manor. The violence peaked in May 1777, when the Livingstons reported that hundreds of their tenants had risen in armed rebellion in anticipation of the arrival of the king's forces. Robert Livingston, Jr., believed his tenants would support the British, hoping that the king's forces would confiscate the

---

[58] Sabine, ed., *Memoirs of William Smith*, 2:265, 267, 295; Robert Livingston, Jr., to George Clinton, 8 Jan. 1778, *Clinton Papers*, 2:654; James Duane to George Clinton, 6 Apr. 1780, ibid., 5:592.

[59] Sabine, ed., *Memoirs of William Smith*, 2:280.

great landed estates and redistribute the land among Tory tenants.[60]

Since early 1776, the Livingstons had tried in vain to keep order at the Manor by warning county and state authorities that their tenants were incorrigible Tories who could be controlled only by outside military intervention. As early as February 1776, Walter Livingston had appealed to the Albany County committee to send three militia companies to the Manor to disarm and capture the alleged Tory rioters. In October 1776, the Manor district committee, of which the Livingston brothers were prominent members, asked the Dutchess County committee to send fifty militamen to quash an expected Tory riot in the Manor's southeastern corner. By the spring of 1777, the committees of the towns of Rhinebeck, Kingston, and Claverack also had been summoned to help quiet the alleged tenant Tories, and Chancellor Robert R. Livingston was writing to Governor Clinton complaining that the Manor was infested with loyalists who could be suppressed only by force of arms.[61] In fact, the Livingstons exaggerated the loyalism, if not the rebelliousness, of the Manor's residents. During the war, several Livingston tenants were accused of recruiting loyalist soldiers, but only five sons of tenants were known to have joined the British forces.[62]

Fragmentary evidence suggests that Livingston leaseholders were not prominent participants in the Revolutionary era uprisings. In the 1770s, Livingston Manor had nearly 400 tenant families, or a population of approximately 2,000 people. William Smith, Jr., claimed that between 400 and 500 people were involved in the rioting at its height in the spring of 1777 and that more than 200 were taken prisoner in the aftermath of the May uprising. Between Feb-

[60] Ibid., 2:127–41. See also Philip Ranlet, *The New York Loyalists* (Knoxville, Tenn., 1986), pp. 125–36, and for a different view see Staughton Lynd, "The Tenant Rising at Livingston Manor, May 1777," in *Class Conflict, Slavery, and the United States Constitution* (Indianapolis, Ind., 1967), pp. 63–77.

[61] *Minutes of the Albany Committee*, 1:336, 795–96; "The Minutes of the Committee of Safety of the Manor of Livingston, Columbia County, New York," *NY Gen. & Bio. Rec.*, 60 (1929): 327; Sabine, ed., *Memoirs of William Smith*, 2:134; Robert R. Livingston, Jr., to George Clinton, 11 Apr. 1777, *Clinton Papers*, 1:709–10.

[62] Livingston Manor Tory assessment, 24 Jan. 1781, *Clinton Papers*, 6:593–94. For the alleged recruitment of loyalist troops at Livingston Manor, see *Minutes of the Commissioners for Detecting and Defeating Conspiracies in the State of New York, Albany County Sessions, 1778–1781*, ed. Victor Hugo Paltsits, 3 vols. (Albany, N.Y., 1909–10), 1:142–43, 347, 2:708.

ruary 1776 and May 1777, however, the Albany County committee and the Manor district committee had questioned only 28 Manor residents about their alleged Tory activities. That sample indicates that the men involved in the riots were overwhelmingly those who had no assets at the Manor—a leasehold, improvements, crops— that could be jeopardized by their misconduct. Of these 28 men, only 4 were themselves leaseholders; another 15 were probably sons of tenants, and the remaining 9 seem to have been squatters near the Manor's disputed eastern border. Of the four suspected Tories who were themselves Manor tenants, three had taken up their leases only within the past three years, and most likely had not improved their farms substantially during that brief period. Only one of the twenty-eight, Hendrick Rypenbergh, was an established tenant farmer whose family had long since settled and proliferated on Livingston land.[63]

A similar if less pronounced pattern emerges from the records of the Commissioners for Detecting Conspiracies, a special body formed in June 1777 for the express purpose of thwarting Tory activity in the Hudson Valley. Between June 1777 and May 1781, the commissioners questioned, charged, or imprisoned a total of 36 men whom they identified as Manor residents. In this case, 20 of the 36 were not Manor tenants. Four of those 20 men were squatters or outsiders whose surnames appeared nowhere in the Manor records. The remaining 16 may have been sons or relatives of farmers who held leases at Livingston Manor.[64]

Overall, the committees' records suggest that established tenant farmers with family responsibilities and material interests to protect were inclined to be neutral, or apathetic, even under the most extraordinary circumstances. The overwhelming majority of the Manor's men consistently avoided militia service, and their unwillingness to appear even for routine musters was a source of profound embarrassment to the proprietary family. The tenants' reluctance to fight

---

[63] Sabine, ed., *Memoirs of William Smith*, 2:132, 134; "Minutes of the Committee of the Manor of Livingston," pp. 239–43, 325–41; *Minutes of the Albany Committee*, 1:336, 444, 503, 505, 669. Tenants and their probable relations have been identified in the Livingston Manor rent ledger, 1767–84, Livingston Family Papers, NYHS, reel 15, and the account book of Robert Livingston, Jr., 1782–87, Livingston-Redmond MSS., reel 13.

[64] *Minutes of the Commissioners for Detecting Conspiracies*, 1:142–43, 152, 239–40, 254, 275, 335, 338–40, 347, 394, 399, 403, 2:509–12, 630, 643, 644, 653, 708, 726.

on either side persisted long after the British forces had come and gone, and they had lost all hope of seizing the Livingstons' land. When the British left the Hudson Valley, more than two-thirds of the Manor's men took the state's loyalty oath, probably to avoid further harassment by the Revolutionary regime. By 1778, most Livingston tenants were willing to pledge their allegiance to the state government, though they continued to ignore the state's calls to serve in the local militia.[65]

The committees' records also raise important questions concerning the role that outsiders played in fomenting or encouraging the violence at Livingston Manor. Despite the apparently large numbers of rioters involved, the disturbances of 1776–77 resembled earlier agrarian unrest—especially that of the 1750s—in two important respects. In both cases, most of the violence occurred at Taghkanic, in the Manor's southeastern corner, adjacent to disputed New York–Massachusetts border.[66] In both cases, New Englanders were involved in the rioting.

In the 1770s, the Massachusetts militiamen, who came to Taghkanic ostensibly to subdue the allegedly Tory mob, played a double hand and added to the Livingstons' problems. The militiamen from western Massachusetts did take twenty prisoners at Taghkanic, but they attacked tenants indiscriminately and continued their attacks even after the rioters had offered to surrender to the Manor committee. As William Smith, Jr., shrewdly observed, the New Englanders had come to the Manor to revive their claims to the Livingstons' land: "The N[ew] E[ngland] People are jealous of the Livingston Family ag[ains]t whom they want a Matter of Accusation and [their behavior] shews that their Alternative was a Junction with the Majority [of rioters] or a Destruction of their Estates and perhaps the Loss of their Lives." Chancellor Robert R. Livingston

---

[65] See, for instance, "Minutes of the Committee of the Manor of Livingston," pp. 325–33, 336–38; Sabine, ed., *Memoirs of William Smith*, 2:17, 26, 59, 84, 114, 126, 304, 350, 372, 397; Order of the provincial congress, 8 Nov. 1776, *DRNY*, 15:136–37; Peter R. Livingston to provincial convention, 2 Jan. 1777, ibid., 15:144; John R. Livingston to Robert R. Livingston, Jr., 12 Aug. 1777, *Clinton Papers*, 2:219; Peter R. Livingston to George Clinton, 13 June 1778, ibid., 3:453–54; Samuel Ten Broeck to Clinton, 15 Sept. 1778, ibid., 4:33–34.

[66] Sabine, ed., *Memoirs of William Smith*, 2:127, 129, 130; "Minutes of the Committee of the Manor of Livingston," p. 327; Robert R. Livingston, Jr., to George Clinton, 11 Apr. 1777, *Clinton Papers*, 1:709–10.

warned his cousins at the Manor of "the Necessity of the Family's appearing to guard ag[ains]t Reproaches" because the New Englanders hoped to discredit the Livingstons and thereby gain control of their land. After the militamen departed, the "N[ew] England Borderers" continued to accuse the Livingstons publicly of loyalism and threatened to confiscate their estate in the name of the Revolution. In February 1778, Peter R. Livingston, who spent much of his time dealing with tenant grievances, reported, "The N[ew] E[ngland] People talk of burning [the] House and Mills & Iron Works" at Livingston Manor.[67]

In the 1770s, as in the 1750s, the violence at Livingston Manor became a three-cornered struggle in which the tenants found themselves increasingly allied with the Livingstons against their New England adversaries. Robert Livingston, Jr., and his sons bitterly opposed the excessive violence of the Massachusetts militia and took great pains to protect their tenants from the New Englanders and their allies. In the spring of 1777, when the unrest at the Manor was gradually increasing, Smith reported that the tenants were "daily applying to [Peter R. Livingston] for Favors." The tenants especially sought protection from the New England forces who had come to Taghkanic, allegedly to restore order, but were instead harassing tenant farmers and confiscating their property. In May 1777, Peter wrote to both the Claverack district committee and the New York Council of Safety, unsuccessfully requesting protection and restitution for the troubled tenant farmers.[68]

The crisis of 1777 passed when British troops left the Hudson Valley that autumn and the militiamen returned home to western Massachusetts. Having abandoned the possibility of winning their land by allying with the king's forces, the Manor's residents stopped rioting and went back to the business of farming. But outsiders continued to cause trouble, and the New England "Borderers" continued to talk openly of confiscating the Manor, justifying their attack on the Livingstons' property by accusing them of toryism.[69] More serious still, in 1778 and 1779, gangs of armed robbers intermittently attacked the homes of Manor tenants. Some, though not

[67] Sabine, ed., *Memoirs of William Smith*, 2:128–32, 139, 312; Ranlet, *New York Loyalists*, pp. 128–30.

[68] Sabine, ed., *Memoirs of William Smith*, 2:130, 132, 139, 312.

[69] Ibid., 2:312.

all, of the gang members were outsiders, probably from Massachusetts. In May 1778, for instance, a gang of thirty men attacked and robbed the home of Harme Koon, a Livingston tenant and captain in the Manor militia; of the three men captured after the Koon robbery, only one resided on the Livingstons' land. These raids and robberies terrified the Livingstons' tenants, the vast majority of whom had adopted a passive but defensive stance by 1778.[70]

After the British had left the area and peace was restored at the Manor, the Livingstons were notably sympathetic to the plight of their tenants, perhaps because they shared many of the tenants' grievances. In 1779, for instance, Chancellor Robert R. Livingston complained to Governor Clinton that state contractors were defrauding his tenants and forcing them to sell their wheat for less than the prices allowed by current government regulations. The contractors pretended that the lower prices of 1777 were still in force and then commandeered the tenants' crops "without paying proper attention to the circumstances of their families." The chancellor's mother kept him informed of the hardships the tenants faced, and in the winter of 1780 she informed him that government policies, plus a bad harvest, most likely would result in famine. Some tenants, she noted, already lacked sufficient provisions, and "the people at Large Complain That they cannot pay [their taxes]; Goods and Cattle are distrained [and] many put to great hardships." Ensign John Pell, a Massachusetts-born soldier in the loyal Queen's Rangers, confirmed Margaret Beekman Livingston's assessment of the situation. In February 1780, Pell reported that the Manor's residents were living in miserable circumstances and wanted nothing more than an end to the war, its taxes, and the requisitions of the Continental Army.[71]

[70] On the Koon incident, see ibid., 2:397. On robbers and attempts to subdue them, in general, see James Duane to George Clinton, 12 June, 13 June, 29 July 1778, *Clinton Papers*, 3:452–54, 593–94; Petitions of the Northern Towns of Dutchess County and Southern Manor Towns for Authority to Raise a Company of Rangers to Protect the Inhabitants from Robbers, [Aug. 1778], ibid., 3:674–76, 685–86; Orders of Governor George Clinton, 23 Aug., 21 Sept. 1778, ibid., 3:686, 4:56; Robert R. Livingston, Jr., to George Clinton, 14 Mar. 1779, ibid., 4:633–34; *Minutes of the Commissioners for Detecting Conspiracies*, 1:143, 254, 399, 403.

[71] Robert R. Livingston, Jr., to George Clinton, 23 Mar. 1779, Misc. MSS., Robert R. Livingston, NYHS; Margaret Beekman Livingston to Robert R. Livingston, Jr., Feb. 1780, Robert R. Livingston Papers, NYHS, reel 1; Report of Ensign John Pell, 5 Feb. 1780, *DRNY*, 8:783–84.

By 1780–81, the Livingstons and their tenants clearly had common economic interests: tenants and landlords alike despised high taxes and price ceilings; landlords realized that overtaxed tenants could not pay their rents and that price regulations discouraged them from working for maximum productivity.[72] In January 1781, more than 300 Manor residents gathered to draw up a list of their manifold grievances. They complained of the high taxes that they were unable to pay, and of the method of assessment that overtaxed the district of Livingston Manor. They protested having to sell their crops to state contractors, who paid low prices in nearly worthless paper money. They condemned the fines extracted from "Whig" tenants whose sons allegedly supported the British. Significantly, the tenants chose two of the Manor lord's sons, Walter and John, with Major Samuel Ten Broeck, to present their grievances to the state legislature.[73]

New York's conservative Whigs knew that the Revolution threatened their way of life. Since 1776, they had seen their political authority challenged, their economic lives regulated, and their customary privileges diminished. They had witnessed the state's confiscation of loyalist estates, an abrogation of property rights, which they believed set an ominous precedent. New York's great landed families worried that their own estates would be the government's next target. In 1776–77, Walter Livingston had invested heavily in land in order to protect his fortune from the ill effects of wartime inflation, but by 1778 he was urging his relatives to sell their speculative landholdings because he believed the state government would invalidate their titles. In 1782, Thomas Tillotson warned his brother-in-law, the chancellor, that "a strong Democratic spirit" was likely to make trouble for New York's remaining great families. "The first stroke," Tillotson predicted, "would be at the Tenanted estates, which the people on the borders of New England have already in

[72] For rental accounts in arrears and credit extended to tenants, see Livingston Manor rent ledger, 1767–84, Livingston Family Papers, NYHS, reel 15; List . . . of Arrearages of Rent Due to Mrs. Margaret [Beekman] Livingston, 1 May 1779, ibid., reel 52; Lists of bonds due to Mrs. Margaret [Beekman] Livingston, 1751–80, Misc. MSS., Margaret Beekman Livingston, NYHS; Account book of Robert Livingston, Jr., 1782–87, Livingston-Redmond MSS., reel 13.
[73] Resolutions at a meeting of above 300 of the Inhabitants of the Manor of Livingston, 6 Jan. 1781, Livingston Family Papers, NYHS, reel 15.

contemplation." Meanwhile, the landlords themselves had become politically impotent and unable to prevent the "Democratic Tyranny" Tillotson expected. "The upper Manor [family] has made a small effort to put a member in the Senate & Assembly," he noted, "but [they] have failed in all."[74]

Aside from the loss of the family assembly seat, however, the Revolution effected few permanent changes in the private world of Livingston Manor. The Livingstons were able to preserve the trappings of power and privilege on their estate, despite their declining influence at the state level. Until the death of Robert Livingston, Jr., in 1790, the Manor's preprinted leases continued to designate the lessor as "Lord Proprietor of the Lordship and Manor of Livingston." The landlords retained both their milling monopolies and their preemptive rights to the crops of their tenants.[75] The great landowners also continued to canvas their tenants on election day, though the absorption of the manors by surrounding electoral districts undermined their ability to influence the outcome of elections. For the time being, at least, the Livingstons thus kept both their land and the prerogatives of landownership.[76]

Beyond their bailiwicks, the old elite's prospects were far less heartening. In 1776, the Livingstons and their friends had expected political society in an independent America to perpetuate the authority and privileges they had enjoyed under the old colonial order. They were bitterly disappointed. By its equitable tax policies, price controls, and aggressive anti-Tory measures, the new regime proved

[74] Sabine, ed., *Memoirs of William Smith*, 2:133, 296, 330; Thomas Tillotson to Robert R. Livingston, Jr., 17 June 1782, Robert R. Livingston Papers, NYHS, reel 2. On the conservative opposition to the government's confiscation of loyalist property, see Young, *Democratic Republicans*, pp. 29, 62–66; Dangerfield, *Chancellor Robert R. Livingston*, pp. 199–200.

[75] See, for example, the lease between Robert Livingston, Jr., and James Van Deusen, 14 Mar. 1785, Livingston Family Papers, Columbia University, ser. II. The use of the title "Lord Proprietor" may have been discontinued only because the Manor was subdivided upon Robert's death in 1790.

[76] On electioneering, see Thomas Tillotson to Robert R. Livingston, Jr., 23 Mar. 1787, Robert R. Livingston Papers, NYHS, reel 3; Margaret Beekman Livingston to Robert R. Livingston, Jr., Apr. 1789, ibid., reel 4; Robert Livingston, Jr., to James Duane, 30 Apr. 1788, Duane Papers, NYHS, box 7; John and Henry Livingston to [Stephen Van] Rensselaer and [Leonard] Gansevoort, 27 Apr. 1787, Misc. MSS., John Livingston (1750–1822), NYHS.

remarkably responsive to popular demands. Annual legislative elections and the government's willingness to entertain and to resolve the grievances of ordinary people—such as the Rhinebeck farmers who accused Robert Livingston, Jr., of extortion—also encouraged popular participation to an extent unparalleled during the colonial era. The Revolution democratized New York's political culture by diffusing authority and influence among men who had previously played only passive roles in the political process.

Some conservative Whigs did not entirely understand the implications of this Revolutionary transformation. Robert Livingston, Jr., and others who had been isolated from the daily give-and-take of Revolutionary politics found the demise of traditional networks of influence most incomprehensible. As late as 1783, Robert was unable to understand why his sons—who had been notably lukewarm toward the Revolution and openly hostile to the state government—could not obtain "lucrative" political appointments in New York. A year later, Livingston's sons were still seeking government appointments "worth their acceptance," and the lord of the Manor was still wondering why their attempts to secure preferment had been so unsuccessful.[77] It never occurred to him that the state of New York did not need his sons' services and that, given their less than exemplary wartime record, the Livingstons were deemed undeserving of political favors.

Although New York's elites believed that the Revolution jeopardized both their property rights and their social status, many hoped that their lot would improve once the war was over. But New Yorkers did not revert to the politics of deference in the immediate postwar era. The state government's persistent prosecution of loyalists continued to challenge the sanctity of property, and the departure of many Tory gentlemen further depleted the ranks of New York's men of quality. Chancellor Robert R. Livingston worried that men of his own class were scarce in the state and suggested, "Perhaps by good training, and by crossing the breed frequently . . . [the loyalists] may be rendered useful animals in a few generations."[78] The

[77] Robert Livingston, Jr., to James Duane, 29 Jan. 1783, 30 Jan. 1784, Duane Papers, NYHS, box 5.

[78] Robert R. Livingston, Jr., to John Jay, 29 Nov. 1783, in Richard B. Morris, ed., *John Jay: The Winning of the Peace* (New York, 1980), p. 653. Hamilton, the Tories' leading defender, made this point even more emphatically. See his letter to Chancellor Livingston, 13 Aug. 1783, Robert R. Livingston Papers, NYHS, reel 2.

reformed tax system and the new popular politics, once thought to be mere side effects of war, also continued to function after the war ended, much to the distress of the great men and their families. Nor did popular unrest cease with the formal restoration of peace in 1783. In western Massachusetts, an area well known to the Hudson Valley magnates as a hotbed of leveling sentiment, Daniel Shays led his famous rebellion in 1786. A year earlier, the New England squatters had revived their claims to Livingston Manor and threatened to murder its aged proprietor.[79]

Soundly defeated at the state level, it was from the arena of national politics that New York's most talented conservatives re-emerged, as Federalists, to lead the last political offensive of the old elite. As early as 1780, conservative nationalists had sought to give Congress the power to tax—a power explicitly prohibited by the Articles of Confederation. When the war ended officially in 1783, Congress found itself too weak and too impoverished to enforce the terms of the Treaty of Paris, thus enabling the British to defy the treaty by maintaining forts in the Ohio River valley. At the same time, merchants and artisans clamored for effective commercial policies in the midst of a postwar depression, though the Articles prohibited Congress from imposing tariffs or adopting national commercial policies. The Constitutional Convention of 1787, which sought to address these issues, thus marked the culmination of years of nationalist efforts to strengthen the central government.

At the same time, however, conservatives were growing increasingly restive under popular rule and looked to an energetic national government to promote stability, peace, and order. Indeed, Alexander Hamilton made the dichotomy between government "energy" and popular "anarchy" the central theme of the Federalists' New York campaign. In his fifty-one *Federalist* essays, Hamilton repeatedly argued that anarchy—or an excess of democracy—posed the greatest threat to American liberties and that only a strong, or energetic, national government could ensure the survival of the Republic.[80] By contrast, the Anti-Federalists—led in New York by the formidable Governor George Clinton—feared the power or "ener-

---

[79] Edwin Brockholst Livingston, *The Livingstons of Livingston Manor* (New York, 1910), pp. 313–16.

[80] [Alexander Hamilton], "Federalist," esp. nos. 1, 6–9, 11, 15–17, 21–23, 26–29, 36, 70, 85, in *The Federalist Papers*, ed. Clinton Rossiter (New York, 1961).

gy" of government far more than they feared the potential for anar-chy among the people. Like many other Anti-Federalists, New York-er Abraham Yates saw the proposed constitution as an aristocratic conspiracy, a plot "to get Power out of the Hands of the People" by diminishing the influence of the popular state governments.[81]

In the fall of 1787, Hamilton, the dynamo of conservative na-tionalism, assessed the prospects of a Federalist victory in New York. He predicted that three types of men could be counted on to sup-port the adoption of the new frame of government: men who traded, men who speculated in government securities, and those "men of property" who would be well disposed toward a govern-ment "able to protect them against domestic violence and the depre-dations which the democratic spirit is apt to make on property."[82]

All three of Hamilton's categories included members of the Livingston family. Both Walter Livingston and the chancellor's brother John R. Livingston were public creditors who had specu-lated extensively in government securities.[83] On the other hand, the lord of the Manor and his merchant sons, like most New York mer-chants, believed that a stronger government would best serve their outward-looking, or "cosmopolitan," business interests. Throughout the war, Robert Livingston, Jr., had worried about the future of overseas trade, and by 1784 he was convinced that Congress needed more power to make "many wholsom Laws to incourage trade . . . & not trade with Britton nor Ireland untill they Sufferd us to trade to their W[est] I[ndian] Islands," New York's most important colonial market. Most New York merchants shared Livingston's concerns and grievances. Consequently, by 1788, virtually all of them were in the Federalist camp, as were the commercially minded landowners of the Hudson River valley.[84]

[81] Lynd, "Abraham Yates's History," esp. p. 232.

[82] Hamilton's Conjectures about the New Constitution, [17–30 Sept. 1787], in Harold C. Syrett and Jacob E. Cooke, eds., *The Papers of Alexander Hamilton*, 26 vols. (New York, 1960–79), 4:275–76.

[83] Robert F. Jones, "William Duer and the Business of Government in the Era of the American Revolution," *WMQ*, 3d ser., 32 (1975): 393–416; Dangerfield, *Chancellor Robert R. Livingston*, pp. 246–47; Young, *Democratic Republicans*, pp. 75–77.

[84] Young, *Democratic Republicans*, pp. 69–75, 77–80; Sabine, ed., *Memoirs of William Smith*, 2:214, 319; Robert Livingston, Jr., to James Duane, 30 Jan. 1784, Duane Papers, NYHS, box 5. For an overview of the Federalists' "cosmopolitan" orientation, as opposed to the "localism" of their adversaries, see Jackson Turner Main, *The Anti-federalists: Critics of the Constitution, 1781–1788* (Chapel Hill, N.C., 1961), and Main,

Finally, Hamilton's third category—the "men of property" who feared democracy—included virtually every member of the Livingston family. In 1787–88, the Livingstons joined with other patriotic but conservative republicans in an attempt to preserve America from the dangers of democracy. Affluent and educated Federalists throughout America saw themselves as the guarantors of public order and civic virtue. They believed that they were their country's "worthy" natural governors. The Constitution was their most impressive effort to undermine the power of the "licentious" state governments.[85]

More than anything else, fear of continuing violence and disorder galvanized the Livingstons and their friends to recreate their united front to protect what remained of their property and privilege and to use their talents to create a more orderly and stable republican world. It was for this reason that men like Robert R. Livingston and John Jay, neither merchants nor speculators, led the Federalist forces at the Poughkeepsie convention, just as they had guided the conservative minority in the provincial convention a decade earlier.

On 19 June 1788, nineteen Federalists and forty-six Anti-Federalists gathered at Poughkeepsie to debate the merits of the proposed Constitution. By then, eight states already had ratified the document; ratification by a ninth would result in the creation of a new national government. Ratification by a ninth state also would force New Yorkers to choose between going it alone or joining the new federal union. The Federalists recognized that both time and momentum were on their side, so they sought to prolong the convention's debates until the decisive ninth state had voted for ratification.[86]

Known for his oratorical skills, Chancellor Livingston delivered his party's opening address to the Poughkeepsie delegates. In a well-

---

Political Parties before the Constitution (Chapel Hill, N.C., 1973), esp. chaps. 12–13. The Hudson Valley tenants also gravitated toward the Federalist camp, as a result of either their landlords' influence or their own hostility toward the largely Anti-Federalist state government.

[85] Wood, *Creation of the American Republic,* chap. 12.

[86] Several accounts of the Poughkeepsie convention include Countryman, *People in Revolution,* chap. 9; Linda Grant DePauw, *The Eleventh Pillar: New York State and the Federal Constitution* (Ithaca, N.Y., 1966), chap. 9, 13–18; E. Wilder Spaulding, *New York in the Critical Period, 1783–1789* (New York, 1932), chap. 14; and Young, *Democratic Republicans,* chaps. 3–5.

argued speech, Livingston stressed the virtues of the proposed frame of government as well as the dire political and economic consequences of refusing to ratify it. The chancellor would make three significant speeches before the convention adjourned in late July. Of these, the most revealing was his oration in defense of aristocratic government.[87]

Led by Melancthon Smith, the Anti-Federalists characteristically exalted the rule of the common man and condemned the Constitution as an aristocratic document that undermined popular government. When the Anti-Federalists denigrated the rule of "rich men," Chancellor Livingston rose to defend his class and its ability to govern. The wealthy, he maintained, were "as honest and virtuous as any class in the community." In response to Smith's charge that the rich were insensitive to the needs of the people, Livingston asserted that affluent men were both more compassionate and less self-interested than their less prosperous countrymen. "Those who are most occupied by their own cares and distresses have the least sympathy with the distresses of others," the chancellor contended. "The sympathy of the poor is generally selfish, that of the rich is a more disinterested emotion."[88]

Chancellor Livingston went on to argue that aristocrats—or uncommon men—were best suited to exercise the powers of government. Livingston's fear of demagoguery and his faith in the wisdom of uncommon men led him to oppose Anti-Federalist proposals to mandate rotation in office and to give state legislatures the power to recall senators who disregarded the popular will. By contrast, Livingston approved of the relatively large congressional districts that the Constitution created, while the Anti-Federalists condemned them as an aristocratic plot to distance the common man from his government.[89]

Chancellor Livingston did not attempt to refute this Anti-Federalist criticism. Instead, he ridiculed his opponents' belief in giving ordinary men extraordinary power. Like most of his

[87] Livingston's speeches appear in Jonathan Elliot, comp., *The Debates in the Several State Conventions on the Adoption of the Federal Constitution . . .* , 5 vols., 2d ed. (New York, 1888), 2:208–16, 274–80, 291–93, 322–23. On the chancellor's contributions to the Poughkeepsie convention, see Dangerfield, *Chancellor Robert R. Livingston*, pp. 225–32.

[88] Elliot, comp., *Debates in the State Conventions*, 2:276.

[89] Ibid., 2:277–80, 291–93.

Federalist colleagues, Livingston hoped to create a government of men of wealth, wisdom, and virtue. That government would be republican—the people would choose their representatives—but it would not be democratic. Having chosen their representatives, the people would then defer to these wise and enlightened leaders, who would govern according to their own understanding of the community's best interests. Livingston scorned his opponents' fears of aristocracy, arguing that only men of superior wisdom and talent—by definition, aristocrats—were fit to wield political power. If Americans rejected their aristocratic leaders, he asked, "Whom, in the name of common sense, will we have to represent us? Not the rich," he retorted sarcastically, "for they are sheer aristocrats. Not the learned, the wise, the virtuous, for they are all aristocrats. Whom then? Why, those who are not virtuous; those who are not wise; those who are not learned: these are the men to whom alone we can trust our liberties." Thus, Livingston mocked the Anti-Federalists' commitment to preserving the common man's political power.[90]

Although the chancellor's arrogance alienated many of his fellow delegates, events outside Poughkeepsie gave the Federalists the impetus they needed to secure ratification. For one thing, commercially oriented New York City threatened to form a separate state and ratify the Constitution on its own if other New Yorkers refused to join the federal union. Moreover, on 21 June, New Hampshire became the ninth state to adopt the Constitution; four days later, Virginia also voted for ratification. When the news from New Hampshire and Virginia reached Poughkeepsie, even most Anti-Federalists conceded that New York could not afford to remain outside the new federal union the Constitution created. For another month, the Anti-Federalists sought to attach conditions to New York's acceptance of the new frame of government, while the Federalists sought unconditional ratification. On 26 July 1788, the Federalists won, but only by a narrow margin. The final tally was 30 for and 27 against; by a margin of three votes, New York became the eleventh pillar of the new constitutional union.[91]

In 1788, as in 1777, however, the conservatives' victory was short-lived and largely illusory. New York's convention ratified the Con-

90 Ibid., 2:277–78.
91 Spaulding, *New York in the Critical Period*, pp. 254–68.

stitution, but even under the new government the old elites were forced to recognize that their aristocratic assumptions had outlived their political usefulness. The federal Constitution had actually enhanced the legitimacy of popular sovereignty by replacing the concept of mixed government with an arrangement that divided government branches by function rather than by social class, making each branch at least theoretically representative of the sovereign people. Theory became practice when the Jeffersonian "revolution of 1800" deposed the Federalists in favor of their more democratically inclined opponents. After 1800, even the most conservative of Americans would have to admit that national affairs also would conform to the rules of popular politics.[92]

Disillusioned by the decline of deference in state politics, conservative Federalists were therefore the ultimate losers in the national government they had fought so hard to obtain. Some did hold office at the national level, but most gravitated toward judicial and diplomatic posts—appointive offices least dependent on popular approval but most befitting unpopular men who possessed the advantages of a gentleman's education. Of the Livingstons, only Edward, the chancellor's youngest brother, participated extensively in the electoral politics of the post-Revolutionary era. Born in 1764, Edward had never basked in the deference of colonial constituents and thus was affected least profoundly by the changes of the Revolutionary era.

For New York's great colonial families, the Poughkeepsie convention and its aftermath marked the end of a century of political dominance and a tradition of political leadership. In the process of building a distinct elite ethos, the Livingstons and their social peers had adopted the aristocratic values of personal honor, public service, and noblesse oblige. The influence of these values, in part, inspired them to lead a revolution that brought changes they were unable to accept. In the post-Revolutionary era, the patriotic remnant of New York's colonial elite abandoned their claims to public leadership, refusing to adapt themselves to an undeferential political world.

---

[92] Wood, *Creation of the American Republic*, chap. 15; David Hackett Fischer, *The Revolution of American Conservatism: The Federalist Party in the Era of Jeffersonian Democracy* (New York, 1965).

Conclusion

For more than a century, the Livingstons had been among New York's most dynamic and visible leaders. The colonial Livingstons had forged dense political and personal networks. They had experimented with new commercial strategies and set a pace surpassed by none for exploiting their landed resources. In time, they embraced new cultural forms as symbols of class distinction, even as they remained true to the work ethic of their less affluent forebears. Innovative as political leaders, they used pamphlets, boycotts, and extralegal committees to pursue their objectives and counter their declining influence within the provincial government. After independence, they were instrumental in the creation of New York's republican institutions. A decade later, they led the state's movement to ratify the federal Constitution.

The post-Revolutionary Livingstons did not sustain their family's tradition of creative and dynamic leadership. Unwilling or unable to accept the rise of democracy, they remained relatively aloof from politics at both the state and the national levels. They also lost their status as entrepreneurial leaders. After the Revolution, the family maintained their interests in land and trade, but they were no longer among America's pioneers of economic development.

The Livingstons gravitated toward the family land in the post-Revolutionary era. By the turn of the century, Chancellor Robert R. Livingston and seven of his siblings had built their mansions within a twenty-mile radius of Clermont; even Edward, who moved to New Orleans in 1803, returned to the valley to spend his summers. Similarly, four of the five surviving sons of Robert Livingston, Jr., chose to reside at Livingston Manor. In the post-Revolutionary era, other Livingston kin also returned to their ancestral roots to settle near the family seat in the Hudson River valley.[1] Intermarriage among kin— rare in the colonial era—became commonplace among members of future generations, who sought to avoid alienating family land and to preserve both the names and the traditions of their illustrious ancestors.[2]

During and after the Revolution, however, matters of pride and property undermined the family's internal cohesion. The physical proximity of family members did not betoken solidarity. Two disputes, in particular, signaled the demise of Livingston family unity. One pitted Chancellor Robert R. Livingston against his Manor cousins, while the other divided the five sons of the third lord of Livingston Manor.

Although they had withdrawn voluntarily from state and local politics, Robert Livingston, Jr., and his sons envied the chancellor's sudden rise to prominence and resented the fact that a member of their family's junior branch had become its de facto political leader. Chancellor Livingston outraged his already nettled kinsmen when, in 1779, he claimed the right to build a sawmill on Roeloff Jansen's Kill, the stream that divided Clermont from Livingston Manor. Although his claim was legally dubious, he built his mill in 1780, ignoring his cousins' adament protests. Two years later, the chancellor compounded his offense by purchasing the timber rights to a farm lying within the Manor's borders, but owned by Major Dirck Ten Broeck, whose ancestor had acquired the land from the first Robert Livingston.[3]

[1] Clare Brandt, *An American Aristocracy: The Livingstons* (New York, 1986), pp. 145–50; Thomas Streatfield Clarkson, *A Biographical History of Clermont* . . . (Clermont, N.Y., 1869), p. 48; John Ross Delafield, "Montgomery Place," *NY Hist.*, 20 (1939): 445–49; John Henry Livingston, "The Livingston Manor," Order of Colonial Lords of Manors in America *Publications*, 1 (1910): 24.

[2] Patricia Joan Gordon, "The Livingstons of New York: Kinship and Class," (Ph.D. diss., Columbia University, 1959), pp. 270–77.

[3] George Dangerfield, *Chancellor Robert R. Livingston of New York, 1746–1813* (New York, 1960), pp. 192–94; William H. W. Sabine, ed., *Historical Memoirs of William Smith*, 2 vols. (New York, 1958), 2:131, 144; Robert Livingston, Jr., to James Duane, 16 Oct. 1779, Livingston-Redmond MSS., reel 8; Peter R. Livingston to Peter Sylvester, 18 Oct. 1780, ibid., reel 10; Agreement between Robert R. Livingston, Jr., and Dirck Ten Broeck, 4 Oct. 1782, Livingston Family Papers, NYHS, reel 29. See also Alexander Hamilton's opinion, 3 Nov. 1783, Duane Papers, NYHS, box 5. Duane had requested Hamilton's opinion on behalf of his father-in-law.

Conclusion

Relations between cousins deteriorated precipitously as the chancellor sent his surveyors to the Manor and old Robert Livingston, Jr., inveighed against the temerity of "this troublesome covetous man." The dispute dragged on for more than a decade without formal legal action, though by 1790 the Manor's proprietor had sought the advice of at least seven different lawyers. In 1795, the disputants finally compromised their differences.[4] By then, however, the death of the eighty-two-year-old Robert Livingston, Jr., had given rise to another bitter family controversy.

As we have seen, Robert Livingston, Jr., had broken the entail on Livingston Manor when he revised his will in 1771. By dividing the Manor among his five surviving sons, Robert hoped to save it from the profligacy of the eldest, thus preserving the family's land and reputation for subsequent generations. Like the first Robert Livingston, who unexpectedly rewarded one son and disinherited another, Robert Livingston, Jr., thus modified custom to fit the merits of his legatees. He diminished the portion of his eldest son, Peter R. Livingston, both to punish Peter and to recognize the greater merit of his more industrious and successful brothers.

The partition of the Manor undermined the spirit of cooperative enterprise that had characterized the Livingstons' family business throughout the colonial era. Robert Livingston, Jr., had depended on his brothers' services to market the produce of the family land as well as to defend that land from the attacks of hostile outsiders. With the division of the Manor, however, the interests of the fourth generation often were competing, not cooperative. Legal obligations overshadowed shared family interests in the years following the death of the third lord of Livingston Manor.

When Robert Livingston, Jr., died in 1790, all of his heirs disputed his will. Peter R. Livingston, the eldest son, claimed that he had been robbed of his birthright, the lordship of Livingston Manor. Peter insulted his father's memory and threatened to contest the will. Old Robert's will also dissatisfied the younger Livingston siblings, who approved the abolition of the entail but complained that their father

---

[4] Dangerfield, *Chancellor Robert R. Livingston,* pp. 237–55. The seven lawyers were Duane, Hamilton, Rufus King, Brockholst Livingston (son of William), John Morin Scott, Theodore Sedgwick, and William Smith, Jr., who was by then chief justice of Quebec. See Robert Livingston, Jr., to James Duane, 1 Mar. 1788, Duane Papers, box 7; William Smith, Jr., to Peter R. Livingston, 2 Jan. 1790, Livingston-Redmond MSS., reel 9; Walter Livingston to Robert Livingston, Jr., 21 Feb. 1790, ibid.

still had given Peter too large a share of the family land. Since old Robert had paid Peter's outstanding debts, they contended, he should have deducted these expenditures from Peter's remaining legacy. Meanwhile, the younger brothers also squabbled among themselves, each contending that the other had received a better portion of Livingston Manor. The protracted dispute was remarkably acrimonious. Eventually, the dissension within the Livingston family became the butt of local gossip.[5]

The efforts of Robert Livingston, Jr., to save the fortune and honor of his family thus became instead a source of disunity and public embarrassment. Dissension, not grief, dominated the funeral services of the last lord of Livingston Manor. Well might Margaret Beekman Livingston observe the pettiness of Robert's children and pray that "heaven has preserved my children from the hatred [that I] see in them."[6]

Within the next seven years, the deaths of Peter R., Walter, and Robert Cambridge Livingston eliminated three of the main disputants and therefore eased tensions somewhat, but deaths in the fourth generation also resulted in a further fragmentation of the family's landed legacy. Of Robert's sons, only John and Henry retained their original portions. By 1797, the remainder of the Manor had been divided among Peter's widow, the eldest sons of Peter and Walter, and the five minor children of Robert Cambridge Livingston.[7] Thus, within less than a decade after the death of Robert Livingston, Jr., Livingston Manor had ceased to exist as a cohesive entity.

Perhaps the diminution of their landed resources discouraged subsequent generations from sustaining their ancestors' entrepreneurial spirit. After the Revolution, New Yorkers developed

[5] See, for instance, Peter R. Livingston to Walter Livingston, 14 Dec. 1790, 10, 12, and 31 Jan., 14 and 25 Feb. 1791, Robert R. Livingston Papers, NYHS, reel 4; Henry Livingston to Walter and Robert [Cambridge] Livingston, 18 Dec. 1790, 16 Jan. 1791, ibid.; Henry Livingston to Peter R. Livingston, 30 Jan. 1791, ibid.; John Patterson to James Duane, 3 Jan. 1791, Duane Papers, NYHS, box 8; Walter Livingston to Peter R. Livingston, 16 July 1791, Livingston Family Papers, NYHS, reel 15. Robert had bequeathed his Saratoga landholdings to his three surviving daughters. See will of Robert Livingston, Jr., 31 May 1784, ibid., reel 3.

[6] Margaret Beekman Livingston to Robert R. Livingston, Jr., 15 Dec. 1790, Robert R. Livingston Papers, NYHS, reel 4.

[7] Ruth Piwonka, *A Portrait of Livingston Manor, 1686–1850* (Germantown, N.Y., 1986), p. 61.

new financial networks and corporate forms; they experimented with new industries and methods of capital formation.[8] Unlike their colonial ancestors, however, the post-Revolutionary Livingstons were not among New York's entrepreneurial leaders. Walter Livingston did invest in the China trade, and the chancellor was deeply interested in the development of the steamboat.[9] By comparison, the business activities of most of their kin were relatively unadventurous.

For most of the Livingstons, settling on the family land represented a retreat, not a bold new adventure into aggressive land development. For one thing, although the population of the Manor continued to grow, the commercial importance of the Hudson Valley diminished in the post-Revolutionary era. Farmers spread the grain belt into western New York and on into the Great Lakes region. In 1825, the Erie Canal connected New York City with the western grain-producing territories. Competition from the West greatly diminished the commercial value of the Livingston family's landholdings. Most Hudson Valley farmers converted to dairying and sold their products in growing urban markets.[10] The switch from grain to dairy products limited the Livingstons' opportunities to participate in international commerce.

The post-Revolutionary Livingstons also had to contend with renewed tenant unrest, which erupted from time to time beginning in the 1790s. In 1795, some 210 Manor residents unsuccessfully petitioned the state legislature for a revocation of the 1686 Dongan patent. They redoubled their efforts in 1811–12, rioting, petitioning, and vainly seeking judicial invalidation of the Livingstons' land titles.[11] The tenants' bargaining position improved in 1821, how-

[8] Dixon Ryan Fox, *The Decline of Aristocracy in the Politics of New York* (New York, 1919), chap. 10; Janet A. Riesman, "Republican Revisions: Political Economy in New York after the Panic of 1819," in William Pencak and Conrad Edick Wright, eds., *New York and the Rise of American Capitalism: Economic Development and the Social and Political History of an American State, 1780–1870* (New York, 1989), pp. 1–44; Gregory S. Hunter, "The Manhattan Company: Managing a Multi-unit Corporation in New York, 1799–1842," ibid., pp. 124–46.

[9] Cathy Matson, "Public Vices, Private Benefit: William Duer and His Circle, 1776–1792," in Pencak and Wright, eds., *New York and the Rise of American Capitalism*, p. 94; Dangerfield, *Chancellor Robert R. Livingston*, pp. 277–97, 403–22.

[10] David Maldwyn Ellis, *Landlords and Farmers in the Hudson-Mohawk Region, 1790–1850* (Ithaca, N.Y., 1946), chaps. 3 and 6.

[11] Ibid., pp. 34–36, 153–55; Petition of Petrus Pulver et al., 7 Jan. 1795, *DHNY*,

ever, when a new state constitution instituted universal manhood suffrage. Tenant grievances acquired new political significance as politicians in both parties scrambled to capture the votes of thousands of leaseholders.

As party competition grew heated in New York, Whigs and Democrats alike came to support the Anti-Rent movement that emerged in the 1840s to take on New York's manorial families. The Livingstons were helpless in the face of renewed tenant unrest; this time the tenants emerged victorious. In 1846, the amended state constitution abolished manorial obligations and long-term leases. Soon thereafter, the state government instituted proceedings to invalidate the faulty colonial patents, and the tenants' leases gradually were converted to fee simple ownership. After seventy years of waiting, the Hudson Valley tenants finally had their revolution. The Anti-Renters' success left the Livingstons with only a small fraction of their ancestral landholdings.[12]

The destruction of the manors represented a triumph of democracy over outdated forms of status and privilege that had somehow survived the Revolutionary era. Before the Revolution, the Livingstons had been members of an entrenched class of untitled aristocrats who were politically, socially, and economically preeminent. After the Revolution, the decline of the manors undermined the old elite's economic interests and social status, while the rejection of their political leadership reversed the late colonial trend toward aristocracy in America.[13]

The Revolution had challenged the elite's image of themselves as the natural governors of their society. While most colonial Americans had deferred to their social betters, the Revolutionary experience politicized many ordinary people, who in time began to question the propriety of aristocratic governance. Revolutionary ideology and institutional changes, together, encouraged ordinary

---

3:839–41; Petition of a few Dam'd Rascals at the Manor of Livingston to the Legislature of New York, 1811, Livingston Family Papers, Columbia University, ser. II.

[12] Ellis, *Landlords and Farmers,* chap. 8.

[13] For a suggestive overview of this trend and the Revolution's decisive impact, see Rowland Berthoff and John M. Murrin, "Feudalism, Communalism, and the Yeoman Freeholder: The American Revolution Considered as a Social Accident," in Stephen G. Kurtz and James H. Hutson, eds., *Essays on the American Revolution* (Chapel Hill, N.C., 1973), pp. 256–88.

Americans to think about politics and to demand that their interests be represented in the political process. They scrutinized the performance of their traditional governors and found that their ideals and interests often clashed with those of the governed.

Like gentlefolk throughout America, the post-Revolutionary Livingstons found themselves unable to reconcile the Revolution's democratic values and ideals with their own notions of noblesse oblige and public service.[14] In the 1790s, Chancellor Livingston and many of his kin abandoned Federalism for Jeffersonian Republicanism, but their change in party allegiance did not signify an acceptance of egalitarian values. Chancellor Livingston resented the fact that the Federalists, acting on Hamilton's advice, had excluded him from patronage at the national level. By 1792, his principled opposition to Hamilton's fiscal policies led him to break openly with the Federalist party. The chancellor's tastes and interests were predominantly agrarian; consequently, he condemned an economic policy that favored speculators and commercial interests at the expense of agriculture. Unlike the Federalists, Chancellor Livingston also preferred France to Britain and admired the French Revolution, at least in its earliest stages. As an agrarian and a francophile, Chancellor Robert R. Livingston thus allied himself with the party of Thomas Jefferson. Like many other Republicans, however, Livingston did not share the Virginian's commitment to political democracy.[15]

In his public life, Chancellor Livingston pursued fame, not popularity. Like many men of wealth, experience, and education, he disdained a political culture that forced leaders to curry the favor of the masses and to submit their ideas and opinions for popular approval. When Livingston returned from France in 1803, after negotiating the Louisiana Purchase, he did not seek popular acclaim for his

---

[14] See David Hackett Fischer, *The Revolution of American Conservatism: The Federalist Party in the Era of Jeffersonian Democracy* (New York, 1965), esp. chap. 1; Rhys Isaac, *The Transformation of Virginia, 1740–1790* (Chapel Hill, N.C., 1982), pp. 259, 264–66, 320–22. If the Livingstons were typical, the political attitudes Fischer attributes to the "old Federalists" also could be found among displaced elites outside the Federalist party.

[15] Dangerfield, *Chancellor Robert R. Livingston*, part 4. On the Republicans, in general, see Lance Banning, *The Jeffersonian Persuasion: Evolution of a Party Ideology* (Ithaca, N.Y., 1978), esp. chap. 7, p. 269n. Many Republicans believed that inequality was natural and inevitable but condemned the Federalists for creating artificial inequalities by aggressively promoting financial and industrial interests.

efforts, but hoped instead for "a bust, or a picture, in the picture chamber of the City hall" to preserve his fame for future genera-tions. Conversely, six years later, he complained that he found him-self "ill-calculated to take a lead among men rendered fastidious by too much courtship, to intrigue with little men, to carry little mea-sures & to hold out lures for the ambition of every scoundrel that had smoked & drank himself into the honourable station of village chieftain."[16] Many members of the old elite shared his sentiments, and during and after the Revolution most withdrew from elective politics, particularly at the state level.

In 1809, an English observer shrewdly noted that America's "men of property and talents have been so annoyed by the servile means necessary to gain power, and by the violence and licentiousness con-nected with it, they are generally shrinking from the [political] scene."[17] He might well have been acquainted with the history of the Livingston family. Only Edward, the youngest Livingston, partici-pated extensively in the electoral politics of the post-Revolutionary era. He served as mayor of New York, as congressman and United States senator from Louisiana, and ultimately as secretary of state and ambassador to France under Andrew Jackson. But Edward was an aberration. His death in 1836 ended the Livingston family's tradi-tion of public service and political leadership.[18]

When Alexis de Tocqueville visited America in the 1830s, he found that the spirit of democracy had driven America's upper class-es out of politics, even at the national level. This process of elite withdrawal had begun, in New York and elsewhere, during the Rev-olutionary era. Tocqueville believed that the elite's withdrawal from political life had divorced them from the society and culture of

---

[16] Robert R. Livingston, Jr., to Janet Livingston Montgomery, 24 July 1803, Robert R. Livingston Papers, NYHS, reel 8; Robert R. Livingston, Jr., to John Armstrong, 29 Dec. 1809, ibid., NYHS, reel 10. See also Douglass Adair, "Fame and the Founding Fathers," in *Fame and the Founding Fathers: Essays by Douglass Adair,* ed. Trevor Col-bourn (New York, 1974), pp. 3–26.

[17] John Howe, quoted in Fischer, *Revolution of American Conservatism,* p. 197.

[18] On Edward's political career, see William B. Hatcher, *Edward Livingston: Jefferso-nian Republican and Jacksonian Democrat* (University, La., 1940). One notable exception was Peter R. Livingston, a distant cousin who married Joanna Livingston, Edward's elder sister. He served several terms in the state legislature in the 1820s and later was active in Whig party politics at the state level (Fox, *Decline of Aristocracy,* pp. 240–48, 332, 422–23).

mainstream America. Consequently, the Livingstons and their social peers formed an insular counterculture in Jacksonian America. America's would-be aristocrats were, Tocqueville surmised, "within the state, a private society with its own tastes and amusements." The old elites had in effect preserved their elitist self-image by accentuating their cultural distinctiveness.[19]

Before the Revolution, America's leaders had forged a distinct elite ethos that combined their inherited bourgeois values with a new regard for honor and gentility. The aristocratic ideal that the Livingstons and their peers sought to emulate was two-sided: one side led them to pursue pleasure and comfort, while the other urged them to exercise their public spirit as enlightened statesmen and community leaders. While the elite's genteel style of living survived the Revolution, aristocracy as a political ethos vanished with the king's functionaries. In the post-Revolutionary era, democratic competition replaced aristocratic noblesse oblige. The Revolutionary transformation meant the downfall of the Livingstons as well as the decline of aristocracy in America.

[19] Alexis de Tocqueville, *Democracy in America*, ed. J. P. Mayer (New York, 1969), p. 179. For a perceptive analysis of cultural separatism among conservative elites after 1800, see Linda K. Kerber, *Federalists in Dissent: Imagery and Ideology in Jeffersonian America* (Ithaca, N.Y., 1970).

Livingston Genealogy

Sources: The standard Livingston genealogy is Florence Van Rensselaer, *The Livingston Family in America and Its Scottish Origins* (New York, 1949). This genealogy has been supplemented and corrected with information from the various collections of family manuscripts as well as from the following published works: Edward P. Alexander, *A Revolutionary Conservative: James Duane of New York* (New York, 1938); Elizabeth Clarkson Jay, "The Descendants of James Alexander," *NY Gen. & Bio. Rec.*, 12 (1881): 13–28; George Kinkead, "Gilbert Livingston and Some of His Descendants," ibid., 84 (1953): 4–14, 99–107, 170–78, 239–45, and 85 (1954): 20–34; Milton M. Klein, "The American Whig: William Livingston of New York" (Ph.D. diss., Columbia University, 1954); Edwin Brockholst Livingston, *The Livingstons of Livingston Manor* (New York, 1910); Livingston Rutherfurd, comp., *Family Record and Events, Compiled Originally from the Original MSS in the Rutherfurd Collection* (New York, 1894); George W. Schuyler, *Colonial New York: Philip Schuyler and His Family*, 2 vols. (New York, 1885); G. M. Waller, *Samuel Vetch: Colonial Enterpriser* (Chapel Hill, N.C., 1960); C. S. Williams, *Jan Cornelis Van Horne and His Descendants* (New York, 1912).

Table A
First and Second Generations

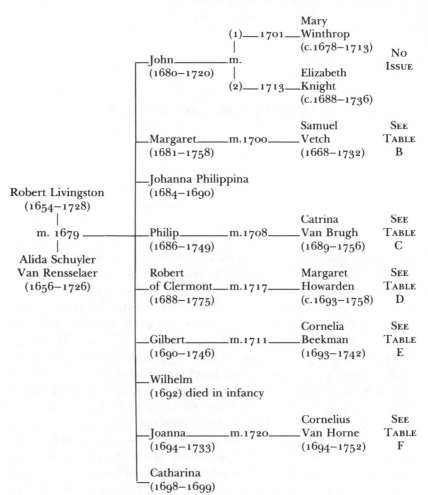

Robert Livingston
(1654–1728)
|
m. 1679
|
Alida Schuyler
Van Rensselaer
(1656–1726)

John
(1680–1720)
m.
(1)——1701——Mary
Winthrop
(c.1678–1713)
(2)——1713——Elizabeth
Knight
(c.1688–1736)
No
Issue

Margaret——m.1700——Samuel
(1681–1758)
Vetch
(1668–1732)
See
Table
B

Johanna Philippina
(1684–1690)

Philip——m.1708——Catrina
(1686–1749)
Van Brugh
(1689–1756)
See
Table
C

_Robert
of Clermont_——m.1717——Margaret
(1688–1775)
Howarden
(c.1693–1758)
See
Table
D

Gilbert——m.1711——Cornelia
(1690–1746)
Beekman
(1693–1742)
See
Table
E

Wilhelm
(1692) died in infancy

Joanna——m.1720——Cornelius
(1694–1733)
Van Horne
(1694–1752)
See
Table
F

Catharina
(1698–1699)

[254]

Appendix: Livingston Genealogy

Table B
Descendants of Margaret Livingston Vetch (1681–1758)

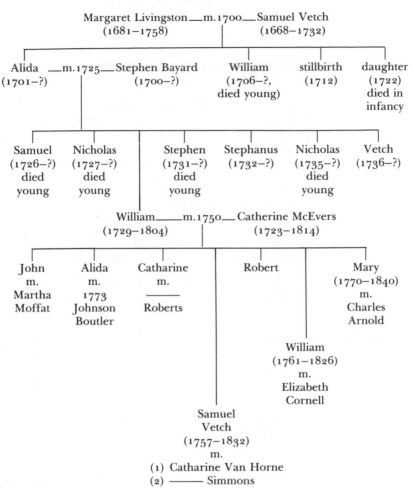

Margaret Livingston—m.1700—Samuel Vetch
(1681–1758)   (1668–1732)

Alida —m.1725— Stephen Bayard   William   stillbirth   daughter
(1701–?)   (1700–?)   (1706–?,   (1712)   (1722)
                    died young)   died in
                                                     infancy

Samuel   Nicholas   Stephen   Stephanus   Nicholas   Vetch
(1726–?)   (1727–?)   (1731–?)   (1732–?)   (1735–?)   (1736–?)
died   died   died   died
young   young   young   young

William———m.1750— Catherine McEvers
(1729–1804)   (1723–1814)

John   Alida   Catharine   Robert   Mary
m.   m.   m.   (1770–1840)
Martha   1773   ———   m.
Moffat   Johnson   Roberts   Charles
         Boutler   Arnold

William
(1761–1826)
m.
Elizabeth
Cornell

Samuel
Vetch
(1757–1832)
m.
(1) Catharine Van Horne
(2) ——— Simmons

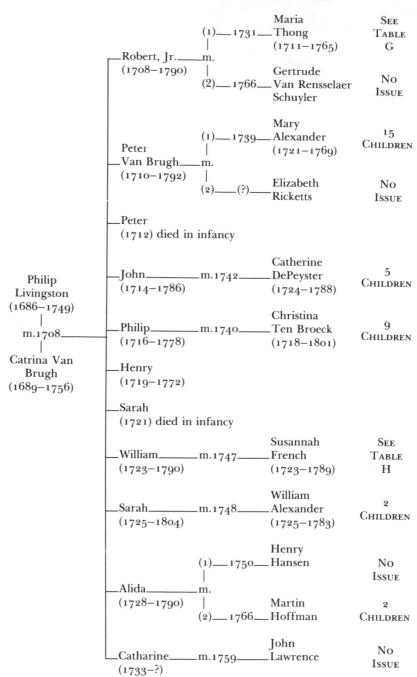

Table C
Descendants of Philip Livingston (1686–1749)

Philip
Livingston
(1686–1749)

m.1708

Catrina Van
Brugh
(1689–1756)

Robert, Jr.____m.
(1708–1790)

(1)___1731___Maria
Thong
(1711–1765)

See Table G

(2)___1766___Gertrude
Van Rensselaer
Schuyler

No Issue

Peter
Van Brugh____m.
(1710–1792)

(1)___1739___Mary
Alexander
(1721–1769)

15 Children

(2)___(?)___Elizabeth
Ricketts

No Issue

Peter
(1712) died in infancy

John____m.1742____Catherine
(1714–1786)   DePeyster
(1724–1788)

5 Children

Philip____m.1740____Christina
(1716–1778)   Ten Broeck
(1718–1801)

9 Children

Henry
(1719–1772)

Sarah
(1721) died in infancy

William____m.1747____Susannah
(1723–1790)   French
(1723–1789)

See Table H

Sarah____m.1748____William
(1725–1804)   Alexander
(1725–1783)

2 Children

Alida____m.
(1728–1790)

(1)___1750___Henry
Hansen

No Issue

(2)___1766___Martin
Hoffman

2 Children

Catharine____m.1759____John
(1733–?)   Lawrence

No Issue

[256]

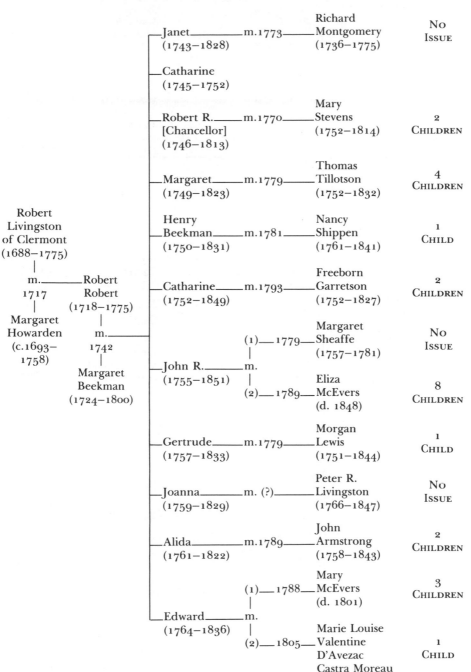

Robert
Livingston
of Clermont
(1688–1775)
|
m.————Robert
1717   Robert
| (1718–1775)
Margaret
Howarden |
(c.1693–   m.————
1758)   1742
           |
        Margaret
        Beekman
        (1724–1800)

Janet————m.1773————Richard
(1743–1828)   Montgomery   No
                     (1736–1775)   Issue

Catharine
(1745–1752)

Robert R.————m.1770————Mary
[Chancellor]   Stevens   2
(1746–1813)   (1752–1814)   Children

Margaret————m.1779————Thomas   4
(1749–1823)   Tillotson   Children
                     (1752–1832)

Henry   Nancy   1
Beekman————m.1781————Shippen   Child
(1750–1831)   (1761–1841)

Catharine————m.1793————Freeborn   2
(1752–1849)   Garretson   Children
                      (1752–1827)

                (1)——1779——Margaret   No
                           Sheaffe   Issue
John R.————m.   (1757–1781)
(1755–1851)
                (2)——1789——Eliza   8
                           McEvers   Children
                           (d. 1848)

Gertrude————m.1779————Morgan   1
(1757–1833)   Lewis   Child
                      (1751–1844)

Joanna————m. (?)————Peter R.   No
(1759–1829)   Livingston   Issue
                    (1766–1847)

Alida————m.1789————John   2
(1761–1822)   Armstrong   Children
                   (1758–1843)

                (1)——1788——Mary   3
                           McEvers   Children
                           (d. 1801)
Edward————m.
(1764–1836)
                (2)——1805——Marie Louise   1
                           Valentine   Child
                           D'Avezac
                           Castra Moreau

[257]

Table E
Descendants of Gilbert Livingston (1690–1746)

Gilbert
Livingston
(1690–1746)
|
m.
1711
|
Cornelia
Beekman
(1693–1742)

- Robert
  Gilbert_____m.1740_____Catharine
  (1712–1789)   McPheades   9
                          (1722–1792)   CHILDREN

- Henry_____m.1741_____Susanna
  (1714–1799)   Conklin   13
                        (1724–1793)   CHILDREN

- Alida
  (1716–1798)
  (1)—1737—Jacob
           Rutsen   4
           (1716–1756)   CHILDREN
  m.
  (2)—1762—Henry   No
           Van Rensselaer   ISSUE

- Gilbert
  (1717) died in infancy

- Gilbert_____m.1748_____Joy
  (1718–1789)   Darrell   7
                                          CHILDREN

- Johannes
  (1720–c.1740)

- Joanna_____m.1748_____Pierre
  (1722–1808)   Van Cortlandt   8
                        (1721–1814)   CHILDREN

- William
  (1724–?)

- Philip
  (1726–1751)

- James_____m.1751_____Judith
  (1728–1790)   Newcomb   3
                        (1733–1808)   CHILDREN

- Samuel
  (1730–c.1756)

- Cornelius
  (1732–1762)

- Catharine_____m.1751_____Jonathan
  (1734–1769)   Thorn   8
                            (1724–1777)   CHILDREN

- Margaret_____m.1764_____Peter
  (1738–1818)   Stuyvesant   11
                          (1727–1805)   CHILDREN

Table F

Descendants of Joanna Livingston Van Horne (1694–1733)

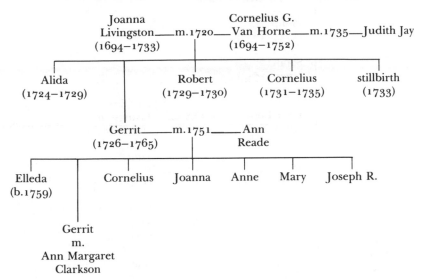

Table G
Descendants of Robert Livingston, Jr. (1708–1790)

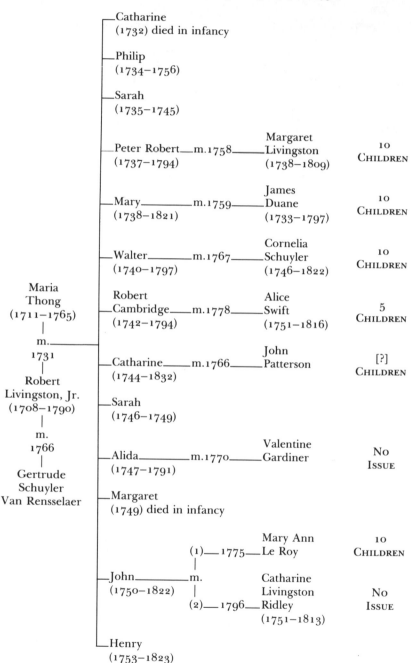

Maria
Thong
(1711–1765)
|
m.
1731
|
Robert
Livingston, Jr.
(1708–1790)
|
m.
1766
|
Gertrude
Schuyler
Van Rensselaer

Catharine
(1732) died in infancy

Philip
(1734–1756)

Sarah
(1735–1745)

Peter Robert——m.1758——Margaret Livingston (1738–1809) — 10 CHILDREN
(1737–1794)

Mary——m.1759——James Duane (1733–1797) — 10 CHILDREN
(1738–1821)

Walter——m.1767——Cornelia Schuyler (1746–1822) — 10 CHILDREN
(1740–1797)

Robert Cambridge——m.1778——Alice Swift (1751–1816) — 5 CHILDREN
(1742–1794)

Catharine——m.1766——John Patterson — [?] CHILDREN
(1744–1832)

Sarah
(1746–1749)

Alida——m.1770——Valentine Gardiner — No ISSUE
(1747–1791)

Margaret
(1749) died in infancy

John (1750–1822)
(1)——1775——Mary Ann Le Roy — 10 CHILDREN
m.
(2)——1796——Catharine Livingston Ridley (1751–1813) — No ISSUE

Henry
(1753–1823)

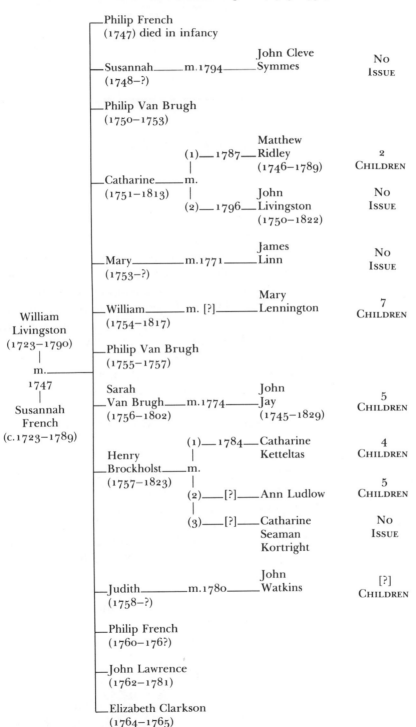

Philip French
(1747) died in infancy

Susannah———m.1794———John Cleve
(1748–?)   Symmes   No
                                          Issue

Philip Van Brugh
(1750–1753)

                    (1)—1787—Matthew
                             Ridley   2
                             (1746–1789) Children
Catharine———m.
(1751–1813) | John
              (2)—1796—Livingston   No
                       (1750–1822)   Issue

Mary———m.1771———James   No
(1753–?)   Linn   Issue

William———m. [?]———Mary   7
(1754–1817)   Lennington   Children

Philip Van Brugh
(1755–1757)

Sarah   John
Van Brugh———m.1774———Jay   5
(1756–1802)   (1745–1829)   Children

                 (1)—1784—Catharine   4
                          Ketteltas   Children
Henry
Brockholst———m.
(1757–1823)   (2)—[?]—Ann Ludlow   5
                                         Children

                 (3)—[?]—Catharine   No
                         Seaman   Issue
                         Kortright

Judith———m.1780———John   [?]
(1758–?)   Watkins   Children

Philip French
(1760–176?)

John Lawrence
(1762–1781)

Elizabeth Clarkson
(1764–1765)

William
Livingston
(1723–1790)
|
m.
1747
|
Susannah
French
(c.1723–1789)

Bibliographical Essay

Most studies of New York's early history stress the colony's peculiarities—its factious politics, ethnic pluralism, vast manors, and agrarian conflicts. The validity of that perspective notwithstanding, this book takes a different approach, attempting to locate both New York and its provincial elite in a broader Anglo-American context. This broadened perspective has shaped the contents of this bibliographical essay, which is neither a complete survey of New York's early history nor an exhaustive list of material pertaining to the Livingston family. Indeed, this essay is not a definitive bibliography for any given topic. It is instead an acknowledgment of my own intellectual debts, as well as a guide for readers who would like to know more about the themes and people discussed in this volume.

Individually and collectively, the Livingstons have been the subjects of several significant studies. Lawrence H. Leder, *Robert Livingston, 1654–1728, and the Politics of Colonial New York* (Chapel Hill, N.C., 1961), is an exhaustive study of the political career of the first Robert Livingston. Leder's discussion of Livingston's entrepreneurial interests should, however, be supplemented with Linda Briggs Biemer's work on the business activities of his wife, Alida Schuyler Livingston. See Biemer, *Women and Property in Colonial New York: The Transition from Dutch to English Law* (Ann Arbor, Mich., 1983), as well as "Business Letters of Alida Schuyler Livingston, 1680–1726," *New York History*, 63 (1982): 183–207. Milton M. Klein, "The American Whig: William Livingston of New York." (Ph.D.

diss., Columbia University, 1954), is a first-rate account of William Livingston's political activities in New York. Readers interested in Livingston's subsequent career as governor of New Jersey (1776–90) should consult Carl E. Prince et al., eds., *The Papers of William Livingston*, 5 vols. (Trenton and New Brunswick, N.J., 1979–88). George Dangerfield, *Chancellor Robert R. Livingston of New York, 1746–1813* (New York, 1960), is a thorough and readable biography of the most interesting and influential of the fourth-generation Livingstons. William B. Hatcher, *Edward Livingston: Jeffersonian Republican and Jacksonian Democrat* (University, La., 1940), discusses the life and times of the chancellor's youngest brother.

On the Livingston family in general, Edwin Brockholst Livingston, *The Livingstons of Livingston Manor* (New York, 1910), is useful if somewhat laudatory. Equally laudatory but less reliable is Clare Brandt, *An American Aristocracy: The Livingstons* (New York, 1986), which carries the family's story into the twentieth century. Patricia Joan Gordon, "The Livingstons of New York: Kinship and Class" (Ph.D. diss., Columbia University, 1959), offers a sociological perspective on six generations of family history. *The Livingston Legacy: Three Centuries of American History,* ed. Richard T. Wiles (Annandale, N.Y., 1987), is a collection of papers presented at a symposium commemorating the tercentary of Livingston Manor. Ruth Piwonka, *A Portrait of Livingston Manor, 1686–1850* (Germantown, N.Y., 1986), is a stunning catalog of Livingston family portraits, which includes an excellent and brief narrative history of Clermont and Livingston Manor.

Useful studies of other prominent colonial families include Richard S. Dunn, *Puritans and Yankees: The Winthrop Dynasty of New England, 1630–1717* (Princeton, 1962); Randolph Shipley Klein, *Portrait of an Early American Family: The Shippens of Pennsylvania across Five Generations* (Philadelphia, 1975); Paul C. Nagel, *The Lees of Virginia: Seven Generations of an American Family* (New York, 1990); Kevin M. Sweeney, *River Gods and Lesser Dieties: The Williams Family of Western Massachusetts* (Chapel Hill, N.C., forthcoming); John J. Waters, Jr., *The Otis Family in Provincial and Revolutionary Massachusetts* (Chapel Hill, N.C., 1968); and Philip L. White, *The Beekmans of New York in Politics and Commerce, 1647–1877* (New York, 1956).

Curiously, most of these family histories focus overwhelmingly on men and their activities, often ignoring gender-related issues and the changing roles of women in elite colonial families. Laurel Thatcher Ulrich, *Good Wives: Image and Reality in the Lives of Women in Northern New England, 1650–1750* (New York, 1980), is the best introduction to the varied experiences of colonial women. On women in the Revolutionary era, see Mary Beth Norton, *Liberty's Daughters: The Revolutionary Experience of American Women, 1750–1800* (Boston, 1980), and Linda K. Kerber, *Women of the Republic: Intellect and Ideology in Revolutionary America* (Chapel Hill, N.C., 1980). Two excellent essays by Ruth H. Bloch discuss sex roles and gender conventions in eighteenth-century America. See her "American Feminine Ideals in Transition: The Rise of the Moral Mother," *Feminist Studies*, 4 (1978): 101–26, and "The Gendered Meanings of Virtue in Revolutionary America," *Signs*, 13 (1987): 37–58.

The members of America's elite families promoted colonial economic growth and were the main beneficiaries of the eighteenth century's commercial revolutions. The best overview of economic development in provincial America is John J. McCusker and Russell R. Menard, *The Economy of British America, 1607–1789* (Chapel Hill, N.C., 1985), which evaluates and synthesizes decades of historical writing on key issues in early American economic history. J. E. Crowley, *This Sheba, Self: The Conceptualization of Economic Life in Eighteenth-Century America* (Baltimore, 1974), examines the colonists' changing attitudes toward work, wealth, and commerce. More recently, scholars have begun to study the impact of economic growth on consumption and material culture. See James A. Henretta, "Families and Farms: *Mentalité* in Pre-Industrial America," *William and Mary Quarterly*, 3d ser., 35 (1978): 3–32, and James T. Lemon, "Comment on James A. Henretta's 'Families and Farms: *Mentalité* in Pre-Industrial America,'" ibid., 3d ser., 37 (1980): 688–700, for an early and important debate on the extent to which consumption and market values shaped the conceptual world of eighteenth-century Americans. A more recent contribution to this debate is Daniel Vickers, "Competency and Competition: Economic Culture in Early America," ibid., 57 (1990): 3–29. Carole Shammas, *The Pre-industrial Consumer in England and America* (Oxford, 1990), is the definitive work on consumption patterns in British colonial America, but readers should also consult *Material Life in America, 1600–1860*, ed. Robert Blair St. George (Boston, 1988), a collection of readable essays on subjects ranging from tea services to domestic architecture. Neil

McKendrick, John Brewer, and J. H. Plumb, *The Birth of a Consumer Society: The Commercialization of Eighteenth-Century England* (London, 1982), offers a British perspective on the commercial revolution, the commodities it produced, and the markets it exploited.

In colonial New York, the fur trade was the first source of profits and commercial development. Thomas Elliot Norton, *The Fur Trade in Colonial New York* (Madison, Wis., 1974), is the standard work on that topic. The success of the fur trade often depended on the settlers' ability to maintain goods relations with their Indian neighbors. See *The Livingston Indian Records, 1666–1723*, ed. Lawrence H. Leder (Gettysburg, Pa., 1956); Allen W. Trelease, *Indian Affairs in Colonial New York: The Seventeenth Century* (Ithaca, N.Y., 1960); and Stephen Saunders Webb, *1676: The End of American Independence* (New York, 1984), on European-Indian relations during the fur trade's heyday. For a more imaginative approach, and one more sensitive to the Indians' perspective, see Daniel K. Richter, "Cultural Brokers and Intercolonial Politics: New York-Iroquois Relations, 1664–1701," *Journal of American History*, 75 (1988): 48–60.

New York's commerce flourished increasingly during the eighteenth century, as traffic in grain and other commodities began to overshadow the colony's trade in furs. Virginia D. Harrington, *The New York Merchant on the Eve of the Revolution* (New York, 1935), remains a useful overview of the varied entrepreneurial activities of Manhattan's merchant community, while David A. Armour, *The Merchants of Albany, New York: 1686–1760* (New York, 1986), is the best source of information on the Hudson Valley's leading commercial center. Bernard Bailyn, *The New England Merchants in the Seventeenth Century* (Cambridge, Mass., 1955), and Thomas M. Doerflinger, *A Vigorous Spirit of Enterprise: Merchants and Economic Development in Revolutionary Philadelphia* (Chapel Hill, N.C., 1986), are two excellent studies of trading communities outside New York that provide a helpful comparative perspective. Jean P. Jordan, "Women Merchants in Colonial New York," *New York History*, 58 (1977): 412–39, shows the extent to which women participated in New York's commercial economy throughout the colonial era. Irene D. Neu, "The Iron Plantations of Colonial New York," *New York History*, 33 (1952): 3–24, examines New York's colonial iron industry and includes a discussion of the Livingstons' facilities. William I. Davisson and Lawrence J. Bradley show the growth and increasing diversity of New

York's eighteenth-century trade in their "New York Maritime Trade: Ship Voyage Patterns, 1715–1765," *New-York Historical Society Quarterly*, 55 (1971): 309–17. A more general survey of colonial shipping is James M. Shepherd and Gary F. Walton, *Shipping, Maritime Trade, and the Economic Development of Colonial North America* (Cambridge, 1972).

In the eighteenth century, a growing demand for colonial grain increased the commercial value of land and of agricultural labor. On land speculation and its role in New York's commercial development, see Ruth L. Higgins, *Expansion in New York with Especial Reference to the Eighteenth Century* (Columbus, Ohio, 1931); Edith M. Fox, *Land Speculation in the Mohawk Country* (Ithaca, N.Y., 1949); and William Wyckoff, *The Developer's Frontier: The Making of the Western New York Landscape* (New Haven, 1988). Walter Allen Knittle, *Early Eighteenth Century Palatine Emigration: A British Government Redemptioner Project to Manufacture Naval Stores* (Philadelphia, 1937), is a detailed account of the Palatine settlements that ultimately played a crucial role in the development of Livingston Manor, though Knittle unfairly blames Robert Livingston and Governor Robert Hunter— rather than the home government—for the failure of the naval stores project. Sung Bok Kim's meticulously researched *Landlord and Tenant in Colonial New York: Manorial Society, 1664–1775* (Chapel Hill, N.C., 1978), shows how landlords promoted economic development in the Hudson Valley, correctly stressing the economic interests shared by landlords and their tenants, but probably exaggerating the manor lords' benevolence.

A generous selection of documents pertaining to New York's manorial grants is found in *The Documentary History of the State of New-York*, ed. E. B. O'Callaghan, vol. 3, (Albany, N.Y., 1850). Irving Mark, *Agrarian Conflicts in Colonial New York, 1711–1775* (New York, 1940), remains the fullest account of the Hudson Valley uprisings. According to Mark, tenant dissatisfaction was the main cause of rural unrest in the pre-Revolutionary era. Two more recent works supporting this interpretation are Staughton Lynd, *Anti-Federalism in Dutchess County, New York: A Study of Democracy and Class Conflict in the Revolutionary Era* (Chicago, 1962), and Edward Countryman, *A People in Revolution: The American Revolution in New York, 1760–1790* (Baltimore, 1981). Other scholars contend that New England squatters, not New York tenants, were primarily responsible for the Hudson

Valley riots. See, for instance, Kim, *Landlord and Tenant,* cited above, as well as Patricia U. Bonomi, *A Factious People: Politics and Society in Colonial New York* (New York, 1971); Dixon Ryan Fox, *Yankees and Yorkers* (New York, 1940); and Philip J. Schwarz, *The Jarring Interests: New York's Boundary Makers, 1664–1776* (Albany, N.Y., 1979).

As landlords, merchants, and political leaders, the Livingstons were part of an increasingly self-conscious provincial elite who, by mid-century, had forged a uniquely genteel culture that distinguished them from their social inferiors. Jack P. Greene, "Search for Identity: An Interpretation of the Meaning of Selected Patterns of Social Response in Eighteenth-Century America," *Journal of Social History,* 4 (1970): 189–220, shows elite ambivalence toward English models of genteel culture, while Richard L. Bushman's important essay "American High-Style and Vernacular Culture," in Jack P. Greene and J. R. Pole, eds., *Colonial British America: Essays in the New History of the Early Modern Era* (Baltimore, 1984), pp. 345–83, describes the growing cultural gap between elites and ordinary people in the late colonial era. Several studies examine the increasingly stratified urban culture of eighteenth-century America. See, for instance, Carl Bridenbaugh, *Cities in Revolt: Urban Life in America, 1743–1776* (New York, 1955); Gary B. Nash, *The Urban Crucible: Social Change, Political Consciousness, and the Origins of the American Revolution* (Cambridge, Mass., 1979); and Frederick B. Tolles, *Meeting House and Counting House: The Quaker Merchants of Colonial Philadelphia, 1682–1763* (Chapel Hill, N.C., 1948). Esther Singleton, *Social New York under the Georges, 1714–1776* (New York, 1902), describes the homes, clothing, and social lives of the city's eighteenth-century gentlefolk. Although Singleton's work is more antiquarian than analytical, it conveys the flavor of urban life among elites in provincial America.

Most scholarly appraisals of the values and culture of rural elites have focused on the Virginia gentry, who shared the social stature and agricultural interests of New York's landed magnates but—because of their reliance on Scottish factors—were less likely to participate directly in an urban commercial economy. T. H. Breen, *Tobacco Culture: The Mentality of the Great Tidewater Planters on the Eve of Revolution* (Princeton, 1985), delineates the gentry's economic ideals and argues that perceived mistreatment by British merchants shaped the planters' response to the imperial crisis that preceded the Revolution. Louis B. Wright, *The First Gentlemen of Virginia: Intellectual Qualities of the Early Colonial Ruling Class* (San Marino, Calif., 1940), examines the gentry's growing taste for learning, which was replicated among elites in other British American colonies. Charles S. Sydnor, *Gentlemen Freeholders* (Chapel Hill, N.C., 1952), describes political practices and values of Virginia's colonial gentry. Jack P. Greene, *Landon Carter: An Inquiry into the Personal Values and Social Imperatives of the Eighteenth-Century Virginia Gentry* (Charlottesville, Va., 1965), summarizes the Carter diaries and offers significant insights into the public and personal values of one unusually loquacious and cantankerous Virginia gentleman. For more information on Carter, his plantation, and his family, readers should consult *The Diary of Landon Carter of Sabine Hall, 1752–1778*, 2 vols., ed. Jack P. Greene (Charlottesville, Va., 1965). Daniel Blake Smith, *Inside the Great House: Planter Family Life in Eighteenth-Century Chesapeake Society* (Ithaca, N.Y., 1980), is a more general account of family life among southern elites, which should be read in conjunction with Jan Lewis, *The Pursuit of Happiness: Family and Values in Jefferson's Virginia* (Cambridge, 1983), and the less persuasive work of Philip Greven, *The Protestant Temperament: Patterns of Child-Rearing, Religious Experience, and the Self in Early America* (New York, 1977). Finally, Rhys Isaac, *The Transformation of Virginia, 1740–1790* (Chapel Hill, N.C., 1982), uses literary evidence, material culture, and anthropological theory to show how the gentry molded the values and culture of colonial Virginia, only to be challenged by evangelicals and democrats in the Revolutionary era.

Although Virginia's gentry was perhaps the most stable of America's colonial elites, over the course of the eighteenth century an entrenched ruling class emerged in all the provinces of British colonial America. John M. Murrin, "Political Development," in Greene and Pole, eds., *Colonial British America*, pp. 416–41, summarizes the stages of each colony's political evolution, as does Bernard Bailyn, *The Origins of American Politics* (New York, 1968). Bailyn's seminal *Ideological Origins of the American Revolution* (Cambridge, Mass., 1973), explores the political culture of late colonial America, stressing the influence of England's eighteenth-century Radical Whig opposition writers.

Several fine monographs discuss the political history of colonial New York, though relatively little work has been done on the ideological dimension of New York's colonial politics. Robert C. Ritchie, *The Duke's Province: A Study of New York Politics and Society, 1664–1691* (Chapel Hill, N.C., 1977), is an excellent narrative that concludes with Leisler's Rebellion. Patricia U. Bonomi's important and influential book, *A Factious People,* cited above, analyzes a half-century of interest group politics and shifting factional alliances. Stanley N. Katz, *Newcastle's New York: Anglo-American Politics, 1732–1753* (Cambridge, Mass., 1968), focuses on the transatlantic connections that shaped the conduct of imperial politics. Carl Becker's classic *History of Political Parties in the Province of New York* (Madison, Wis., 1909), is still the best account of partisan conflict in the pre-Revolutionary era.

Two contemporary histories of the province, both written by future loyalists, provide unique perspectives on New York's political history. William Smith, Jr., *The History of the Province of New-York,* ed. Michael G. Kammen, 2 vols. (1757; Cambridge, Mass., 1972), sympathizes with the Livingstons and their party. See also *Historical Memoirs of William Smith . . . ,* ed. H. W. William Sabine, 2 vols. (New York, 1956–58), which include Smith's accounts of the imperial crisis and his wartime sojourn at Livingston Manor. Thomas Jones, *History of New York during the Revolutionary War,* ed. Edwin Floyd DeLancey, 2 vols. (New York, 1879), finds the origins of the Revolution in the religious controversies of the 1750s and ardently supports DeLancey and his partisans. William Livingston et al., *The Independent Reflector; or, Weekly Essays on Sundry Important Subjects More particularly adapted to the Province of New-York,* ed. Milton M. Klein (Cambridge, Mass., 1963), is an accessible sample of the triumvirate's most significant polemics, preceded by a fine introductory essay. For more information on the activities and writings of Livingston, Smith, and Scott, see Dorothy Rita Dillon, *The New York Triumvirate: A Study of the Legal and Political Careers of William Livingston, John Morin Scott, William Smith, Jr.* (New York, 1949).

Patricia U. Bonomi explores the relationship between religion and political culture in *Under the Cope of Heaven: Religion, Society, and Politics in Colonial America* (New York, 1986). Carl Bridenbaugh, *Mitre and Sceptre: Transatlantic Faiths, Ideas, Personalities, and Politics, 1689–1775* (New York, 1962), examines colonial fears of ecclesiastical tyranny and opposition to Anglican schemes to establish an American episcopate in the pre-Revolutionary era. Randall Balmer,

A Perfect Babel of Confusion: Dutch Religion and English Culture in the Middle Colonies (New York, 1989), shows how the Dutch Reformed churches adapted to anglicization, while Richard W. Pointer, *Protestant Pluralism and the New York Experience: A Study of Eighteenth-Century Religious Diversity* (Bloomington, Ind., 1988), traces the evolution of a culture of religious dissent in provincial New York. Pointer's book, along with the works by Milton Klein and Dorothy Dillon, cited above, include detailed discussions of the King's College controversy. But see also David C. Humphrey, *From King's College to Columbia, 1746–1800* (New York, 1976), for a useful account of the college's origins and early history.

In a series of essays, Milton M. Klein examines the evolution of New York's legal community and explains the legal and judicial controversies of the pre-Revolutionary era. See his "From Community to Status: The Development of the Legal Profession in Colonial New York," *New York History,* 60 (1979): 133–56, on the rise of New York bench and bar during the eighteenth century. Klein, "Prelude to Revolution in New York: Jury Trials and Judicial Tenure" *William and Mary Quarterly,* 3d ser., 17 (1960): 439–62, discusses the legal crises of the 1760s, while "New York Lawyers and the Coming of the American Revolution" *New York History,* 55 (1974): 383–407, shows how the province's lawyers led the fight against imperial tyranny. John M. Murrin describes a similar scenario for pre-Revolutionary Massachusetts. See Murrin, "The Legal Transformation: The Bench and Bar in Eighteenth-Century Massachusetts," in *Colonial America: Essays in Politics and Social Development,* ed. Stanley N. Katz and John M. Murrin (New York, 1983), pp. 540–63.

Leopold S. Launitz-Schürer, Jr., *Loyal Whigs and Revolutionaries: The Making of the Revolution in New York, 1765–1776* (New York, 1980), chronicles the politics of resistance in colonial New York, supplementing but not supplanting Carl Becker, *History of Political Parties.* Edmund S. Morgan and Helen M. Morgan, *The Stamp Act Crisis: Prologue to Revolution* (Chapel Hill, N.C., 1953), is the best account of the first phase of the imperial crisis in New York and elsewhere, while Pauline Maier, *From Resistance to Revolution: Colonial Radicals and the Development of American Opposition to Britain, 1765–1776* (New York, 1972), traces the development of an intercolonial popular resistance movement during and after the Stamp Act crisis. On New York's Sons of Liberty and their most illustrious leader, see

Roger J. Champagne, *Alexander McDougall and the American Revolution in New York* (Schenectady, N.Y., 1975). See also Bernard Mason, *The Road to Independence: The Revolutionary Movement in New York, 1773–1777* (Lexington, Ky., 1966), for a detailed account of the final phase of the imperial crisis, following the Boston Tea Party. Paul David Nelson, *William Tryon and the Course of Empire: A Life in British Imperial Service* (Chapel Hill, N.C., 1990), is a recent account of the troubled career of New York's last colonial governor. Readers should consult Philip Ranlet, *The New York Loyalists* (Knoxville, Tenn., 1986), for a reassessment of the province's reputation as a hotbed of toryism. In "The American Revolution as a *Crise de Conscience:* The Case of New York," Michael Kammen addresses the problem of allegiance in Revolutionary America, maintaining that many New Yorkers sought to avoid involvement in the Revolution and chose sides only under duress (in *Society, Freedom, and Conscience: The Coming of the Revolution in Virginia, Massachusetts, and New York*, ed. Richard M. Jellison [New York, 1976], pp. 125–89).

In "Feudalism, Communalism, and the Yeoman Freeholder: The American Revolution Considered as a Social Accident," Rowland Berthoff and John M. Murrin argue that the Revolution reversed the elitist, anglicizing trends that prevailed in late colonial America (in *Essays on the American Revolution*, ed. Stephen G. Kurtz and James H. Hutson [Chapel Hill, N.C., 1973], pp. 256–88). Countryman, *A People in Revolution*, cited above, is the best account of New York's internal revolution, while the work of Jackson Turner Main illustrates the democratization of politics in all thirteen of the former colonies. Especially useful are Main, "Government by the People: The American Revolution and the Democratization of the Legislatures," *William and Mary Quarterly*, 3d ser., 23 (1966): 391–407, and *Political Parties before the Constitution* (Chapel Hill, N.C., 1973). On tax reform in Revolutionary America, see Robert A. Becker, *Revolution, Reform, and the Politics of American Taxation, 1763–1783* (Baton Rouge, La., 1980).

Gordon S. Wood's magisterial *Creation of the American Republic, 1776–1787* (Chapel Hill, N.C., 1969), has shaped my general understanding of politics and political culture in Revolutionary America. The best account of politics in Revolutionary New York is Alfred F. Young, *The Democratic Republicans of New York: The Origins, 1763–1797* (Chapel Hill, N.C., 1967), though E. Wilder Spaulding, *New*

York in the Critical Period, 1783–1789 (New York, 1932), is also useful. Along with the works by Countryman, Young, and Spaulding cited above, Linda Grant De Pauw, *The Eleventh Pillar: New York State and the Federal Constitution* (Ithaca, N.Y., 1966), describes New Yorkers' debates on the federal Constitution and the Federalists' ultimately successful struggle for ratification. For the reminiscences of a leading Anti-Federalist, see Staughton Lynd, "Abraham Yates's History of the Movement for the United States Constitution," *William and Mary Quarterly*, 3d ser., 20 (1963): 223–45.

Several important studies discuss the decline of aristocratic politics in post-Revolutionary America. David Hackett Fischer, *The Revolution of American Conservatism: The Federalist Party in the Era of Jeffersonian Democracy* (New York, 1965), and Linda K. Kerber, *Federalists in Dissent: Imagery and Ideology in Jeffersonian America* (Ithaca, N.Y., 1970), examine the Federalists' reaction to the success of their more egalitarian adversaries. Dixon Ryan Fox, *The Decline of the Aristocracy in the Politics of New York* (New York, 1919), describes the downfall of the state's old elites and the democratization of politics in nineteenth-century New York, epitomized by the victorious Anti-Rent movement of the 1840s. David Maldwyn Ellis, *Landlords and Farmers in the Hudson-Mohawk Region, 1790–1850* (Ithaca, N.Y., 1946), is the best analysis of the Anti-Rent movement, its origins, and the settlement and development of New York's frontier during the first half of the nineteenth century.

Index

Index

Craftsmen, 136–37, 139–40
Crown Point, 74, 169
Cruger, Henry, 187
Cuyler, Henry, 67

Dairying, 247
Dancing, 140, 150
Dartmouth, Earl of, 205
Davis, Joseph, 52
Decker, Gerrit, 94–95
Decker, Isaac, 99
Declaration of Independence, 8
Declaratory Act, 188
Defense policy, 2, 15–17, 62, 165, 169–70
Deference, 183; decline of, 184, 202, 205, 212–14, 221, 228, 236, 242, 248–49
DeLancey, James, 55, 113, 121, 135, 172, 179; influence of, 169, 171, 173–74, 176–77
DeLancey, James, Jr., 186–88, 190, 193–94, 198–99. See also DeLancey party
DeLancey, John, 195
DeLancey, Oliver, 174, 187
DeLancey, Stephen, 67, 69
DeLancey party, 165, 169–70, 172, 174–78, 185, 190, 197, 202–3, 206; and Colden, 190–93, 195–96; and Sons of Liberty, 187–88, 195
Democratic party, 248
Democratization, 211, 221, 236, 242–43, 251; elite resentment of, 212–15, 221–24, 234–35, 239, 248–50
"Deputy husbands," 50
DeWitt, Charles, 110
DeWitt, John, 96
Dissenters, religious, 153, 166, 188–89; and King's College controversy, 173–76; legal disabilities of, 177–78, 189–90, 197; New York Society of, 189, 193
Distilleries, 79
Dominion of New England, 28–29
Dongan, Thomas, 32, 34, 65, 115; as patron of Robert Livingston, 5, 25–26, 28
Dongan patent (1686), 26, 28, 115, 247
Douglas, Henry, 67
Douglas, James, 67
Duane, James, 123, 135, 150, 197, 206–9, 213, 216, 227

Duer, William, 213
Dutchess County, 43–44, 61, 106, 116, 118
Dutch Reformed Church, 8, 15, 106–8, 163–64, 189
Dutch West India Company, 13

East Camp, 108
East River, 135, 141
Economic growth, 79, 130–31, 142; in New York, 48, 66, 247
Economic regulations: under Burnet, 45–46, 55; during Revolution, 224–28, 233–35
Edinburgh, 56
Education, 6, 145–47, 157–58; of daughters, 50, 148–52; of fourth generation, 75–76, 144, 150, 152–54; of second generation, 49–53, 56, 58, 67; of sons, 51, 53, 56, 58, 69–71, 75–76, 145–47, 152–53; of third generation, 69–71, 144–45, 147, 150, 152; of young children, 49
Elections, 183, 195–96, 199, 236; of 1761, 174–75; of 1768, 186; of 1769, 187–89; of 1777, 211–13; at Livingston Manor, 110, 196, 235
Elites, 166, 199–200, 242, 248–51; as civic leaders, 109–10, 157–59, 161–63; values of New York, 1–4, 6–7, 9, 46, 86–87, 128–29, 143–47, 154–57, 159–60, 164, 249–51; in Virginia, 2, 139, 155–56
England: economic growth in, 130–31; Robert Livingston in, 34–35, 38–39; trade with, 22–23, 65–66, 130–31. See also London
Entrepreneurial ideals, 48, 77. See also Work ethic
Entrepreneurs, 48, 77, 84–85, 87, 95, 224
Episcopacy controversy, 188–89, 199
Episcopalians. See Anglicans
Erie Canal, 247
Erving, John, 74
Eviction, 95, 102–3, 124

Factions, 12, 31, 36, 62, 160, 165, 174, 187, 190–91, 197–99, 201–2; ambivalence toward, 166–68, 173. See also DeLancey party; Livingston party
Fairfield, Connecticut, 31

[275]

Index

Index

Livingston, William (cont.)
193–94; in New Jersey, 202, 206,
218; as promoter of education, 147,
150, 154, 158; as social critic and
polemicist, 132, 143–44, 161–63,
166, 185, 188–89
Livingston, William (son of Gilbert),
61
Livingstone, John (father of Robert
Livingston), 10–11
Livingston family, 89, 165, 198–99,
206–7, 217–18; as Federalists, 202,
239; in post-Revolutionary era, 242–
47, 249–50; religious affiliations of,
153; reputation of, 223, 225–27,
232, 236, 246; Scottish ancestry of,
10
Livingston Manor, 27, 44, 106–10,
127, 235, 244; agrarian unrest at,
110–19, 228–32, 247–48; as commercial hinterland, 5, 66, 74, 78–79,
87; creation of, 5, 24, 26; development of, 41–43, 65–67, 79–80, 87,
91; division of, 57, 64, 125, 245–46;
as family seat, 125–26, 218, 244;
faulty title to, 26, 113, 115–16, 119,
247–48; general store at, 41–42, 74,
83, 93–94; Palatine settlers at, 41–
43, 93, 106; political representation
of, 44, 61, 195–96, 210, 221; population of, 43, 90–92, 229; during
Revolution, 126, 217–20, 228–34
Livingston party, 7, 167, 190–92, 203–
4, 206; links to Morrisites, 165, 178;
origins of, 165–66, 173–76; strength
in assembly, 174–75, 186, 188, 195–
97
Logan, James, 156
London, 38, 46, 51, 56, 58, 75, 136–
37, 153; trade with, 22–23, 67, 73,
78, 226n.
Loomis, Josiah, 111, 114, 123–25
Loonenburg, 108
Lords of Trade and Plantations, 34–
35. See also Board of Trade
Louisiana, 250; purchase of, 8, 249
Low, Isaac, 204
Lower Manor. See Clermont
Loyalists. See Tories
Lumber: as trade commodity, 5, 66,
79, 244
Lutherans, 108, 177
Luxury: as source of corruption, 143–
44, 159, 162

McDougall, Alexander, 192–94, 203–4
Madeira: and wine trade, 72
Main, Jackson Turner, 100–102
Mancius, George Wilhelmus, 106
Manhattan. See New York (city)
Manors, 26, 89–91, 116, 134, 210,
247–48; political representation of,
44, 61, 196, 210, 221
Mansion-building, 132, 134–35, 243–
44
Manufacturing, 48, 79; promotion of,
80, 159
Marston family, 135
Massachusetts, 11, 13, 125, 202, 233,
237; disputed boundary with New
York, 111–13, 115–16, 119, 174;
General Court of, 111, 116, 122,
187; land scarcity in, 83, 92, 115;
Robert Livingston's contacts in, 18–
19, 21
Massachusetts Circular Letter, 187
Material culture, 6, 102–3, 128, 130–
39
Mediators, 15, 17
Merchants, 209, 237–38; in Albany,
40–41, 45, 65, 67; in New York, 45–
46, 163–64, 184, 187, 192, 194–95,
204–6. See also Trade
Methodists, 164
Milbourne, Jacob, 29–31
Military contracts, 32–34, 36, 40, 68,
74–75, 131–32, 224–26
Militia, 229; in Livingston Manor, 94,
230–31, 233; from Massachusetts,
231–32
Milling tolls, 92–93. See also Gristmills
Mills. See Gristmills; Sawmills
Ministers, 107–8, 146
Ministry Act (1693), 177–78; at-
tempted repeal of, 189–90
Mohawk River, 40
Mohawk Valley, 54, 88
Monckton, Robert, 180, 182
Monopolies, 29–30, 80, 96
Montgomery, Richard, 207, 213–14
Montressor, John, 117
Moore, Sir Henry, 117, 186–87, 190
Moravians, 163
Morris, Gouverneur, 209, 212–13,
216
Morris, Lewis, 45, 55–56, 58, 62, 168
Morris, Lewis, III, 74, 190, 195–96
Morris, Roger, 135
Morris-Cosby dispute, 55–56, 121;

Library of Congress Cataloging-in-Publication Data

Kierner, Cynthia A., 1958–
    Traders and gentlefolk : the Livingstons of New York, 1675–1790 /
Cynthia A. Kierner.
        p.   cm.
    Includes bibliographical references and index.
    ISBN 0-8014-2638-3 (alk. paper)
    1. New York (State)—History—Colonial period, ca. 1600–1775.   2. New York
(State)—History—1775–1865.   3. Elite (Social sciences)—New York (State)—
History—18th century.   4.   Gentry—New York (State)—History—18th
century.   5. Merchants—New York (State)—History—18th century.   6. Elite
(Social sciences)—New York (State)—History—17th century.   7. Gentry—New
York (State)—History—17th century.   8. Merchants—New York (State)—
History—17th century.   9. Livingston family.   I. Title.
F122.K54   1992
974.7′02—dc20   91-55565